English Fiction

Longman Literature in English Series

**General Editors: David Carroll and Michael Wheeler
Lancaster University**

For a complete list of titles see pages viii and ix

# English Fiction of the Romantic Period 1789–1830

Gary Kelly

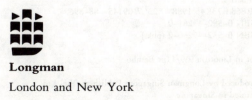

**Longman**

London and New York

**Longman Group UK Limited**
Longman House, Burnt Mill, Harlow,
Essex CM20 2JE, England
*and Associated Companies throughout the world.*

*Published in the United States of America
by Longman Inc., New York*

© Longman Group UK Limited 1989

First published 1989
Third impression 1993

BRITISH LIBRARY CATALOGUING-IN-PUBLICATION DATA
Kelly, Gary
  English Fiction of the Romantic period, 1789–1830.
  1. Fiction in English, 1745–1837 — Critical Studies
  I. Title    II. Series.
  823′.6′09

ISBN 0-582-49261-0  CSD
ISBN 0-582-49260-2  PPR

LIBRARY OF CONGRESS CATALOGING IN PUBLICATION DATA
Kelly, Gary.
  English Fiction of the Romantic period, 1789–1830.

  (Longman Literature in English series)
  Bibliography: p.
  Includes index.
  1. English fiction — 19th century — History and
criticism.   2. Romanticism — Great Britain.   3. English
fiction — 18th century — History and criticism.   I. Title.
II. Series.
PR868.R73K45 1988   823′.7′09145   88-8969
ISBN 0-582-49261-0
ISBN 0-582-49260-2 (pbk.)

Set in Linotron 9½/11pt Bembo

Produced by Longman Singapore Publishers (Pte) Ltd.
Printed in Singapore

# Contents

# Editors' Preface

The multi-volume Longman Literature in English Series provides students of literature with a critical introduction to the major genres in their historical and cultural context. Each volume gives a coherent account of a clearly defined area, and the series, when complete, will offer a practical and comprehensive guide to literature written in English from Anglo-Saxon times to the present. The aim of the series as a whole is to show that the most valuable and stimulating approach to literature is that based upon an awareness of the relations between literary forms and their historical context. Thus the areas covered by most of the separate volumes are defined by period and genre. Each volume offers new informed ways of reading literary works, and provides guidance to further reading in an extensive reference section.

As well as studies on all periods of English and American literature, the series includes books on criticism and literary theory, and on the intellectual and cultural context. A comprehensive series of this kind must of course include other literature written in English, and therefore a group of volumes deals with Irish and Scottish literature, and the literatures of India, Africa, the Caribbean, Australia, and Canada. The forty-seven volumes of the series cover the following areas: pre-Renaissance English Literature, English Poetry, English Drama, English Fiction, English Prose, Criticism and Literary Theory, Intellectual and Cultural Context, American Literature, Other Literatures in English.

David Carroll
Michael Wheeler

# Longman Literature in English Series
**General Editors:   David Carroll and Michael Wheeler**
**Lancaster University**

## Pre-Renaissance English Literature

⋆ English Literature before Chaucer *Michael Swanton*
  English Literature in the Age of Chaucer
⋆ English Medieval Romance *W. R. J. Barron*

## English Poetry

⋆ English Poetry of the Sixteenth Century (Second Edition) *Gary Waller*
⋆ English Poetry of the Seventeenth Century (Second Edition)
  *George Parfitt*
  English Poetry of the Eighteenth Century, 1700–1789
⋆ English Poetry of the Romantic Period, 1789–1830 (Second Edition)
  *J. R. Watson*
⋆ English Poetry of the Victorian Period, 1830–1890 *Bernard Richards*
  English Poetry of the Early Modern Period, 1890–1940
⋆ English Poetry since 1940 *Neil Corcoran*

## English Drama

  English Drama before Shakespeare
⋆ English Drama: Shakespeare to the Restoration, 1590–1660
  *Alexander Leggatt*
⋆ English Drama: Restoration and Eighteenth Century, 1660–1789
  *Richard W. Bevis*
  English Drama: Romantic and Victorian, 1789–1890
  English Drama of the Early Modern Period, 1890–1940
  English Drama since 1940

## English Fiction

⋆ English Fiction of the Eighteenth Century, 1700–1789
  *Clive T. Probyn*
⋆ English Fiction of the Romantic Period, 1789–1830 *Gary Kelly*
⋆ English Fiction of the Victorian Period, 1830–1890 (Second Edition)
  *Michael Wheeler*
⋆ English Fiction of the Early Modern Period, 1890–1940   *Douglas Hewitt*
  English Fiction since 1940

**English Prose**

★ English Prose of the Seventeenth Century, 1590–1700 *Roger Pooley*
English Prose of the Eighteenth Century
English Prose of the Nineteenth Century

**Criticism and Literary Theory**

Criticism and Literary Theory from Sidney to Johnson
Criticism and Literary Theory from Wordsworth to Arnold
Criticism and Literary Theory from 1890 to the Present

**The Intellectual and Cultural Context**

The Sixteenth Century
★ The Seventeenth Century, 1603–1700 *Graham Parry*
★ The Eighteenth Century, 1700–1789 (Second Edition) *James Sambrook*
The Romantic Period, 1789–1830
★ The Victorian Period, 1830–1890 *Robin Gilmour*
The Twentieth Century: 1890 to the Present

**American Literature**

American Literature before 1880
★ American Poetry of the Twentieth Century *Richard Gray*
★ American Drama of the Twentieth Century *Gerald M. Berkowitz*
★ American Fiction 1865–1940 *Brian Lee*
★ American Fiction since 1940 *Tony Hilfer*
★ Twentieth-Century America *Douglas Tallack*

**Other Literatures**

Irish Literature since 1800
Scottish Literature since 1700

Australian Literature
★ Indian Literature in English *William Walsh*
African Literature in English: East and West
Southern African Literature in English
Caribbean Literature in English
★ Canadian Literature in English *W. J. Keith*

★ *Already published*

# Author's Preface

This book is a descriptive and interpretative study of the fiction of the Romantic period in Britain. For the purposes of this book, the Romantic period opens with the outbreak of the French Revolution in 1789, a decisive event in British life for the entire period, and one that revealed significant conflicts and contradictions in British culture and society, especially in the 1790s and early 1800s; the period ends with the death in 1830 of George IV, a figure who represented in his character, career, and social and cultural influence some of the major conflicts and contradictions of the 'high' Romantic period, the 1810s and 1820s. The novel and other kinds of prose fiction were major vehicles for setting forth and arguing about the issues centred around the French Revolution debate in Britain, the Prince Regent (later to become George IV) and Regency culture, and other important events and social transformations of the period. Indeed, the Romantic period saw the rise of the novel not only to literary status but to become the most widely disseminated form of writing in society, apart from newspapers and magazines.

Yet the novel also remained, for many readers and critics, popular in a negative and pejorative sense – merely widely read and commercially exploited rather than deeply serious or highly artistic. At the same time there were major changes in other kinds of prose fiction – chapbooks and 'street literature' – as well as organized attempts to use this popular fiction – 'popular' in the sense 'of the common people' – to assist the social programmes and to achieve the social objectives of the middle and upper-middle classes, that is, those who constituted, during the Romantic period, the 'novel-reading classes' of Britain. Thus the Romantic period revealed, by bringing into play, contradictions and oppositions between popular fiction of two different sorts – the novel and 'street literature'. Yet the Romantic period also saw the rapid development of the major kinds and techniques of nineteenth-century fiction and the development of prose fiction into mass literature. The Romantic period in Britain is now thought of as an age of poetry; in fact, it was, if not the age of the novel, then the age of prose fiction.

This book, then, treats Romantic fiction as a product, or rather articulation, of major social and cultural issues and changes of the Romantic period. These issues and changes were many and various, but were dominated, I argue, by the situation of the novel-reading classes – mainly the urban professional middle classes – as social groups rapidly growing in numbers and confidence and still emulating but increasingly resisting the hegemonic social class, the landed gentry, while both these social groups were faced with challenges from the urban and rural labouring and artisan classes. The changing relations among these classes during the Romantic period were decisive in shaping modern British society and culture, and initiated, produced, or perfected many of our major social and cultural institutions and myths, including: the institutions of professionalization; 'national' literature and a 'standard' national language; education for literacy and participation in the new 'national' print culture; the nuclear family as we know it; childhood as we know it; the subjective self; gender differentiations substantially as we know them; class differentiations as we know them; the commercialization of culture and cultural distinctions; and – a major delineator, definer, and enacter of all of these institutions and myths – the novel as it was known throughout the nineteenth century and as it is still known to the majority of novel readers. My main concern here is with Romantic fiction and the Romantic novel in their time, but I suggest that their time still seems to have been a formative one for us in many ways, and not just in Britain but, with important variations, throughout the linguistic and literary social world covered by the *Longman Literature in English Series*.

There is my claim. In being able to define the grounds of that claim in the chapters that follow I have acquired many debts. First I am indebted to the general editors of this series for their patience and encouragement. My wife Jennifer has borne with me and this book beyond the call of duty or even love. The students in my graduate seminar in Romantic fiction at the University of Alberta in 1983–84, namely Kabelo Keakile, Rhoda Zuk, Rick Martin, Janz Lim, Steve Scott, and Kelly Hewson, made essential contributions to the formation of the ideas in this book, as also did my colleagues and the students in the English Department who listened to and challenged an earlier version of the arguments contained herein, in the Edmund Kemper Broadus Lectures for 1984 at the University of Alberta. Catrin Owen, Barbara Miron, Richard Gooding, and Michelle Jones helped greatly with research and my wife, Linda Pasmore, Flora Pavich, and Nora Potts transformed messy and hesitant-looking manuscript into confident-looking and readable typescript. The University of Alberta and the Social Sciences and Humanities Research Council of Canada provided indispensable time for research. For essential help with that research I am very grateful to the University of Alberta Bruce Peel

Special Collections Library, presided over by John Charles, and the British and Bodleian Libraries. Finally, I could not have done without the moral and material help of Vera and Albert Levine, Sue and Dave Coles, and Irene and Tom Stanley. I dedicate this book to my wife and to my students.

Gary Kelly
Edmonton, August, 1987

# Chapter 1
# Fiction and British Society 1789–1830

Why do people read fiction? Out of interest, is one obvious answer. As Henry James put it: 'The only obligation to which in advance we may hold a novel . . . is that it be interesting'.[1] But 'interest' is a complex word. Its first sense, from the sixteenth century, has to do with relations to property: to have an interest in something is to have a claim to or share in it. The relation generates an attitude: to have a claim to something gives one a concern in or about it. This sense was developed further during the late eighteenth century: to be interested meant to have concern for or curiosity about a person or thing. Almost immediately, the attitude was transferred to the object of the attitude, in a third sense: to interest is to arouse curiosity or attention, to matter or make a difference.[2] People read fiction – or anything, including this book – because what they read is matter of interest, in all these senses; they read fiction because it is about the kinds of things, persons, or attitudes in which they have, in real life, an interest. Of course, not all groups in society have the same interests, and so the themes and the forms of fiction in Britain during the Romantic period were determined in large part by the interests, real or imagined, of its readers, writers, and publishers. This chapter will specify some of the most important of those interests.

The themes and artistic forms of fiction are, however, also determined in part by the material forms and circumstances of the production, distribution, and marketing of fiction. These forms and conditions during the Romantic period were in some respects similar to but in important respects quite different from those that prevail now. In the first place, fiction was distributed in three main material forms – magazines, chapbooks, and books. There was also serial publication in parts – purchase on the instalment plan – and reprinting of fiction of the past ('classic' fiction) in cheaper formats than were allowed for 'fiction of the day'. All of these physical forms of fiction could be bought by individuals and groups, or rented by individuals, and in general the cheaper forms or serial forms were purchased, whereas the expensive, multi-volume 'novels of the day' were rented, principally because they were considered ephemeral reading, 'mere' entertainment, and not usually worth buying to keep, unlike much 'solid' or 'serious' reading, such as the 'classics' (including 'classic' novels), history, poetry, *belles lettres*, and so on. Thus all of the material forms by which fiction was disseminated were already surrounded by social values and represented major social and cultural differences, partly because of price, but partly, too, because of social and cultural attitudes and values. During the Romantic period many of these values shifted and changed, like the themes and artistic forms of the fiction, in response to major social and cultural changes.

There was noticeable change in magazine fiction, for example. By the late eighteenth century magazines had an enormous sale and virtually universal distribution. They were by then also highly specialized according to local, regional, professional, social, cultural, and political differences in British society. They were the chief channels for dissemination of information of all kinds, as well as for dissemination of such cultural movements as the Enlightenment and Sensibility. In short, they were the leading manifestation of what was referred to at the time as 'the rise of the reading public' – the apparent turning of the upper and middle ranks of society, and even many of the lower ranks, to reading, especially reading fiction. The most common variety of magazine in the late eighteenth century, the 'miscellany', for example, contained a good deal of fiction, and after 1800 there were increasing numbers of magazines devoted entirely to fiction. The miscellany magazine served the rapidly increasing urban professional classes and brought together between the covers of the monthly periodical such discourses of knowledge as history, current events, biography, moral essays, fashion, exploration, science, agricultural and industrial 'improvements', the arts – including painting, theatre, gardening, *belles lettres* – and guidance in matters of manners, fashion, taste, and criticism.

More important, in such magazines there was a fusion of genteel and professional values, and many of the miscellany magazines relied heavily for their fiction and poetry on readers' contributions. In other words, they relied on the desire of their readers to be writers, to participate in the apparently genteel culture of authorship in the *belles lettres*, even if – or perhaps especially if – it meant doing so for nothing, since writing for pay was still considered ungenteel. This urge to be published reached its height in the 1790s and was associated with the 'pseudo-genteel' nature of the miscellanies, when 'thousands of amateurs came to regard writing for the magazines as a sign of arrival in cultivated society'.[3] Nevertheless, during the Romantic period this situation changed radically. For with the rise of the great literary miscellany periodicals in the early nineteenth century, the *Edinburgh*

*Review* (1802), the *Quarterly Review* (1809), *Blackwood's Magazine* (1817), the *London Magazine* of John Scott (1820), the *Westminster Review* (1824), *Fraser's Magazine* (1830), and others, with well-paid professional writers, the age of the genteel amateur in the literary periodicals came to an end. As literature was constructed as a major social institution of middle-class culture it was given over to professionals, including professional writers of fiction.

Fiction in book form, and books in general, were expensive, and were still regarded largely as upper-class property. Yet acquisition of books by the gentry as a form of conspicuous consumption was only a few generations old, as reflected in the larger size, the more public function, and the more prominent position libraries came to have in the architecture of country manors and town houses in the mid-eighteenth century. According to the historian of the English country house, Mark Girouard, for example, 'in big houses the main informal living room was usually the library. In the late eighteenth and early nineteenth century the country-house library was at its apogee',[4] and there the new upper- and middle-class social culture of domesticity and informality joined hands with the new culture of books. Thus reading or even owning books became fashionable, and during the Romantic period more and more booksellers began manufacturing and marketing relatively inexpensive versions of the books owned by the well-to-do gentry. These 'elegant' reprints, often embellished with engravings by fashionable artists, were aimed at upwardly mobile professional and middle-class people who aspired to possess 'polite' literature. It was at this time that some novels of the past century were canonized as 'classics', to join the already established reprint classics of *belles lettres* in non-fiction prose and verse. Books remained expensive, however, partly because bookselling remained a fairly conservative trade, though it became much less so during the Romantic period. Another problem was the financial system, and the complicated system of exchanging promissory notes between booksellers and printers, which contributed to the disastrous series of bankruptcies in 1826. The main cause of the crash of 1826 as well as one cause of the great boom in bookselling was the new entrepreneurial spirit in bookselling, and especially the selling of fiction. For the rapid growth in demand for books, and above all for novels, seemed to dispel the traditional caution of the book trade.[5]

There were several ways eager participants in the 'rise of the reading public' could get around the high cost of novels in book form. One was the book club, formed primarily to share the cost of getting books of the day and to enable its members to participate in the century's movements of professionalized intellectual inquiry and rational 'improvement'.[6] Often the distribution of books was part of a programme of discussion and other literary and cultural socializing. These clubs were formed at all levels of society, from upper classes to working classes, and on the whole the members of an individual club came from the same social or religious section of society. Books could also be obtained through subscription libraries, a kind of closed-membership circulating library, usually operated from a bookseller's shop, or coffee-house, or public house. Public houses and coffee-houses also offered their own small collections of books, as well as newspapers, for rental, serving the lower social levels of the town readership.

Then there was a very active market in books through selling of parts or numbers: for a few pennies a week or month someone who could not afford a single outlay of several shillings could acquire books, mostly reprints. In the nineteenth century this form of distribution became for a while the normal way of marketing new fiction. The main way of obtaining books, and especially novels, however, was the circulating or rental library, for if books could be bought by only a few, they could be rented by many many more.[7] Circulating libraries had appeared by the 1720s, spread rapidly throughout Britain, and were commonplace by the second half of the eighteenth century. Thus the rise of the circulating libraries coincided with the rise of the professional classes and with urbanization and the commercialization of leisure. The larger and more elegant libraries were located in places of fashionable resort, suggesting that reading had become a prominent part of the commerce of culture. By 1800 humble circulating libraries could be found even in small towns and villages, suggesting that reading was being commercialized for almost all classes of society. The majority of titles were usually from 'polite literature' such as history, travels, essays, poetry, and *belles lettres*; but the majority of the total stock was usually fiction, both 'classics' and fashionable novels, and it was generally believed that most of the borrowings were from the stock of fiction. By 1789, circulating libraries were a central institution in the rapidly expanding leisure industry and a controversial element in the world of fashionable consumption where class attitudes, values, and cultures met, came into conflict, and were worked out.

Meanwhile, fiction in chapbook form for the labouring, artisan, and lower middle classes also underwent significant changes during the Romantic period. From half to three-quarters of the lower classes could read (and up to half the women of those classes could read) though not many were therefore avid or even occasional readers. Partly this was because books or even magazines were simply too expensive for poorer readers, until the very end of the Romantic period. Partly it was because customary or traditional oral culture still dominated the experience of most of the common people, especially in the countryside, and partly it was because reading and books were seen as class property – the property of the upper and middle classes.[8] Nevertheless, the lower classes did have their own popular print, or 'street literature'.[9] 'Street literature' was in many ways another embodiment of the world-view of the traditional oral culture of the common people.[10] It included a great deal of 'non-fiction' material, such as dream and prophecy books, folk-medicine, science and how-to books, magic, 'godly books', jest-books, and so on; but a large part of it was fiction. Chap-book tales were sold in town and country by chapmen, or pedlars of miscellaneous goods – hence the name chapbook. Similar kinds of chapbook fiction were sold all over north-western Europe almost from the advent of print until well into the second half of the nineteenth century. Its modern descendants are comic books and story magazines, pop records and pulp novels, and chapbooks similar to the original ones are still sold in market-places of Africa.[11] The popular narrative chapbooks were *Jack and the Giants, Tom Hickathrift, Dick Whittington, Valentine and Orson, Fortunatus, Fair Rosamond*, and prankster-tales featuring a variety of tailors, weavers, petty thieves, and other lower-class jokers. Closely associated with these stories was a group of adventure tales, some borrowed from middle-class literature, such as *Robinson Crusoe, The English Hermit, Baron Munchausen*, and even *The Pilgrim's Progress*. Scotland in particular was rich in chapbook literature, some of it in written forms of Scots dialect.[12] In the late eighteenth century new matter was added to the centuries-old 'street literature', but these additions were adapted to the themes and the world-view of the traditional material.

In fact, what the middle and upper classes of late eighteenth-century Britain knew of popular culture was mostly what they could find in chapbooks and broadsheets. They 'discovered' this literature as a major social fact in the 1790s and they began to suppress it and to appropriate it for their own fiction, but popular print and fiction continued to develop and grow in country and town, shaking off all attempts to control and channel it. Hardly had middle-class reformers such as Hannah More and the Religious Tract Society begun to attempt to uproot traditional popular fiction, and working-class radicals also begun to condemn it as a vestige of paternalistic society in the 1790s and early 1800s, when lower-class readers, especially in towns, began to leave behind the traditional chapbooks and purchase cheap, cut-down versions of the fashionable novelties – mainly sentimental tales and Gothic romances – being read by their betters. This dramatic change in the format as well as the content of popular fiction was part of larger and broader changes in working-class leisure and culture, and the development of a new, commercialized culture of those classes.[13]

Thus the material form and distribution of fiction and changes therein reflected and even transacted complex and shifting social and cultural differences during the Romantic period. These differences, tensions, and conflicts, already alluded to in the previous pages, show up dramatically in critical attitudes to and reaction against fiction of various kinds during the Romantic period. Yet the ambivalence and the controversy about fiction were signs of fiction's central place in the ideological conflicts of a society in the process of restructuring and redefining itself.

Probably the fiction most complacently accepted by its readers was chapbook fiction, and there is plenty of evidence of the impact that the traditional small books made on their readers: they marked them for life. Besides the traditional chapbooks, the fictions that helped shape the sense of self and world for common readers were *The Pilgrim's Progress* and *Robinson Crusoe*. Crusoe appealed to young boys and apprentices as much as Jack the Giant-Killer, Dick Whittington, Christian the Pilgrim, and Joseph in the Bible, for very similar reasons. They turn up in one working-class autobiography after another, not just as heroes of stories, but as informing models for encountering the world, as versions of a myth about the self and society.[14] When the lower-class readers tried to go beyond the traditional chapbooks and associated novels, however, they found the same social stratifications, relativities, and obstacles that they would find in their working lives, their pursuit of leisure and recreation, and their attempts to make the country's political and cultural institutions responsive to their own aspirations. Novels and any kind of books of the day, let alone learning, scholarship, and 'classic' literature, were class property. The world beyond cheap print was a fallen and divided world: the paradigm haunted political as well as religious consciousness. On the other hand, as we have seen, and will see again in more detail in the next chapter, middle-class hostility to popular chapbook fiction was strong, and resulted in several projects to uproot it and replace it with fiction of 'the right sort', fiction which modelled a middle-class version of self and social relations (apparently without much success) for lower-class readers. Significantly, though, reformers such as Hannah More and the Religious Tract Society turned to fiction only with the greatest reluctance and distaste, as the only way to engage the interest of the common people. Fictionality and narrativity were still closely associated with 'irrational' and 'immoral' forms of oral, communal, popular culture.

Reformers and moralists such as Hannah More were just as hostile, however, if not quite so attentive, to the fiction of the middle and upper classes, the 'circulating-library novel' or 'modern novel'. In the widespread condemnation of 'modern novels' several commonplace themes were repeated (and had been repeated for several decades before

1789): that circulating-library novels raised false expectations of life and thus made one unfit to survive this vale of tears, that women of the middle classes were its usual devotees and victims, that it was similar in its effects to excessive drinking, and that novel reading affected one's personal, inward self in some way that was dangerous to both self and society.[15] In fact, research indicates that there were as many men as women patrons of circulating libraries and that most came from the professional middle classes.[16] What they found in 'the ever-pouring stream of high-flown and sentimental fiction from the circulating library' were mostly images of their fear and their fantasy, fictions of love and property where what was supposed to be aristocratic and decadent court culture met the culture of the professional and middle classes. For novels had, since the seventeenth century, been associated with aristocratic and gentry values and culture.

The principal danger, as far as such commentators were concerned, was that novels would become an instrument of ideological penetration by what was seen as decadent aristocratic or gentry culture, depicted as either glamorous libertinism or its transmuted form of sensibility or sentimentalism, into the lives and consciousness of those lower down the social scale. Such penetration, it was thought, would help to ensure the continued ideological and social hegemony of the upper classes. In 1793 a reader wrote to the editor of the *Gentleman's Magazine* to denounce the modern novel's preoccupation with fashionable vices, libertine loves, and high feeling: 'This contagion is the more to be dreaded as it daily spreads through all ranks of people; and Miss the Taylor's Daughter talks now as familiarly, to her confident [i.e., confidante] Miss Staytape, of swains and sentiments as the accomplished Dames of genteel life'.[17] Twelve years later in October 1805 a writer in the same magazine argued that the pleasure of novel reading consists 'in the reader's being introduced into the acquaintance of a class of personages of superior wealth and rank, of extraordinary virtues and extravagant vices, with whom he is not likely to become familiar in any other way'.[18]

Defenders of the novel were in a minority. They focused on the qualities of a bourgeois domestic realism, such as was to be found in Defoe and a few others, for, like the majority of critics, they rejected the novel of sensibility and of fashionable life. This line of defence frequently involved making a distinction between 'modern novel' and 'modern romance', celebrating the potential for domestic realism of the former, and denouncing the decadent aristocratic extravagance suppos-edly found in the latter. Thus Robert Alves, in his *Sketches of a History of Literature* (1794), designed as a guidebook for the middle-class aspirant to literary culture, preferred history to fiction, as more 'solid' and 'useful' (terms repeated many times).

> Novel-writing, however, [he admitted] as containing the
> history of man in a private capacity, with his various
> peculiarities, foibles, and good qualities, may, though less
> solemn in its objects, become, in able hands, peculiarly
> interesting in detail, from those domestic incidents and
> peculiar situations which are more or less the lot of all.
> (p. 232)

Three years later, in the *Monthly Magazine*, which often represented
the values of liberal professionals, professional intellectuals, and liberal
Dissent, Mary Hays wrote:

> The business of familiar narrative should be to describe life
> and manners in real or probable situations, to delineate the
> human mind in its endless varieties, to develope the heart,
> to paint the passions, to trace the springs of action, to
> interest the imagination, exercise the affections, and
> awaken the powers of the mind. A good novel ought to
> be subservient to the purposes of truth and
> philosophy. . . .

Two months later, another reader of the *Monthly Magazine* wrote to
agree with Mary Hays that the novel ought to be a vehicle for social
and political information and enlightenment, as it was in Dr John
Moore's *Zeluco* (1789) and recent novels by the 'English Jacobins'.
Such novels

> have probably diffused more liberal, and more just moral
> ideas, than could, in the same space of time, have been
> inculcated upon the public by a thousand sermons, or by
> as many dry political disquisitions. . . . Those who are
> afraid of philosophy, when she speaks in the language of
> the schools, are glad of her acquaintance, and proud of
> being able to converse with her, when she talks *plain
> prose*.[19]

   The mainstream of criticism, however, continued to be hostile, and
to focus on the ideological dangers of novel reading by emphasizing
its negative moral and intellectual effects. Novels were condemned for
corrupting the morals, taste, and intellect of their readers and then
these effects were supposed to have further, social consequences. The
anonymous author of *The Evils of Adultery and Prostitution* (1792)
declared that, 'The increase of novels will help to account for the
increase of prostitution and for the numerous adulteries and elopements
that we hear of in the different parts of the kingdom.'[20]

These criticisms are testimony to the power fiction was thought to have in shaping the inner self of the reader and thus affecting ethical action and social relations – if the fact of the huge consumption of fiction by all classes were not testimony enough. But these criticisms of the novel and other kinds of fiction articulate the specific role fiction, more than any other form of print or literary culture, was supposed to have in affecting and mediating social relations and conflicts of the Romantic period. Now it is time to look more closely at those relations and conflicts. In the chapters that follow I will then explore in more detail the great variety of ways in which Romantic fiction embodied, modelled, and mediated the competing and conflicting values, visions, and relations of self and society during the years 1789 to 1830.

As we have seen, although most novel readers and writers during the Romantic period belonged to the professional and middle classes, most novels of the period, from the 1790s through to the 1820s, continued to dwell, favourably or unfavourably, on the way of life, culture, values, and power of the dominant class in society, the gentry – those who owned a landed estate large enough to support a life of leisure and conspicuous consumption of certain traditional kinds. The gentry were divided into the smaller or 'local' gentry and the larger, more cosmopolitan 'county' gentry, they included the aristocracy (or those with both land *and* a title), and they dominated almost all aspects of society in the eighteenth century.[21] Their wealth made them social leaders in country society and in their urban places of resort and recreation. They dominated the leading professions because their younger sons, those not destined to inherit the family estate, were often disposed of by being set up in one of these professions. The gentry controlled local administration of law and social services and, indirectly, the educational system.

Throughout the eighteenth century they enjoyed a 'golden age' of influence and prosperity, based on their domination of the social institutions just described, a long-term rise in the prices for agricultural commodities, and certain important if often localized 'improvements' in agricultural productivity and transportation. The gentry were often in a position to benefit from early forms of industrialization because of their ownership of resources and capital and their political power and local influence. Furthermore, since they had a culture of conspicuous consumption, their increasing power and prosperity inspired a commercial revolution in comfort, leisure, and entertainment of all kinds (including novel reading) in the latter part of the eighteenth century.[22] In fact, there was felt to be a conflict between the demands of capitalist practices of estate management and improvement on one hand and the culture of free-spending – luxury – on the other. The gentleman who lost his estate by foolish extravagance or unproductive 'improvement' was a commonplace in the fiction of the century.

The very 'success' of the gentry, however, led to a challenge to their domination from that section of society closest to them, the professional middle classes. The growth in wealth and complexity of British society in the eighteenth century led to the rapid increase in the numbers, wealth, variety, prestige, and power of professional men (and a few women) of all kinds – lawyers, teachers, poets, architects, doctors, scriveners, estate managers, dentists, landscape designers, civil servants, authors, military men, and so on.[23] Throughout the eighteenth century some professional men found it easier to gain entry to the gentry class by amassing enough money to buy estates left vacant by the accidents of mortality or encumbered with debt by the gentry's proverbial extravagance and mismanagement. Certainly it was widely believed that the professions were one of the main avenues by which a family might advance, by exercise of proper middle-class prudence and self-discipline, over several generations, from lower levels of society to the highest. This system of apparent and actual social mobility seemed to make British society both stable and open to a degree not found anywhere else.[24]

By 1789, however, many professional middle-class people had come to question and to challenge the hegemony of the gentry. Not every professional man could expect to rise to gentry estate and status; yet more and more professional men and women were socialized, in their families and at school and university, to attitudes of limited egalitarianism and worth by personal merit. They were then reinforced in principles of independence and meritocracy by their frustrating experiences in a world still dominated by the patronage system of gentry hegemony and court politics.[25] By the mid-eighteenth century many professionals had become critical of gentry society and patronage; by the later part of the century they had developed their own centres of association and power in the towns, and their own channels of communication and self-expression, especially newspapers and novels. Significantly it was during these years that many professions began to establish internal organization and self-government in order to sustain their social autonomy.[26]

More important than institutional developments, however, were changes in attitudes, values, and beliefs – in the ideology of the professional middle classes, especially as thematized in four main issues: the nature and importance of the individual self; the changing nature and role of the family and the 'domestic affections' (including childhood and the role of women); relations between different social classes and ranks; and 'national' history, culture, identity, and language (including the relation of speech and writing and the nature and function of literature). This is where fiction was important, for, as we shall see, in its guise as 'mere' entertainment and in its wide readership prose fiction was ideally suited for the role of ideological communication in an age of social change and conflict. Furthermore, the social and ideological differentiation of the professional middle classes was expressed in several different areas of social practice, including intellectual, cultural, and religious movements, but all of these movements, too, were expressed in fiction, among other kinds of written discourse, including historiography, scientific and philosophical work, social studies and social criticism, and polemics, or overt propaganda, culminating in fiction of the Romantic period.

The eighteenth-century Enlightenment, for example, was a complex intellectual and cultural movement led by professional men, many of them in universities (in Scotland) or places of higher education (in England), in the law (especially in Scotland), or in the clergy (in England, in the Dissenting clergy). It is true that the Enlightenment had important patrons and participants among the aristocracy and gentry, especially where the Enlightenment extended Renaissance humanism or took part in neo-classical culture, and assisted or justified agricultural and social 'improvement' – various schemes to improve economic productivity and social order – and early forms of industrialization. Indeed, 'improvement' and 'progress' became by-words for many kinds of social change in the later eighteenth century, both positive and negative. Many Enlightenment writers argued that 'progress' and 'improvement' could take place and have positive results only if professional middle-class values of reason, order, self-discipline, social and religious toleration, free inquiry, and free enterprise prevailed against the 'superstitions', mystifications, prejudices, censorship, self-indulgence, and 'unreason' which the Enlightenment writers associated with the court governments, patronage system, fixed hierarchical social structures, economic monopolies, and oppressive institutions of the *ancien régime*.

Enlightenment writers often stressed individual moral and intellectual worth or merit against 'artificial' social categories such as rank or other forms of ascribed or unearned status. They often argued for an egalitarian moral, affective, and intellectual sympathy as the social bond between individuals in a family, community, or nation, rather than what they saw as the *ancien régime*'s system of patronage and dependence, which supposedly deformed and denatured relations between husband and wife, parents and children, friends, members of a profession, and members of different social classes, nationalities, races, or even species.[27]

The eighteenth-century Enlightenment in Britain was a diverse, interrelated set of movements. The Scottish Enlightenment was centred in Edinburgh (the 'Athens of the North') and the Scottish universities and legal profession.[28] The English provincial Enlightenment was centred in towns such as Norwich, Birmingham, and Manchester and the new mercantile and industrial classes there. The English Nonconformist Enlightenment, which was closely connected to the provincial Enlightenment, was centred in the Dissenting academies and in certain towns with large Dissenting communities or historic associations with religious Dissent. Many men of the Nonconformist Enlightenment were, at least nominally, clergymen, but many of them were also heavily influenced by certain writers of the French Enlightenment. Nevertheless, these Enlightenment movements, perhaps like Renaissance humanism in an earlier period, gave expression and self-definition to the increasingly confident professional classes. Dissent had, since the seventeenth century, been a way in which self-conscious middle-class and artisan groups could differentiate themselves from a society dominated by court culture and patronage at every level.[29]

During the late eighteenth century, elements of liberal and rational Dissent played an active role in political movements directed against court politics and gentry hegemony. In the 1790s many liberal Dissenters actively supported the French Revolution, and often formed the leadership of reformist political societies.[30] Thus liberal, Enlightenment Dissent could also turn into secular forms of social differentiation and protest. Liberal Dissent was a cultural and social model for many early Romantic writers; and as we shall see, several leading Romantic novelists and critics, such as William Godwin and William Hazlitt, came directly from the culture of the English provincial and Nonconformist Enlightenments. Furthermore, the Scottish Enlightenment, revised and disseminated through such major Romantic periodicals as the *Edinburgh Review*, the *Quarterly Review*, and *Blackwood's Magazine*, and revised and fictionalized by such major Romantic novelists as Walter Scott and John Galt, had a great influence in shaping Romantic culture, as a specifically professional middle-class culture, in all parts of Britain – indeed, in many parts of Europe. These revisions and disseminations will be traced in several of the chapters that follow.

The specifically cultural and aesthetic (as distinct from scientific, scholarly, and philosophical) expressions of professional and middle-class consciousness in the later eighteenth century are to be found largely in the complex movement known as Sensibility or Sentimentalism (formerly called 'Pre-Romanticism' by some scholars).[31] To some extent Sensibility expressed reaction against certain Enlightenment views, values, and ideas; in other respects it was a continuation, development, and further expression of them, especially the ideas of the autonomous subjective self and sympathy as the social bond.

Writers of both the Enlightenment and Sensibility turned to the novel as a way of dramatizing as well as popularizing their ideas – writers such as Voltaire, Diderot, and Rousseau in France, Goethe in Germany, Smollett and Henry Mackenzie in Scotland, and (with reservations) Goldsmith, Sterne, Horace Walpole, Henry Brooke, William Beckford, Thomas Day, and Robert Bage in England.

Sentimental fiction in particular, with its elements of sentimental (rather than satirical) social criticism, its rapid development of techniques of writing the inward self, its philanthropic and benevolent optimism, its resistance to the culture of the social élite, its reformist zeal, its emphasis on inner moral and intellectual worth, its celebration of an aristocracy of feeling, its sympathetic treatment of the 'domestic affections', including the new importance and role of childhood and of women, did much to define and promote, for readers who were mostly members of the professional and middle classes, the ideas and ideals of those classes, against the social and cultural values and practices of the courtly, aristocratic, and gentry classes and their emulators. Novelists of the Romantic period, from Godwin to Scott, continued to draw on the formal and thematic repertory of Enlightenment and Sentimental novelists, for the same reasons. Indeed, one could argue that, while many Romantic writers were hostile to certain values and techniques of the Enlightenment and Sentimental writers, Romanticism itself largely continued the social and cultural project of the Enlightenment and Sensibility: to redefine the individual and society in ways different from what were thought to be the definitions and practices of the power-holding or hegemonic classes, the aristocracy and gentry.

The professional and middle classes did not break with the gentry and aristocracy, however, far from it. During the Romantic period, in particular, the exchange between the middle and upper classes clearly entered a new and important phase. On one hand, many professional and middle-class ideologues and writers – including novelists – argued for and presented models for the professionalization of the ruling classes, indeed, of all of society. On the other hand, many of these writers also pictured and promoted the gentrification of the professional and middle classes. As we shall see, in Chapters 4 and 5, the two foremost novelists of the Romantic period, Jane Austen and Walter Scott, depict and argue for this kind of exchange and mutual modification of ideology and social practice by the ruling classes and their nearest competitors. This was a social dialectic that would have a long history, reaching down to the present.[32]

Furthermore, as culture became increasingly commercialized, social mobility and social emulation were marketed through the ever-changing field of social practice known as fashion – a complex language of social differentiation and distinction. As William Hazlitt wrote in 1830, 'Fashion is gentility running away from vulgarity and afraid of being overtaken.'[33] Significantly, the novel (along with magazines) was both a major vehicle for disseminating information about and criticism of fashion, and itself a major and controversial item of fashionable consumption. Thus the novel had a central place in the culture and social practices of the upper and professional middle classes – that is, of the classes who could afford to buy or rent novels – during the Romantic period. Yet, as we have seen, these readers had a deeply ambivalent attitude to the novel, precisely because of its participation in the culture of fashion and emulation that mediated relations between the upper and middle classes.

Social emulation and conflict between upper and middle classes formed a large part of the subject matter, and formed the basis for the commercial viability of the novel. But these classes did not conduct their negotiations in isolation from the rest of society, the majority. On the contrary, their relations with one another, especially during the Romantic period, were profoundly influenced by their perceptions of the nature of and challenges from the lower classes, and these perceptions also exercised a powerful shaping force on the Romantic novel. The actual condition of the lower classes of Britain in the late eighteenth and early nineteenth century is a complex and controversial issue. In the first place, far more than upper- and professional middle-class culture, the culture of the labouring classes was highly local and subject to local conditions of economic production as well as to local tradition, custom, and social conflict.[34] Obviously there were great differences between the situation, experiences, and culture of London labourers and Scottish crofters, Irish peasants and East Anglian farm workers, town artisans and town labourers, workers in small shops and workers in factories.

Nevertheless, one piece of evidence that there was a broadly national lower-class culture is the remarkably homogeneous body of cheap popular print, and especially cheap fiction, which flourished in England, Scotland, and Ireland from the late sixteenth to the early nineteenth century.[35] Most labouring people in the late eighteenth and early nineteenth century probably benefited little from the improved economic conditions that were benefiting their 'betters'; and there was an increasing sense of class alienation, and resentment of the conspicuously consuming gentry and their professional associates, the Anglican clergy.[36] Enclosure of common lands and capitalist practices in land management continued to be viewed by the common people as an abandonment by the gentry of their traditional responsibilities.[37] Furthermore, the Romantic period saw a great increase of pressures on the labouring classes and their culture from new forces of urbanization, population increase, industrialization, the stresses of war-time economy, commercialization of popular culture, and more powerful engines of state control and social supervision.[38]

These changes showed up less in the popular fiction of the common people than in civic disturbance and in the new mass literature of lower-class political radicalism. At the same time, as we have seen, these forces also led to a decline in the older culture of custom, reflected in the popular chapbook literature or 'street literature' of the common people, which had remained virtually unchanged since the seventeenth century. Furthermore, these forces led to the rise of new forms of 'street literature', while middle-class reformers tried to uproot both this 'traditional' popular literature and its parallel oral culture, seeing both as manifestations of an irrational popular culture that had to be extirpated in the interests of progress, morals, and public order.

Meanwhile, middle-class novelists gave greater attention to the character and culture of the common people, as they saw them. In the 1790s some novelists, such as William Godwin and Isaac D'Israeli, gave attention to the problem of lower-class radicalism, in 'Jacobin' and 'Anti-Jacobin' novels (see the next chapter). After 1800 other novelists, such as Maria Edgeworth and Elizabeth Hamilton, attacked the popular culture of 'superstition', tradition, and custom, while other novelists, such as Jane Porter and Sir Walter Scott, appropriated elements of 'traditional' popular culture, such as folklore, folksong, and the folktales, to the project of describing – or rather inventing – a 'national' culture that would bridge social gaps and reconcile social conflicts in a vision of a transcendental national character and destiny (see Ch. 3). Other novelists, such as Mary Mitford, tried to present a version of the rural lower classes imbued with middle-class virtues, while novelists of the 1820s such as Pierce Egan and Edward Bulwer Lytton (in his 'silver-fork novels' and 'Newgate novels') celebrated the urban underworld and the lower-class 'folk' and their culture as the modern site of 'Merrie England' (the Romantic period also saw a revival of interest in the Robin Hood legend), anticipating the work of Dickens and other novelists of the 1830s and later (see Ch. 6). For just as the idea of autonomous and inward selfhood implicitly subverted ideas of status by ascription, tradition, and birth, so the idea of the nation as a historical fact yet also a transcendental reality or cultural essence implicitly subverted the hierarchical model of social structure and diminished the importance of divisions of rank or class. This idea of the nation could be used to undermine paternalism; it could also be used to head off middle- and lower-class discontent as 'unpatriotic'.

Such was the case during the 1790s, for example, when war broke out between Britain and a militantly nationalistic and revolutionary France. Nationalism was used to block solidarity between French revolutionaries and the artisans, Nonconformists, and discontented middle-class clerks and professionals who were described contemptuously as 'English Jacobins'. Later still, in the post-war years, nationalism was appropriated by reformers of all classes in order to imply that their calls for political reform were in the name of restoring the identity of state and people.

Nationalism of the new type had a profound effect on Romantic literature and especially fiction precisely because this kind of nationalism had to be written, though it was supposed to originate in the oral culture of the nation. For the modern 'nation' is an 'imagined community', unlike the actual communities of family and immediate society, 'because the members of even the smallest nation will never know most of their fellow-members, meet them, or even hear of them, yet in the minds of each lives the image of their communion'.[39] The image of the nation did not reflect and serve the interests of all of British society, but only those parts that had or were actively seeking social domination and leadership. Since these social elements constituted most of the well-to-do and literate classes, it was the two forms of print most commonly used by these classes, the newspaper and the novel, which, according to Benedict Anderson, 'provided the technical means for "re-presenting" the *kind* of imagined community that is the nation'.[40]

One further important point for the destiny of the novel during the Romantic period is that British national identity had to be constructed in writing and print because there was as yet no British national dialect of spoken English. Written English was the only common language of Britain for all classes and regions. At the same time, written English was being made the basis for a 'standard' spoken English, and this language was in the hands of professionals, especially the increasingly important professions of teaching, journalism, and literature.[41] Indeed, literature itself was becoming increasingly important as the repository for national identity. Literature would later be organized into a canon so that it could form the basis for national education and for the 'serious' literature of the day, by which ideological communication could be effected between the administrative and professional élites scattered throughout the three kingdoms. But speech itself, the local and regional dialects and sociolects which revealed instantly the social stratification of language in Britain, had to be dealt with. Crude and conventionalized versions of dialect-in-writing had been used in literature and especially drama for some two centuries, but increasingly so in the eighteenth century. Sociolect, especially the 'jargon' and 'cant' of professions, had also been well used in eighteenth-century fiction, for example in the novels of Fielding and Smollett. With the creation after 1800 of the kind of fiction called the 'national tale', dialect and sociolect were appropriated by writing in a thorough and comprehensive way.

The social and historical novels of the early 1800s presented their professional and middle-class readers with a linguistic model of the desired British national identity. The standard written English of the narration of such novels (almost always some form of third-person narration) contains and subordinates the various kinds of non-standard English used to represent and to characterize individuals from various classes and regions. Furthermore, the fact that the 'serious' characters in such novels tend to 'speak' in the same standard English used by the narrator only reinforces the implicit argument of such novels: full selfhood is shown in standard written English; marginal or merely social selfhood is shown in non-standard or 'deviant' forms of English. The social and historical novel deals decisively with the problems of class and regionalism by positing, in its linguistic structure, a model of comprehensive national identity couched in the language used and commanded by the professional middle classes.

Related to this use of language to present a certain image of social order, and of equal importance for the social function of fiction, was the development of obvious techniques of literariness, particularly in the novel but also in the 'art tale' or short story in its modern form. For the Romantic period saw the rise of prose fiction – or at least well-made and 'serious' fiction – from being considered sub- or quasi-literary to full literary status. The evident signs of literariness in fiction took several forms. In the 1790s, for example, the 'English Jacobins' used quotation and allusion, as well as names of characters, to draw parallels from classic English literature and history to support their fictional arguments. Another kind of 'philosophical' literariness is seen in such novels as those of Dr John Moore, a literariness one might expect from a Scot who lived through the golden age of the Scottish Enlightenment. Moore published his first novel, *Zeluco*, in 1789, and he gave it all the features of a fiction suitable for intellectually serious and well-educated professional people. It is full of philosophical dialogues and brief essays by the narrator, and its persistent narrative figure is the movement from a general maxim or observation to the particular example in the story – philosophy teaching by examples, as Bolingbroke defined historiography. Moore also uses epigraphs at the head of many of his chapters to suggest the matter to follow. This tactic was taken up and given a different twist by Ann Radcliffe, who uses classic English poets and eighteenth-century Sentimental poets rather than the Latin classics and older English writers favoured by Moore (see the next Chapter).

Another major technique of literariness came after 1800 – what one might call the footnote-novel or novel of social and historical description. The first footnote-tale was Maria Edgeworth's *Castle Rackrent* (1800), with its three layers of editorial apparatus mediating the details of Irish folkways for an English reading public; and the antiquarian novel with footnotes, appendices, and glossaries, prepared readers for Scott's thorough appropriation of historical discourse in fiction, in the Waverley Novels (see Chs 3 and 5). Not only did Scott bring into the novel the principal kinds of non-fiction discourse of learned professional culture, namely history, biography, law, political economy, and human geography, but Scott's enormously well-stocked mind enabled him to fill his novels with a rich and sophisticated literary allusiveness, ranging from the Bible to the English 'classics' and including a good deal of 'world literature'. This enabled him to go beyond the self-conscious documentary referentiality of Edgeworth and Strutt, beyond the elegant literary decoration of Radcliffe or her imitators, and beyond the somewhat stolid philosophical authoritativeness of Dr John Moore. The all-encompassing literariness of Scott's novels made the 'modern novel' more acceptable to more kinds of readers than ever before.

Finally, a third kind of literariness proved more decisive still in establishing the novel and certain forms of short fiction as literature, a position they had to achieve in order to participate in and effectively disseminate professional middle-class versions of self, society, nation, and language. Jane Austen's novels are, in themselves, the best criticism of late eighteenth- and early nineteenth-century fiction we have, and to read Austen fully we should have a good knowledge of the novel of her day, including the 'trash of the circulating libraries'. For Austen in all of her novels (not just the early semi-parodies of Gothic and Sentimental fiction) plays with the novel-reader's habits and expectations and expertise in novel reading; she repeatedly flirts with utter conventionality in order to test the reader's skill and judgment. One might say that the more 'trash of the circulating library' one has read, the more easily one is fooled by Austen, at the same time the better equipped one is to read Austen's novel correctly. In spite of the allusions to Byron, Scott, Gothic novels, and so on, Austen deliberately avoids the *belles lettres*; the literariness, the intertextuality she uses to generate meanings, intrigue the reader, and dignify her work is that of the 'modern novel' itself. Certainly she has her moral purpose and designs on the reader; but the means she uses are not those of Radcliffe or Moore or Scott. They are the means used by any writer of 'modern novels', but turned back on themselves, as a test and a potential trap for the novel reader, including the novel readers within her novels.

It is not surprising that it was Austen rather than any of the more intellectual and literary novelists of her day who should have written what is probably the best-known statement in English about novels, at the end of the fifth chapter of *Northanger Abbey*:

'And what are you reading, Miss – – ?' 'Oh! it is only a
novel!' replies the young lady; while she lays down her
book with affected indifference, or momentary shame. –
'It is only Cecilia, or Camilla [both by Fanny Burney], or
Belinda [by Maria Edgeworth];' or, in short, only some
work in which the greatest powers of the mind are
displayed, in which the most thorough knowledge of
human nature, the happiest delineation of its varieties, the
liveliest effusions of wit and humour are conveyed to the
world in the best chosen language.

This is praise indeed, and corresponds to the modern idea of the high moral and artistic potential of the novel; but from this statement, with its happy generalities – 'the greatest powers of the mind', 'human nature', 'the world', 'the best chosen language' – one would not suspect what the preceding pages of this chapter have aimed to show: that the novel and all fiction of the Romantic period were socially and culturally relative, partial, and in some way, to a greater or lesser extent, implicated in and expressive of the social divisions and conflicts of the time, divisions and conflicts that in fact shaped Romantic fiction, as they shape fiction of any period.

Austen is, in the view of much modern criticism, the one acknowledged classic novelist of the Romantic period in Britain. She is also the representative Romantic novelist because, as we shall see in Chapter 4, she deals superbly with the central thematic and formal issues of the novel of the period – the gentrification of the professional classes and the professionalization of the gentry, the place of women in a professionalized culture that denies them any significant role in public or professional life, the establishment of a 'national' culture of distinction and discrimination in the face of fashion and commercialized culture, the re-siting of the authentic self in an inward moral and intellectual being so cultivated as to be able to negotiate successfully the varieties of social experience and cultural discriminations, the establishment of a standard speech based on writing, and resolution of the relationship of authoritative narration and detailed representation of subjective experience. Austen 'predicted' the identity and the literary culture of the gentrified professional classes which came to dominate society and culture in Britain and elsewhere during the nineteenth century. More important, however, she conceals or rather transforms the basis of her art in the rhetorical structure – the formal elements and their ordering and relationship – of the 'trash of the circulating libraries'. In doing so, she concealed the partial, relative character of her own fiction, if not from her contemporaries then from the successive generations of readers who saw themselves in her version of the novel as moral art and therefore concluded that her novels were and are normal, natural, and normative – in a word, classic literature.

Part of the task of the five chapters that follow will be to uncover aspects of Romantic fiction obscured from us by Austen's success in fulfilling Romantic fiction's drive to become the consummate yet most widely disseminated form of verbal art of and for the gentrified professional classes. Another task will be to account for the rich variety thus uncovered. In these chapters, then, emphasis will be not only on formal elements and the exercise of artistic options in particular novels and novelists, but also on the issues of the times to which these novels and novelists responded and which they helped to enact. The formal elements that will be emphasized are the usual ones of character, plot, setting, dialogue, description, and narrative 'voice' or method, but attention will also be given to elements of fiction discussed less often, namely structures of language and methods of literariness. The issues kept in view will be the central ones of most Romantic fiction, indeed much fiction from the age of Sensibility to the late nineteenth century – the nature of the individual self, the 'domestic affections', social class, and national identity.

And so the next chapter will examine the major continuities and transformations of prose fiction in the 1790s, the decade of the French Revolution, by considering particular issues or topics – the legacy of Enlightenment and Sentimental novelists; the great form of the late eighteenth-century novel of manners, sentiment, and emulation; the innovations, real or apparent, of the Gothic and Jacobin novelists; and reaction to these by Anti-Jacobin novelists, by expropriators of popular fiction, and by a fiction writer associated with the early phase of English Romanticism in poetry, Charles Lamb.

The third chapter will turn to the chief varieties of fiction in the decade and a half after 1800 and up to the appearance of the best work of Jane Austen and the phenomenal success of the 'Wizard of the North', Sir Walter Scott. Much of the fiction of this decade and a half tried to transcend the conflicts and the fictional rhetoric of the 1790s with formal and thematic innovations such as the 'national tale' and revisions of earlier fictional forms such as the tale of fashionable life, the sentimental tale, the tale of rural life, and the Gothic romance. This will also be the place to take some brief notice of that great nineteenth-century fiction industry, the tale for children and the tale for youth.

Chapters 4 and 5 deal with the major novelists of the Romantic period, Austen and Scott, whose work was the culmination of developments in late eighteenth- and early nineteenth-century fiction, representative of two major strains of Romantic fiction (the novel of selfhood and the novel of social life), and the basis for the great tradition of Victorian fiction.

The last chapters then turn to novels and quasi-novels of the decade and a half before 1830, the death of George IV, and the end of a cultural era. Here the focus will be on further fictional versions of the two major thematic complexes of Romantic art, the subjective self and the 'national' community (including the themes of the exotic and imperialism). But another focus will be on the limits of Romantic fiction, and those writers, principally the writers of quasi-novels such as Hazlitt, satirical novelists such as Peacock, and the one deconstructionist Romantic novelist, James Hogg. With Hogg we come to the opposite end of the artistic scale from Jane Austen – a novelist who lays bare the partial, class-based nature of the assumptions derived from Enlightenment sociology and history and developed with great variety in Romantic fiction, assumptions about the nature of the self, the family, the community, the nation, and the orders of language and written discourse. Not surprisingly, Hogg's novels sank without a trace, while the achievements of other Romantic novelists exercised their diverse energies in fiction and culture through the nineteenth century and into our own time, when Hogg's best novel has been exhumed, to speak to us again about our formation in and by English fiction of the Romantic period.

## Notes

*Place of publication is, unless otherwise stated, London.*

1. Henry James, 'The Art of Fiction' (1888), in *The Art of Fiction and Other Essays* (New York, 1948), p. 8.

2. All definitions from the *Oxford English Dictionary*.

3. Robert D. Mayo, *The English Novel in the Magazines 1740–1815* (Evanston Illinois and London, 1962), p. 323.

4. Mark Girouard, *Life in the English Country House: A Social and Architectural History* (1978; Harmondsworth, 1980), p. 234.

5. A. S. Collins, *The Profession of Letters: A Study of the Relation of Author to Patron, Publisher and Public, 1780–1832* (1928), p. 156.

6. Paul Kaufman, 'English Book Clubs and Their Social Import', in Paul Kaufman, *Libraries and Their Users* (1969), pp. 36–64.

7. On the circulating libraries, see Devendra P. Varma, *The Evergreen Tree of Diabolical Knowledge* (Washington D.C., 1972).

8. See David Vincent, *Bread, Knowledge and Freedom: A Study of Nineteenth-Century Working Class Autobiography* (1981), part III.

9. On chapbook literature, see Victor E. Neuburg, *Popular Literature: A History and Guide* (Harmondsworth, 1977), and the works listed in Neuburg's bibliography.

10. See Peter Burke, *Popular Culture in Early Modern Europe* (1978), pp. 256–57.

11. On African chapbooks, see Emanuel N. Obiechina, *An African Popular Literature: A Study of Onitsha Market Pamphlets* (Cambridge, 1973).

12. See William Harvey, *Scottish Chapbook Literature* (Paisley, 1903).

13. See Hugh Cunningham, *Leisure in the Industrial Revolution* (1980), and J. M. Golby and A. W. Purdue, *The Civilization of the Crowd: Popular Culture in England 1750–1900* (1984).

14. For some representative testimony to the power of popular print, see Samuel Bamford, *The Autobiography*, vol. I, *Early Days*, edited by W. Chaloner (1848–49; reprinted 1967), pp. 90–91; *John Clare's Autobiographical Writings*, edited by Eric Robinson (Oxford and New York, 1983), pp. 56–57; and Hugh Miller, *My Schools and Schoolmasters* (1877), ch. 2.

15. Surveys of reaction to the novel may be found in Joseph Bunn Heidler, *The History, from 1700 to 1800, of English Criticism of Prose Fiction* (Urbana Illinois, 1928); John Tinnon Taylor, *Early Opposition to the English Novel: The Popular Reaction from 1760 to 1830* (New York, 1943); W. F. Gallaway, Jr, 'The Conservative Attitude toward Fiction, 1770–1830', *PMLA*, 55 (1940), 1041–59; and Gary Kelly, '"This Pestiferous Reading": The Social Basis of Reaction against the Novel in Late Eighteenth- and Early Nineteenth-Century Britain', *Man and Nature*, 4 (1985), 183–94.

16. Paul Kaufman, 'In Defence of Fair Readers', in Paul Kaufman, *Libraries and Their Users*, pp. 223–28.

17. *Gentleman's Magazine*, 63 (Apr. 1793), 294.

18. *Gentleman's Magazine*, 75 (Oct. 1805), 912.

19. *Monthly Magazine*, 4 (Sept. 1797), 181; (Nov. 1797), 349.

20. *Evils of Adultery* (1792), p. 54. The author's name is not known.

21. On the gentry, see G. E. Mingay, *The Gentry: The Rise and Fall of a Ruling Class* (London and New York, 1976); see also Lawrence and Jeanne F. Stone, *An Open Elite? England 1540–1880* (Oxford, 1984).

22. On the commercialization of culture, see Neil McKendrick, John Brewer, and J. H. Plumb, *The Birth of a Consumer Society: The Commercialization of Eighteenth-Century England* (1982).

23. On the rise of the professional classes, see Geoffrey Holmes, *Augustan England: Professions, State and Society, 1680–1730* (1982).

24. Cf. Lawrence and Jeanne F. Stone, *An Open Elite?*, pp. 283–89.

25. On the sociology of the professions of the Scottish Enlightenment, see Charles Camic, *Experience and Enlightenment: Socialization for Cultural Change in Eighteenth-Century Scotland* (Chicago, 1983). See also Philip Elliott, *The Sociology of the Professions* (London and Basingstoke, 1972), p. 12.

26. See A. M. Carr-Saunders and P. A. Wilson, *The Professions* (Oxford, 1933), part II.

27. On the Enlightenment, see (among many others) Lester G. Crocker, *An Age of Crisis: Man and World in Eighteenth Century French Thought* (Baltimore and London, 1959), and Ernst Cassirer, *The Philosophy of the Enlightenment*, trans. (Princeton, 1951); on treatment of animals, see Keith Thomas, *Man and the Natural World: Changing Attitudes in England 1500–1800* (1983), chs 3 and 4.

28. On the Scottish Enlightenment, see Anand Chitnis, *The Scottish Enlightenment: A Social History* (London and Totowa New Jersey, 1976), and *Wealth and Virtue: The Shaping of Political Economy in the Scottish Enlightenment*, edited by Istvan Hont and Michael Ignatieff (Cambridge, 1983).

29. See Alan D. Gilbert, *Religion and Society in Industrial England: Church, Chapel and Social Change, 1740–1914* (London and New York, 1976), pp. 27–42.

30. See Albert Goodwin, *The Friends of Liberty: The English Democratic Movement in the Age of the French Revolution* (1979) and the works listed in its bibliography.

31. See R. F. Brissenden, *Virtue in Distress: Studies in the Novel of Sentiment from Richardson to Sade* (1974); Louis I. Bredvold, *The Natural History of Sensibility* (Detroit, 1962); and Janet Todd, *Sensibility: An Introduction* (London and New York, 1986).

32. See Martin J. Wiener, *English Culture and the Decline of the Industrial Spirit, 1850–1980* (Cambridge, 1981).

33. Quoted in N. McKendrick, J. Brewer, and J. H. Plumb, *The Birth of a Consumer Society*, p. 39.

34. See Bob Bushaway, *By Rite: Custom, Ceremony and Community in England 1700–1880* (1982).

35. See Bernard Capp, 'Popular Literature', in *Popular Culture in Seventeenth-Century England*, edited by Barry Reay (London and Sydney, 1985).

36. Pamela Horn, *The Rural World 1780–1850: Social Change in the English Countryside* (1980), pp. 35, 38. See, however, the arguments of R. M. Hartwell, in 'The Standard of Living Controversy: A Summary', in *The Industrial Revolution*, edited by R. M. Hartwell (Oxford, 1970), pp. 167–79.

37. E. P. Thompson, 'The Moral Economy of the English Crowd in the Eighteenth Century', *Past and Present*, 50 (Feb. 1971) 76–136. See also Bob Bushaway, *By Rite*.

38. See Philip Corrigan and Derek Sayer, *The Great Arch: English State Formation as Cultural Revolution* (Oxford, 1985), chs 5–6.

39. Benedict Anderson, *Imagined Communities: Reflections on the Origin and Spread of Nationalism* (1983), p. 15.

40. Anderson, *Imagined Communities*, p. 30.

41. Dick Leith, *A Social History of English* (1983), ch. 2.

## Chapter 2
# The 1790s: From Enlightenment and Sensibility to Romanticism – 'Modern Novels' and 'Tales of the Times'

The 1790s were a decade of social and political crisis in Britain and Europe. Not only did the French Revolution inspire a renewal of social criticism directed at the system of court politics, aristocratic patronage, and gentry hegemony, but a number of other social conflicts converged to shake 'Old Corruption'. Yet 'Old Corruption' recovered and did not seem to loosen its grip on power until the end of the Romantic period; and so movements of protest and reform continued to arise throughout the 1790s and beyond, to the 1820s. These movements were several, and they were to some extent interrelated. In the 1790s there was 'Jacobinism' or specifically political protest in which artisans, 'enlightened' Dissent, elements of the professional middle classes, and a few aristocrats and gentry formed a temporary coalition against 'Old Corruption.'[1] At the same time there was the sudden rise to prominence of Evangelicalism, a largely professional middle-class religious, moral, and social reform movement, within the Church of England but with objectives that went far beyond the Church to the whole of society. Emerging in the 1790s from elements of late Enlightenment and Sentimental culture, and influenced by liberal Dissent, was a broad movement in the arts, and especially literature, which is now called Romanticism.[2]

This movement attempted to redefine secular culture in the image of the progressive professional middle classes, by redefining the idea of the self, the 'domestic affections', the experience of community, the nation, and nature, and by transcendentalizing these ideas through art as a social practice free from both old forms of aristocratic patronage and new forms of vulgar commercialization. Thus, while some aspects of Romanticism grew out of Jacobinism or were sympathetic to it, and were later sympathetic to various liberal political goals, many Romantic writers were or became socially conservative in the face of continuing plebeian political protest and such later 'progressive' intellectual and philosophical movements as Utilitarianism. Broadly speaking, therefore, Romanticism was always in one way or another an 'Anti-Jacobin' movement, even when it was politically liberal or radical. Finally, from certain aspects of the English and Scottish Enlightenments, tempered by the philosophical radicalism of the 1790s, the movements known as Utilitarianism grew to prominence after 1800, associated with increasing professionalism in political economy, government and administration, social policy, and science and technology. These were not separate movements, but rather colleagues and rivals for leadership of the professional middle classes in their increasingly aggressive attempts to remake the whole of British society in the image – the ideal image – of the professional middle classes themselves.[3]

Of these diverse movements, Jacobinism, Evangelicalism, and Romanticism found immediate expression in fiction during the 1790s. Nevertheless, much of the fiction published during the 1790s was largely similar to and continuous with fiction of the various Enlightenments and the fiction of Sensibility – especially the latter. Here, too, gender differentiation in the varieties of fiction – the association of gender and genre – continued to be an important shaping influence. For the Enlightenments in Britain were staffed almost entirely by men, whereas Sensibility had particularly a place for women, albeit women still subject to definition by patriarchal values. Because intellectual and public activity were still associated with men and the emotions still associated with women, wherever subjectivity was the subject of discourse women or the female would tend to be placed in the foreground. During the 1790s elements of Enlightenment and Sensibility converged momentarily in the work of certain middle-class feminist writers such as Mary Hays and Mary Wollstonecraft. For the most part, however, Enlightenment and Sentimental fiction, when extended into the 1790s, retained their previous gender differentiations.

'Philosophical novels' or 'novels of ideas' of the 1790s, by writers such as Dr John Moore and Robert Bage, and Jacobin novels by writers such as Thomas Holcroft and William Godwin, drew on elements of the thematic and formal repertories of Enlightenment fiction, while novels of manners, sentiment, and social emulation by writers such as Fanny Burney, Elizabeth Inchbald, Charlotte Smith, and many others, 'Gothic romances' by writers such as Ann Radcliffe and a host of followers, Evangelical tales by writers such as Hannah More and her sister, and Romantic tales by writers such as Charles Lamb used elements of the thematic and formal repertories of Sentimental fiction. There was, of course, a considerable amount of overlap in use of Enlightenment and Sentimental fiction for new purposes and emergencies, as the rapid intensification of social and cultural crisis in the 1790s forced writers to find new and more striking ways of using fiction to intervene in the social history of their present.

## From Enlightenment to English Jacobin fiction

Probably the most controversial novels of the 1790s were those written by the 'English Jacobins', a number of intellectuals and miscellaneous writers of liberal social views who were deeply indebted to the Enlightenments and to Sensibility and who, inspired by revolution abroad and political protest in Britain, gave a much sharper edge to the social criticism usually found in Enlightenment and Sentimental fiction. These writers included Thomas Holcroft, William Godwin, and Mary Wollstonecraft; associated with them were older writers such as Dr John Moore and Robert Bage and novelists more indebted to Sensibility, including Charlotte Smith, Elizabeth Inchbald, Mary Hays, and Mary Robinson. But though the late Enlightenment and Jacobin novelists were the most prominent social critics in fiction of the 1790s, elements of their social criticism can be found in such Gothic novelists as 'Monk' Lewis and even Ann Radcliffe, in conservative, loyalist novelists such as Fanny Burney, in a Romantic fiction writer such as Charles Lamb, and in Anti-Jacobin novelists such as Isaac D'Israeli.

Dr John Moore was personally connected with leaders of the Scottish Enlightenment; he was also a friend of the Burney family. His novels were issued by leading publishers of Scottish and English Enlightenment thought in Britain, and included a wide range of Enlightenment themes of social analysis and criticism, particularly in his first novel, *Zeluco: Various Views of Human Nature, Taken from Life and Manners, Foreign and Domestic*, published in the epochal year of 1789. It was read with attention by many intellectuals in the 1790s, and was widely respected, partly for its anti-hero, Zeluco, a study in the perversion of an individual by unnatural and arbitrary social codes and institutions, especially court culture and politics, irrational religion, the subservience of women, chivalric codes of 'honour' and revenge, patronage, the slave system, and cruelty to animals. To give his novel a historical resonance, Moore even compares Zeluco to historical self-tormented tyrants such as Nero. Against his dark portrait are set a number of enlightened, independent, and sensitive professional men. Although Moore spends less time describing subjective experience than do novelists in the line of Sensibility, then, he shares with them an emphasis on the inner self as the 'real' self, grounding and validating social expressions of the self in ethical conduct, in the face of false or misleading social categories of identity.

As we saw in Chapter 1, it is this emphasis which carried the burden of professional and middle-class attack on hierarchical and paternalistic social values of aristocratic and gentry culture. The same emphasis is found in novels of manners, sentiment, and emulation and Gothic romances. Yet, as many readers and critics confessed, Moore's villain-hero, Zeluco, retained a degree of fascination in its mediterranean otherness from British virtues (later developed into Romantic Orientalism – see Chapter 6), revealing a deep ambivalence about this moral and social alien that is so similar to the villains of Gothic romance.

And so Moore's novels, like Ann Radcliffe's, use fictional form and certain formal devices to contain this fascinating alternative to the values promoted by the enlightened professional middle classes of late eighteenth-century Britain, such as plotting the self-torment, reform, or destruction of the courtly and aristocratic villains; use of contrasting virtuous characters; repeated variations on themes of aristocratic decadence and extravagance and foolish middle-class emulation of them; philosophical dialogues, modelled on those of Swift and Voltaire, to expose superstition, prejudice, and folly; authoritative moralizing narrators (in two of Moore's three novels); use of classical allusions and quotations as well as maxims to reinforce this authoritativeness; satirical character sketches; and, finally, the same narrative figure found in Ann Radcliffe's novels – the retrospective explanation that illuminates some puzzle, mystery, or paradox – this is the figure of enlightenment, demystification, and knowledge. The 'philosophical' and learned range of allusion, reference, formal devices, and structuring of language in Moore's novels was a major contribution to establishing the 'modern novel' as serious discourse during the 1790s.

If Moore was a novelist of the late Scottish Enlightenment, his contemporary Robert Bage was just as much a novelist of the English provincial Enlightenment. Bage was closely connected with leading philosophers, scientists, and industrialists of the English midlands; he himself owned and managed a paper factory in Staffordshire. He published four novels of Enlightenment social satire and liberal political views in the 1780s, and his two novels of the 1790s, *Man As He Is* (1792) and *Hermsprong; or, Man As He Is Not* (1796), carry these themes and techniques into the decade of the French Revolution, and represent late Enlightenment social criticism with unusual clarity, vivacity, and wit. His novels were certainly known to leading Jacobin novelists of the decade, even Jane Austen knew his work,[4] and Scott decided to reprint his earlier novels in the 1820s.

Bage's novels are novels of character (in the sense of the Enlightenment satirical portrait, or Theophrastan Character), the plots are kept loose enough to permit the kind of social survey suitable for a wide sweep of satiric observation, and Bage employs the knowing, worldly-wise, authoritative narrator, too, though his narrators are less 'philosophical' and detached than those of Dr John Moore. Bage deals with public themes familiar in late eighteenth-century fiction, and he tries to show the relationship between grand historical events and individual lives and destinies – also a project of the major Romantic social-historical novelists such as Scott. But, as with Moore, Bage takes aim at decadent court culture and its manifestations at the local level of everyday life and ordinary (upper- and middle-class) characters. Thus in *Man As He Is* Bage depicts a young man, Sir George Paradyne, almost ruined by false courtly values of fashionable society, and in *Hermsprong* he shows tyranny operating at the local and familial level in Lord Grondale and his dependents. Sir George, significantly, is rescued by love of a good woman as well as the inspiring spectacle of cultivated, conscientious, civic-minded French aristocrats working for the French Revolution (albeit in its earlier, moderate phase); Hermsprong, just as significantly, comes from the free spaces and egalitarian society of the young American republic to break up Lord Grondale's local tyranny, marry Grondale's virtuous daughter, and take over Grondale's estate (he turns out to be the long-lost true heir). In both novels it is individual rather than institutional or systemic change that sets the local world to rights, even though radical social change is discussed and applauded.

The same ambivalence about revolution is seen in the more carefully constructed and more radical 'English Jacobin' novels of Thomas Holcroft, William Godwin, and Mary Wollstonecraft.[5] Holcroft was one of that class favoured by certain Romantic literary sociologists, the 'writers sprung from the people'. Of low birth, he was self-educated and had been a stable-boy, shoe-maker, teacher, and actor. His life story would have made a fine Romantic novel. By the 1790s he was a leading playwright and miscellaneous writer and a disciple of French Enlightenment thought. He was one of the leading 'English Jacobins' of the early 1790s, and he was put on trial for treason, along with other middle-class and artisan radicals, in 1794, probably as the Government prosecutor's representative writer and intellectual in the group. Together, Holcroft and Godwin worked out a comprehensive political philosophy of anarchism and democracy based on reason and benevolence; thus, in a sense they fused the major elements of Enlightenment and Sentimental ideas and values. In the early 1790s Holcroft published his version of this philosophy in a novel, *Anna St. Ives* (1792); a year later Godwin put the same ideas into a comprehensive philosophical treatise, *An Enquiry Concerning Political Justice* (1793); a year after that Godwin published his own fictional reformulation of those ideas in *Things As They Are; or, The Adventures of Caleb Williams* (1794) and Holcroft published the first half of another novel aimed at 'Old Corruption', *The Adventures of Hugh Trevor* (completed 1797). A couple of years later, the feminist and professional writer Mary Wollstonecraft, author of *A Vindication of the Rights of Woman* (1792), began working on her fictional fusion of Enlightenment and Sensibility for an age of Revolution, *The Wrongs of Woman; or, Maria* (uncompleted and published posthumously in 1798).

Meanwhile, various friends of this inner circle of English Jacobin ideologues and novelists also published novels influenced more or less by English Jacobin ideas and the Godwin circle's recension and development of themes and literary forms from the Enlightenments and Sensibility – particularly the French Enlightenment and the English Nonconformist Enlightenment. Elizabeth Inchbald, for example, who was very close to both Holcroft and Godwin, published an early novel of passion, *A Simple Story* (1791), which became a best-seller, but in 1796 she also published a more thorough and very sharp fictional attack on courtly values and culture in *Nature and Art*, a book which she first entitled a 'Satire upon the Times' and which led to her being described in 1800 by the *Anti-Jacobin Review and Magazine* as '*the scavenger of democracy*'.[6] Mary Hays, a close friend of both Godwin and Wollstonecraft, was influenced by both the English Nonconformist Enlightenment and the great French writer of the culture of Sensibility, Jean-Jacques Rousseau. She published two novels of Sentiment, *Memoirs of Emma Courtney* (1796), partly based on her intellectual relationship with Godwin, and *The Victim of Prejudice* (1799). Like Wollstonecraft, she also published a feminist polemic. Her novels, in their foregrounding of female desire and passion, resemble the later tales of another member of what was called 'Godwin's seraglio' by his enemies.

Amelia Alderson, later Amelia Opie, was another child of the English Nonconformist and provincial Enlightenments, in Norwich. She published a conventional novel of manners, sentiment, and emulation in 1790, *The Dangers of Coquetry*, and in the mid-1790s she was closely associated with the Norwich Jacobins as well as Godwin's circle; indeed, in 1796 Godwin proposed marriage to her. But after 1800 when she became a leading fiction writer, Opie also became more critical of her former English Jacobin friends, especially Godwin and Wollstonecraft (see Ch. 3). Then there was Eliza Fenwick, another intimate of the Godwin circle in the mid-1790s. Her one novel, *Secresy; or, The Ruin on the Rock* (1795), 'By A Woman', examines critically the social condition of middle- and upper-class women, within Godwin's and Wollstonecraft's radical critique of court culture as it affected women at all levels of society.

The impact of these English Jacobin novelists on novel readers and critics in the 1790s was very strong, and raised a countervailing school of 'Anti-Jacobin' novelists, even though the English Jacobins only expressed professional middle-class criticism of 'Old Corruption' in a particularly aggressive, sharp, and comprehensive way. The term Jacobin itself was a smear applied to them by their more conservative rivals within the professional classes; in fact, the English Jacobins' ideas had much more in common with the moderate, late-Enlightenment values of the French Girondins, who were overwhelmed by the Jacobin faction in France in 1793. Furthermore, even Anti-Jacobin novelists in the 1790s, and many other Romantic novelists after 1800, learned from the English Jacobins; and, thanks to their controversial work, the novel itself gained new prestige as a vehicle for ideological communication in an age of crisis.

Yet the English Jacobin novelists were thorough and careful students of the art of the novel in and before their own day. After all, they believed, as Mary Hays put it in the pages of the *Monthly Magazine*, that 'A good novel ought to be subservient to the purposes of truth and philosophy', and, as another writer put it, 'Those who are afraid of philosophy, when she speaks in the language of the schools, are glad of her acquaintance, and proud of being able to converse with her, when she talks plain prose' (see Ch. 1, p. 8). By 'philosophy' here is meant the thought of the Enlightenment *philosophes* of both France and Britain. Holcroft, for example, was both an avowed follower of the *philosophes* and an astute scholar and critic of eighteenth-century fiction, which he wished to restructure for his own rhetorical and political purposes. In his novels he exploits the achievements of Richardson and Fielding, as well as Smollett and Sterne, in order to disseminate his 'New Philosophy'.

*Anna St. Ives* is a revision of Richardson's classic novel in letters, *Clarissa*, and like *Clarissa* it is a study of the corruption of individual, domestic, and social life by the courtly culture of love, gallantry, chivalry, 'honour', and sexual intrigue. For example, the heroine's first name, Anna, suggests Donna Anna, victim of the decadent courtly gallant, Don Juan, a well-known story which had been recently dramatized and frequently represented on the London stage. (Mozart's opera did not come to London for some years, but Holcroft probably knew of it anyway.) Her last name, St Ives, is an allusion to the place where Oliver Cromwell whiled away a few years in quiet domesticity and rural retreat, before he plunged into the English Civil War, a revolution with which the social conflicts of the 1790s were being compared. Anna's surname holds a prophecy. Thus the novel embodies a broad spectrum of late eighteenth-century social criticism bearing on the relations of gentry and middle classes. It depicts fashionable follies of social emulation, from Sir Arthur St Ives's passion for 'improvement' of his estate to his desire to see his daughter married to a man of rank, however morally corrupt. It depicts that man of rank (Coke Clifton) as a fashionable courtly libertine, with a decadent chivalric code of revenge. It depicts the fashionable decadence of pre-Revolutionary France. It exposes the professional classes' overt dependence on but covert exploitation of their social superiors, the gentry, in the character of Sir Arthur St Ives's steward and the hero's father, the fawning and hypocritical attorney and Dissenter, Abimelech Henley. It also shows the effect of brutal exploitation of the common people, in the character of the Irish criminal Mac Fane.

The main focus of the novel's attention, however, is not on this rather conventional material of late eighteenth-century social satire, but rather the love triangle of Anna, Abimelech Henley's virtuous son Frank, and Coke Clifton. Holcroft has added the virtuous hero to the duo of Clarissa and Lovelace in Richardson's novel *Clarissa*, and thus written an implicit criticism of Richardson's tragic fiction, though Frank Henley is also a middle-class version of Richardson's idealized and professionalized landed gentleman, Sir Charles Grandison – a character much imitated in late eighteenth-century novels of manners.[7] Holcroft's intention, like Richardson's, however, is to expose the moral corruption of the code of gallantry and chivalry and to replace it with a code of transcendent virtue located in the mind of the enlightened and rational individual. Thus Frank is already enlightened, Anna is enlightened but thinks it her social duty selflessly to redeem the unenlightened Clifton, and Clifton is finally enlightened and reformed by the example of the combined virtues of Frank and Anna.

'Mind', an Enlightenment version of the inward self as moral-intellectual authenticity, is the basis for self-transcendence, exposes the insufficiency of merely social and selfish moral codes, and leads to gradualist social reform through the 'spread of truth' from one individual mind to another. In order to give this plot of self-transcendence full weight, Holcroft appropriates both religious language and the language of contemporary neoplatonism, and a range of literary allusion from Dante and Petrarch to Shakespeare and Milton. At the end of the novel Frank and Anna marry and look forward to a life of egalitarian domesticity and mutual happiness as well as expanded social usefulness. The paternalist social structure is not replaced, only reformed from within.

Formally, *Anna St. Ives* aims to fuse elements of the eighteenth-century philosophical tale with elements of the epistolary Sentimental novel of domestic and psychological realism. Although the novel is in the epistolary form, there are the same philosophical dialogues and brief essays, satirical incidents, generic and ironic naming of characters, and intermingling of political language with domestic incident found in philosophical novels with third-person or objective narration, such as those of Moore and Bage. But Holcroft also exploits the epistolary form to the full for display of motive and for dramatization of individual feeling and psychology, the traditional strengths of the novel in letters, and he uses the overlapping of letters to achieve the effect of epistolary irony, which is the novel's version of dramatic irony. The epistolary form is used effectively by Holcroft to give to *Anna St. Ives* a degree of formal realism usually lacking in 'novels of ideas', and *Anna St. Ives* is nothing if not a novel of ideas.

Holcroft wrote two more novels, both quite different from *Anna St. Ives*. *The Adventures of Hugh Trevor* (1794–97) is, like Godwin's novel of the same year, a first-person narrative describing the picaresque adventures of a young man trying to make his way in the world. Holcroft's subject is the choice of a profession; Trevor (whose early years are quite similar to Holcroft's) explores all the windings of the patronage system and concludes that all professions are dependent on the upper classes, and all individuals are reduced to playing roles in a desultory plot over which they have no control, because they have no power, no matter how much knowledge and merit they may have. Eventually the plot of romantic comedy is resolved in the usual way, and Trevor is enabled, by the appearance of a *deus ex machina* (somewhat like that in *Tom Jones*), to avoid a profession altogether and become a gentleman. *Hugh Trevor* is a vigorous, varied, and humorous novel, adapting two of Holcroft's favourite eighteenth-century predecessors, Fielding and Smollett, to the ideological aims of Holcroft's social criticism, as Holcroft had already adapted Richardson in *Anna St. Ives*. But it reveals clearly the deep ambivalence of professional middle-class reformers about the classes whose moral and intellectual fitness and general political right to rule they were criticizing and questioning. Finally, *Hugh Trevor*, like Bage's *Hermsprong*, settles for individual rather than systemic change. Moreover, *Hugh Trevor* sees the world entirely from the point of view of the upwardly mobile middle classes – the sort of people likely to read novels. Significantly, the lower classes are depicted as overly emotional, imitative, and corruptible or improvable depending on the kind of example they are set by their 'betters' – this is not much different from the depiction of the lower classes in such conservative fictions as Hannah More's Cheap Repository tracts of 1795 to 1798. By the end of the 1790s, Holcroft, like many Jacobin writers and English Jacobinism itself, was a spent force, though he wrote one more novel, an interesting experiment in Sternean satire, *Memoirs of Bryan Perdue* (1805).

Holcroft's success in *Anna St. Ives* encouraged his friend William Godwin to embody the same beliefs and arguments in a novel. But Godwin found, as he wrote his novel in 1793–94, in the midst of the most serious political and social crisis in Britain since the seventeenth century, that the optimism of Holcroft's vision of social transformation might have to be seriously qualified. In his *Enquiry Concerning Political Justice, and Its Influence on General Virtue and Happiness*, published in 1793, he argued that man is naturally benevolent and rational, and that

only government (or the whole range of political and social institutions) perverts this good nature; therefore, we should work toward the
abolition of all government and all constraint on individual action
except individual persuasion. This kind of philosophical optimism was
received warmly by intellectuals of the time, and was thought to have
given a death blow to Edmund Burke's defence of irrational prejudices,
traditions, and associations of feeling, in his *Reflections on the Revolution
in France* (1790). After the success of his treatise, Godwin planned to
go on to write a massive work of Enlightenment 'philosophical
history', history as rational *exposé* of superstition, prejudice, tyranny,
and 'priestcraft'. But he soon dropped this project, as the political crisis
in Britain deepened, and turned instead to the novel in order both to
expose the 'unreason' of the chivalric culture celebrated by Burke and
to rouse his countrymen to the truths of 'political justice' and thus to
avoid a violent political confrontation such as had occurred in France.

Things As They Are; or, The Adventures of Caleb Williams* (1794) is
the major English Jacobin novel and one of the major novels of the
Romantic period. Yet it is thoroughly imbued with Enlightenment
ideas. It translates the principal ideas of the *Enquiry Concerning Political
Justice* and Enlightenment critical historiography into the form of
fiction, and, as the full title suggests, it illustrates general social
conditions in the experiences of one individual. After 1800 this would
become the classic technique of the social-historical novel; but, as we
have seen, even before 1800 it was a common method of novelistic
social criticism of contemporary life. It is immediately obvious that
*Things As They Are* is another critique of gentry culture and hegemony. Caleb's employer, Ferdinando Falkland, is named after a
chivalric king of Spain and after a hero of the Civil War period, Lucius
Cary, Viscount Falkland, a liberal, intellectual, artistic gentleman, the
best representative of his class and culture, but because of his loyalty
to his king – a chivalric and feudal prejudice – he destroyed himself.
Godwin's Falkland represents the chivalric traditions of the gentry,
their broad, not to say cosmopolitan literary culture, and liberal Whig
political values – in other words, gentry culture at its best, as celebrated
in the anti-Revolutionary and anti-Enlightenment writings of the
decade's outstanding defender of the gentry, Edmund Burke. Quite
distinct from Falkland is Barnabas Tyrrel, another country gentleman,
but of the old sort – conservative, boorish, uncultured, and tyrannical
– in short, an example of the provincial 'local' gentry rather than the
cosmopolitan 'county' gentry.

Their struggle and its consequences are recounted in volume one
of the novel, as a narrative heard by Caleb from Falkland's steward,
Mr Collins. Collins also describes how Falkland's education, especially
his reading of chivalric romances, made him the person Caleb now

knows. Since Godwin believed in the 'necessitarian' doctrine that circumstances produce character, he names Collins after the early eighteenth-century philosopher of necessity, Anthony Collins. What Godwin's Collins does not know, however, is that Falkland murdered Tyrrel in secret, after having been insulted and humiliated by him in public. Falkland's irrational prejudice is his concern for his reputation, the merely social image of the self held by public opinion, which may be quite different from the 'real' self, the inward private self. In the eyes of the public, Falkland is the paragon of the gentleman; in fact he is a murderer; he has committed the crime of Cain, the original sin of social rupture. Moreover, Falkland has acted on a principle of merely personal, rather than public and social justice, namely revenge. Revenge is a recurring motive and motif in fiction of the Romantic period, and it signifies destructive selfhood, excessive individualism, like emotional or financial extravagance. It also signifies aristocratic excess, the extreme of egotism or selfishness in one's personal relations with others, and it stands for the socially destructive possibilities of selfhood. It is usually deplored, yet it fascinates, precisely because it is a form of excess that transgresses rational, orderly, bourgeois limits to self. This excess and transgression, already evident in Moore's *Zeluco*, will become a master theme of high Romantic prose fiction and verse narrative (see Ch. 6).

Caleb is certainly fascinated by Falkland's outward signs of inward suffering for his moment of selfishness, and this fascination spurs Caleb to discover his master's 'secret'. Caleb's passion is not for reputation (Falkland's obsession), or power (Tyrrel's), but truth. This is *his* selfish folly, and it stands for the dangerous and socially disruptive passion for truth in the heroes of revolutions in the past, including the Protestant Reformation and the eighteenth-century Enlightenment. Caleb learns Falkland's secret; he 'demystifies' Falkland's social image, if only for himself, since he does not intend to expose his master's guilt. But knowledge is power, and Falkland's self cannot stand to be in the power of another; and so Caleb becomes another object of Falkland's social power and private vengeance. Caleb the obsessed seeker of truth becomes Caleb the victim and fugitive.

After a public confrontation between master and man, Caleb is imprisoned, escapes, joins a gang of bandits (led by a social philosopher), and flees to London, where he becomes a writer of popular literature, and where he finds he is the villain-hero of a popular semi-fictional chapbook hawked about the streets at Falkland's instigation as a way of keeping Caleb both concealed in scandal and on the run. Discovered, Caleb flees to Wales, finds moments of happiness and perhaps even love; he is 'exposed' again by Falkland's agents and the cursed chapbook. Finally, realizing that Falkland is forcing him to be as alone in society as Falkland feels himself to be, Caleb turns in desperation and seeks a final public confrontation with his 'enemy'. Godwin's original ending was to have Caleb lose again, and to close his narrative with his life; but this ending, affirming the novel's social protest against the power of the gentry, was abandoned, and instead Godwin had Caleb move Falkland to a public confession and to throw himself into his erstwhile victim's arms in a last gesture of reconciliation before death. Falkland does die, wasted by remorse, and Caleb remains to revile himself for his impetuous act of public self-vindication and for being the 'murderer' of Falkland. The novel lodges a protest against a society based not on 'political justice' but on forms of false consciousness that generate mutually destructive acts of selfishness.

Furthermore, this society is incapable of discovering the true individual self. There are two major elements in this exposure of the abyss between the private and the social self. First there is Caleb's narrated self, his description and analysis of his own thoughts, motives, and feelings as he sets about investigating the truth about Falkland, and later his descriptions of his feelings as he tries to find a new place in society and fails. These descriptions are interspersed in his account of his 'adventures of flight and pursuit'. Added to this material are Caleb's digest of Collins's account of Falkland's vicissitudes and Caleb's speculations on Falkland's inner anguish. This psychological description and analysis show that Caleb and Falkland are equal selves. On the other hand, there are successive incidents of social representation – or rather misrepresentation – of the self. Some of these incidents are direct confrontations between Caleb and Falkland in a most public place, the legal or quasi-legal tribunal drawn up to discover the truth. Ironically but significantly, the tribunals never do make such a discovery.

At first Caleb is reluctant to reveal his secret knowledge about Falkland, even though his master has had him apprehended on spurious charges. Later, Caleb reveals what he knows. Finally, he seeks vindication once and for all. But until Falkland himself publicly acknowledges his guilt, the tribunal, faced with a choice of believing a gentleman's testimony or that of his servant, consistently base their estimate of truth on grounds of social rank. Not only does the social institution established to find out the true character of the individual (innocent or guilty) fail to do so, but so too do all the individuals Caleb meets in the novel – Mr Collins, Mr Forrester (Falkland's half-brother), Caleb's helpers in London, and Laura Dennison, his friend in Wales. In spite of the fact that Caleb repeatedly declares and explains his innocence in face-to-face confrontations with patrons, friends, and fellow-servants, they all accept Falkland's version of Caleb's character (and the version in the semi-fictitious but damning chapbook), rather than the evidence of their own personal knowledge of Caleb. His 'true' self is permanently masked or imprisoned by his social self. Only Caleb's last peroration, rather inexplicably, persuades Falkland to confess the truth about himself and Caleb.

This theme of failed sincerity in *Things As They Are* probably owes a great deal to the master of the European literature of Sensibility and adopted father of the Revolution, Jean-Jacques Rousseau; but Godwin gives a political purpose to the self-vindicating text. His first aim is to depict individual history and experience, the particular and individual self produced by collision with the whole range of social institutions, from mere opinion and convention, to ideological constructions or prejudices – especially of rank or class – to law and imprisonment. Then Godwin aims to make that individual history historically reformative by making it into a narrative for others, an oral narrative and a self-vindicating written testimony within the novel, and a text inserted into the world of historical process outside the novel. Godwin's novel is designed for the emergent class of professional writers because it envisages social change by change of mind, not revolution in the existing institutional order; and changing minds is to be accomplished through individual association (in a 'philosophical' circle or coterie) and through texts. Revolution is to be accomplished in the salon and the study, not at the barricades. That is why Godwin is interested in the novel as literature, or in making the novel into literature.

We know from his manuscript journal that Godwin was one of the first writers to do detailed research for his novels, and *Things As They Are* has its own kind of literariness – historical allusions, parallels with Rousseau's autobiographical writings, similarities to the form and themes of Defoe's novels, appropriation of 'Gothic' settings and atmosphere, and adoption of the tone of Dissenting spiritual autobiography. But this is not the feminine literariness of, say, *The Mysteries of Udolpho*, published the same year. It is the literariness of professional social critics and men of letters, the kind of men whom Edmund Burke thought were responsible for the Revolution in France and who were fomenting revolution in Britain. Burke was right in one sense, but wrong in another. Men of letters such as Godwin, Holcroft, Bage, and Moore were not fomenting revolution. They were only developing a more radical version of the 'modern novel's' attack on gentry power, ideology, and culture, and a more politically pointed advocacy of authentic and independent selfhood, the culture of writing and the book, and the social leadership of the professional middle classes.

Godwin wrote five more novels, and his career as a novelist lasted until the early 1830s and the threshold of the age of Dickens; but even before the 1790s were over he had shifted from novelist of late Enlightenment social criticism to Romantic novelist of alienated selfhood. *St. Leon: A Tale of the Sixteenth Century* (1799) seems to be a late Enlightenment 'historical romance', availing itself of certain supernatural and Gothic elements. Here Godwin went back to the age of the Protestant Reformation for his analogy to hiṡ own age of revolution, and to 'old philosophy' – that is, alchemy and occult science – for his analogy to the 'new philosophy' – that is, late Enlightenment social criticism.[8] *St. Leon* has a grand historical design, anticipating (if only in this respect) the later achievements of the writers of 'national tales' (see Ch. 3) and Walter Scott. *St. Leon* also registers Godwin's sense, acquired from personal experience since publishing *Things As They Are*, of the cost in social ostracism and domestic loss of being a 'philosopher' and 'philanthropist'. Godwin depicts his hero's tormented subjectivity and his ruined 'domestic affections' as the products not so much of a society ignoring or ignorant of principles of 'political justice' as of the hero's own rage for social improvement. Here Godwin clearly anticipates the fable of his daughter Mary Shelley's first novel, *Frankenstein* (see Ch. 6).

With *St. Leon* Godwin was already moving away from Enlightenment critical history of contemporary life toward a sociology of the origins of the present in the past, and his interest in applying historical analogy to the present had already become less fervent and pointed than in *Things As They Are*. This was especially obvious in his third triple-decker novel, *Fleetwood; or, The New Man of Feeling* (1805), which was much influenced by Godwin's attempts to write a Rousseauistic autobiography in the late 1790s and early 1800s, and by his close friendship with Coleridge, then at the height of his advocacy of Wordsworthian Romanticism. Godwin continued to participate in the central issues of liberal Romanticism in his novels, especially the antagonistic relation of authentic selfhood to a society still dominated by court culture and gentry hegemony; and he continued to provide a model and inspiration for Romantic social critics and lyricists of the self, from Amelia Opie and Lady Caroline Lamb to Edward Lytton Bulwer – not to forget his powerful and pervasive influence on his daughter Mary Shelley. Godwin was one of the most important artists and thinkers of the early Romantic novel – indeed, of early Romantic literature, and especially the transition from Enlightenment and Sensibility to Romantic culture.

The Enlightenments of England and Scotland were dominated by public and social issues and by men; Sensibility was dominated by private, domestic values and well-populated by women writers. In the Godwin circle and in English Jacobin utopian visions, Enlightenment and Sentimental ideas and values mixed and new models for the intellectual, amorous, and sexual relations of men and women were advanced. Godwin's wife, Mary Wollstonecraft, was the leading feminist voice in the 1790s, not so much for the kind of Enlightenment utopian speculations in which Godwin and Holcroft indulged as for her trenchant criticism, partly rooted in Enlightenment and Senti-mental ideas but partly reacting against them, of the condition of women in a courtly system of values which had penetrated to every level of society. These ideas she developed in a series of diverse texts, including a polemic, a history, a sociological travel book, and a novel.[9]

Her novel, *The Wrongs of Woman*, begins *in medias res*. Maria Venables, the narrator tells us, awakes to find herself imprisoned in a madhouse, her daughter taken from her, alone. Gradually she stirs the interest and sympathy of her warder, the ex-prostitute Jemima, and makes contact with a fellow-prisoner, Darnford. They exchange books, including Rousseau's *La Nouvelle Héloïse*; they meet, and become lovers. Oppression produces transgression as liberation: for some reason the keeper of the madhouse runs away and his prisoners are free. Maria and Darnford leave together, but then separate to tend to their particular legal problems, including a suit for seduction laid by Maria's husband against Darnford. The novel breaks off; sketches of possible conclusions suggest Maria is abandoned by Darnford, tries suicide, is reunited with her daughter by Jemima (now her loyal servant and follower), and persuaded to live for her child. As is often the case in novels of social criticism of this period, however, the plot, while presenting an argument about the fate of the individual (im-plicitly any individual) in particular circumstances, is outweighed in importance by the novel's descriptive material and narrative structure. Wollstonecraft intended to show the 'wrongs of woman' in the different classes of society, and this descriptive project is accomplished by having a number of different women tell of their personal wrongs in inset narratives of different lengths.

Maria represents woman of the class on the border between the middle class and the gentry, while Jemima represents lower-class woman; for both women oppression has forced them beyond the limits of the legal or conventional, to excess or transgression. Their narratives are therefore exemplary in several senses, and take up most of what was completed of the novel; however, the experiences of a few middle-class women are briefly represented. Maria's own tale, intended for her daughter, is told in retrospect. Because of incorrect education, Maria developed excessive sensibility, a culture of emotional excess which men can exploit in women. She was courted by George Venables, who hid a deep-dyed libertinism beneath a mask of virtuous sensibility, and only wanted Maria for her inheritance. Once they were married, he revealed his true character and extorted money from her to continue his extravagances and to repair failed business speculations. He even tried to sell Maria to one of his creditors. When Maria refused further supplies of money, he locked her up, claiming his legal rights over her person and her money. She escaped, but was pursued, and eventually abducted and immured in the madhouse, while her husband held the daughter who will inherit Maria's estate. This takes Maria's story up to the start of the novel.

In her feminist polemic, *A Vindication of the Rights of Woman*, Wollstonecraft had dealt with the ideological and cultural condition of woman, and promised a further volume of the *Vindication*, dealing with the legal wrongs of woman; this volume turned out to be the the novel she did not live to complete, but the legal researches were embodied in the story of Maria Venables. Jemima, who is induced by Maria's kindness, the first she has ever experienced, to tell her own tale, recounts a history of lower-class seduction and betrayal by men, and of ruthless oppression by other women, who can see her only as a rival. What the narratives of Maria and Jemima accomplish in this novel, then, is an exposé of the true nature and causes of the faulty and fallen condition of women, represented here, as in many novels over the next century and more, by sexual harassment and exploitation, and imprisonment for crime or 'madness'.

This exposé gains strength from the kind of historical and literary allusiveness-for-argument that Godwin practised in *Things As They Are* (which Wollstonecraft studied while writing her own novel). For example, when Maria turns in disgust from a book on the philosophy of mind to recreate herself with Dryden's 'Guiscard and Sigismunda', we may suspect she is enjoying Sigismunda's spirited defence of women in that poem; when Maria quotes Calista from Nicholas Rowe's 'she-tragedy', *The Fair Penitent*, we are encouraged to read the feminist protest of that play into the situation of Wollstonecraft's novel. There is a powerful historical allusion, too. Maria is a revision of Mary, the heroine of Wollstonecraft's first, Sentimental novel (published in 1788); she is her author; she is the notorious and celebrated woman of feeling from the past, Mary Queen of Scots (another actual prisoner of sex) – an association reinforced by the name of Maria's lover Darnford, a remake of lord Darnley, the second husband of Mary Queen of Scots. There is also a parallel to the leading woman of the early revolution in France, Marie Roland – like Wollstonecraft, an ambivalent Rousseauist and self-confessed woman of feeling; like Wollstonecraft, a feminist who blamed court culture for the oppression and exploitation of women throughout society; and like Wollstonecraft's Maria, an autobiographer who addressed the text of her life to her absent daughter, as a self-vindication, a legacy, and a warning. Sons may inherit estates; daughters, unjustly deprived of estates by customs of male primogeniture, inherit texts designed to raise a feminist self- and social consciousness.

Maria's life echoes two centuries of the lives of women as prisoners of sex, on both the domestic and the national scale. The public, political implications of domestic oppression and the domestic consequences of social, cultural, and institutional injustice are the over-riding interests of feminist social criticism in Wollstonecraft's day, be the feminists women or men. When Maria defends in court her right to choose a mate according to her own tastes and desires, the judge declares that Britons 'did not want French principles in public or private life' (ch. 17). Like Godwin, Wollstonecraft also fills her novel with facts, in this case about 'things as they are' for women – not only the laws of marriage, property, divorce, and custody of children, but wages for women, conditions of work, the realities of domestic service, prostitution, and so on. This is, like *Things As They Are*, in the most important sense a historical novel; it, too, attacks ideological and social structures that oppress, but it does so in terms of the social institutions of both gender and class. It argues that the 'wrongs of woman' are found in every class, but aims to show that all of those wrongs are rooted in the false consciousness of a society dominated by court and gentry notions of property, family, and gender, and in the internalization of that false consciousness by women, in the social construction of their selves. This internalization is especially marked in that culture of courtliness in disguise – Sensibility. Wollstonecraft's novel goes further than any other of the period in attempting to expose the ways sexual inequality is rooted in the class structures of society and reproduced by ideological dissemination. Women are left only two roads to travel – submission or transgression.

Finding the road to liberation is more difficult. There are two directions that can be discerned in this fragment, however. First there is the very self which professional middle-class ideology had constructed and situated in the centre of human nature. This self is shown to be designed, developed, and experienced differently for women than for men because men and women are socialized differently into the ideology of the self. The self's burden of sensibility was supposed to be greater for women, and in Wollstonecraft's polemical writings of the early 1790s she agreed that it was, and that it was used to suppress and oppress women in new ways. Yet she also argued, first, that women have a special burden of self because of their limited, desultory, and largely 'domestic' education, their expected silence in public or absence from public life, their enforced limitations of experience and observation, and their being limited as readers and thinkers to the merely literary. Secondly, Wollstonecraft argued that these limitations could be converted by an act of will into literary polemical forms of authentic self-expression, and thus of liberation.

Wollstonecraft's two earlier *Vindications* had been essays in demonstrating and developing this rhetorical method of 'turning the tables';

so, too, was her 'travel-book' of 1796, *Letters* from Scandinavia; these different kinds of discourse were restructured into fictional narrative form in *The Wrongs of Woman*. The argumentative element in polemical writing is transformed into the structural relationship of serial inset narratives; the personal and expressive element is transformed into the particular life-stories of the novel. At the same time, the persuasive relationship between polemicist and reader is represented in certain of the personal relationships within the novel. Maria's memoir, intended for her daughter, is read by Darnford and Jemima, and moves him to love Maria and moves Jemima to help her. As in *Things As They Are*, expressive self-vindication may have considerable persuasiveness, in the right circumstances. But while Caleb wishes to move his fellows and his judges, Maria intends to instruct her daughter in order that she may avoid the errors of Sensibility, which have made Maria just another victim of society's various institutions of deformation and oppression of the self.

Like Holcroft and Godwin, Wollstonecraft believed that 'the mind is its own place', and like Godwin she believed that the mind always has a history – indeed, that the first task of mind is to know its own history so that the future may be directed by the reason and the will. Autobiography is the central form of the Godwin–Wollstonecraft fictions because in one's self are written the evils of 'things as they are', and the institutionalized 'wrongs of woman'. The autobiographical text then becomes enlightening and thus reformative for others, as in seventeenth-century spiritual autobiography, which is one of the sources for this kind of writing. Self-knowledge is textualized, and results in social change, if only on the level of other individual lives; but since society is an agglomeration of these individual lives, that is how society will change, through 'the spread of truth' from mind to mind, self to self.

Nevertheless, in Wollstonecraft's novel there is a special problem, which is not broached in Godwin's novels until after he had learned of it from her. Maria's narrative 'converts' Jemima, and liberates her from her misanthropy, revives her female feelings, and makes of her an ally and assistant – it is Jemima who finds Maria's daughter at the end. Maria's self-narrative moves Darnford to love; he reads her before he woos her. The narrative, the text of oppression becomes a source of power, rhetorical power, releasing love. But after their unforeseen release from the madhouse, and after their tilt with the outmoded laws of divorce and marital property, apparently (for the novel *is* incomplete) Darnford abandons Maria, precipitating her attempt at self-destruction, from which she is redeemed by Jemima's appeal to live for her daughter. If in its several incidents and inset narratives the novel warns women to beware women, the novel as it stands holds out no hope at all for self-rescue through men. The closure of the novel seems to leave us with this image: a liberated and enlightened woman from the margin between the professional and gentry classes, with her enlightened and emancipated voluntary woman servant, and her rescued and educable daughter, abandoned by law and man but united and ready to go on. According to *The Wrongs of Woman*, conventional married domesticity leads to exploitation and imprisonment, love is an illusory liberation, and unconventional domesticity based on it will fail. What remains is a social unit probably meant to be socially prefigurative: two women of different classes, disburdened of socially imposed false selves, ready to educate the next generation of women for a necessarily embattled future.

# From Sensibility to Gothic

## The Novel of Manners, Sentiment, and Emulation

Sharp generic distinctions were not part of Romantic literary culture; on the contrary, breaking the bounds of form was a recurrent rhetorical gesture. In any case, the novel itself had always been a loose and open generic system. Thus the late Enlightenment and English Jacobin novels described in the preceding pages shared many themes and elements with other widely read kinds of prose fiction in the late eighteenth century and the Romantic period, especially with the commonest varieties of fiction in the last few decades of the eighteenth century, the Sentimental tale and the novel of manners, sentiment, and emulation.[10]

Here authentic selfhood, thematized as romantic love, is seen to conflict with 'merely' social categories such as rank and wealth. Women characters are prominent as protagonists because of their supposedly finer, more emotional natures. The plot form is usually that of romantic comedy, resolving social conflict and validating the authentic subjective self in a social institution, marriage, but marriage for love. Both the Sentimental tale and the novel of manners, sentiment, and emulation, but especially the latter, are also fictions of social criticism, specifically criticism of the fashion system, pride of rank, the gentry culture of conspicuous consumption, patronage and dependence, the 'mistress system' of courtly gallantry, and emulation of these 'merely' social and economic institutions by other classes. More broadly, Sentimental tales and novels and the novel of manners, sentiment, and emulation exhibit a deep suspicion of the social; they do so principally in plots featuring a sensitive young heroine harassed or persecuted by upper-class men or vulgar relations, as she tries to learn and to negotiate the various languages of social being and identity, and the social conflicts and relativities they embody, without compromising or losing her social identity (respectability) or – more important – her sexual and subjective integrity, her wholeness. Often there is a sense that society or 'Society' (i.e., the fashionable world) constitutes a conspiracy to disrupt that integrity, and there are numerous incidents or scenes of confinement, ranging from the constrictions of false social conventions to actual imprisonment (for the unlucky or those who lose their integrity). In some cases, Sentimental literature, both fictional and non-fictional, deals with actual forms of social oppression of the individual, such as the prison system (exposed by the reformer John Howard), slavery, even cruelty to animals.[11]

When Sentimental tales and novels and novels of manners, sentiment, and emulation are set in distant times or climes they become 'Gothic romances', and virtue in distress, the classic figure of much Sentimental literature, becomes the heroine threatened with rape or enforced marriage, and faced with various kinds of confinement and adventures of flight and pursuit, or becomes the hero deprived of social standing or his true identity, confined, as it were, in a false social self, or in prison of one kind or another, such as the dungeon of a tyrant or the cells of the Inquisition. Clearly, these figures could and did have strong political overtones, especially in the first heyday of the Gothic novel, the 1790s, and we have seen already how leading English Jacobin novelists of that decade employ images of conspiracy, tribunals, confinement, imprisonment, or banishment to figure the ways false social institutions oppress the individual. It is often difficult to determine if the false social institutions are merely those of an inherently malign social structure and régime, such as court culture or 'Old Corruption', or are the characteristic of society and the social in general. The latter would be the paranoia of a Sentimental or Romantic culture that saw only subjective selfhood as authentic and natural and all social categories as irredeemably relative and conflicted. This kind of culture leads to a cult of individualism, implicit in late eighteenth-century capitalist and bourgeois ideology, perhaps, but co-ordinated, too, with various ideas of the transcendental, be it Nature (especially sublime nature), History, Nation, or God. All of these forms of the transcendental are found in Romantic literature and fiction, though History and Nation are less prominent in the literature of Sensibility and Nature may have different expression. A further, and most important form of the transcendental, and one directly related to the idea of authentic selfhood and very prominent in Romantic fiction, is passion – the plenitude or excess of self that seems to lead inevitably to transgression of limits, especially social conventions, codes, and laws.

These topics will be raised again in the chapters that follow, especially Chapter 6; here the subject will be some forms of the Sentimental tale and novel of manners, sentiment, and emulation in the 1790s, including the 'Gothic romance', and their relation to the particular issues of that decade of public crisis. In the last decades of the eighteenth century the Sentimental tale was most often found in the miscellany magazines; the novel of manners, sentiment, and emulation, on the other hand, was sometimes serialized in the magazines but more usually published in book form, as the 'triple-decker' novel or the 'circulating-library novel', and it was the kind of novel usually meant by the phrase 'the modern novel'.

The novel of manners, sentiment, and emulation is more often called simply the novel of manners, although this name suggests that such fiction treats what are now considered to be fairly trivial matters of social conduct in polite society. These matters *are* treated in novels of manners, sentiment, and emulation, but they were by no means considered trivial by the majority of novel readers in the late eighteenth century and Romantic period. Indeed, it would be difficult to over-estimate the importance of such matters, for 'manners' had a much broader meaning and greater significance then than it does now. It had the force of both senses of the French 'mœurs' – morals and conduct – and referred to the whole range of social practices of a particular society. Thus it is significant that in the latter part of the eighteenth century there were increasing numbers of 'conduct books' or guides to etiquette, social discrimination, and ethical conduct, especially for women.[12] There was a close connection between novels of manners and these conduct books: in an age of rapid social change, novels of manners were the most widely available guides to changing social standards and values, and so there could not be a more interesting form of literature for readers of the time. The novel of manners is in effect the novel of social emulation.

Not all novels of manners and sentiment deal with successful mastery of manners, however; indeed, the novel of manners had always been as interested in inward sensitivity as in outward conduct. This was especially true in the late eighteenth century, when Senti-mental tales were being widely read as providing models for inward cultivation and gentility of soul, if not of breeding. Furthermore, such novels sometimes deal with excessive individualism, individuality that breaks social codes, conventions, and even laws, or they depict the unsuccessfully socialized, the alienated, estranged, or exiled individual, for, as we have seen, the drama of the self in society takes place in the collision of the rights of individuals and the duties demanded by social convention. In the 1790s this collision could be read as an allegory for larger political collisions. The novel of manners is in effect the novel of social politics, necessarily including the politics of the subjective self.

During the last two decades of the eighteenth century the acknowledged master of the novel of manners and sentiment was Fanny Burney and she set a mark for dozens of followers, from Elizabeth Inchbald and Charlotte Smith to Maria Edgeworth (see Ch. 3) and Jane Austen (Ch. 4), and even Sir Walter Scott (Ch. 5). All of Burney's novels rely on the classic situation of novels of Sensibility, namely 'virtue in distress', or 'female difficulties'; and like most Gothic novels, too, their form provides, through this situation, what Horace Walpole described as 'a constant vicissitude of interesting passions'.[13] Burney's novels expose a young, inexperienced, and sensitive heroine to the perplexing relativities of a complex and conflicted social world, relativities that the heroine must negotiate in order to reach her true or rightful place in society. This place turns out to be a home and husband of her own, a domestic refuge from the social relativities traversed with such peril to the self, its moral integrity, and its social identity. Burney's heroines suffer two kinds of social affliction in particular: unwanted attention from decadent courtly men and women, and 'contamination' by vulgar social-climbing relatives or acquaintances. Thus in Burney's novels the adventures of the self in society encompass the two major ranges of social criticism in late eighteenth-century fiction: criticism of decadent court culture and of gentry and middle-class emulation and dependence, and criticism of the intellectual and social narrowness of professional and middle-class people.

The novel of manners, sentiment, and emulation incorporates this repertory of themes, character types, and incidents in a repetitive rather than a cumulative form. The basic narrative figure of the perplexed heroine or hero could be multiplied to five volumes or limited to a brief tale without damage to its rhetorical structure. In this repeated narrative figure the unsocialized self is led into conduct that appears immoral at worst, morally ambiguous at best; and the resulting embarrassment drives the insouciant self back on itself, for reflection, self-examination, and self-reconstruction, as preparation for yet further essays in ethical action in social life of all kinds, from high society to the cottages of the poor. This figure is repeated until at last the comic universe turns up trumps, as the reader expected it would. Such a moral and ethical vision of human life combines an Anglican emphasis on ethics and 'good works' with Nonconformist emphasis on conviction, endurance, fortitude, integrity, and fullness of moral and intellectual being. Thus the plot of Burney's sentimental novel of manners formulates a cultural and ideological common ground for novel readers from both the mainstream and the most important subsidiary cultural

traditions in late eighteenth-century Britain. Other attempts to formu-
late that common ground were the religious movement known as
Anglican Evangelicalism and the broad cultural movement later called
Romanticism.

The narrative mode participates in the same shaping of common
ground. Whereas Burney's first novel, *Evelina; or, A Young Woman's
Entrance into the World* (1778), is written in the intimate, immediate,
and confessional epistolary form, and thus is associated with the
tradition of the Nonconformist Samuel Richardson, Burney's next
three novels were all written in a form of the omniscient and third-
person narration the great eighteenth-century practitioner of which was
the Anglican Henry Fielding. In *Cecilia; or, Memoirs of an Heiress*
(1782), Burney adopts a philosophical and detached third-person
narration, but she focuses a good deal on the thoughts and feelings of
her heroine and thereby retains some of the intimacy and immediacy
of the epistolary form. While writing her next novel, *Camilla*, she was
probably influenced by the success of John Moore's philosophical novel
*Zeluco* (Moore was a family friend). For in *Camilla* the narrator
becomes even more philosophical than in *Cecilia*, with occasional brief
essays and frequent aphorisms on various topics moral and ethical. The
most important feature of the third-person narration in Burney's
novels, however, is the use of filtered or mediated consciousness, the
reporting by the narrator of the thoughts and feelings of the heroine,
in almost the language that might be used by the heroine were she to
speak inwardly to herself. This technique of narration retains omniscient authoritative control for the narrator, but brings the consciousness of the protagonist very close to the reader. It is a technique used,
with variation, by Ann Radcliffe, Maria Edgeworth, Jane Austen,
Walter Scott, and many of the major Victorian novelists.

Characterization in *Cecilia, Camilla*, and *The Wanderer; or, Female
Difficulties* (1814) relies on authoritative character portraits, with a tendency toward the moral-satirical 'Character' of the type written by La
Bruyère in France and Samuel Butler and others in England, and
commonly found in the late eighteenth-century miscellany magazines.
On the other hand, Burney's novels abound in variety of characters
and so she uses characteristic speech to individualize them, especially
the minor characters. By contrast the novel's serious and morally
correct characters speak in standard English that is usually highly
formal. Significantly this style is also that of the novel's narrator, and
the language that is closest to the acknowledged standard for discursive
moral writing is the most likely to bear truth and authority. Style
distributes authority in *Camilla*, as in most novels of manners, sentiment, and emulation. A good example is the opening of chapter 1 of
*Camilla*, titled 'A Family Scene':

Repose is not more welcome to the worn and to the aged,
to the sick and to the unhappy, than danger, difficulty,
and toil to the young and adventurous. Danger they
encounter but as the forerunner of success; difficulty, as
the spur of ingenuity; and toil, as the herald of honour.
The experience which teaches the lesson of truth, and the
blessings of tranquillity, comes not in the shape of
warning nor of wisdom; from such they turn aside,
defying or disbelieving. 'Tis in the bitterness of personal
proof alone, in suffering and in feeling, in erring and in
repenting, that experience comes home with conviction, or
impresses to any use.

The next paragraph begins, 'In the bosom of her respectable family resided Camilla.' This opening could have come from any moralistic periodical essay of the century; even the introduction of a narrative in the second paragraph, presumably as illustration of the maxims uttered in the first, was commonplace in serious periodical essays, and resembles Bolingbroke's well-known definition of history – 'philosophy teaching by examples'. Clearly, this style of narration is at some remove from the epistolary novel's 'writing to the moment'. A more significant example of the privileging of authoritative, didactic, essay discourse is the 'little sermon upon the difficulties and the conduct of the female heart', which Camilla's father, Mr Tyrold, leaves for his daughter to read and live by, rather than any spoken counsel he might give (Book V, ch. 5). The writing, we are to suppose, has a power speech does not. The rhetoric of moral seriousness in this novel, for both narrator and authoritative characters, takes the form of the maxim, the essay, and the sermon, forms of discourse commanded by late eighteenth-century professionals of letters, particularly the clergyman and his secular counterpart, the moral essayist.

Burney's novels, then, and especially her novel of the 1790s, *Camilla*, use the elements of fiction within a structure dominated by authoritative moral discourse. Although they are novels of contemporary life, they treat that life in general, philosophical-literary terms, structured by values that are particular to the culture of writing, a professional middle-class culture. But *Camilla* is also a novel of 1796 and as such its silences are as significant as what it describes and inscribes. For a five-volume novel of 1796 to omit any reference to the events and controversies of this revolutionary decade was not unusual. On the other hand, the author was known to be married to a French *émigré* nobleman and former member of the Revolutionary Constituent Assembly, and she was known to be a former officer of the Royal court (the novel is dedicated to the Queen). Contemporary politics were precisely what Burney did not want to appear in her novel, though eighteen years later she put the Revolution into the plot of *The Wanderer*. When the Royal Princesses told her that *Camilla* had been well received at court, especially since so many 'bad' novels had been published by 'Democrats' recently, Burney explained to their Royal Highnesses

> that *Politics* were, *all ways*, left out: that once I had had an idea of bringing in such as suited *me*, – but that, upon second thoughts, I returned to my more native opinion they were not a *feminine* subject for discussion, & that I even believed, should the little work sufficiently succeed to be at all generally read, it would be a better office to general Readers to carry them wide of all politics, to their domestic fire sides, than to open new matter of endless debate.[14]

In *Camilla*, the absence of 'politics' of any kind is a riposte to the 'Democrats', the English Jacobins who were busy appropriating the 'modern novel' to a radical form of social criticism. It was also, as Burney says, an assertion of what she saw as the centrality of the domestic – the normality, naturalness, and authenticity of 'the domestic fire side' in relation to the relativities of political controversy and public events, and an assertion of the feminine role in the public activity of writing. This function of the domestic was widespread in fiction of the period, and by no means apolitical, in fact. The *topos* runs through all of the 'serious' novelists of the Romantic era, through Edgeworth, Austen, Scott, and many others, on into Victorian fiction. Appropriately enough, then, the profits from *Camilla* (the first edition was sold by subscription so as to maximize those profits) enabled Burney and her husband to build a country retreat, of ideal egalitarian domesticity, which they named 'Camilla Cottage'. Nevertheless, in refusing to write a 'tale of the times', Burney only wrote a 'tale of the times' of a somewhat different kind.

## The 'Gothic Romance'

As we saw in Chapter 1 readers and critics of the Romantic period thought that the novel of manners specialized in 'real life' (though in high society), the familiar, the contemporary, and to a large extent, the domestic, whereas the 'Gothic romance' dealt with the exotic, the extravagant, the extraordinary, the sublime, and the 'not English' or 'not British'. In fact, both the novel of manners, sentiment, and emulation and the 'Gothic romance' were about issues of self and society at the heart of late eighteenth-century and Romantic fiction. In some ways, indeed, the 'Gothic romance' is a version of the novel of manners, sentiment, and emulation, and there is no surprise in the fact that the most important Gothic novelist of the Romantic period, Ann Radcliffe, was a subscriber to Fanny Burney's *Camilla* in 1796. For just as novelists and narrative poets of the 1810s and 1820s used exotic settings and alien cultures to comment on contemporary Britain, so Gothic novelists used things 'not English' to deal with the same issues presented in novels of manners set in contemporary England. Furthermore, in the 1790s in particular there were novelists such as Charlotte Smith and Elizabeth Inchbald who combined elements of both 'Gothic romance' and the novel of contemporary life. In the same fertile decade there were novelists such as Thomas Holcroft, William Godwin, and Mary Wollstonecraft, who, as we have seen, made the same combinations and used Gothic elements in overtly political novels; and there were other novelists, discussed in the next section of this chapter, who appropriated Gothic elements to counter the fiction of the 'English Jacobins'.

After 1800 the 'Gothic romance' seemed to become ever more extravagant, verging at times on self-parody, as it joined with elements of the newly popular melodrama, and was adapted to the novel of passion of the 1810s and 1820s; these developments will be examined in Chapters 3 and 6. Elements of the Gothic were taken up by poets such as Shelley and Byron, and were even adapted by writers of 'national tales' and 'historical romances', such as the Porter sisters (see Ch. 3) and Sir Walter Scott (Ch. 5). Elements of the 'Gothic romance' can be found in much of the literature and art of the Romantic period, for, although some twentieth-century critics see the Gothic as an expression of fundamental human nature,[15] the 'Gothic romance' was not so much a coherent and authentic genre as an ensemble of themes and formal elements which could be taken over and adapted in whole or part by other novelists and writers and by artists in other media.

The sources of the 'Gothic romance' of the 1790s and the next three decades were diverse, but very important were certain forms of seventeenth-century court literature which had a continuing if precarious existence with late eighteenth-century readers, particularly the 'Heroic Dramas' of Dryden, Otway, and Lee; later plays, by Nicholas Rowe and others, called 'she-tragedies' because they focused on the plight of a heroine; some earlier tragicomedies, particularly those of Beaumont and Fletcher; and both the short novels and much longer '*romans à longue haleine*' (long-winded romances) imported from France after the Restoration in 1660 and dealing with plots of courtly intrigue and gallantry (in the sense of both courtly love and chivalric valour). The dramas were enjoying a revival on the late eighteenth-century stage; furthermore, books of plays were often read as if they were novels. In such plays there is usually a woman caught in complex intrigues both political and domestic, and facing powerful men and other women ruled by strong passions which the heroine must fend off by exercise of self-discipline and self-denial. The Heroic Dramas, 'she-tragedies', and prose romances influenced the grand air and somewhat operatic dialogues, the complex intrigues, exotic and 'historical' settings, and basic character repertory of Gothic novels, as well as conflicts of domestic and public loyalties and duties, conflict of the generations, and the theme of romantic love as a personal absolute running against social and political institutions and motives.

These elements had been used to depict the plight of the individual in a court society during the later seventeenth century, and they continued to retain a certain glamour in the late eighteenth century, when they were adapted to issues of interest to a theatre-going and novel-reading public that was predominantly professional and middle class and, like the gentry, profoundly suspicious of courts and court culture. Seventeenth-century anxieties about Catholic designs on Protestant England and fears of royal dynastic ambitions and failings could be revived in the 'Gothic romance' of the 1790s as fears of international secret conspiracies (supposedly instrumental in causing the French Revolution), fears of excessive social ambition and conflict, and fears of excessive individualism. Finally, the materials of court literature, transformed into 'Gothic romance', could have special relevance for middle-class women with little legal power or material independence, women supposed to be entirely domestic in their experience and in need of special curtailments of their 'natural' tendency to emotional extravagance.

Certainly these themes and materials are exploited to the full by the most important Gothic novelist of the Romantic period, Ann Radcliffe. Little is known of her education and background, but her novels show that she was very well read in the literature of Sensibility, including Sentimental tales, poetry, and *belles lettres*, as well as aesthetic theories of the sublime and picturesque; the English 'classics', such as Shakespeare and Milton; and such earlier 'Gothic' experiments as Horace Walpole's *Castle of Otranto* (1765). In his preface to *Otranto*, Walpole asserted his aim was to combine 'old' romance, meaning romances of chivalry, with the 'new', meaning the novel of manners in contemporary life. In fact, Walpole had really only written a particular kind of novel of Sensibility, for he used disjunction of plot and sudden changes of direction to present the reader with 'a constant vicissitude of interesting passions', that is, a display of inward subjectivity. At the same time, the pride of rank, social ambition, and associated aspects of aristocratic culture are made to seem incomprehensible and futile, yet unpredictable and dangerous.

Radcliffe took this structure and rearranged it, adding elements from the courtly literature described earlier, from Sentimental literature and aesthetic theories, and from the Burney novel of manners, sentiment, and emulation.[16] Like her contemporaries Charlotte Smith and Elizabeth Inchbald, Radcliffe emphasizes the subjectivity of her heroine at the expense of plot. Subjectivity is also opposed to merely social modes and codes of being. Society and social life are portrayed as full of confusing relativities, mysterious conspiracies, and hidden dangers for the sensitive and socially inexperienced heroine. Even the action and adventure are often treated in a perfunctory way. Radcliffe's novels represent a woman's impression of male swashbuckling and portray the male-dominated public and social world as confused, confusing, dangerous, and pointless – except as a test for the moral and intellectual character of the heroine and as an exercise of her moral and aesthetic sensibility. Furthermore, in Radcliffe's novels the heroine's feeling yet disciplined inwardness is contrasted to the hero's tendency to impulsive action, impetuousness, giving way to his passions – significantly, supposed to be a national trait of the revolutionary French. Radcliffe's novels oppose subjectivity to sociability, disciplined inwardness to impulsive action, and endurance to rebellion, along the lines of gender differences.

Thus the heroine's subjectivity is the central signifying and structural principle in Radcliffe's novels, as in Burney's. In Radcliffe's novels, however, this subjectivity is often stimulated by moral and aesthetic rather than moral and social causes – chiefly picturesque and sublime nature, the 'domestic affections', love, and the arts (especially music). Near the beginning of *The Mysteries of Udolpho*, for example, we are told that:

> It was one of Emily's earliest pleasures to ramble
> among the scenes of nature; nor was it in the soft and
> glowing landscape that she most delighted; she loved more
> the wild wood-walks, that skirted the mountain; and still
> more the mountain's stupendous recesses, where the
> silence and grandeur of solitude impressed a sacred awe
> upon her heart, and lifted her thoughts to the GOD OF
> HEAVEN AND EARTH. In scenes like these she would often
> linger alone, wrapt in a melancholy charm, till the last
> gleam of day faded from the west; till the lonely sound of
> a sheep-bell, or the distant bark of a watch-dog, were all
> that broke on the stillness of the evening. Then, the

gloom of the woods; the trembling of their leaves, at
intervals, in the breeze; the bat, flitting on the twilight; the
cottage-lights, now seen, and now lost – were
circumstances that awakened her mind into effort, and led
to enthusiasm and poetry. (vol. I, ch. 1)

Here the detached, authoritative narrative voice of the opening of the
paragraph gives way to a piling up of details, almost as Emily, too,
would notice them, for an effect of immediacy of perception; this in
turn leads to a clear statement of the moral consequence of the aesthetic
moment, activity of feelings and intellect taking the particular, expressive yet disciplined form of lyric poetry (later in the novel some of
Emily's poems are quoted for the reader's benefit).

The emotions felt by Radcliffe's heroines are also more dramatic
than those of Burney's heroines, and include fear and terror caused by
apparently supernatural events. Unlike her imitators, however,
Radcliffe always explains the supernatural by reference to 'reality' and
reason. Radcliffe's novels use a repeated plot-figure of enlightenment,
and their structure is a repetitive arrangement of discrete episodes of
various kinds of subjectivity, loosely held together by the plot of
courtship. Thus Radcliffe writes novels of description, and in this
respect she left a rich legacy for later descriptive novelists such as
Walter Scott. Scott made different uses of description, however; for
in Radcliffe's novels the emphasis in the descriptive passages is on the
heroine's 'taste'. According to Edmund Burke in his treatise on the
sublime and the beautiful (1757), 'taste' is the result of strong sensibility disciplined by reason and reflection.[17] Thus, in their way, too,
Radcliffe's novels are 'philosophical', and would have been recognized
as such by well-informed readers. This fact partly explains the high
estimation of Radcliffe's novels in their time, even with professional
intellectuals, for in them subjectivity is everywhere to be dominated
by reason and self-discipline. For example, as in Burney's novels, the
moral-aesthetic subjectivity of the heroine remains hidden to all but
the reader; she must conceal from others her real feelings and her real
self, in order to preserve them. The heroine is a patient, not an agent,
and patience, fortitude, endurance (moral rather than physical) are her
virtues, appropriately feminine ones – again, according to Burke's treatise on the sublime and the beautiful.[18] As the heroine of *The Mysteries
of Udolpho* is told by her dying father, ' "Always remember how much
more valuable is the strength of fortitude, than the grace of sensibility" ' (vol. I, ch. 7).

Fortitude is equated with strength of mind, normally to be
considered the appropriate speciality of men, and the villain of
*Udolpho*, Montoni, compliments Emily for displaying ' "a strength

of mind seldom observable in your sex"' (vol. II, ch. 3). In fact, it is seldom observable in anyone other than the heroine in Radcliffe's novels. The heroine's function is to be a field of disciplined subjectivity, and the central characters in Radcliffe's novels are young women for the same reason they are so in Burney's novels: women are supposed to be more inward, more subjective, more passive than men – in short, better subjects, in several senses, for the novelist. But their disciplined inwardness clearly indicates that they are heroines of a particularly professional middle-class culture and ideology, albeit a culture and ideology coloured by courtly aristocratic literature depicting nobility of sentiment. Thus Radcliffe uses elements of seventeenth-century courtly literature – dramas as well as fiction – to set forth the actual 'condition of upper middle-class women in the late eighteenth century: for better or for worse, women have no public or legal existence in society; they have only their selves. They are entirely private and domestic beings or they are means of transferring property and power from one man to another. But Radcliffe also uses these elements of earlier aristocratic literature to give new zest and an additional degree of literariness of her version of the 'modern novel's' treatment of self and society.

The narrative mode of Radcliffe's novels filters in a particular way all of the vicissitudes that constitute the self's experience in the temporal and social world. This narrator, like Burney's in her last three novels, is authoritative and omniscient, delivering definitive character portraits and explanations of mysteries. More important, however, the narrative voice exhibits a model consciousness of chastened sensibility toward which the heroine aspires, and chastens in effect the feelings of all kinds that the heroine experiences and which are reported to us in a relatively unvarying narrative 'voice'. This is seen in the passage quoted a few pages earlier, or in the following description of Emily's first view of the castle of Udolpho:

> Emily gazed with melancholy awe upon the castle,
> which she understood to be Montoni's; for, though it was
> now lighted up by the setting sun, the gothic greatness of
> its features, and its mouldering walls of dark grey stone,
> rendered it a gloomy and sublime object. As she gazed,
> the light died away on its walls, leaving a melancholy
> purple tint, which spread deeper and deeper. . . . Silent,
> lonely and sublime, it seemed to stand the sovereign of the
> scene, and to frown defiance on all, who dared to invade
> its solitary reign. (vol. II, ch. 5)

The emphasis here is less on the sublime and terrible of the castle, as it appears to Emily, than its value as an aesthetic object of a particular kind, and an object with moral and social associations ('silent, lonely and sublime'; 'the sovereign of the scene'; 'to frown defiance'). Furthermore, the picturesque and sublime are rendered in the same measured, stately prose, immune to whatever terrors the castle may suggest or, within the story, disclose.

This narrative 'voice' is the normal – the norm-setting – tenor of the Radcliffe novel.[19] It is not ironical or witty or genteelly learned; in fact, wittiness is expressly attacked in *Udolpho*, as in Burney's *Camilla*, as a sign of superficiality, mere sociability, or worse. To be ironic and learned would smack too much of the social values and culture that Radcliffe's novels explicitly expose and condemn. Nor is the narrative 'voice' in her novels expressively sentimental and personal. In fact, sentiment is warned against in *Udolpho*, as the self's danger to itself. Radcliffe's narrator is a model of the woman of the professional middle classes, a lady from the inside, not the outside; from the inward self, not the social personage.[20]

Radcliffe's novels are ladylike in another important way, too – in their use of verse for effects of literariness, though this literariness participates in the pseudo-genteel amateur *belles lettres* of the miscellany magazines rather than in the literariness of the Romantic poets of the 1790s. Verse is used frequently in Radcliffe's novels, and articulates meaning and form in several ways that Radcliffe made her own, and then gave to the novelists, especially the women novelists, of the Romantic period. In the first place, as epigraphs to each chapter, verse provides an outside border for the narrative and all that it contains. The prose – one can say the despised prose – of the novel is hedged, framed, or marked off with bits of 'serious literature', mostly short quotations from Shakespeare, Milton, Thomson, and Sentimental poets such as Collins, Gray, Mason, Rogers, and so on.

This canon of sources constitutes very much a late eighteenth-century lady's bookshelf of recognized 'classics' along with 'modern' poets of moral feeling. Furthermore, the epigraphs participate in the form of the novel by foreshadowing the chief events of the chapters themselves: they pre-figure; they are pretexts; they 'literarize' the novel. There are also original poems and songs within the chapters, which perform a number of functions. The lyric effusions of the heroine constitute just about the only form of emotional self-expression she allows herself; but since she indulges herself this way only when alone, they remain personal and private, documents of the self for itself. Then there are the songs, sung by various characters, which may be tales or lyrics, which may simply interrupt and punctuate the narrative, but which may also communicate something from one character to another, may be a kind of personal signature, a sign of unseen presence and propinquity. Still, they too remain personal, and intimate, if not private. In Radcliffe's novels verse, as the literary or the expressive, marks the outer and the innermost borders of narrative, the plane of the social and cultural institution on one hand, and the personally expressive on the other. This use of verse reinforces the emphasis on aesthetic experience – 'taste' – as one of the main varieties of the inward subjectivity of the heroine. Thus, in their use of verse, too, Radcliffe's novels clearly advertise their character as texts designed to represent a particular kind of inward self, the self of the lady of the professional middle classes.

The self-damaging or self-destructive tendencies of masculine self-hood, let alone its danger to the family and the community, are important though secondary elements in Radcliffe's novels, but become central in 'Gothic romances' written by men. The outstanding example is Matthew Gregory Lewis's *The Monk* (1796), so successful that the title of Lewis's novel became his nickname. *The Monk* presents an ambivalence about excessive individuality that persists right through the Romantic period. What is condemned is desired; what is repeatedly refused is repeatedly returned to, and when Lewis brought the Radcliffe villain into the centre of his novel he created a sensation with readers of fashionable novels and stole leadership in the line of 'Gothic romance' from Ann Radcliffe. Her reply to him was a restatement of her own form of Gothic, in *The Italian* (1797), but henceforth it was *The Monk* which set the pattern for a host of imitators at all levels of the market for fiction, from the circulating library to the chapbook hawker.

Lewis was the dandified son of a rich professional civil servant, he was another subscriber to Burney's *Camilla*, and he knew many of the leading liberals and English Jacobins in the 1790s. Like theirs, his novel contains much explicit social criticism. It satirizes and exposes the vices, pride of rank, and abuse of power of the nobly-born, or at least those who follow the 'old ways' of aggrandizement of the estate and the family name at all costs, and who toady at court and tyrannize at home in order to achieve their narrow class interests and selfish ends. *The Monk* also exposes and satirizes the vanity and social ambitions of the emulative middle classes, the ignorance, superstitiousness, gulli-bility, and violence of the common people (there are several scenes of mob violence in the novel), and of course the hypocrisy of religion and the evils of monastic life. In short, *The Monk* is thematically quite similar to most 'modern novels' of the day, and even exhibits some of the ideas and assumptions of the more liberal social criticism of the 1790s, including late Enlightenment sociology of court culture found in the English Jacobin writers.

The focus of the novel's attention, and the cause of its celebrity and notoriety, is the character of the monk himself, Ambrosio. Ambrosio's history, like that of John Moore's *Zeluco* (whom Ambrosio resembles), illustrates the English Jacobin principle that circumstances form character. Sequestered from the world at a tender age, and educated by monks, Ambrosio is of necessity ignorant of himself and society. Thus, from being a paragon of passionate piety, the marvel of Madrid as a pulpit orator, and sought-after confessor, he is easily seduced into becoming a monster of private – indeed secret – lust, the inverse of his public character and the reputation he holds with both the town and his religious order. Publicly he represents religious law and limit; privately he gives way to excess and transgression. Having abetted terrible cruelties in the name of religion, he is led unwittingly to murder his mother and rape and murder his sister. The virtuous characters in the novel, who act on the periphery of all this emotional extravagance, and who are in any case utterly static and uninteresting, almost all survive to enjoy domestic happiness while Ambrosio perishes alone after an ingenious set of tortures implemented by the devil himself. Thus there is a contradiction between the structure of the novel and what it appears to argue: corruption and passion, including erotic passion, are at the centre; virtue and domesticity are victimized, disrupted, or remain on the periphery of the novel's main interest – the passion (in several senses) and excess of the monk.

Formally, therefore, the novel's main element, and its centring compositional and thematic element, is the description of Ambrosio's thoughts and feelings as he 'progresses' from solitary but innocent paragon to solitary and secret villain. The narration is third-person, as in Radcliffe's novels; but whereas Radcliffe's narrator describes the heroine's perceptions and feelings with an even-tempered detachment, Lewis's narrator employs conventions of 'excited' and sympathetic expressivity in describing Ambrosio's inward experiences, conventions which had been well developed by the principal writers of Sensibility of the previous generation, Mackenzie and Sterne, though Lewis does not go as far as they did in this respect. In the following passage, for example, the reader is at one moment the observer, at another moment invited to see through Ambrosio's own eyes. Matilda, who has disguised herself as the young monk Rosario in order to seduce Ambrosio, threatens to kill herself if Ambrosio continues to reject her:

> She lifted her arm, and made a motion as if to stab
> herself. The Friar's eyes followed with dread the course of
> the dagger. She had torn open her habit, and her bosom
> was half exposed. The weapon's point rested upon her left
> breast: And Oh! that was such a breast! The Moon-beams
> darting full upon it, enabled the Monk to observe its

> dazzling whiteness. His eye dwelt with insatiable avidity
> upon the beauteous Orb. A sensation till then unknown
> filled his heart with a mixture of anxiety and delight: A
> raging fire shot through every limb; The blood boiled in
> his veins, and a thousand wild wishes bewildered his
> imagination. (vol. i, ch. 2)

This is a long way from Burney's, Radcliffe's, or Austen's mastery of filtered inward speech and of its alternation with reported thoughts.

On the other hand, like later Gothic novelists of the 1800s and 1810s and like the novelists of passion of the 1810s and 1820s, Lewis places corrupted rather than virtuous consciousness at the centre of his fictional structure. Thus, while Radcliffe describes sensibility, Lewis describes passions, including both the erotic passions and the conventional inward conflict or psychomachia of the villain. Drawing on a broad range of earlier eighteenth-century erotic art and literature (much of it, ironically, influenced by court culture), Lewis contributed to the developing language of psychological description in this period what one might call the Sentimental erotic. At the beginning of volume 3, for example, Ambrosio approaches the bed of Antonia, whom he has enchanted into a sleep so that he can enjoy her unresisted:

> He now ventured to cast a glance upon the sleeping
> Beauty. A single Lamp, burning before the Statue of St.
> Rosolia, shed a faint light through the room, and
> permitted him to examine all the charms of the lovely
> Object before him. The heat of the weather had obliged
> her to throw off part of the Bed-cloathes: Those which
> still covered her, Ambrosio's insolent hand hastened to
> remove. She lay with her cheek reclining upon one ivory
> arm; The Other rested on the side of the Bed with
> graceful indolence. A few tresses of her hair had escaped
> from beneath the Muslin which confined the rest, and fell
> carelessly over her bosom, as it heaved with slow and
> regular suspiration. The warm air had spread her cheek
> with higher colour than usual. A smile inexpressibly sweet
> played round her ripe and coral lips, from which every
> now and then escaped a gentle sigh or an half-pronounced
> sentence. An air of enchanting innocence and candour
> pervaded her whole form; and there was a sort of modesty
> in her very nakedness, which added fresh stings to the
> desires of the lustful Monk. (vol. iii, ch. 1)

The attitude evoked from the reader is one of connoisseurship rather than lust, however, so that this 'Object' may be enjoyed for its aesthetic properties, a would-be refined blend of opposite qualities ('a sort of modesty in her very nakedness') often found in Sentimental literature, and a replacement for, rather than a prelude to, any real or imagined physical enjoyment of the 'Object'. The point of view is that of the third party, observer or voyeur, who appears in so much of the genteel pornography of the late eighteenth century. Such passages are, in a way, *The Monk's* counterpart to the descriptions of Emily's perception of the beauties of landscape, or music, in *The Mysteries of Udolpho*. They were removed by Lewis in later editions, but the energetic and expressive portrayal of Ambrosio's passions remained, passions apparently condemned and terminated by the novel's argument, but in fact occupying central importance and attention in the novel's structure, and inviting, however obliquely, the (male) reader's participation.

This is not to say that depiction of social institutions, relations, and relativities is unimportant in *The Monk*. Indeed, without its elements of social criticism, this novel, along with the other 'Gothic romances' and novels of passion, could not have enjoyed its great popularity during the Romantic period. Lewis's depiction of society is also very close to that of the more liberal novelists of the time, including, as already noticed, the English Jacobins; and certain social practices and institutions are clearly shown to be hostile to rich selfhood, whether virtuous or vicious. The inset narratives in *The Monk*, as well as its main story, clearly show how the institutions of property and noble rank suppress individuality, in the form of romantic love – this is a very old theme in literature. But just as clear is the way excessive institutional power and order, as in a monastery or in an autocratic state, pervert individual natures, enforce outward conformism but inward rebellion, or destroy virtuous and authentic individuality. For *The Monk*, like many 'Gothic romances', appropriates conventions of courtly intrigue from the courtly novels and Heroic Dramas of the seventeenth century.

On the other hand, and very aptly for a decade of popular revolution, *The Monk* shows that the common people, the 'populace' or 'mob', are also lacking in individual selfhood and are therefore dangerous. The populace of Madrid follow undiscriminatingly such 'popular' orators as Ambrosio, or they go to the other extreme and rise up angrily to destroy monastic institutions when their own irrational faith is shown to have been mere credulity. As in Godwin's *Caleb Williams* and *St. Leon* (1799), the mob is shown to be collectively passionate and violent, just as the individual deprived of 'normal' affective and domestic life and 'a proper education' (to quote the last words of Inchbald's *A Simple Story*) will become either a slave to the power of others or tyrannical in his or her turn. Lacking a 'true' self, both the 'populace' and the individual lack a stable inward or outward identity – indeed, the individual will experience a self-destructive conflict between inward and outward identity.

These themes were major issues during the Romantic period, and go a long way to explain the popularity of 'Gothic romance' and the later novels of passion, where they were developed, perhaps, in their most striking and dramatic form. It can be said that these themes were bound up with the very notion of individual identity constructed in literature during the late eighteenth and early nineteenth century, and still very much with us, as is 'Gothic' fiction of various kinds. Nevertheless, the themes had their own specific, yet developing character during the Romantic period. The 'Gothic romance', particularly of the type of *The Monk*, exhibited a profound ambivalence toward the culture of Sensibility that had been developing in western Europe for four or five decades. The ambivalence is seen clearly in the reception of Byron's major narrative and dramatic poems; other notable examples are novels of passion (examined later, in Ch. 6), such as Lady Caroline Lamb's *Glenarvon* and Mary Shelley's *Frankenstein*, Godwin's *Fleetwood* and his pupil Bulwer Lytton's *Pelham*. Even more is it seen in the 'sensation-Gothic' or 'terror-Gothic' novels by Charlotte Dacre, W. H. Ireland, Francis Lathom, Percy Shelley, Louisa Stanhope, and Charles Maturin; in the thirty-page Gothic chapbooks by Isaac Crookenden, Sarah Wilkinson, and a host of anonymous hacks; and, of course, in translated 'German romances'. For Sensibility is both a version and a subversion of the extravagance of the aristocratic hero, and thus to be feared and desired as opening a way back to what it replaces; but it is also to be feared and desired as individuality *in extremis*, as extra-social being *par excellence*, as freedom from the relativities and constraints of merely social existence, but consequently as a terrible solitude.

## Against Enlightenment, Sensibility and Revolution: Anti-Jacobinism and Romanticism

By 1795 the English Jacobins were in retreat. Government repression and intimidation broke up the nascent coalition of aristocratic, middle-class, and artisan reformists, and turned many Nonconformists – leaders in calls for institutional reform – back to evangelism and emotional religious revival. But 'Jacobinism' remained a source of fear, especially since Britain remained at war with a militantly revolutionary

France – now, quite clearly, anything labelled Jacobin, even if of native British growth, could be characterized as 'not British'. In the second half of the decade replies and counters to Jacobinism at home were multiplied, and included novels to instruct the novel-reading classes in the dangers of liberalism of any kind, as well as short fiction for the common people – the real threat to both the 'privileged orders' and those in the professional and middle classes who wished to collaborate with privilege or to take it over themselves. Immediately after 1800, the novel would be turned whole-heartedly to the task of modelling a collaboration of gentry and professionals, and artists pursuing this same task produced the great fiction of the 1810s.

Meanwhile, 'Anti-Jacobin' novelists lashed out with personal satires against leading English Jacobins, in novels such as Elizabeth Hamilton's *Letters of a Hindoo Rajah* (1796) and *Memoirs of Modern Philosophers* (1800), Isaac D'Israeli's *Vaurien* (1797), and Edward Dubois's *The Travels of St. Godwin* (1800) – a parody of Godwin's *St. Leon* (1799). In spite of their satire on ideas and characters of the English Jacobins, however, these novels continued many of the themes of social criticism developed in English Jacobin fiction. Other novels such as Jane West's *The Advantages of Education* (1793) and *A Tale of the Times* (1799), Amelia Opie's *Adeline Mowbray* (1804), and Charles Lamb's *Rosamund Gray* (1798) did not so much satirize Jacobinism and its supposed disguises, Sensibility and 'philanthropy', as seek alternatives to Jacobinism by exploiting elements of the Sentimental tale such as themes of rustic simplicity, religious quietism, the 'domestic affections', aesthetic transcendence, and subjective, personal narration.

The first and most lastingly influential Anti-Jacobin fiction, however, was not aimed at the novel-reading classes but at the readers of 'street literature'. As early as 1792, Hannah More, a leading Evangelical and campaigner for lower-class literacy, decided that increasing social insubordination was based on popular print culture, and that this print and the culture it embodied could only be eradicated by reading-matter of a similar kind. As More's biographer put it, since

> the school of Paine [i.e., the English Jacobins] had been
> labouring to undermine, not only religious establishments,
> but good government, by the alluring vehicles of novels
> [i.e., short fiction in chapbook form], stories, and songs
> [i.e., broadsheets], she thought it right to encounter them
> with their own weapons. . . .[21]

Very reluctantly, she tried her hand at fiction for the people, but her first essay in this genre, *Village Politics: Addressed to All the Mechanics, Journeymen, and Day Labourers, in Great Britain*, 'By Will Chip, A

Country Carpenter' (1792), was such a success, bought in the hundreds and thousands by the well-to-do and given away to the common people, that she set up a more comprehensive plan, the Cheap Repository, launched in 1795 with the help of supporters in the upper classes and the Church of England. Most of the chapbooks were written by Hannah More and her sister Sarah. More prepared carefully for her task, collecting a wide range of street literature, or her 'sans-culotte library', as she called it. She also planned to take over the usual distribution channels of street literature, by bribing or coercing small bookstall holders and travelling chapmen into carrying her wares along with or in place of their usual stock. As printers she employed two men, one the proprietor of a circulating library at Bath, and the other a prominent printer and distributor of street literature.

Of the Cheap Repository tracts themselves, a few attack Jacobinism directly, as in *Village Politics* and *The History of Mr. Fantom, the Newfashioned Philosopher and His Man William* (1797); but the majority are aimed at various aspects of popular culture, or the 'moral economy of the common people' – the lottery-of-life mentality, tolerance of 'small sins' such as pilfering and poaching, the lower-class culture of amorous courtship and marriage after pre-marital pregnancy, interest in dreams and prophecies, the idea of the 'fair wage' and the 'fair price' based on traditional relationships of social interdependence, and popular acceptance of the social structure of gentry hegemony and rural paternalism. Examples are *The Shepherd of Salisbury Plain* (1795), *Hints to All Ranks of People* (1795), *Black Giles the Poacher* (1796), *The Hubbub; or, The History of Farmer Russell the Hard-Hearted Overseer* (1797) and *Tawny Rachel, or, The Fortune Teller; with Some Account of Dreams, Omens and Conjurers* (1797). Almost all of the tracts are written from an authoritative third-person narrative point of view, and have as hero, social model, and *deus ex machina* a good middle-class Evangelical – often an Evangelical clergyman. The plots are simple: reward for conversion and humility, and punishment for sins (however small) and proud independence or rebelliousness.

Often the lowly – children, the very poor, servants, and the elderly – are made instruments of conversion in their families and neighbourhoods, and thus have spiritual greatness attributed to them – another version of the 'trivial sublime' of Wordsworth, Charles Lamb, and other Romantic poets and writers of the 1790s. For More's work and that of her follower, Rev. Legh Richmond (*Annals of the Poor*, 1809–14), has much in common formally and thematically with the writings of the early Romantic poets and essayists; More and Richmond are Romantic Evangelicals. In both More's and Richmond's tracts, too, the narrator and the Evangelical characters 'speak' the same dialect, standard written English, and while there is not much use of

dialect (restricted to lower-class characters), there is some use of sociolect for characterization. The virtuous poor usually 'speak' the dialect
of religious literature – the Bible, hymns, and tracts. In other words,
they have internalized 'the Word' as understood by Evangelical culture;
they have been removed from oral culture into the particular culture
of writing promoted by Evangelicalism. In general, they turn out to
be diminutive versions of the middle-class Evangelical characters.

The increasingly nervous upper and middle classes responded with
enthusiasm to Cheap Repository, buying the tracts in bulk lots to
distribute to the poor, probably with the hope of heading off social
disaffection as well as saving souls. No doubt, too, the tracts presented
such purchasers with a fantasy version of ideologically disarmed
common people gratefully accepting leadership and patronage from
their virtuous, self-disciplined, Evangelical social superiors. Almost
immediately, for example, there were calls for editions of Cheap
Repository on 'superior' paper with good quality press-work, suitable
for binding and shelving in the libraries of the well-to-do. As More's
biographer remarked, 'The success [of Cheap Repository] surpassed
her most sanguine expectation. Two million of the publications were
sold in the first year – a circumstance perhaps new in the annals of
printing.'[22] How many were actually bought by the common people
is uncertain; but each of the tracts bore on its title page the price for
a single copy as well as the price for 25, 50, or 100 copies. More
conducted Cheap Repository until 1798. Others imitated its plan and
format, and the original tracts were reprinted again and again by
various printers, in Ireland and America as well as in Britain, down
into the 1840s, and they were translated into many languages. In 1799
the Religious Tract Society was founded to carry on More's work in
a more thorough and systematic way; but the persistence of the Cheap
Repository tracts far beyond the social crisis they were designed to
address strongly suggests that their real task was not so much to defeat
Jacobinism as to erase what was seen as the seed-bed of Jacobinism –
the popular oral and print culture, the traditional, centuries-old 'moral
economy' of the common people.

Meanwhile, other writers were reacting in various ways against use
of the 'modern novel' to spread Jacobinism amongst the upper and
middle classes. Elizabeth Hamilton, Jane West, and Isaac D'Israeli are
the most notable Anti-Jacobin novelists, but there were many by the
end of the 1790s, and there were others who adopted some Anti-
Jacobin elements in novels with different objectives, including John
Moore in *Mordaunt* (1800) and Fanny Burney in *The Wanderer* (1814).
The Anti-Jacobin novels of the 1790s share a number of themes and
characteristics. First, of course, there are direct attacks on the characters
and writings of leading English Jacobins, especially intellectuals,

philosophers, polemicists, and novelists such as William Godwin, Thomas Holcroft, and Mary Wollstonecraft. Anti-Jacobin novels often fall back on the techniques of earlier satirical fiction, such as *Don Quixote, Gil Blas,* and the novels of Fielding and Smollett. The most intellectual Anti-Jacobin novelists also draw on the classical Lucianic tradition of satire against various kinds of idealism and enthusiasm. Anti-Jacobin novelists tend to rely in part on the plot of the novel of education: a young man or woman enters the world, is taken in by the Jacobin villain, and is either destroyed in consequence or saved by a mentor or wise lover. The survivors learn to see things as they really are, and so in this kind of Anti-Jacobin novel there is an equating of Jacobin idealism with delusion and fantasy. Often, too, the Jacobin deluder is shown to be a hypocrite, mouthing liberty, equality, and philanthropy, but actually motivated by mere self-interest, by excess of merely personal ambition, desire, lust, passion. Thus the Jacobin villain is an intriguer and a machiavel, and hence associated, paradoxically, with the great evil in middle-class ideology, court politics and culture, or at least courtly practices.

Character in Anti-Jacobin novels is usually one-dimensional, based on rather old-fashioned ideas of the ruling passion and drawing, again, on the satirical Character-books of earlier writers such as Butler and La Bruyère. Much of the action, too, is in dialogue, as the Characters talk through the themes of the Revolution debate. The didactic and polemical elements dominate these novels, then, especially the novels of the more conventionally intellectual and philosophical men writers. Women Anti-Jacobins such as Jane West and Elizabeth Le Noir tend to emphasize themes of rural simplicity and domestic affections as opposed to urban, courtly, fashionable decadence. Sympathy for the Revolution is treated as just another fashionable vice of the decadent upper classes. Women Anti-Jacobin novelists also tend to rely more on techniques of domestic realism, fearing to appear too intellectual and philosophical, for that would associate them with English Jacobin feminism. Sensibility is also criticized severely by Anti-Jacobin novelists of both sexes; this criticism, of course, is found in much Jacobin fiction.

Nevertheless, there are significant differences in treatment of this theme. Conservatives regarded the culture of Sensibility as a contributory factor in the outbreak of the French Revolution; many conservative moral critics in the 1790s associated Sensibility with aristocratic libertinism, with things 'not English', with 'French principles', with excess and transgression justified by delusive or impractical ideals. Women, then, became the centre of the struggle between 'traditional', 'English' values and new political, social, and cultural values, in a model of social conflict that can be traced back to the seventeenth century at least: the social enemy intrigues to seduce the women of another class, as a way of exercising power over that class and, at the same time, as a way of getting at the other class's property. Thus many Anti-Jacobin novels include an intriguing Jacobin villain; but many also dwell on the internal struggle of a hero or heroine to resist the false values, the ideological penetration of the intriguer, the subjugation of the self by the other. As in most late eighteenth-century literature, sensibility, defined as the unique inwardness of each person, is differentiated according to gender, and the sensibility of women (or impressionable and naive young men) is then depicted as particularly susceptible to exploitation by unscrupulous seducers bent on acquiring power over the minds, bodies, and property of women (or perhaps effeminate men) while masquerading as libertarians and enemies of 'artificial' social boundaries and constraints. Thus Anti-Jacobin novels, too, debate the nature of individuality and individualism, and begin to develop the fictional study of the perils, fragility, and excesses of selfhood, major themes of fiction for the next three decades, when the threat of Jacobinism had receded.

Charles Lamb's *A Tale of Rosamund Gray* is also a 'tale of the times', even though it does not refer to the political and social crisis of the 1790s at all. For, as with Burney's *Camilla*, this absence could be just another kind of political statement. In fact, *Rosamund Gray* excludes both Jacobin and Anti-Jacobin politics as a way of rebuking and rising above or going beyond both, but this rhetorical function will only appear if the tale is considered in its historical context. At the time he published the tale, Lamb was closely associated with the young English Romantic poets Wordsworth, Coleridge, Southey, and others, and he had already published some poems himself. *Rosamund Gray* was his first work of prose and was published in the same year as Wordsworth's and Coleridge's *Lyrical Ballads*, the work supposed to have inaugurated the Romantic period in English poetry. In spite of its prose form, then, *Rosamund Gray* is thoroughly implicated in Romantic poetry of the late 1790s, when the Romantic poets were withdrawing from English Jacobinism and turning to transcendental nature, transcendental selfhood, the 'domestic affections' as authentic social experience, authentic language, and transcendental literariness after the apparent collapse of political idealism and the defeat of political reform in the mid-1790s. *Rosamund Gray* participates in this literary movement by reconstructing the Sentimental prose tale, just as the Romantic poets were reconstructing Sentimental lyric and narrative poetry.[23]

Lamb identified the genre of *Rosamund Gray* in the full title as 'a tale', and to readers of the time this designation would suggest a short narrative, probably dealing with rustic or provincial life and with daily and domestic reality, celebrating values of simplicity, naturalness, and candour, and perhaps featuring an eccentric storyteller as mediator of the simple matter. For example, one source of *Rosamund Gray* is the popular ballad of 'street literature', which also provided models for *Lyrical Ballads*, and Lamb claimed that the inspiration for his tale was just such a ballad.[24] But like the Romantic poets, Lamb gives this popular original some distinctly literary attributes, just as German Romantic writers transformed the 'folk-tale' into the 'art-tale'.[25] Lamb emphasizes the storyteller as much or even more than the story, and, like Wordsworth in 'The Ruined Cottage', places a feeling and humane narrator between the story matter and the reader – indeed, it soon becomes clear that the narrator is the real subject of this fiction. His feelings, tastes, observations, and values are always in the foreground; he narrates the story at the same time that he finds it exercising his feelings and his judgment. In short, the subject of the tale is the subjectivity of its teller, and in this and in its desultory and digressive form, *Rosamund Gray* resembles not only Wordsworth's tales and Coleridge's conversation poems (one of which was dedicated to Lamb), but also several of Lamb's favourite books – Walton's *Compleat Angler*, Burton's *Anatomy of Melancholy*, Thomas Amory's novel *The Life and Opinions of John Buncle* (1756–66), Cowper's *The Task*, and Sterne's *Tristram Shandy*.

Thus *Rosamund Gray* belongs to a particular tradition of overt literariness, of the text as medley, and it might be characterized as a 'rhapsodic narrative'. But *Rosamund Gray* also adapts this tradition to the circumstances of the 1790s. The literary genre known as 'rhapsody' is a farrago, a mixture of discourses of different kinds, and thus it works against the kind of argumentative connectedness well-informed novel readers of the 1790s would have associated with the fiction of the English Jacobin novelists, such as William Godwin. Indeed, Lamb wrote to Godwin in 1803,

> Ten thousand times I have confessed to you . . . my utter inability to remember in any comprehensive way what I read. – I can vehemently applaud, or perversely stickle at *parts*: but I cannot grasp at a whole. This infirmity (which is nothing to brag of) may be seen in my two little compositions, the tale [*Rosamund Gray*] & my play [*John Woodvil*]. In both which no reader, however partial, can find *any story*.[26]

This is not to say that *Rosamund Gray* is apolitical, however, for it does participate in the politics of subjectivity inherited from the culture of Sensibility. Rhapsody is expressive, elevated, and enthusiastic, deliberately personal and individual rather than objective and general in its rhetorical mode. Thus, whereas in the earlier part of the century 'rhapsody' often meant something like 'nonsense', after mid-century and the rise of Sensibility it was associated with the individual, the unique, the original, the sublime, the prophetic and visionary.[27] The two great rhapsodists of the 1760s and 1770s, Sterne and Rousseau, established it as a characteristic discourse of the transcendentally individual and personal, as the characteristic writing of 'genius', writing itself, writing for the sake of writing. Yet in this respect again rhapsody is paradoxical: in its expressiveness, apparent immediacy and spontaneity, and purposive disorder, rhapsody pretends to recapture the quality of 'voice' lost in the great cultural shift from orality to writing, from 'folk-tale' to 'art-tale'. Rhapsody mimics inspired speech, and inspiration comes from on high or from the authentic self within. Thus rhapsody also claims to transcend writing by returning to writing's supposed origin, speech. The pseudo-vocal authenticity of rhapsody, its condition as a kind of anti-writing, is also necessary for it to function as supra-writing, and as a critique of mere writing-for-a-purpose, in political or polemical writing or novels of purpose.

In rhapsodic narrative, then, the nominal element (narrative) is a pretext and the modal element (rhapsodic) becomes the *raison d'être* of the text. For in its characters, incidents, and low-intensity melodrama, *Rosamund Gray* would seem to be not much different from the fiction found in the amateur literary magazines, in cheap and sensational chapbooks, or in popular collections of tales by professional or semi-professional authors. Even the social criticism and social ideals embodied in Lamb's story are, for the late 1790s, familiar enough. What makes *Rosamund Gray* an art-tale, and sets it quite apart from the false simplicity of the magazine tale or the crude simplicity of the street ballad, is the handling of the story matter. This has two aspects, the attitude of the narrator to the story and the style of narration itself.

The pervasive attitude of narrator to story in *Rosamund Gray* is a subtle combination of sympathy and ironic detachment – precisely the kind of rhapsody of memory and loss, change and return so characteristic of Lamb's essays of Elia. Reliving the past enables one to live *in* the present but not be *of* the present; and part of that reduced but transcendent living is writing. For the narrator tells us that he began writing the tale of Rosamund Gray in order to revivify memory. The revivifying aroused the desire to return to the scenes, and the return brought him back to 'the purity and simplicity of childhood',[28] back to a world that is/was whole and harmonious, unlike the world of social inequality and evil described in the story the narrator tells. But this return to wholeness leaves the actual fallen and divided world of adulthood exactly as it was/is.

The second aspect of *Rosamund Gray* as rhapsodic narrative is the

variety and artfulness, the energy and vivacity of the narrative voice
– a play of voice that more than compensates for the pathos and gloom
of the story matter itself. In the Romantic period, this peculiar 'voice'
is conventionally a trait of the artistically self-conscious tale, anecdote,
or sketch, or literarized genres of popular narrative literature. *Rosamund
Gray* is particularly notable for this literary foregrounding of the
storyteller's personality. One could even say that the tale's protagonist
is its narrator, who exhibits all the characteristics of the conventional
rhapsodist.

The narrative manner ranges from Wordsworthian aggressive
simplicity to chatty informality to lyrical expressiveness, and deploys
numerous devices of immediacy found in Sterne's novels – frequent
dashes, exclamation marks, use of italics for 'vocal' emphasis,
repetition, apostrophe, rhetorical questions, sentences broken off, and
parenthetical asides. An example is the narrator's reflections on the
gravestones in the cemetery of his native village, where he goes to pray
at his father's grave:

> Having performed these duties, I arose with quieter
> feelings, and felt leisure to attend to indifferent objects. –
> Still I continued in the church-yard, reading the various
> inscriptions, and moralizing on them with that kind of
> levity, which will not unfrequently spring up in the mind,
> in the midst of deep melancholy.

So far the language and the ideas are Wordsworthian; but the very next
paragraph is the unmistakable voice of Elia:

> I read of nothing but careful parents, loving husbands,
> and dutiful children. I said jestingly, where be all the *bad*
> people buried? Bad parents, bad husbands, bad children –
> what cemeteries are appointed for these? do they not sleep
> in consecrated ground? or is it but a pious fiction, a
> generous oversight, in the survivors, which thus tricks out
> men's epitaphs when dead, who, in their life-time,
> discharged the offices of life, perhaps, but lamely? – Their
> failings, with their reproaches, now sleep with them in the
> grave. *Man wars not with the dead.* It is a *trait* of human
> nature, for which I love it. (ch. 11)

The last sentence is a clear echo of Yorick in Sterne's *Sentimental
Journey*. But there are also a few ploys taken from another major writer
of Sensibility, Henry Mackenzie, such as the narrator's having personal
knowledge of the main characters and their story, the narrator's regular

reminders of his limited knowledge of characters' private thoughts and motives, and the breaking off of the narrative so that the narrator can exclaim his own thoughts, feelings, and experiences, or deliver a lyrical passage. Furthermore, throughout the narrative there is a degree of belletristic literariness, seen in the use of specifically literary quotation and allusion, that also distances the narrative voice from the mere pathos and emotionalism of formula Sentimental writing. The odd archaism and occasional use of the archaic form of the third-person singular verb help to give a literary quality to the prose, too, thus drawing attention, as both Sterne and Mackenzie do, to the actual making or composition of the text. An example is the long digression on the moon at the end of chapter 3:

> The moon is shining in so brightly at my window,
> where I write, that I feel it a crime not to suspend my
> employment awhile to gaze at her.
> See how she glideth, in maiden honor, through the
> clouds, who divide on either side to do her homage.
> Beautiful vision! – as I contemplate thee, an internal
> harmony is communicated to my mind, a moral
> brightness, a tacit analogy of mental purity; a calm like
> *that* we ascribe in fancy to the favored inhabitants of thy
> fairy regions, 'argent fields.'

Here is heard, too, the voice of Coleridge's 'conversation poems'.

The devices Lamb uses in his narrative, then, are drawn from Sterne, Mackenzie, and others, but they are put to uses pursued by Lamb's friends among the Romantic poets. These devices deliberately distinguish Lamb's prose from both late Enlightenment philosophical detachment and Sentimental emotionalism. More particularly, Lamb's style is a deliberate refusal of philosophy and history, the discourses making deepest inroads into serious fiction during the 1790s; it is a deliberate refusal of the connectedness, the 'philosophical' use of plot-as-argument in the novels of Godwin and the English Jacobins. The form of *Rosamund Gray* is 'Romantic' in the specific sense of the efforts of this first generation of English Romantics to create their own repertory of form and style from the literature of Sensibility, the discourses of liberal English Dissent, and the material of popular print culture. These efforts were partly a reaction against English Jacobinism and its writings, but partly, too, a development of them. In particular, through the form of *Rosamund Gray*, Lamb tried to transcend both the Jacobin and Anti-Jacobin novel, their themes and their rhetoric of fiction. In trying to do so, Lamb created one of the most interesting fictional experiments of the Romantic period; but though he began another novel in 1806, Lamb abandoned prose fiction for the essay, and after 1800 attempts to move beyond the fictional debate of the 1790s took the form of 'village anecdotes', 'tales of the heart', and social-historical 'national tales'.

## Notes

1. See Carl Cone, *The English Jacobins* (New York, 1968).

2. I use Enlightenment(s) to refer to the intellectual and cultural movements of social criticism in history, philosophy, literature, antiquarianism, sociology, linguistics, and so on, especially in England, Scotland, and France of the mid and late eighteenth century. I use Sensibility (with the adjective Sentimental) for the literary and cultural movement of the 1760s to 1780s that focused on inward subjectivity and criticism of court and aristocratic society, while recognizing that Enlightenment and Sensibility are not clearly distinct movements and that they are complex and even self-contradictory. For an introduction, see James Sambrook, *The Eighteenth Century: The Intellectual and Cultural Context of English Literature, 1700–1789* (London and New York, 1986).

3. See M. S. Larson, *The Rise of Professionalism: A Sociological Analysis* (Berkeley, 1977), ch. 12.

4. Marilyn Butler, *Jane Austen and the War of Ideas* (Oxford, 1975), p. 85.

5. See Gary Kelly, *The English Jacobin Novel 1780–1805* (Oxford, 1976).

6. *Anti-Jacobin Review and Magazine*, 5 (Feb. 1800), 152.

7. See Gerard A. Barker, *Grandison's Heirs: The Paragon's Progress in the Late Eighteenth-Century English Novel* (Newark New Jersey, 1985).

8. See Kelly, *The English Jacobin Novel*, pp. 209–36.

9. *A Vindication of the Rights of Woman* (1792), *A Historical and Moral View of the French Revolution* (1794), *Letters Written during a Short Residence in Sweden, Norway and Denmark* (1796), and *The Wrongs of Woman; or, Maria* (1798).

10. See R. F. Brissenden, *Virtue in Distress* (1974), Part 1, ch. 3.

11. See Keith Thomas, *Man and the Natural World* (1983), pp. 173–81; Edith F. Hurwitz, *Politics and the Public Conscience: Slave Emancipation and the Abolitionist Movement in Britain* (London and New York, 1973), pp. 21–47.

12. Joyce Hemlow, 'Fanny Burney and the Courtesy Books', *PMLA*, 65 (1950), 732–61.

13. Horace Walpole, *The Castle of Otranto* (1765), preface.

14. *The Journals and Letters of Fanny Burney*, vol. III, edited by Joyce Hemlow with Patricia Boutilier and Althea Douglas (Oxford, 1973), p. 186.

15. See for example Elizabeth MacAndrew, *The Gothic Tradition in Fiction* (New York, 1978).

16. Gary Kelly, '"A Constant Vicissitude of Interesting Passions": Ann Radcliffe's Perplexed Narratives', *Ariel*, 10 (Apr. 1979), 45–64 (pp. 46–47).

17. Edmund Burke, *Enquiry into the Origin of Our Ideas of the Sublime and Beautiful*, edited by James T. Boulton (London and New York, 1958), p. 23.

18. Burke, *Enquiry*, pp. 110–11.

19. See Kelly, '"A Constant Vicissitude of Interesting Passions"', pp. 60–61.

20. Mary Poovey, 'Ideology and *The Mysteries of Udolpho*', *Criticism*, 21 (1979), 307–30 (p. 317).

21. William Roberts, *Memoirs of the Life and Correspondence of Mrs. Hannah More*, second edition, 4 vols (London, 1834), II. 425.

22. Roberts, *Memoirs of More*, II. 426.

23. See Mary Jacobus, *Tradition and Experiment in Wordsworth's Lyrical Ballads (1798)* (Oxford, 1976).

24. Charles Lamb to Robert Southey, 29 Oct. 1789, in *The Letters of Charles and Mary Anne Lamb*, edited by Edwin W. Marrs, Jr, vol. I (Ithaca New York and London, 1975), p. 132.

25. See Jack Zipes, *Breaking the Magic Spell: Radical Theories of Folk and Fairy Tales* (1979), chs 2 and 3.

26. Charles Lamb to William Godwin, 10 Nov. 1803, in *The Letters of Charles and Mary Lamb*, edited by Edwin W. Marrs, Jr, vol. II (Ithaca and London, 1976), p. 128.

27. *Oxford English Dictionary*.

28. *Rosamund Gray*, in *The Works of Charles and Mary Lamb*, edited by E. V. Lucas, 6 vols (London, 1903–05), I. 26.

## Chapter 3
# 1800–1814: Beyond 'Tales of the Times'

The controversies and divisions of the 1790s, as embodied in the themes and forms of fiction, continued to exercise a powerful influence on novelists and other fiction writers throughout the Romantic period, and to some extent even acted as a filter through which classic eighteenth-century fiction had to be viewed. Yet, as we saw with Lamb's *Rosamund Gray*, even in the 1790s some writers tried to find formal and thematic resolutions and transcendences for the alarming conflicts and divisions revealed and exacerbated during the Revolutionary decade. After 1800 such efforts would become more strenuous. Although the threat of Jacobinism seemed to have been headed off at home, the war continued to intensify deep-seated social conflicts, and the rise of Napoleon, self-proclaimed embodiment of the Revolution, gave new menace to the international situation of Britain and its empire. These domestic and foreign anxieties led to renewed, if not necessarily open criticism of the power-holding classes and their institutions within Britain, and to renewed attempts to find a 'national' consensus in transcendental values or 'national' culture. Some novelists turned to depicting transcendence through subjectivity or the 'domestic affections', in 'tales of the heart', or subjectivity as social isolation, in Gothic romances or 'tales of wonder'. Others turned to the challenge of representing reformed, harmonious communities, either local, in 'village anecdotes', or national, in 'national tales'.

In this fiction – the Gothic romances apart – there was an increased emphasis on techniques of domestic realism and 'fact'; fictionality was seen as a sign of the impractical, the speculative, the imaginative, and moral or artistic excess – qualities associated with the French Revolution and Jacobinical utopianism, especially in the writings of Edmund Burke and his followers, including, as we have seen, the Anti-Jacobin novelists. On the other hand, a taste for fictionality and narrativity was also supposed to be a sign of the unenlightened mind, unregenerate moral self, or – worse – the 'pre-modern' or even pre-literate consciousness of the childlike common people. Somehow fiction and fictionality were still thought to impede the development of the rational, disciplined self idealized by the professional middle classes and to encourage different varieties of moral, subjective, imaginative excess, including excessive novel reading. Byron, for example, claimed he had read 4000 novels, as well as history, poetry, and *belles lettres*, by late 1807.[1] According to Thomas Medwin, Percy Shelley 'greedily devoured' chapbooks and then went on to Minerva Press novels and the 'trash of the circulating libraries' while he was still at school, and Shelley himself reported to a friend that on rainy days he would 'read Novels & Romances all day, till in the evening I fancy myself a Character' in one of them.[2] Many novel readers regarded that practice as a kind of addiction, even though other great novel readers, such as Jane Austen and her family, found nothing to be ashamed of or deplore in it.

At the same time, with the rise of Napoleon and the prolonging of war with France, with naval mutinies and social and economic crises at home, there were increased anxieties about social control and the quality of social leadership given by the hegemonic classes. Thus, paradoxically, even conservative writers took up English Jacobin criticism of aristocratic and courtly excess and middle-class emulation, in 'tales of fashionable life' that would develop into novels of passion in the 1810s and 'silver-fork novels' in the 1820s. On the other hand, there was increasing concern about lower-class culture, and its apparent dependence on gentry-dominated and paternalist social structures and ideologies of custom and tradition. Through the 1800s, then, various fiction writers tried to show how rural society in particular, and at all levels, should be reformed from within by professional middle-class values and domestic and social practices. This reform would have the added advantage of transcending increasingly sharp class divisions and creating a national community that was disciplined, harmonious, and purified of 'not British' elements within, and united against the external foe (not to mention better able to defend or even expand an extensive colonial empire). Fiction could have an important role not only in depicting this 'imagined community' and remaking all classes in the image of the professional middle classes, but it would also have an instrumental role in educating children and re-educating the upper, middle, and lower classes to the name and nature of these new modes of individual being and social relationship.

Two further remarks should be made before turning to more detailed consideration of some of the leading fiction writers of this central decade and a half in the development of Romantic fiction in Britain. In the first place, as we have noticed, many of the prominent varieties of fiction just after 1800 took the generic name 'tale', and there was generally a concern by authors to affirm the realism or basis of their fictions in fact. A reviewer of Jane Taylor's *Display: A Tale for Young People* asked in 1815:

> What is the difference between a Tale and a Novel? Is it
> that a tale is supposed to be a shorter and less laboured
> production than a novel; that a tale is designed to relate
> the natural occurrences and simple incidents of life; while a
> novel sets real life and probability at defiance, and
> demands, as its essential features, a heroine, a lover, a
> plot, and a catastrophe? – Is the novel necessarily of a
> more epic character than the tale, or are both to be
> referred to the same class of productions? How comes it
> that novels are, with few exceptions, the most pernicious
> in tendency of any works; while, under the generic title of
> Tales, we have some of the most instructive and profound
> compositions in the language?[3]

'Anecdotes' and 'sketches' were other terms used to distinguish fiction that was often short, usually desultory in form, apparently modest in its subject matter and scope, and more or less realistic in its method, as distinct from the greater artistic pretensions, settings in high society or exotic places, and more obviously fictional character of the 'modern novel'.

A second point to note is the dominance of women writers in the fiction of this decade and a half, and in the market for the prose fiction tales, be they 'tales of the heart', 'tales for youth', 'village anecdotes', or 'national tales'. Women had, of course, been prominent as writers of courtly novels in the late seventeenth and early eighteenth century, with figures such as Aphra Behn and Delariviere Manley; in Sentimental fiction and novels of manners, sentiment and emulation, with figures such as Eliza Haywood and Fanny Burney; in English Jacobin novels, with writers such as Mary Wollstonecraft and Mary Hays; in children's fiction, with writers such as Dorothy Kilner and Sarah Trimmer; and in religious tales, with writers such as Hannah More and her sister. But after 1800 the prominence of women and fiction, and thus the association of gender and genre, was even stronger. And the association was a mutually degrading one, and shown in such fictional satires as Eaton Stannard Barrett's *The Heroine* (1813). Women were supposed to be the main producers and consumers of fiction and fiction was supposed to be intellectually undemanding (therefore, it was supposed, fit for women's lesser intellectual capacities), overly stimulating to the emotions, and actually distracting from more 'solid' and 'improving' reading matter, 'solid' and 'improving' being characteristic of reading that fitted one for (male) professional life. This mutual degradation persisted in spite of the praise of some fiction, such as that quoted above in the review of Jane Taylor's *Display*. Moreover, it persisted in spite of the evident national, public importance of the ideological work undertaken in 'tales for youth', 'village anecdotes', and 'national tales' – nothing short of an entire moral social reformation of Britain. Here in fiction, then, women could participate in public life and national issues under the guise of writing 'mere' fiction, or 'only a novel' (to use a well-known phrase from chapter 5 of Jane Austen's *Northanger Abbey*).

## 'National Tales', 'Moral Tales' and 'Tales of Fashionable Life'

Maria Edgeworth was the most respected new fiction writer in the very early nineteenth century, the major woman novelist between Burney and Austen; and although she wrote both Burney-style triple-deckers (she was yet another subscriber to Fanny Burney's *Camilla*) and tales for adults and youth, it was in her 'Irish tales' that she did her most original work. As a child and young woman she had been forbidden by her father, Richard Lovell Edgeworth, to read novels at all. When she did begin to publish, her fiction was very much tied up with his ideas, interests, and experiences. He was thoroughly versed in the vices and follies of fashionable society, though educated to the bar as a preparation for the responsibilities of a landed gentleman in Ireland, and he was personally connected to leading figures in the English provincial and Nonconformist Enlightenments.[4] In all of her fiction, Edgeworth argues for the same thing, that which her father represented in his own career and his active life: the professionalization of the gentry, the remaking of a social class to fit it for social leadership of the other classes in a single, 'national' interest.

Maria Edgeworth's first work of fiction to embody this vision was published in 1800, almost by accident. Its sources were in the early history of the Edgeworth family and in a parlour-piece imitation, performed by Richard Lovell Edgeworth, of the oddities of speech of a servant on the Edgeworth's estate in Ireland. *Castle Rackrent, an Hibernian Tale Taken from Fact, and from the Manners of the Irish Squires before the Year 1782* was well received by readers and critics alike, inspired a small host of imitators, and launched Edgeworth on a career of fiction writing that lasted into the 1830s. Along with her later 'Irish tales' in *Tales of Fashionable Life* (1809–12), it gave many hints to Walter Scott – so much so that some critics referred to Scott's first novel, *Waverley*, as 'a Scotch *Castle Rackrent*'.[5]

*Castle Rackrent* is a tale, and like Lamb's *Rosamund Gray* it foregrounds the voice of the tale-teller, Thady Quirk, loyal steward and retainer of the Rackrent family. Thady's task is to narrate 'the family's' decline over four generations, and his narrative has the quality of speech rather than writing, being loose and conversational, full of asides and oblique observations on the facts of the story, full of dashes suggesting an improvised discourse, and full of Irish expressions, though there is not much attempt to render dialect pronunciation through spelling. The narrative proceeds at an even tenor and is rarely expressive, for, apart from his loyalty to 'the family' (a good feudal characteristic), Thady does not have an inward self to express, let alone to describe in the way and with the fullness that, say, Caleb Williams, another gentleman's retainer, does. There is thus an ironic distance between Thady and the reader, and his substandard English is the index to a variety of ways in which the reader is not meant to share his point of view. Yet, in his loyalty and human sympathies, and the sheer power of first-person narrative, there is also much to attract the reader.

These contradictory qualities can be seen in Thady's description of the climactic scene in the novel, the confrontation between Sir Condy and Jason over the payment of the estate's debts – in effect, the transfer of the estate from the Rackrents to Jason:

> The execution came down, and every thing at Castle
> Rackrent was seized by the gripers, and my son Jason, to
> his shame be it spoken, amongst them – I wondered, for
> the life of me, how he could harden himself to do it, but
> then he had been studying the law, and had made himself
> attorney Quirk. . . .[6]

There then follows a long list of the bills, constituting a picture of the extravagance and folly of the unprofessionalized gentry, which both Thady and the reader will shake their heads at. Yet as the scene develops, Thady's sympathy for his 'master's' distresses is evident, and evidently meant to be shared by the reader, especially in the face of Jason's relentless pursuit of the now ruined master of Castle Rackrent. The conclusion is: better to be Sir Condy with all the faults of his class than to be the new man, Jason Quirk, attorney, with all his professional virtues. Thus there is a formal ambiguity in the narrative voice of Thady, which Edgeworth tries to offset by hedging the narrative with three different framing structures of mediating editorial matter; in her later fiction, she dropped this kind of narrative altogether.

Plot and character in Thady's story carry the by-now-overly familiar themes of the decline of the old-style gentry, too preoccupied with traditional gentry pleasures – family honour, family 'rights', and noble living – to manage its affairs and thereby the affairs of its many dependents. The hard-drinking Sir Patrick Rackrent, the litigious Sir Murtagh, the fashionable Sir Kit, and the sentimental Sir Conolly manage to run the estate down until it ends up in the hands of Thady's own son, Jason (appropriately and ironically named for the hero of the Greek legend of the golden fleece). Jason is, significantly, an attorney and the Rackrent's last steward. Like Aby Henley in Holcroft's *Anna St. Ives* and a host of other petty professionals in eighteenth-century fiction, Jason exploits the moral weaknesses and class culture of his employer in order to take over his estate. Poor Thady, thoroughly penetrated by the ideology of gentry hegemony and its decayed code of feudal loyalty, is torn between sorrow for the decline of the family honour – the Rackrent family honour, that is – and a sneaking pride in the success of his own family in the person of his anti-feudal, thoroughly middle-class son.

For the plot and characterizations of the novel also show how the peasantry or common people and the old-style extravagant gentry in effect victimize each other, though they also unite (vainly) to resist the representative of rising middle classes. When Sir Conolly is finally forced to sign over the estate to Jason, a 'mob' of Irish peasants gather outside the manor house, 'in great anger against my son Jason, and terror at the notion of his coming to be landlord over them, and they cried, No Jason! No Jason! – Sir Condy! Sir Condy! Sir Condy Rackrent forever!' (p. 79). Even Jason is terrified, and forced to make a concession to the Rackrent family honour. In this incident, middle-class readers could readily see a frightening alliance between gentry and vulgar mob to resist rational pursuit of the profit motive and to keep the middle classes from the power and position they had earned; yet they could not disapprove entirely. Moreover, Sir Condy's weakness is his identification with the improvident lottery mentality of the common people, since he grows up being allowed to mix freely with them. For example, to choose a bride he flips a coin, and he dies as the result of a foolish bet that he can drink a horn of ale without stopping for breath. Even the fashion-conscious and cosmopolitan gentry are made fun of, though major development of this theme was reserved for Edgeworth's novels of manners and another 'Irish tale', 'The Absentee' (1812).

In *Castle Rackrent*, as in Edgeworth's other fiction, fashion of all kinds is the special province and failing of the women of the gentry.

In *Rackrent* Sir Condy's wife Isabella is a typical upper-class female novel reader and really only marries Sir Condy because her father has forbidden her to do so and because she wants to be eloped with, just like the heroine of a novel (p. 66). After marriage, she prefers to read *The Sorrows of Werther*, a classic Sentimental novel by Goethe, rather than concern herself in what her husband calls '"the sorrows of Sir Condy"', that is, his financial distress, which is not helped by her ignorance of household economy and her extravagant, fashionable tastes (p. 48).

In short, there is no hero of *Castle Rackrent*; the moral of Thady's tale is implicit and not embodied in some wholly admirable figure. Thus Thady's tale in effect argues for what it doesn't actually describe, a renewed (certainly not supplanted) landed gentry, a gentry with the professional training and self-discipline necessary for social leadership, for effective direction of both the peasantry and the middle classes, and for protection of each from the other. But if the model does not appear in the story of *Castle Rackrent*, it nevertheless appears in the text, in that triple-layered framing material referred to earlier. Having written her *tour de force* of literary ventriloquism, Edgeworth drew back, and framed Thady's monologue with an 'editor's' Preface in which she offers the narrative as an 'anecdote' illustrative of passed-away attitudes and practices, as an example of 'vernacular idiom', and as a refreshingly simple and natural, 'plain unvarnished tale', 'preferable to the most highly ornamented narrative' (i.e., preferable to 'modern novels').

But this apparent tribute to the quality of Thady's narrative in effect distances and diminishes it. Furthermore, the narrative itself is persistently undermined by the 'editor's' footnotes and by the Glossary, originally published at the front of the novel (it was moved to the back after the first London and Dublin editions of 1800). This editorial apparatus repeatedly draws attention to the irrational, improvident nature of Irish popular culture, and emphasizes the 'otherness' of this culture further by notes on Irish peculiarities of pronunciation and phrasing. These notes and the style of Thady's discourse clearly establish the character of Irish popular culture as oral and 'pre-modern' (a term now used by historians to refer to pre-industrial, non-urbanized, and feudal or semi-feudal societies).

For example, in the note on Irish mourning practices the editor points out the great waste of time for work by the practice of every relative, however distant, participating in the mourning and the wake for a dead person. The note reveals the editor's inability to comprehend the value of these periodic re-affirmations of relatedness and community to the common people who are condemned to a subsistence economy with no one to rely on for help but each other. The impression that the editor is an enlightened, rational, practical-minded person is reinforced by the mock-antiquarianism of many of the notes (anticipating the mocking of antiquarianism in Scott's novels), as if to suggest that antiquarians' loving, laborious, and bookish recording of particularities of folklore and folksay is beside the point in a world that needs reason, order, and 'improvement', and not superstition, prejudice, and unexamined tradition, if modernization is to take place.

The narrative 'voice' in the apparatus is also highly allusive, discriminating, well-informed about history and economics, at times humorous, and (because of the large number of anecdotes from personal observation) widely and personally acquainted with Irish society. Thus the apparatus exhibits the only model consciousness in the text as a whole; and if *Castle Rackrent* is to have a hero, the kind of person necessary to reform and renew the degenerate Irish gentry and their equally and mutually degenerate dependents, while controlling the rapacity of the professional middle classes, then this person can only be the 'editor'. Moreover, the 'editor' dominates the text as a whole while operating from its margins (i.e., 'preface', footnotes, and 'glossary'), and the mere narrative is continually interrupted, controlled, or supervised by the notes, which represent a literate and learned consciousness very different from that of the 'illiterate' narrator.[7] In *Castle Rackrent* textual structure is meaning.

While the Edgeworths were enjoying the unexpected success of *Castle Rackrent*, Maria Edgeworth was in fact preparing a much more conventional novel for the press, one in the tradition of Fanny Burney and concerned not with a geographically and politically marginal part of Britain and British society, but with the centre: English high society in its metropolitan setting. *Belinda* (1801) and its successors *Patronage* (1814) and *Helen: A Tale* (1834) were regarded by Edgeworth as her major works, while her enormously popular tales for children and young people, her 'Irish tales', and moral tales and tales of fashionable life were treated by her as important but minor genres. This may seem curious in the light of her disavowal on moral grounds of the genre of the 'modern novel' and preference for the 'moral tale', in the 'Advertisement' to *Belinda*:

> The following work is offered to the public as a Moral Tale – the author not wishing to acknowledge a Novel. Were all novels like those of madame de Crousaz, Mrs. Inchbald, miss Burney, or Dr. Moore, she would adopt the name of novel with delight: But so much folly, errour, and vice are disseminated in books classed under this denomination, that it is hoped the wish to assume another title will be attributed to feelings that are laudable. . . .

But like most of her contemporary women novelists, including Jane Austen, Edgeworth regarded the novel of manners, sentiment, and emulation as developed by Fanny Burney as the most important and challenging literary form available to her – 'literary' form, because women writers were only accepted as professional writers in minor forms of practical and didactic writing, such as books both fictional and non-fictional for children, as genteel amateurs in minor forms of the *belles lettres*, and as authors of the 'trash of the circulating library', such as Minerva Press novels.

*Belinda*, like *Patronage* and *Helen*, is indeed a 'modern novel' and not a tale, in spite of what subtitles and prefaces may say. With its successors, *Belinda* represents a slight advance on Fanny Burney's third-person novels, in its lighter, more flexible, less didactic narrative tone, its finer touches of comedy, and its sense of the essential artifice of the novel form itself – in these respects Edgeworth's novels of manners achieve a level of artistry not much below Austen's. In variety of characters, distribution of characteristic speech, handling of dialogue, and range of topical matter Edgeworth is at least the equal of Burney. In the development of the novel of manners, sentiment, and emulation, then, Edgeworth is midway between Burney and Austen; but Edgeworth was also an important model for Walter Scott, and while it is true that her 'Irish tales' were most in Scott's eye when he conceived his 'Scotch novels', he recognized the achievement of her triple-deckers, too. For the relation of self and society was Edgeworth's main matter in all her fiction, and, like Scott and Austen, she was more suspicious of subjectivity than Burney and other late eighteenth-century novelists had been.

Furthermore, unlike other women novelists of the 1800s and 1810s, such as Amelia Opie and Mary Brunton, who shared her suspicion of Sensibility and individualism as causes of social disruption on the domestic and national levels, Edgeworth did not indulge in prolonged treatment, description, and representation of what her novels claimed to discredit. In her 'modern novels' Edgeworth dramatizes the triumph of reason and self-discipline over both social folly and individual self-excess. Edgeworth was, after all, heir to the powerful liberal and rationalist thought of the eighteenth-century English provincial and Nonconformist Enlightenments.

*Belinda*, like *Camilla* and *Emma*, is a novel named for its heroine; but Belinda is not the central 'problem' in Edgeworth's novel. Rather, the other female characters are the problems, for Belinda is already a paragon when the novel opens. She is an ideal representation of the late eighteenth-century Enlightenment in female form. She is a rational social critic and reformer operating on the personal and domestic planes rather than on the public and professional planes. She chastens the folly of other women and restores them to domestic peace and local social usefulness, rather than struggling much with her own rebellious feelings or social aspirations. This, of course, is what sets Belinda apart from at least half of Austen's heroines, and perhaps all of them in a way. Belinda is almost a *deus ex machina*, repairing and reconciling from a height of reason and inward perfection that is preternatural. This precocious wisdom and goodness in the Edgeworth heroine is what Austen objected to and avoided, thus moving the novel of self and society from Edgeworth's achievement in treating the woman's mind to the greater achievements of Elizabeth Gaskell, Charlotte Brontë, George Eliot, and Virginia Woolf. Edgeworth's strength as a novelist in the Burney tradition is in her psychological realism, even when dealing with a figure of female perfection such as Belinda, even when eschewing Radcliffean depiction of inward sentimental struggle and turmoil in her heroine.

In *Belinda* Edgeworth also voices many of the points made – more sharply and polemically, it is true – by Wollstonecraft in *A Vindication of the Rights of Woman* and *The Wrongs of Woman* (Wollstonecraft and Edgeworth shared the same publisher, Joseph Johnson): women must be well educated and rational if they are to resist the influence of aristocratic court culture which, in its culture of gallantry, seems to offer them a superior social position, but which in fact would turn them into mere coquettes and the playthings of men who still retain all the power. Furthermore, women must have independence of judgment, moral and intellectual if not physical and professional equality with men, if they are to conduct the rational, intimate, 'egalitarian' domestic life that is supposed to be the foundation of the social order, as reconstructed in the image of the professional middle classes. Finally, Edgeworth shows a sense of the limitations of the usual 'modern novel' and the high demands of the novel as art that is equal to Austen's. This formal self-consciousness marks not so much an uneasiness about fictionality in a daughter of the English provincial Enlightenment, but rather a well-read, well-educated imaginative artist's sense of the particular status and limits of the novel as moral discourse operating by techniques of the representation of 'reality'. In short, *Belinda* is a very well made novel indeed, in spite of its heroine, but that was just the sort of character problem Jane Austen would take on, and solve, in *Mansfield Park*.

In a sense Edgeworth combined the achievement of *Castle Rackrent* and *Belinda* in her next major project of fiction for adults, *Tales of Fashionable Life*, published in two sets in 1809 and 1812. Here she continues to argue for the renewal of the gentry, by infusion of professional middle-class values and practices, in a variety of tales, some dealing with the social setting of *Belinda*, others returning to the matter of Ireland, and the latter had the greatest influence and popularity. The renewal of the gentry, inwardly and socially, by internalization of professional values and practices is argued most thoroughly in 'The Absentee', published in the second set of *Tales of Fashionable Life*. After *Castle Rackrent*, this is Edgeworth's best known tale, and in it she is more ambitious, though less original, than she had been in the first of her Irish tales. Moreover, 'The Absentee' was written in 1811–12, after the publication of her and her father's *Essays on Professional Education* (1809), in which he argues that the proper landed gentleman is a professional, rather than the professional man being an inferior version of the gentleman. At around the same time, Maria was working on a conventional triple-decker novel with the significant title *Patronage* (1814), dealing with relations of aristocratic court culture, gentry, and professions. It seems likely, too, that in 'The Absentee's' depiction of 'fashionable life' Edgeworth was responding to the commercial success of novels such as Thomas Surr's *A Winter in London; or, Sketches of Fashion* (1806; eight editions in that year alone), which criticize the fashion-system of London upper-class social life, and represent, by contrast, the virtuous, genteel, and professional type of hero found in many earlier novels, including the 'philosophical romances' of John Moore and Anti-Jacobin novels such as Isaac D'Israeli's *Vaurien*.

Certainly 'The Absentee' is resolutely didactic and critical, for, even more than *Rackrent* or 'Ennui', it tries to tie broad issues of moral corruption and social conflict to the faults of aristocratic court culture, particularly conspicuous consumption and the code of gallantry and intrigue, and it adds the further complication of 'the Irish problem'. The solution to all of these issues is seen to be professionalization of the gentry and the creation of a 'British' rather than merely English, Irish, or Scottish ruling class. By the time she began 'The Absentee', Edgeworth could also profit from the treatment of 'the Irish problem' by Lady Morgan, whose *Wild Irish Girl* was published in 1806, and from Elizabeth Hamilton's treatment of the common people of Scotland in *The Cottagers of Glenburnie* (1808), one of Edgeworth's favourite books.[8]

The plot of 'The Absentee' argues for the renewal of gentry hegemony by a particular kind of 'civil courage' in resisting the tyranny of fashion and decadent court culture, a kind of courage no less important in the modern age than the martial courage required by the gentry's medieval ancestors in resisting the tyranny of monarchy or the oppression of barons. But 'The Absentee' also deploys a great deal of social description, of fashionable society in London and of lower-class, middle-class, and upper-class society in Ireland. Here Edgeworth employs traditional kinds of social satire, using socially and morally representative characters. As in Lady Morgan's *The Wild Irish Girl* (1806) and Jane Porter's *The Scottish Chiefs* (1810), landscape does play an important part, if not in constructing the hero's self as a nationalist, then in reinforcing his interest in and dedication to Ireland, that is, an Ireland led by a nationally conscious, self-disciplined, resident Anglo-Irish gentry. Topographical and sociological description play a major role in the central section of 'The Absentee', Colambre's romance journey of self-discovery and social enlightenment through Ireland, from which he returns dedicated to a professional kind of paternalistic social leadership and middle-class kind of domestic harmony.

'The Absentee' argues what many 'modern novels' had argued for the past few decades, and would continue to argue throughout the Romantic period, and it uses many devices of plot and character already developed in the late eighteenth century, but it uses those devices with particular skill and freshness. More important, its treatment of the Irish theme was widely thought to have added a new kind of social realism to prose fiction. It did this primarily by its deployment of language, sharply discriminated characteristic speech applied to a very broad range of socially representative characters, a technique Edgeworth adapted from Burney. But Edgeworth goes beyond Burney in deploying language as a model of the *national* social reconciliation, professionalization, and cultivation for which the novel argues in its plot and character relations. Whereas in *Castle Rackrent* the first-person narrator and a substandard form of English are at the centre of the fictional structure, though framed and undermined by an authoritative 'voice' working in standard English, in 'The Absentee' the case is reversed. An omniscient and authoritative third-person narrator, delivering character portraits, descriptions, and social-historical explanations in standard written English, presides over an astonishing range of sociolects and dialects. Every socially representative character has characteristic speech, usually a jargon (over a score of these are presented) that signifies the character's narrowness of interest and outlook.

The Irish characters participate in their own community through dialect, though this community and its speech are not as severely criticized or mocked as they are in *Castle Rackrent*, probably because the authoritative narrative structure in 'The Absentee' lessens the danger of the reader sympathizing too much with the culture and values of the lower-class Irish. Moreover, the Irish accent links the Irish gentry with their dependents. Significantly, Lady Clonbrony has to try to lose her Irish brogue in order to be accepted by 'the World', or fashionable London society. She only makes herself more ridiculous, of course, advertising the intensity of her desire in emulation by her attempts to speak upper-class English – itself depicted as a narrow and substandard form of English. Thus language is tied in to the theme of emulation. The virtuous and fully human characters 'speak' standard written English, the same dialect the narrator uses, and they speak only when they have something worth saying, for Edgeworth, like Fanny Burney and Jane Austen, employs a scale of volubility in her fiction as an index to the moral weight of certain characters.

Furthermore, the standard written English, transcending all merely personal or local variants of English, serves as a sign of possession of that transcendental 'British' consciousness that is to be the unifying culture of the nation's leaders. Not surprisingly, then, in the face of this symbolic role for standard written English, familiarity with and proper discrimination in book culture are important indexes of a character's authoritativeness and worth, as they are in Austen's novels (although Edgeworth does indulge herself in a few cuts at mere novel reading). Finally, there is the persistent tendency of the narrator and the main virtuous characters to deliver themselves of crisp apothegms or maxims, a form of discourse strongly associated with both philosophical and moral, familiar and cultivated writing, and appealing to experience rather than to ratiocination for assent (and also associated with the education of women).[9] The maxim is to be discriminated from the proverb, or 'folksay' as folklorists call it, for the latter is the token of membership in a popular and oral culture whereas the maxim is the token of participation in the culture of writing. In short, the deployment of and relationship between varieties of English in 'The Absentee' display 'The Absentee's' right to participate in the culture it advocates as the proper culture of the social leaders Britain must have in order to move beyond the old – or the new – social particularities, prejudices, and conflicts.

## 'Tales of the Heart' and 'Tales of Real Life'

One prominent aspect of Romantic fiction was relatively neglected by Maria Edgeworth, however – inward subjectivity. Even more than Burney, Edgeworth sees the inward self as moral and intellectual rather than emotional. That dimension of selfhood was the special province of Amelia Opie in the 1800s and 1810s. During those years, in fact, Opie was generally considered second only to Edgeworth among new fiction writers who wrote something more than 'the trash of the circulating libraries'. Her reputation waned quickly as Jane Austen's

grew; yet her tales contain brilliant touches of dialogue, characterization, and incident, equal at times to Austen and very similar in
character. On the other hand, some of her tales contain touches of
realism very similar to those of her fellow East Anglian, the Rev.
George Crabbe. For the most part she dealt with emotion rather than
the fine feelings of the literature of Sensibility or the strong passions
of 'Gothic romance' or the novel of passion. At her best, she has a
subtle grasp of psychological realism which is probably rooted in her
Dissenting cultural background and its practices of self-examination
and spiritual autobiography and which is almost equal to the best in
Romantic writing. Unfortunately, these touches are buried in her
collections of tales – *Simple Tales* (1806), *Tales of Real Life* (1813), *New
Tales* (1818), and *Tales of the Heart* (1820) – or in places in her novels
– *Adeline Mowbray* (1804), her commentary on the domestic politics
of English Jacobinism, *Temper; or, Domestic Scenes: A Tale* (1812),
*Valentine's Eve* (1816), and *Madeline: A Tale* (1822).

For, like many fiction writers of the Romantic period, from Charles
Lamb to Mary Mitford, Opie preferred the desultory form of the 'tale'
– as it was understood in that period – to the formalities and unfor-
tunate associations of the novel. In order to foreground displays of
feeling, these 'tales of the heart' abandon the plausibility of plot and
consistency of characterization found in the Burney novel, the individualized or even eccentric narrator found in the *conte* or the self-
consciously literary tale, and the topographical and social description
found in the 'national tale'. Opie's tales usually consist of a string of
incidents or situations in which a character experiences intense
emotion, usually, though not always, in the presence of others, for
Opie is not very interested in the solitary subjectivity dwelt on by
Radcliffe, Godwin, and others. In order to arrage her situation, Opie
goes through some perfunctory manipulations of plot, including
extraordinary coincidences, in order to display the characters' emotions
through description and dialogue.

These descriptions and dialogues are Opie's *forte* as a fiction writer.
The incidents are usually domestic, and she avoids the public, the
picturesque, the Gothic, and the comic incident, though she
occasionally devotes a whole tale to one of these modes. Opie's
interest, especially in *Adeline Mowbray, Temper*, and *Valentine's Eve*, is
in domestic heroism, the moral drama of the home, of conjugal and
family life, and she often sets these scenes and motifs against the arti-
ficialities and intrigues, the hypocrisy, self-interest, and vice of the
public and social world, the world of manners. In short, she locates
moral drama in the home, drama of manners in 'the World'. Opie uses
fiction to depict the social and psychological drama of the home, a
topic of increasing interest to the professional and middle-class people

– and especially women – who formed the majority of the novel-reading classes. This fact probably explains her popularity and her influence, though later achievements of Elizabeth Gaskell, Charles Dickens, the Brontë sisters, and George Eliot in this area eclipsed what she had done in preparing the ground for their work.

Opie also wrote about and for women, with an ambivalence of theme and form that must have reflected the ambivalence of women of her class toward their identity and role in professional middle-class society and values. The human problems in Opie's tales usually revolve around the moral identity of a young woman who leaves, is deprived of, or is banished from the protection of home and parents because of fate, her own moral inadequacies, inexperience, or blindness (as in *The Father and Daughter*), or because of the moral errors and inadequacies of home (as in *Adeline Mowbray*). In 'the World', she is preyed upon by the envious, the unscrupulous, and the self-interested, who wish to ruin her for their own motives. The ruin usually involves seduction and is to be achieved by drawing the young woman into financial or moral debts, or both, or by creating the false appearance that she is ruined already (as in *Temper* and *Valentine's Eve*). In other words, as in seventeenth-century courtly sentimental 'novels' (which Opie, like Radcliffe, probably read and borrowed from), the 'intrigue' creates a disparity between the heroine's 'true', inner character and the outward appearance, her social character or reputation. This disparity generates a variety of feelings, mostly shame, guilt, and remorse, which overpay the moral debt – at least, the reader, privileged with 'inside' knowledge of the heroine's moral character, can see that her suffering and her punishment are overpayment.

Thus the narrative structure of Opie's tales usually requires an especially intimate relationship between reader and heroine, a fact which must also help to account for the tales' popularity. For whether or not the heroine has transgressed a moral or social code, her suffering and humiliation seem incommensurate with her real or supposed crime, and she remains to be bathed in the reader's sympathy alone. The centre of Opie's tales is this 'passion', in the Christian sense: 'the sufferings of a martyr'.[10] This is not the passion felt by the heroines of Lady Caroline Lamb and the 'silver-fork' novelists of the 1810s and 1820s; it is more acceptable to conservative religious and social morality; it is self-condemning rather than self-aggrandizing, passive rather than active, domestic rather than amorous and erotic in its nature. Yet in its own way it is as much a celebration of the 'female character' as the later novels of amorous passion (see Ch. 6, below), and, to many of their female readers, Opie's tales must have reflected the ambiguities and contradictions of the female condition in social classes that were increasing rapidly in numbers, strength, self-

consciousness and power and that were leading in the professionalization of society, professionalization from which women were
excluded by their supposedly domestic, private, and subjective
'natures'.[11]

The structure of feeling in Opie's tales – overpayment of suffering
for real or imagined transgressions – seems to reflect the apparently
intimate and 'egalitarian' but in fact highly stressful family structure
that was being constructed everywhere in middle-class homes of
Britain and western Europe, and Opie's representation of it in fiction
must have spoken to the experience of many of her women readers.
But Opie was also ambivalent toward her own work as a literary artist,
as seen in the moments of self-conscious playfulness with the very
conventions she is working for emotional effects, her deliberate disregard of formal plausibility and symmetry, and her overwriting in
several places. These aspects of her literary work reveal her ambivalence about her own social identity as a woman yet a very public sort
of woman: an author.

## 'Village Anecdotes'

This ambivalence was not, however, shared by other women novelists
of the first decade and a half of the new century. For, as we shall see
in the next two sections of this chapter, some women writers took
eagerly and enthusiastically to the task of delineating new myths of
social structure and national identity for the novel-reading classes of
Britain; these myths became central to nineteenth-century Britain, in
effect depicting, on the local and national levels, the embourgeoisement
of British society.

A large part of the appeal of some of Maria Edgeworth's and
Amelia Opie's tales was their naturalistic depiction of country and
village life. As we have seen already, the *topos* of rural simplicity was
an important element in Sentimental fiction, and it was available
during and after the 1790s as a refuge from the political struggles of
that decade, and as a source for a new model of the national
community, a community thoroughly penetrated by professional and
middle-class values. But country and village had for centuries been the
domain of a coalition of gentry and common people, where the middle
classes hardly figured at all. If British society were to be remade in the
image of the professional and middle classes, the country and village
had to be so remade.

One of the first novelists to attempt to do so systematically was Elizabeth Le Noir. She was the daughter of the country clergyman and Sentimental poet Christopher Smart. Her two novels, *Village Anecdotes* (1804) and *Clara de Montfier* (1808), take up themes of rural simplicity and domestic affections developed in Sentimental fiction by Mackenzie and Goldsmith in the 1760s and 1770s and turned against English Jacobinism and Romantic individualism by Jane West and others in the 1790s. Her work also had some connection with Fanny Burney, for the second edition of *Village Anecdotes* was dedicated to Burney's father and acknowledged his support of Le Noir's early work (he was probably responsible for the novel's first publication). Le Noir's novels are not like Burney's, however; in fact, Burney's last novel, *The Wanderer* (1814), shows signs of indebtedness to the kind of middle- and lower-class domestic realism of rural life developed by Le Noir and West in the few years after *Camilla* was published. Jane Austen, too, may have learned from West and Le Noir: like Austen, Le Noir was from Hampshire, and there are interesting echoes of *Village Anecdotes* – names, character types, and situations – scattered about in Austen's novels.

Nevertheless, the connection between these novelists was also part of a general movement in fiction after 1800 to develop and explore the theme of rural domesticity as the basis for an important ideological consensus among professional and middle-class people. This theme was, in short, made an important aspect of self-definition for the novel-reading classes after the crisis of the 1790s, and was the basis of the 'national tale' for England, defining the country as it was to be defined for the rest of the century – rural, not urban; agrarian, not industrial; but a rural England no longer under the hegemony of the gentry.[12] Unlike Burney and Austen, but like Hannah More and Mary Mitford, Le Noir depicts a rural England from which the gentry are virtually excluded, and in which social leadership is assumed by the moral and self-disciplined middle classes.

*Village Anecdotes; or, The Journal of a Year, From Sophia to Edward: With Original Poems* resembles the 'national tale' in being largely descriptive, though it does not describe a particular ethnic culture but rather the social types of rural England, excluding the gentry. As it is a first-person narrative – Sophia Willars writes her journal to her husband who is at sea with the navy – it is also personal and expressive. To some extent, it is a rhapsodic narrative, since its form is anecdotal, descriptive, and personal; at times it is lyrical, reflective, and moralizing: and it includes letters, poems, and inset narratives. There are many characters, and many different 'voices' in this novel, social stereotypes with their sociolects and idiolects, all 'centred' by the 'voice' and the consciousness of its narrator, whose name means 'wisdom'. Sophia is not, however, like the traditional village 'wise woman', mistress of folklore, folk medicine, occult knowledge, and prophetic insight. Rather, she is a literary, rational, moralistic social leader, the moderator and mediatrix of the petty provincialisms·of rural society. Her leadership ranges through politics, religion, fashion, moral standards and ethical conduct, manners, literature, domestic economy, sentiment, gender roles, and of course language itself. Her style is familiar and familial, mildly moralizing, morally literary, chastely sentimental, and good standard written English; it represents fully her moral and social authority, her centrality in this social world full of different standards and values.

What she describes is a rural England which is the 'real' and authentic England, but in need of moral, social and cultural reform. This England is central in two senses. First, it is a microcosm of national issues and conflicts. Jacobinism appears in the village and is dismissed by Sophia, definitively refuted in a monologue that repeats the arguments of Hannah More's first Anti-Jacobin tract, *Village Politics* (1792). Class conflict and social emulation appear as snobbery and intolerance on one hand and extravagance and pursuit of fashion on the other. Sophia attacks both, and argues instead for self-discipline, social and religious tolerance, professional competence, and intimate, 'egalitarian' domesticity. These are, of course, the values she and her Edward represent in their own relationship and conduct. The popular culture of chance and superstition and popular amorous culture are seen to infect some of the middle classes, and Sophia exposes those fallacies, too. Harsh treatment of animals, another point of middle-class attack on popular culture, is dealt with several times. A striking point is the condemnation of novel reading, a commonplace in novels and magazines of this period. Finally, there is the novel's and Sophia's treatment of language. Sophia writes the entire narrative, of course, in standard written English, thus exhibiting her command of that central professional middle-class discourse. She and the other virtuous characters also 'speak' in standard written English, in contrast to the relatively deformed sociolects and idiolects employed by the characters labouring under some form of false consciousness.

While the novel insists on the centrality of rural life and domesticity, these are to be reconstructed in terms of a national moral-intellectual culture, a culture of rationalism and writing that is in direct contradiction both to the culture of the courtly, fashionable, extravagant, and socially irresponsible gentry (and their emulators in other classes) and to the superstitious, semi-literate, improvident lower classes. The professional middle classes are seen to replace the falsely cosmopolitan gentry and the merely local lower orders, the predominant elements in eighteenth-century agrarian society. The virtuous urban middle classes (and professionalized gentry) re-situate themselves in the

English countryside, henceforth the site and source of English national consciousness and culture, resisting both the fashionable towns dominated by the gentry and the industrial towns dominated by the working classes and their middle-class employers. *Village Anecdotes* represents an important revision of eighteenth-century genteel Horatianism into the increasingly powerful myth that the 'real' England, the authentic England, is a rural England reformed by professional middle-class culture and values. In her second novel, *Clara de Montfier*, Le Noir made the political implications of her treatment of rural life even more explicit, by placing that life in the context of the French Revolution, seen as a conflict between the decadent aristocracy and the viciously self-interested among the lower orders.

*Village Anecdotes* was not, however, nearly as successful and as widely read as Elizabeth Hamilton's fiction with the same purpose, *The Cottagers of Glenburnie; A Tale for the Farmer's Ingle-nook* (1808). Here the countryside is Scottish, but the fictional argument is the same as in *Village Anecdotes*, only clearer, starker, more militant. Because of this clarity and aggression, *The Cottagers* became a best-seller, and was reprinted many times in the next few decades. In the 1790s Hamilton was a major Anti-Jacobin novelist, with *Letters of a Hindoo Rajah* (1796) and *Memoirs of Modern Philosophers* (1800). Then she met Maria Edgeworth, and in *The Cottagers of Glenburnie* she joined *Castle Rackrent*'s depiction and criticism of the culture of the rural common people with Hannah More's even more 'reformist' approach to the same topic in her Cheap Repository tracts. *The Cottagers* was one of Edgeworth's favourite works, and probably influenced her own depiction of rural life in her Irish tales. Because of its 'realism' *The Cottagers* was read by many people who would never touch a novel. Like *Village Anecdotes* it presents a fantasy of the reformation of rural life and the common people by middle-class values and practices. *The Cottagers* also clearly advertises the idea of literature being used in the service of *national* 'improvement'.

The 'story' is told by Mrs Mason (an appropriate name for a social engineer), who has been educated by hardship. After a life of service to the upper-class Longlands family and the family of their steward, Mr Stewart, she plans to retire to live with some relatives in Glenburnie. Like Sophia in Le Noir's novel, Mrs Mason is sad witness of the follies of emulation in the Stewart family and of the courtly decadence and extravagance of the Longlands family, and her work in reforming the upper classes and their professional middle-class dependents forms an important sub-plot in *The Cottagers*. The real task Mrs Mason faces, however, as the title of this 'Tale for the Farmer's Inglenook' suggests, is to reform not just the upper and middle classes but the rural farmers and their dependents as well. This she succeeds in doing to a great extent. In this part of the tale, which is largely descriptive, Mrs Mason has the same role as Sophia in *Village Anecdotes* – a stable, rational, methodical, self-disciplined, norm-setting centre for the faulty human world she describes. Her programme of reform in Glenburnie is the same as that of Hannah More's middle-class Evangelical protagonists in the Cheap Repository tales (Hamilton's acknowledged models for *The Cottagers*), and her attitude to popular culture is the same as that of the 'Editor' of *Castle Rackrent*.

She attacks the popular culture of *carpe diem*, improvidence, and reliance on luck instead of self-help and self-improvement to get on in life. She advocates continual self-discipline, through resistance to even the smallest 'sin' as leading inevitably to worse crimes. She demonstrates efficient and economical household management, neatness, and cleanliness. This habitual self-discipline will replace the sloppy and wasteful 'customs' of rural life, and at the same time lead to inward transformation of the reforming individual. Everywhere Mrs Mason uses reason and personal example to counter the dead hand of 'custom', the basis of traditional culture. Significantly, perhaps, Hamilton herself had converted from Presbyterianism to Anglicanism and its doctrine of faith *and* works as the means to holy living and the life hereafter. Reason and example, reason and conduct conformable to its dictates are the secular correlatives to this doctrine in *The Cottagers*, as they are in the novels of the Anglican Jane Austen and the Episcopalian-inclined Walter Scott. Indeed, the centrepiece of *The Cottagers* is Mrs Mason's discourse on faith and works, which is delivered in the very middle of the tale. Finally, reform of the popular culture of Glenburnie is to be institutionalized through the founding of a school, based on the Lancaster monitorial method, by which the newly literate teach the as-yet illiterate. The previous school-master, a merely academic pedant, is replaced, and the structure of classes in the new school reflects the social divisions of rural society.

Thus the social structure itself remains, but social transformation is achieved from within through education uprooting oral culture and its ways of thought. Education for literacy, a diminished version of the culture of writing of the professional middle classes, is made a method of social control and of reproduction of the new individual and social type, at the lowest cost. Social emulation, previously directed to false, genteel types of conduct, will now be directed at 'true' models and will spread from Mrs Mason and those she has converted, as well as from the school, to effect a complete transformation of Glenburnie.

The depiction of Glenburnie is not just an exercise in 'realism'; it is also to be read as a figure, representing Scotland, Britain, and the world, for *The Cottagers* had its versions in several countries and continents. Furthermore, this local transformation of everyday life has been effected, appropriately, by a woman, for the conventional role of women was domestic, local, quotidian. They were excluded from public, political, and national life. But as Hannah More had demonstrated in the 1790s – and Mrs Mason is modelled on More – women working at the local level and within their 'traditional' spheres of activity could perhaps effect a social transformation from the grass roots, from the ground up, could perhaps effect what men, working through politics at the local or national level, could not. *The Cottagers* is in a sense a reply to Amelia Opie's depiction of the wasteful subjectivity left to women by patriarchy, for Mrs Mason brings about nothing less than the 'modernization' and professionalization of a traditional society, at all levels. *The Cottagers* is not overtly feminist, even though Mrs Mason's work is conformable to the kinds of new social roles and leadership, developed from women's traditional areas of expertise, advocated by Mary Wollstonecraft and practised by Hannah More.

Nevertheless, there is an important if hidden contradiction in *The Cottagers*. To make her work more effective rhetorically, Hamilton devotes a degree of 'realism' to her portrayal of rural Scotland, and this includes use of 'dialect' for her rural types. Indeed, this kind of domestic realism must have constituted a large part of the appeal of *The Cottagers* to readers of the day, for several Scottish proverbial expressions in the book passed into contemporary usage, especially the unredeemed characters' repeated dismissal of Mrs Mason's proposed 'improvements' with the excuse that they could not 'be fash'd [i.e., troubled] wi' it'. Another proverbial expression offered by the unredeemed in defense of custom is the phrase, 'Ilka place has just its ain gait' – every place has its own way of doing things. Mrs Mason's rightness of thought in the face of this kind of oral obtuseness is clearly signalled by her use of a fully literate standard written English, in both her narrative and her 'speech' to the cottagers. Scots, it appears, is to be equated with lower-class rank and the ignorance and stubbornness of oral culture, at least in the early part of the tale; wisdom is expressed in standard written English.

The new school of Glenburnie, with its programme of reading aloud from books and memorization of passages of writing, is supposed to make the local folk bilingual – Scots and English – but English or standard written English remains the central, the dominant 'tongue'. Here was a problem for writers of 'national tales' of any kind, for dialect is to be associated with national consciousness, too – indeed, a 'national language' is indispensable to the new kind of nationalism. This problem was not confronted until after 1830, though various compromises were struck by Scott in his novels in the 1810s and 1820s, and James Hogg laid bare the contradiction for all to see in his Scottish novel, *The Confessions of a Justified Sinner* (1824). Certainly the available evidence suggests that many readers of the time relished the 'realistic' portrayal of old-fashioned Scottish folk-ways and repeated the Scottish expressions, and perhaps, too, soon forgot Hamilton's programme for modernization of the common people.

## 'National Tales' and 'Historical Romances'

While 'village anecdotes' were representing what authentic social life should be, other kinds of fiction were developed to define the broader scale of national social identity, as it was supposed to have originated in some major crisis of the past. These kinds of fiction were known as 'national tales' and 'historical romances', though they did not necessarily deal with parts of the United Kingdom (known as Great Britain before the Act of Union with Ireland in 1800). Significantly, however, the most successful of these novels dealt with 'marginal' domains in the United Kingdom, especially Ireland (following the example of Maria Edgeworth), and Scotland. It was as though England as the political and social centre and norm did not need to be defined as socially authentic and historically original in the way that the other regions, or 'provinces' of the United Kingdom did. Certainly there was very little in the way of a regionalized market for fiction dealing only with a particular locale or district. Book culture and novel culture, insofar as they were aspects of professional middle-class culture, were much the same wherever found in Britain and Ireland. Perhaps it was the case here that the margin defined the centre, and furthermore that the centre was already being defined satisfactorily in 'tales of fashionable life' set in England's capital and 'village anecdotes' set in England's countryside. Later novels of rural description such as Mary Mitford's *Our Village* (1824–32) and novels of exotic places such as Morier's *Hajji Baba* (1824) would define more precisely the supposed essence of things English.

Sydney Owenson, Lady Morgan, was the best known of the authors of 'national tales', apart from Edgeworth, and like Edgeworth she, too, took up the 'matter of Ireland'. Morgan develops the novel of description and the footnote-novel, supporting the social, historical, topographical, and linguistic information in her novels with substantial footnotes from a variety of documentary sources, as well as from personal observation. She combines all this 'useful' information with familiar plots of love and elements borrowed from European Sentimental fiction such as Rousseau's *La Nouvelle Héloïse*, Goethe's *The Sorrows of Werther*, and Mme de Staël's *Corinne*. *The Wild Irish Girl: A National Tale* (1806) was her most influential novel in its time. So much was it identified with her own literary mode that she herself was referred to as 'the wild Irish girl' and was called by her heroine's name, Glorvina, as Matthew Lewis was always 'Monk' Lewis. She even had to carry her Irish harp about with her to receptions and routs, and perform Irish folksongs for fashionable and aristocratic audiences, after the style of the heroine of *The Wild Irish Girl*. This literary lionizing reveals how ready social leaders were to receive the fictions of national culture, national origins, and national harmony based on such common (if invented) 'traditions'.[13] Certainly *The Wild Irish Girl* embodies a particularly simple and forceful concept of national culture as the basis for social reconciliation and progress, through a revival of the past. This embodiment of a national culture (the Wild Irish Girl) is wedded (literally and symbolically) to an embodiment of English aristocracy (the decadent son of an absentee owner of Irish estates) in such a way as to represent a solution to social divisions within England itself, and not just divisions between Ireland and the rest of the United Kingdom.

Several themes of social reform and reconciliation, short of revolution, could be read into this fable: the inward, moral reform of decadent aristocracy by the pure springs of a national culture, with a return to social responsibility and benevolent, paternalist social leadership; the restoration of Ireland and its people to human dignity (national liberation being the order of the day on the Continent); a renewed harmony of common people and their 'natural' leaders; and, of course, resolution of the 'Irish question'. Setting and landscape description are related to this theme of authenticity. They are used not just to display the rich subjectivity of the novel's first-person narrator, but to bear a major burden of the novel's nationalist theme. Since, however, most of the land is owned by foreigners, absentees who do not know and cannot be influenced and re-formed by their land, the 'natural' relationship between the Irish and their country is distorted, and the land itself is as exploited and denatured as its people. The organic wholeness of landscape, people, and culture is strongly asserted, implying that national culture is unique yet natural, the product of the interaction of local particulars and human universals. National culture, which unites all individuals and ranks in a society, is social and historical, yet universal and beyond social relativities.

Response to the Irish landscape by the hero-narrator is made more forceful and immediate through the novel's epistolary narrative mode. Lyrical flights, emotional apostrophes, and outbursts of passion are frequent in this novel, usually addressed to landscape, examples of Irish virtues, and Glorvina – inspiring objects, apparently, in the reeducation of the narrator-hero, H.M., which it is one purpose of the novel to track for us. Another effect is created by the fact that the narrator's letters are addressed to one J.D. Esq., M.P., a 'man of the world', companion in H.M.'s former career of fashionable dissipation, and, significantly, a Member of Parliament. J.D. Esq., M.P., is the representative of England's (and Britain's) decadent and genteel ruling class. J.D. never does reply to H.M.'s missives; but it is significant, too, that the series of correspondence in the novel concludes not with a letter from H.M. but with the combined blessing on and lecture to H.M. and Glorvina from the wise, virtuous, English aristocrat, the Earl of M——, H.M.'s father (and now Glorvina's father, too), outlining the proper conduct for Anglo-Irish (in a new sense) landlords toward their 'people'.

Thus the structural relationship of speech to writing in the novel is the reverse of the thematic relationship. Whereas H.M. is reformed by his contact with the oral and musical culture of Ireland, his writing surrounds that culture, as quoted by him in the text. What corresponds to – speaks to – the oral authenticity of Irish culture is the lyrical, expressive element in H.M.'s epistolary style. This is the element in his letters that comes from what is authentic and natural in him – his passions, his inner self, rather than his merely social, fashionable self. The correspondence of H.M.'s 'true' self and authentic Irish oral culture is validated by the footnotes, which serve the function they do in non-fiction discourse (rather than the satirical and critical function they serve in *Castle Rackrent*) and which are written in the formal, learned style appropriate to such matter. Lyricism in the text and learnedness in the notes collaborate to assure the reader of the novel's truthfulness. The structure of language in *The Wild Irish Girl* represents the conjunction of the Romantic ideology of selfhood and the ideology of Romantic nationalism. This was a significant formal achievement, even though Lady Morgan lacked the ability to see it through to the construction of the social-historical novel as we know it. That task would fall to Walter Scott, who had already begun a draft of a novel that would be published in 1814 as *Waverley*.

Besides Lady Morgan, the chief writers of 'national tales' between *Castle Rackrent* and *Waverley* were Jane and Anna Porter. They added the quest for the historical origins of national culture to the developing 'national tale', giving the novel some of the authority already enjoyed by historiography, using history as more than the scenic backdrop provided by Radcliffe and other Gothic novelists, and tracing the values of the novel-reading classes of the present back, apparently, to their 'origins' in the past. In 'historical romances' such as *Thaddeus of Warsaw* (Jane Porter, 1803), *The Hungarian Brothers* (Anna, 1807), *Don*

*Sebastian* (Anna, 1809), and *The Scottish Chiefs* (Jane, 1810), the Porter sisters gave medieval and renaissance history the character of idealized modern-day bourgeois life, thereby expropriating the 'national' past for the professional middle classes' vision of present and future. Jane Porter also took the decisive step of adding the 'matter of Scotland' to the 'matter of Ireland' in the developing fiction of nationalism in Britain. In a certain sense, then, all an enterprising writer had to do after 1810 was to combine elements of Edgeworth's *Castle Rackrent*, Hamilton's *The Cottagers*, Morgan's *Wild Irish Girl*, and Jane Porter's *The Scottish Chiefs* and the social-historical novel as we know it would be delivered to an awaiting reading public.

*The Scottish Chiefs* presented novel readers with a particularly clear and forceful dramatization of the relation of authentic selfhood, domestic affections patterned on 'egalitarian' intimacy and the nuclear family, and the national community conceived of as ideally homogeneous and harmonious. The novel focuses on the moral nature of a real historical character but one who was also a long-standing hero of chapbook literature, Sir William Wallace. Porter's Wallace, however, is above all a supremely autonomous self, above the merely human passions, such as lust and revenge, greed and pride, that motivate his enemies. Porter depicts Wallace as an independent landed gentleman, aloof from court intrigues, an ideal family man, deeply religious, and, after his wife Marion is brutally murdered by an English nobleman, absolutely devoted to the cause of Scottish independence. Thus a personal cause issues into a national one, and both are linked to transcendental religious values, for God is declared to approve Wallace's struggle for his country's freedom, at the same time that Wallace's inner moral nature, domestic virtues, and loyalty are declared to accord with the divine will. Indeed, on several occasions Wallace is even compared with history's greatest transcendental self, Jesus Christ.

The plot of the novel also follows the trajectory of Christ's mission on earth. On the surface, the plot is simply that of the liberation of Scotland from English rule; but in fact it follows the pattern of an Evangelical moral *and* social crusade. In the first place, Wallace frees Scotland from the consequences of corrupt court politics: the loss of Scottish independence occurred because contending factions of Scottish nobles could not agree on succession to the throne, and gave the matter to adjudication by the English king. Like a true court politician, the English king then gave the crown to the contender who accepted subservience' and vassalage to himself. Thus a nation was enslaved by the self-interest of one man and his followers. Wallace's rebellion reverses this event, and in the process arouses the courtier-like selfishness, envy, and intrigues of some Scottish noblemen, but converts others to his form of authentic selfhood, domestic purity, and selfless personal dedication to the national cause.

Most notable of his converts are young Robert Bruce (son of one of the original two contenders for the Scottish throne), and an English knight, who becomes disgusted with corrupt and decadent English court culture and transfers his allegiance, himself, and his family to Scotland, thus founding the Scottish noble house of Hamilton. In fact, almost all the other characters recognize Wallace's nobility – even his royalty – of soul; but since he lacks royal family connections, Wallace declines to accept the crown. The lesson is clear: inward qualities are far more important than mere social rank or breeding, as Sentimental and Romantic novels had been arguing for several decades. Eventually, of course, Wallace is betrayed by court intriguers, and sent to the English king to be put to death. His spirit, however, lives on in his convert, Bruce, who completes his work of national liberation.

This fable combines a transcendental yet real-life hero with a plot of liberation from combined foreign domination and court politics, and was the basis of all the Porter sisters' novels of the first decade of the nineteenth century. Clearly, it was a timely fable, too, as Napoleon, self-appointed representative of France and the French Revolution, was busy bringing liberation from court tyranny and foreign rule to the oppressed but emergent nations of Europe. But the fable also had its implications for Britain, its culture, and politics. *The Scottish Chiefs* continues the critique of court politics and decadent aristocratic and gentry culture already seen in eighteenth-century fiction, culminating in the English Jacobin novels of the 1790s, and continued in 'tales of fashionable life' after 1800. But *The Scottish Chiefs* also presents a heroic version – a martial and sublime version – of the idealized professional middle-class man. It could be said that Sir William Wallace passed into the figure of the English gentleman–professional as projected in the late 1820s at Rugby School and for decades afterwards in the institutions of elite education and culture.[14] Looked at another way, Wallace is a secular version of the clergyman–hero of tract tales by the Evangelical writers such as Hannah More, and Legh Richmond, and the young heroes of 'tales for youth' by Barbara Hofland and Mary Sherwood – exemplary in personal life, perfect in profession, dedicated to ideals not of this world, converting others to those ideals by example, rising above all merely social distinctions and divisions and conflicts, and – in short – transforming the world around him by personal conviction and ethical action. The difference is that the Porter sisters add the exotic and historical settings formerly the property – in the theatrical sense – of the Gothic novel. The past has heroes like those of the present, but more 'heroic' in a precisely literary sense – that is, they are like heroes of both romance and history (as the history of great men).

Characterization and plot in *The Scottish Chiefs* thus present a fantasy of social reconstruction and reform through idealized and individual middle-class virtues. The fantasy bears a relation to contemporary political realities insofar as it proposes personal self-discipline, religious piety, domestic virtue, and nationalistic self-dedication as solutions to political and social conflicts in the modern world. The historical 'romance' pretends to find these solutions in the past, in historical reality. This use of the past gives secular validation to the solutions; the religious element gives transcendental validation. But insofar as the novel gives heroic literary-historical form to the solutions, it also represents an alternative to social action in the present: sensational and exciting 'romance' (the novel's subtitle) in the past can be an escape from rather than an addressing of present-day social and political realities.

The literary dimension of *The Scottish Chiefs* has a simplicity that must go a long way to explain the novel's great popularity. The elements Porter draws on are four: Ossian, 'factual' history, 'tradition', and the Bible. The connection with Ossian, James Macpherson's forgeries of ancient Gaelic heroic poetry, is advertised in the epigraph on the novel's title page, and there are several references to Ossian's 'works' through the novel. Ossian was, of course, the inspiration for several nationalist literary forgeries throughout Europe, and the inspiration for the German philosopher Herder's seminal essay on nationalism.[15] On the other hand, 'factual' history is also claimed as a major source by Porter in her preface to *The Scottish Chiefs*, where she declares, 'I have not added to the outline [provided by historical fact], excepting, where time having made some erasure, a stroke was necessary to fill the space and unite the whole.' In fact, historical and antiquarian scholarship are not much in evidence in *The Scottish Chiefs*, though there are plenty of footnotes explaining characters and events or asserting the factual truth of a particular matter in the story. More important is the authoritative, historically informed narration, and both these aspects of formal historiography would also be used by Scott. In general, however, the elements of historiography in the Porter sisters' novels are lighter than in Scott's. Jane Porter also claimed to be assisted in her touching-up of historical fact by 'tradition', the orally transmitted or reconstructed folklore and balladry of Sir William Wallace's legend, especially as found in two authors of Wallace narratives, Thomas the Rhymer (who is used later by Scott) and 'Blind Harry'. This conjunction of 'tradition' and historiography would be the basic material for Scott's Waverley novels and was vital to the founding of national literature in the Romantic period. Finally, there are frequent references to and quotations from the Bible – significantly, also an important 'literary' reference in Scott's novels. The Biblical quotations in *The Scottish Chiefs* tend to attach to Wallace, and serve a function of characterization, reinforcing Wallace's divinely appointed mission of national redemption, his Christ-like personal virtues, and his piety.

As historical novels the works of the Porter sisters are perforce also novels of description. They had to fill many pages with descriptions of characters and events, and especially historical costume and furniture, the kind of thing made popular, familiar and sometimes notorious through novels such as Scott's *Ivanhoe* and its imitators. In fact the Porter sisters are restrained in their descriptions of the theatrical properties of historical fiction. Rather, they emphasize character and incident, especially battles (homage, perhaps, to their father's military profession). More important, they took the topographical descriptive elements of the Gothic novel and put them in relation to the national theme by relating topography to national character. In *The Scottish Chiefs*, for example, the highlands and hill country of Scotland are associated with a Swiss-like independence of spirit and simplicity of life. Landscape and description (including description of war-ravaged countryside) are also used for the kind of sublime effects found in Gothic novels, but the Porter sisters are far less interested in landscape as a stimulus for Sentimental subjectivity than in the connection between landscape and subjectivity of a different kind – 'national character' – a connection long established, of course, in Enlightenment sociology. Novels such as *The Scottish Chiefs* put this relatively new element in prose fiction at the disposal of the literature of Romantic national consciousness, one of the most powerful forces in the modern world.

## 'Tales for Youth'

The kinds of fiction described so far in this chapter were written for adults, to set forth the interests and the visions of reality of the professional middle classes, which constituted the novel-reading public in the early nineteenth century. But just as the 1790s saw a number of projects, such as Hannah More's Cheap Repository, to create kinds of fiction that would purvey those social interests and visions to lower-class readers, so in the late eighteenth century there developed kinds of fiction to purvey those things to younger readers of all classes, but principally of the middle classes. Significantly, this fiction was designed for the most part to supplant the traditional kinds of stories given to children of all classes for over a century, namely the traditional story chapbooks of the common people – *Jack and the Giants, Fair Rosamond, Dick Whittington*, and so on. At the same time, parents were warned not to let illiterate servants fill children's heads with 'superstitious' tales, that is, folklore. If such fictions were dangerous for the common people, how much more so must they be for middle-class children, or any children.[16]

By 1800, then, fiction for children and 'tales for youth' had become a highly specialized and rapidly expanding industry, and since this was, once again, a minor branch of writing, women were very active in it. Writers such as Dorothy Kilner, Sarah Trimmer, Anna Letitia Barbauld, Mary Wollstonecraft, and Maria Edgeworth, working for firms such as the Newberys, Joseph Johnson, and others, had been active in the last few decades of the eighteenth century.[17] After 1800 many more women pushed into this rapidly expanding market, working for publishers such as Harris, Newman, the Dartons, Mary Jane and William Godwin, Houlston of Wellington, Kendrew of York, and many others. This literature is too vast and varied to receive more than a glance here, but its social and historical importance and influence can hardly be over-estimated; moreover, the best authors in the field, such as Maria Edgeworth, Mary Sherwood, and Barbara Hofland, often show a remarkably fine sense of how to employ the rhetoric of fiction to promote their views.

Some general remarks can be made, however. Tales for children and tales for youth draw heavily if selectively on the thematic and formal repertory of the Sentimental tale, especially as refashioned into such pseudo-popular fiction as the Cheap Repository tales of Hannah More. Children, like the common people (and perhaps women), were supposed to be irrational, incomplete as inward beings, and given to mere sociability. Hence narrative and fiction were supposed to be, unfortunately, necessary in order to secure their attention and interest. Nevertheless, fiction for the young would preferably include large amounts of factual, 'solid' information and be in a mode of formal realism, and set in common life. Where the historical or the geographical and social exotic were used they would be primarily for information and education. Usually there is an authoritative narrator, often represented as an adult character within the story supervising the children. Dialogues are used often, for didactic purposes – this coincides with a revival of catechism and catechetics among the Evangelicals (who were leaders in writing fiction for the young, as for the lower classes). Other devices had also been used in didactic literature for centuries: contrasting pairs of characters, good and bad; stereotype characters; inset illustrative anecdotes; and explicit moralizing.

Moreover, in fiction for the young of the Romantic period there is, as in pseudo-popular fiction for the lower classes and moralistic fiction for women, heavy emphasis on what might be called the sliding scale of sin – the idea that small errors and transgressions would lead to major ones. Thus there is also a heavy emphasis on the desirability of following right authority, though this may be female as well as male (as in Hamilton's *The Cottagers of Glenburnie*) and thus another covert assertion of the potential power of women in a culture that celebrates the domestic sphere as the origin and first shaper of the individual self, and the continuing domain of authentic meaning throughout life. Furthermore, the sliding scale of sin, reinforced in the stories by practical illustrations of precise rewards and punishments, has its counterpart in what might be called an investment mentality, to replace, as in fiction for the lower orders, the lottery mentality or attitude of instant gratification and *carpe diem* supposed to be characteristic of irrational and hence improvident young people.

The investments depicted in the stories are mainly moral and intellectual, but this is after all the central concern of professional middle classes whose economic and social achievements are more dependent on participation in intellectual service industries rather than inherited wealth or patronage, or even entrepreneurial or industrial skills and activity. Nevertheless, the investment mentality does participate in a general capitalist ideology because it requires self-discipline and avoidance of forms of personal or financial extravagance associated with gentry culture; at the same time it requires planning and forethought and an expectation that life will, if proper investments are made, be progressive, cumulative, and upwardly mobile rather than repetitive and static. Finally, many of these stories recommend forms of social duty, especially charitable work and missionary endeavour, that are versions of active social control of lower orders at home and exercise of colonial control and imperial expansion abroad.

Mary Sherwood's *Little Henry and His Bearer* (1814) is a good example, not just of these general points, but of Sherwood's own extensive *œuvre* (she published over 300 separate works[18]), the Evangelical tale for children, and the formal sophistication and ideological comprehensiveness this kind of fiction could achieve. The story concerns an English orphan in India, Henry L——, who is raised by a fine lady in a condition of such neglect that he dresses like a native and doesn't even speak English. Needless to say, he cannot read and is ignorant of Christianity. A virtuous and Evangelical young woman arrives from England with a box of Bibles and children's books, and in a year and a half has taught Henry to speak and read English and to consider himself a Christian. His social behaviour also changes; he becomes humble, docile, contented with his lot. The young lady leaves, enjoining Henry to bring his faithful Indian bearer, Boosy, to the true faith. Henry's efforts impress the virtuous Mr Smith in Calcutta; Mr Smith holds Henry up as an example to his fashionable wife and to Henry's equally fashionable step-mother, and teaches him Persian script and gives him translations of parts of the Bible into Hindi. Henry teaches Boosy to read this text, but Boosy persists in his dangerous religious pluralism, believing there are many streams, not just one, which run to the ocean of God. Only when Henry falls ill and nears death is Boosy's mind affected, and he rejects his caste and desires conversion. Henry's step-mother is also moved to become less worldly, and more 'serious', by Henry's example. When Henry dies, he entrusts Boosy to Mr Smith, who oversees Boosy's conversion. The narrator steps forward at this point and from personal knowledge describes Boosy's fate as well as Henry's funeral monument, a woodcut of which appears at the end of the story.

Simple as the story is, it contains a rich and complex fable of social transformation. Henry is neglected by his fashionable worldly guardian and almost absorbed by the lowest social class, but made literate, transformed from within, and thus made an agent of literacy and transformation for others. His example spreads to a member of the very class that had once almost absorbed him, as well as to a worldly member of the class that had neglected him. His death, which he embraces gladly and which moves others to emulate him, is the transcendental validation of his worldly significance to others left behind, including the reader. Social class (Boosy's caste) and merely social interests (Henry's step-mother's worldliness) are thrown aside in a grand social reconciliation in the light of the eternity to which God's agent has already departed.

Formally *Little Henry* uses the same techniques found in Hannah More's Cheap Repository fiction and Legh Richmond's *Annals of the Poor* – the authoritative narrator, the descriptions of nature as God's text, the generous use of Biblical quotations to illustrate or to nail down a point of the narrative's argument, the limited repertory of characters (the virtuous lowly, the irresponsible worldly, and the discriminating well-to-do), the use of dialogue modelled on catechism, the use of certain favourite hymns, the central place of literacy in the plot of conversion, the emphasis on the 'good death', the use of emblems, and so on. One of the appealing features of the tale was its exotic setting, though this is based not so much on descriptions of India as on use of Hindi words and reference to Indian customs, all explained in brief footnotes, which in turn lend authority and authenticity to the narrative.

But the importance of a scale of language, or language used in a figural way, is as great here as in the social-historical novels of the

1800s and 1810s. As Henry learns English he learns through the Evangelical canon of texts: the King James Bible, the Church of England Book of Common Prayer (especially the Catechism, which the Evangelicals were eager to revive), the hymns (which Evangelicals also wished to revive), and tracts, especially fictional ones written for children (and distributed by Evangelical societies). When Henry has learned to quote these texts, he is fully transformed within, and can teach Boosy. But Boosy is not given command of the master language or direct access to its texts; they are translated for him and he receives them at one remove, permanently in a margin of the true faith. In this world he will never enter the space of canonical language of the Church of England in its Evangelical version, a space to which Henry gains access by Evangelical social action and which frees him to be a social agent in his turn.

In Sherwood's tale there are in a sense no social injustices or inequalities, only errors and ignorance, and once these are cleared up by literacy and evangelizing the individual looks beyond this world for salvation from the world's evils and relativities. This myth of transformation of the individual life could be applied both at home in Britain, as in the Cheap Repository tales and *Annals of the Poor*, and in Britain's overseas empire, as in *Little Henry*, to head off calls for social and institutional reform. Certainly this myth gave central importance in a period of profound social conflict and change to the activities of the Evangelicals, many of whose leading ideologues were women. For, as in *The Cottagers of Glenburnie*, the significant agents as well as the ignorant opponents of reform are women.

Barbara Hofland was not an Evangelical and usually wrote for somewhat older readers than those Sherwood aimed at, including adults, but the project of her 'tales for youth' is very similar to that of Sherwood's tales for children and More's, Hamilton's, and Richmond's tales for the common people. Moreover, Hofland always had a keen sense of what the market demanded, and she immediately fell in with the line of the two most successful women writers of the 1800s, Maria Edgeworth and Amelia Opie – the 'tale', especially the tale of domestic life. In the 1810s she even tried her hand at a 'national tale'. Eventually, in the 1820s, she replaced Opie as a supplier of volumes of tales for the publisher Longman, and by the 1830s she was producing conventional triple-decker 'modern novels' for Colburn and Bentley. Throughout her career, she went with the most popular lines of fiction and the most enterprising publishers, producing over sixty works that sold a total of over 300,000 copies.[19] She was thoroughly given to the commercial spirit in writing, yet careful to avoid any appearance of mere commercialism, and careful to preserve her status as a lady.

Her tales may be located somewhere between the simple methods and obvious didacticism of the short fictions of the Cheap Repository and Religious Tract Society and the more complex forms and literariness of the 'modern novel'. Plot and character are the dominant formal elements, and the narrative is almost always third-person omniscient, with authoritative character portraits, explanations of motive and action, and moralizing. Plot and character form a closed system, an economy that is moral, financial, and cosmic. A character or family finds itself in poverty through no fault of its own, and no fault of social injustice or institutional oppression, either. Self-discipline and hard work, together with complete lack of social ambition, attract the attention and patronage of social superiors, and seem to draw a degree of good fortune as well, suggesting Providential validation of the virtuous, as in *The Good Grandmother* (1817), and *The Blind Farmer* (1816). Modest well-being within the protagonists' natural social sphere is the greatest material reward allowed. This is the basic form of Hofland's first success, a cycle of three 'widow' tales – *The Officer's Widow* (1809), *The Clergyman's Widow* (1812), and *The Merchant's Widow* – of other tales of distressed families, such as *The Son of a Genius* (1812), *The Blind Farmer* (1816), and *The Good Grandmother* (1817), and of a number of moral tales of the 1820s, such as *Integrity* (1823) and *Decision* (1824).

These tales plot self-control operating through time-as-work and such practices as frugality, moderation, humility, and even a modest kind of capitalism – ploughing the profits of one stint of work into enhancing the profits of the next, and avoiding any kind of self-indulgence, extravagance, or wasteful emulation of merely fashionable 'betters', as seen in the example of the adolescent female iron-dealer in *Decision* (1824). In all of Hofland's 'tales for youth', education and self-improvement are recommended as moral and monetary investments. There is a strong emphasis on family loyalty and solidarity, as a form of mutual self-defence and advancement, which also have the benefit of drawing the admiration and patronage of one's 'betters'; outstanding bad characters are the irresponsible parent and the undutiful child. In Hofland's tales the national economic and social institutions seem to operate in distant and mysterious ways, beyond human control, indifferent to individual destiny. As in Sherwood's tales, there is no such thing as systemic social injustice, only individual self-government, domestic fidelity, hard-earned social patronage, and gratitude to God's Providence in rewarding merit through His earthly agents, the pious and morally discriminating well-to-do. Lower-class characters appear mainly to reward the deserving middle-class protagonists, too, with awe at the latter's self-control and loyalty to their moral (not social) superiority. Thus in Hofland's tales the moral, social, and monetary economies coincide, and this coincidence is validated from above by Providence and one's moral social superiors and from below by admiring emulation.

In spite of the early reluctance of the pious and evangelistic to use fiction for their own purposes, then, by the mid-1810s fiction was well established as a means of disseminating certain kinds of professional and middle-class values and attitudes to children and the lower classes – in fact, it was seen as the principal means. Of course, 'tales for youth', like Cheap Repository and Religious Tract Society tales, were not written by the same kind of people that were their intended readers, or their intended buyers. The people who bought these tales to give to others could find therein fantasies of what they wanted children, the lower classes, colonized races, and society at large to be. Perhaps this fantasy element was responsible for the large sales of these fictions, rather than the actual enthusiasm of their intended readers for them. Autobiographies of the period, apart from strictly religious ones, give testimony to the will of children and the lower classes to find enough fiction of the 'wrong' kinds, kinds that satisfied their real interests rather than the interests others would impose on them.

## Excess and Transgression: 'Tales of Wonder'

It would be wrong, however, to suggest that all fiction during these years was marshalled against the values, ideology, and institutions of both upper and lower classes, or used simply to defend and advance professional and middle-class versions of those things. The 'Gothic romance' in particular continued to offer overt criticism of courtly values and practices, usually set in exotic places, especially Catholic and Mediterranean Europe or feudal Germany and occasionally incorporating elements of the mysterious East – a major theme in the later 1810s and 1820s. In short, that which was 'not British' continued to be condemned, in various forms, and continued to fascinate. Put another way, 'tales of wonder' treat those things excluded from 'village anecdotes', 'tales of real life', and 'tales for youth', though not necessarily from 'tales of the heart' or 'tales of fashionable life'; yet 'tales of wonder' really deal with the same issues that all of these kinds of fiction deal with, but from a different angle and with different techniques and emphases.

The first decade and a half of the nineteenth century confirmed what had already begun to appear in the 1790s – that writers of 'Gothic romance' were following 'Monk' Lewis rather than Ann Radcliffe in depicting the vicissitudes of the self and things 'not English'. Moreover, by the early 1800s elements of 'Gothic romance' had been taken up in other kinds of fiction and literature. For example, as we have seen in the previous chapter, an intellectual and political novelist such as William Godwin read Gothic novels as well as seventeenth-century Heroic Drama in preparation for writing his *St. Leon: A Romance of the Sixteenth Century* (1799). Soon after, Godwin attempted to write Gothic Heroic Dramas of his own. His next novel, *Fleetwood; or, The New Man of Feeling* (1805), is also related to Gothic fiction of the early 1800s in being a novel of passion, power, and intrigue on the domestic plane. In 1800, Dr John Moore's last novel, *Mordaunt*, included a Gothic tale of flight and pursuit during the French Revolution; Fanny Burney's *The Wanderer* (1814) used similar material. At the other end of the fiction market, hack writers and enterprising publishers quickly reduced popular Gothic novels and stage melodramas to chapbook form, format, and price, embellished with sensational and garishly coloured frontispieces. Elements of the Gothic were used by poets such as Shelley and Byron; and much of the newly collected folk literature contains elements that could be read as Gothic, for example in folk ballads that exhibit strong passions of love, revenge, loyalty, and betrayal, as well as the supernatural and preternatural.

It is true that there were no significant artistic achievements in the 'Gothic romances' of writers such as Regina Maria Roche, Francis Lathom, Charlotte Dacre, Anna (not Agnes) Maria Bennett, Eliza Parsons, and young Percy Shelley in the 1800s and early 1810s. Indeed, in some ways the most significant achievement of early nineteenth-century 'Gothic romance' was to be found in the parodies, burlesques, and satires it inspired or partly inspired, such as Austen's *Northanger Abbey* (written by the early 1800s; published 1818), Eaton Stannard Barrett's *The Heroine* (1813), and Thomas Love Peacock's *Nightmare Abbey* (1818). Nevertheless, the Gothic novelists of these years were prolific; they were widely read, if widely condemned; their work was related to significant developments in other branches of literature and the arts; and they prepared the way for the significant novels of passion of the late 1810s and 1820s, such as Mary Shelley's *Frankenstein* and Maturin's *Melmoth the Wanderer* (both discussed in Ch. 6).

Charlotte Dacre's *Zofloya; or, The Moor: A Romance of the Fifteenth Century* (1806) stands out slightly as an example of the direction in which 'Gothic romance' was developing in these years. It had an impact on such young readers as George Gordon, soon to be Lord Byron but in 1806 still a student at Cambridge, and Percy Shelley, then a schoolboy at Eton. *Zofloya* was published by Amelia Opie's publishers, Longman, Hurst, Rees, and Orme, and it has several important similarities to Opie's novel of passion and domestic estrangement, *Adeline Mowbray*, published in 1804. Its major source, however, was Lewis's *The Monk*, though such novels as Moore's *Zeluco* and Godwin's *St. Leon* may have been in Dacre's mind, too, and there are even elements of Wollstonecraft's feminist sociology of court culture. *Zofloya* certainly has striking characters and themes, and considerable narrative energy; but it is hopelessly self-contradictory on the causes of the evil, both individual and social, it depicts. Perhaps this contradiction in itself appealed to readers who wanted to have both the late-Enlightenment rationalism the novel begins with and overtly defends and the mystery, supernatural, and rather trite pieties with which the novel ends; this contradiction can, after all, be found in much literature of the Romantic period, both high and low.

*Zofloya* opens with an authoritative account of the aristocratic court culture of fifteenth-century Venice and the way this culture deforms social relations, family life, and individual character. This is a typical piece of late-Enlightenment historical sociology, and can be found in the novels of Godwin and Scott alike. Dacre shifts this kind of sociology toward Wollstonecraft's account of the denaturing of women when she then accounts for the character of the protagonist, Victoria di Loredani, formed into a passion-dominated, unself-aware coquette by a mother unable to control her own passions. Dacre attempts to define the social construction and the moral economy of an individual with the same comprehensiveness found in Godwin, though without the same detail, and in Austen, though without the same subtlety and unobtrusiveness. Moreover, Dacre develops the psychological economy of her anti-heroine by suggesting that the inner conflict from which Victoria now suffers (her bosom is said to 'ache' with conflict) opens a fissure in her personal identity through which arise dreams of a Moor who comes to help her achieve her desires. The dream-Moor turns out to be Henriquez's servant, Zofloya, who, in several scenes in a garden offers her his knowledge, gained in exotic places, of poisons and philtres. These potions give one a secret power over another, and as instruments are probably meant to be a material correlative for psychological forms of such power. They may even suggest the invisible way in which much or most power is exercised in a society; but Dacre does not know how to make effective use of this way of imaging the influence of knowledge and power in individual relationships or society at large.

Henceforth the narrative charts Victoria's descent into all 'the stormy passions of the soul', and her consequent succumbing to Zofloya's power over her and her destiny. This part of the novel is full of descriptions of the sublime of obscurity, power, and awesomeness (prime categories of the sublime in Edmund Burke's treatise on the subject, as Ann Radcliffe and other Gothic romancers well knew). There are also many allusions to *Paradise Lost*. This part of the novel also has many dialogues between Victoria and Zofloya, in which, like the dialogues between Eve and Satan in Milton's poem, the woman cannot understand the full significance, the equivocation in Zofloya's words. The reader does understand, however, and this fact establishes a narrative irony by which the reader alone sees what is 'really' going on. As Victoria says to Zofloya later in the novel, '"Oh inscrutable Moor! – thy language is ever indefinable!"' (ch. 30). Equivocation is an ancient characteristic of Satan, but here it may simply represent a woman's perception of male language of desire and power as opaque and problematical, just as Zofloya's understanding of poisons and philtres could represent a woman's perception of the mysteries of male ways of power.

As Victoria relies on the Moor to achieve her desires she passes from one transgression to another: poisoning her husband; declaring love to his brother (hints of incest); imprisoning, torturing, and finally murdering the orphan Lilla (conventional figure for virtue in distress). Victoria's abandonment of social values and institutions is represented by the sublimely terrifying alpine scenery and the 'almost pathless forest'. Here she suffers the agonies of passion or meets with Zofloya to plot her passions' fulfilment. Appropriately, then, Victoria finds herself and Zofloya in the hands of banditti, themselves outcasts and rebels against society. The leader turns out to be her brother, thus degraded from his potentially noble and useful social position by his own passions and the machinations of Victoria's former rival, now Leonardo's mistress. When the banditti are betrayed to the authorities by one of Leonardo's rivals for leadership (even outcast society is a divided society), Zofloya offers Victoria escape once again, on condition she become wholly his. When she agrees, he reveals he is Satan, and hurls her down a mountainside in a scene reminiscent of the ending of *The Monk* and anticipating that of *Melmoth the Wanderer*.

The central irony here, which is remarked on by Victoria several times, and which is fully apparent to the reader, is that Victoria, a flower of aristocratic culture and a child of passion, has been mastered by 'the other' – a creature trebly below her. As a Moor and a servant, Zofloya is 'beneath' Victoria on two counts, racial and social; as Satan he is beneath her morally and, as it were, cosmologically: appropriately, having mastered her he casts her from a height into an abyss at the end of the novel. There is an obvious moral point here; but readers might also have relished or been revolted by the social implications of Victoria's fall. It is possible to read a great deal into novels such as *Zofloya* – another reason, perhaps, for their popularity in their own time and their continuing fascination for some modern critics. Nevertheless, and paradoxically, *Zofloya* remains undecided about the final cause of Victoria's fall into the power of the other, in spite of the apparent forthrightness of its concluding moral: 'Reader – consider not this as a romance merely. – Over their passions and their weaknesses, mortals cannot keep a curb too strong.' Clearly, it is not court culture, operating through all its insidious penetrations into society, the family, and the individual consciousness, which is to blame for crimes and sufferings, but an extra-social *diabolus ex machina*. Satan may, of course, work through false social structures and ideologies such as those of a court society; but no one could imagine that the overthrow of court society would end his potential for power. Suitably enough, in light of the nature of its eponymous villain, *Zofloya* is an equivocating novel; and, like so many 'Gothic romances' – indeed, like so many novels of manners and novels of passion of the Romantic period, it remains fundamentally ambivalent and ambiguous about what it condemns. As with these other novels, such ambivalence gives *Zofloya* an interest beyond its actual literary qualities.

*Zofloya* has some additional interest for literary history because it was the quarry for Percy Shelley's *Zastrozzi: A Romance* (1810), written when Shelley was still at school. The plot, characters, and major incidents of *Zastrozzi* are very similar to those of *Zofloya*, though Shelley disrupts the plot line even further in order to fore-ground the passionate subjectivity of the novel's protagonist, Matilda. Shelley takes the element of crime and transgression in Dacre's novel and pushes it further (a process followed by the Gothic novel in general from the 1790s to the 1820s) in an attempt to write the sublime as a plane of experience beyond social conventions, including language. Shelley's project fails, but it is interesting in its anticipation of major themes in Shelley's later work, in its attempt to push beyond language, in its exhibition of the tendencies of the line of the Gothic horror-novel, and in its being typical of the slap-dash, headlong quality of Gothic novels – part of their appeal to readers interested in the Gothic precisely as a repository of the unhomely, the unfamiliar and unfam-ilial, the unconventional, the sublime, the 'not English', excess, and transgression. Thus *Zastrozzi* is a further development of the fiction of transgression from Moore's *Zeluco*, through Lewis's *The Monk*, and Dacre's *Zofloya* (the letter Z apparently represents the alien, 'not English' element in naming the Other).

*Zastrozzi* may be an example of what one could call tearaway Gothic – fiction for and by rebellious adolescence – but it also antici-pates Shelley's later interests in erotic and platonic love as transcen-dental and inwardly authentic values, in the relation of language and the sublime, in absolute selfhood, in transgression against laws and conventions both human and divine in order to achieve the subliminal and absolute self, and in the problem of creating and disseminating revolutionary consciousness through the medium of language and literary forms that are already politically and socially relative through and through. To the young Shelley, 'Gothic romance' of the kind of Dacre's *Zofloya* must have seemed precisely the genre for representing the absolute and transcendental, precisely because of its interest in excess and transcendence, in relation to decadent courtly and aristocratic values and practices. Furthermore, the extravagant language of Shelley's novels, their frequent recourse to the figure 'words cannot express', and their often ludicrous attempts to transgress the limits of Dacre's already transgressive Gothic all anticipate a central concern of Shelley's later poetry – the paradox of trying to express the sublime – by definition trans-social and trans-linguistic – in language and literary form.[20] Like Charles Lamb, then, Shelley abandoned the quest for authentic language through prose fiction; he turned, however, not to the sociable form of the familiar essay, which Lamb remade for the Romantic age, but rather to the traditionally sublime form and language of poetry.[21]

## Notes

1. Leslie A. Marchand, *Byron: A Biography*, 3 vols (1957), I. 85.

2. Thomas Medwin, *The Life of Percy Bysshe Shelley*, edited by H. Buxton Forman (1913), pp. 24–25. See also Kenneth Neill Cameron, *The Young Shelley: Genesis of a Radical* (1951), ch. 1.

3. *Eclectic Review*, new series, 4 (Aug. 1815), 158–67 (p. 158).

4. See Desmond Clarke, *The Ingenious Mr. Edgeworth* (1965).

5. Marilyn Butler, *Maria Edgeworth* (Oxford, 1972), p. 350.

6. *Castle Rackrent*, edited by George Watson (Oxford, 1964, 1980), pp. 71–72. All subsequent references are to this edition.

7. Thady is described as 'illiterate' in the author's Preface, p. 3.

8. Butler, *Maria Edgeworth*, p. 199.

9. Gary Kelly, 'Expressive Style and "the Female Mind"': Mary Wollstonecraft's *Vindication of the Rights of Woman*', *Studies on Voltaire and the Eighteenth Century*, 193 (1980), 1942–49 (pp. 1947–48).

10. *Oxford English Dictionary*.

11. See Gary Kelly, 'Amelia Opie, Lady Caroline Lamb, and Maria Edgeworth: Official and Unofficial Ideology', *Ariel*, 12 (1981), 3–24.

12. See Martin Wiener, *English Culture and the Decline of the Industrial Spirit* (Cambridge and New York, 1981), ch. 4.

13. See the essays in *The Invention of Tradition*, edited by Eric Hobsbawm and Terence Ranger (Cambridge, 1983).

14. See Mark Girouard, *The Return to Camelot: Chivalry and the English Gentleman* (New Haven and London, 1981).

15. See William A. Wilson, 'Herder, Folklore and Romantic Nationalism', *Journal of Popular Culture*, 6 (1973), 819–35.

16. See F. J. Harvey Darton, *Children's Books in England*, third edition, revised by Brian Alderson (Cambridge, 1982), ch. 6.

17. See Geoffrey Summerfield, *Fantasy and Reason: Children's Literature in the Eighteenth Century* (1984), chs. 6 and 7.

18. See Nancy Cutt, *Mrs. Sherwood and Her Books for Children* (1974), bibliography.

19. *Dictionary of National Biography*, 'Barbara Hofland'.

20. See Robert F. Gleckner, 'Romanticism and the Self-annihilation of Language', *Criticism*, 18 (Spring 1976), 173–89 (pp. 177–78).

21. In 1814 Shelley began a 'romance' entitled 'The Assassins', but abandoned it; see *The Complete Prose Works of Percy Bysshe Shelley*, edited by Roger Ingpen and Walter E. Peck, (reprinted London and New York, 1965), vi. 155–71. Later Shelley began another 'romance', 'The Coliseum'; *Prose Works*, vi. 299–306.

## Chapter 4
# 'Only a Novel': Jane Austen

Novel reading and the nature of the 'modern novel' are at the heart of Jane Austen's novels, both formally and thematically. She came from a large family of avid and enthusiastic and discriminating novel readers. She began to write short parodies of 'modern novels' in the late 1780s, when she was in her teens, and she wrote mostly epistolary novels of manners and sentiment in the 1790s. She subscribed to a circulating library wherever she lived, and she subscribed to Burney's *Camilla* in 1796. She rewrote some of her novels in the 1800s, sold one novel (in which the bad effects of novel reading was a theme) as early as the mid-1800s, and published six novels between 1811 and 1818, two posthumously. Yet she seems to have a paradoxical status as a Romantic novelist. On one hand, many critics regard her as the single novelist of the Romantic period who was a literary artist of the first order: according to F. R. Leavis, for example, her works are the first 'modern classics' of the English novel.[1] On the other hand, this view of her began to develop only at the end of the Romantic period in Britain, with the republication of her novels in the early 1830s in Richard Bentley's Standard Novels, and even in the Victorian period there were important 'romantic' novelists who did not like her work. Charlotte Brontë, for example, who was moved by George Eliot's companion, G. H. Lewes, to read Austen, did so, and found her fiction to be quite unromantic.[2] Yet, as discerning and definitively Romantic a novelist as Sir Walter Scott paid tribute to her artistry,[3] and some modern critics suggest affinities between her work and that of the Romantic poets.[4] Certainly one can argue that Austen's novels do what many Romantic novels do – represent a version of the coalition of gentry and professional middle classes, for Austen knew both the 'modern novel' and the interests of the novel-reading classes very well. In that sense, at least, Austen's novels are central to the Romantic period.

In the first place, she was a member of a family that had been moving steadily through the professions toward gentry status for two generations at least. Her father was a well-to-do country clergyman and her brothers were quite successful in the professions they took up – the clergy and the navy – and one of them was even adopted by a childless gentry family and himself became a landed gentleman in 1797. The two Austen daughters, Jane and her older sister Cassandra, did not marry, and so remained dependent first on their father and then on their successful gentleman brother, Edward Austen Knight. This leisured though dependent life took Austen from Steventon to Bath and Southampton, occasionally to London, and other places, before she settled at Chawton in Hampshire in a cottage owned by her brother Edward. Thus she had plenty of opportunity to live in and observe the lower reaches of 'county society'. In the second place, as the granddaughter, daughter, and sister of Anglican clergymen she was very well placed to have a daily, living familiarity with the mainstream of English culture and ideology. Thirdly, as a woman of the professional middle classes, she was well placed to understand the main points of the debate on women of the middle and upper classes in her time, though she herself was not a feminist.[5] For example, her letters show that she was very knowledgeable in the domestic domain appropriate to women of her class, and well skilled in the minute and local observation that even a feminist such as Mary Wollstonecraft argued was a special attribute of women in their (to Wollstonecraft, unreasonably) restricted social range of knowledge and experience.

Like feminists of her day, Austen too was suspicious of decadent court and aristocratic culture, especially its codes of amorous gallantry and coquetry. Moreover, Austen must have been aware that both Anglican theology and liberal social ideology could not allow for a distinction between men and women in the domain of intellectual and moral nature: if all were to be able to exercise reason and free will to choose good over evil and thus win eternal salvation, then women, and other subject and marginalized social groups such as the poor and slaves, had to be educated and freed from legal and social restraints to the extent that their free will could operate and therefore have moral meaning and ethical consequences.[6]

Most important, Austen was very well placed to know the literary culture of the day and its relation to social life and reality, to the moral and ethical traditions of her Anglican culture, and to the contemporary debate on women. The members of the Austen family were very interested in 'polite literature', especially *belles lettres*, novels, and plays, and they were familiar with both 'classic' English literature and whatever was recently published and making a stir in the world. Furthermore, their interest in literature was part of their everyday familiar and familial lives. Austen's letters show that she and others in her family persistently regarded characters and incidents in fiction and plays as if they were members of the Austen world of social reality, and they saw people and incidents in their circumambient social world in terms of characters and incidents in novels or plays they had read or acted in. And although she did portray the conventional 'dangers of novel reading' in her first novel, *Northanger Abbey*, and parodied and burlesqued novel conventions in her early writings (produced for the amusement of her family), Jane Austen could be impatient with the usual, easy dismissal of novels, as seen in the narrator's outburst in praise of novels at the end of chapter 5 of *Northanger Abbey*, and Austen's own sharp remark when solicited ·to subscribe to a new circulating library in 1798:

> As an inducement to subscribe Mrs. Martin tells us that
> her Collection is not to consist only of Novels, but of
> every kind of Literature, &c. &c. – She might have spared
> this pretension to *our* family, who are great Novel–readers
> & not ashamed of being so; – but it was necessary I
> suppose to the self-consequence of half her Subscribers.[7]

This remark is doubly worth quoting because it shows both Austen's clear sense of the interrelation of social and cultural values and her contempt for the merely conventional or fashionable response. These two principles are of major importance in Austen's novels and have a great deal to do with the relation of Austen's novels to those of her time, in several major ways.

First, Austen reveals in her letters an acute sensitivity to established conventions and changing discriminations in society and culture, including such topics as the relative status of different professions, incomes and property, inherited or acquired social rank, manners of all kinds, language (both speech and writing), 'improvement' (both capitalist and aesthetic estate development), literature of the day (including novels), the delivery of sermons, performance in music, dress and fashion, and, most important of all, courtship and marriage. These are major issues and major fields of discrimination, of the relation of self to society, for both Jane Austen and her fictional heroines, in both Austen's real world and her heroine's fictional world. More than novelists of manners and more even than 'silver-fork' novelists, Austen is a novelist of discrimination, discrimination as not just a set of social codes and languages, but as the central practice of the self engaged in society.

Secondly, then, Austen not only makes such discriminations important matter within her novels, she foregrounds the act of discrimination in her heroines' minds and in her plots of love and courtship. Austen eschews the Romantic art of writing the self as transcendental and supra-social in order to develop (from the earlier work of Richardson in *Sir Charles Grandison*, Fanny Burney, Charlotte Smith, Elizabeth Inchbald, Maria Edgeworth, and others) the art of writing the self in relation to the 'languages' of discrimination in society. Like Maria Edgeworth, she eschews the novel of passion to write the novel of moral and intellectual perception, and consequent ethical action. Thus, like Edgeworth, she tries to re-found the novel of manners, sentiment, and emulation. Like Burney, Austen depicts the self's struggle both to master these 'languages' and to use them to create an independent place for the self in society; like Burney, Austen images this place as a marriage of true minds *and* important social status and responsibility for the heroine as wife of a landed gentleman or dedicated professional man. But more than Burney or the other novelists whose tradition she followed, Austen is also interested in the problem of self-knowledge and self-mastery. In her own way, Austen, like other important novelists of the Romantic period, is interested not only in the social enemies of the self, but in the enemy within – conventionally, in eighteenth-century thought on woman's condition, the enemy to which women were most susceptible. In this way, Austen is responding directly to the Romantic culture of the self. Thirdly, Austen uses novel reading in particular as a major metonymy for both discrimination in general and the problem of mediating self and society within a professional middle-class culture of self and writing. Here she takes up the conventional criticisms of novel reading and of women as novel readers in her day and shows how reading is both constitutive of the self and one case of the self reading itself and the world around it. Reading, for Austen as for some hermeneutic philosophers and some post-structuralist critics, is a dialectic between the self and the text, between the individual 'temper' (both innate and acquired inward character) and a world or a book (as a world) with its own independent, 'objective' reality but always, of necessity, subject to interpretation and thus in the root sense a fiction – something fashioned or formed. But such fashioning, Austen argues, should not be merely arbitrary (the later, usual sense of fiction). Fashioning the world and the book is bad and dangerous when it is selfish and egotistical, good when it recognizes the autonomy of the world and the book and, more important, the inherited, social and cultural codes of reading. But neither should such fashioning be merely conventional, for that is abdication of the self in face of the world and the book. Discrimination (understood) as self-knowledge and knowledge of the world and self-mastery are in accord with both Austen's Anglican culture and the contemporary professional middle-class idea of woman.

Finally, Austen makes discrimination or reading an exercise for the reader, too, precisely by engaging in continual play with both social

and fictional conventions in her novels, so that the reader's work with
the novel parallels that of the heroine with herself and her social world
within the novel.[8] That is why reading is such a powerful representative for discrimination of all kinds in Austen's novels, and why her
own art of fiction is, like the experiences of her fictional heroines, a
continual dialectic between originality and convention, the familiar and
the new. It is also why Austen's novels are re-readable and meant to
be re-read in a way that much Romantic fiction is not and was not
meant to be. As Austen's remark on Mrs Martin's circulating library
shows, she knew very well that the 'modern novel' was a despised
article of consumption marketed according to a culture of fashion and
novelty. In her own novels, then, she clove to the apparently old-
fashioned and conventional, but in order to be novel in her own fashion
and thereby transcend mere fiction and novelty with an art the recognition of which depends on knowledge of precisely those fashions and
novelties being denied, transformed, and transcended. By being deliberately old-fashioned (for the 1810s), she sought to elude the topicality
of many 'modern novels', and thus to be, in her own way – hallmark
of the Romantic artist – more profoundly topical in relation to the
Romantic culture she writes against (as opponent and as necessary
background).

Jane Austen's art of fiction is, then, first of all one of reduction and
intensification relative *to* the fiction of her day.[9] Her own well-known
comments on the limited scope of her novels show she was fully
conscious of this fact. For example, her confession that she worked on
a 'little bit (two Inches wide) of Ivory' was made to her nephew in 1816
in relation to his manuscript novel, itself obviously very much *à la
mode*. 'What should I do with your strong, manly, spirited Sketches,
full of Variety and Glow? – How could I possibly join them on to the
little bit (two Inches wide) of Ivory on which I work with so fine a
Brush, as produces little effect after much labour?'[10] Earlier in the same
letter, she makes a jest about intending to include more extraneous
material in her novels, after the manner of Scott in his *The Antiquary*
(published only six months before). And in April of the same year, she
wrote to the Prince Regent's domestic chaplain declining a suggestion
from His cultivated Royal Highness that she write 'an historical
romance, founded on the [royal] House of Saxe Cobourg' (that was
the sort of proposal that might have been accepted by Sir Walter Scott
and was accepted by Jane Porter). Such a work, Austen replied, 'might
be much more to the purpose of profit or popularity than such pictures
of domestic life in country villages as I deal in. But I could no more
write a romance than an epic poem.'[11] We notice the thoroughly
Romantic rejection of the commercialization of fiction, here.

Finally, in her letters to her niece Anna Austen in 1814, Aunt Jane

persistently employs a standard of plausibility and refers to her own
minute and detailed knowledge of a wide range of languages of social
life in order to 'correct' Anna's manuscript novel, and makes, moreover, the flattering and famous remark about one part of Anna's novel,

> You are now collecting your People delightfully, getting
> them exactly into such a spot as is the delight of my life;
> – 3 or 4 Families in a Country Village is the very thing to
> work on – . . . You are but *now* coming to the heart &
> beauty of your book. . . .[12]

Austen's deliberate self-restriction in her novels is not, of course,
merely a negative gesture toward the participation of the 'modern
novel' in commercialized novelty, fashionable consumption, and social
emulation; like Jane West, Elizabeth Le Noir, Mary Mitford, and
others, Austen reduces and suppresses in order to criticize both the
glamorous treatment of decadent court culture as emotional and financial extravagance in 'modern novels' and the dangerous alternative of
Romantic individualism, be it political, cultural, or 'sentimental', in
Romantic 'tales of the heart' and novels of passion.

Austen had assembled her own formal and thematic repertory by the
late 1790s, when she abandoned the epistolary mode and rewrote two
of her as yet unpublished novels as third-person narratives. Thereafter,
her repertory hardly changed throughout her six published and two
incomplete novels. Settings are in contemporary 'county' society
(particularly of the Home Counties), its houses, estates and places of
resort in country and town, and the private, familial, and domestic
scenes of such society and their socializing. The incidents are limited
to the usual events of county social life – visits, dinners, dances,
excursions – with much dialogue, the chief device of characterization,
along with authoritative narrative description.[13] Dramatic or melo-
dramatic incidents of the kind found in many 'modern novels', such as
secret marriages, elopements, abductions, duels, sudden moral or
financial ruin, and surprising revelations, are rejected, or put at a
distance from the main plot and characters, or kept to a minimum.
Even uncivil conduct and domestic accidents are few and far between.
These suppressions and restraints tend to make Austen's novels seem
'realistic' relative to the ruck of 'modern novels' and, as her letters on
novel writing to her niece and nephew make clear, her standard for
plausibility in fiction was what was conventional in her own social
world. But social settings, scenes, and incidents are not the only ones
in her novels. Like Burney's, her novels also contain many mental

events and dramatic scenes enacted in the mind of the heroine. Usually, these events are related to the social ones, as the heroine reflects on what she has seen and heard, what she has said and done, and what she should do in the future.[14] These inward scenes often alternate with social ones, in a chain of ethical action and moral reflection that constitutes the line of plot development in Austen's novels.

Thus there is a double plot in Austen's novels. On the one hand, all her novels are romantic comedies of love and courtship, historically and traditionally a plot form dealing with social renewal and reconciliation, as the errors, prejudices, and hostilities of an older generation are overcome by the power of love in the younger generation, with marriage as the symbol of social reunion and rejuvenation. In this period, however, as we have seen, romantic comedy focuses on love as an individual absolute, opposed by social inequalities associated with an old social order ripe for reform, if not revolution. Austen's romantic comedy is not revolutionary and does not hold up romantic love as a value transcending all social convention and tradition. Rather, the plots of her novels enact the integration of the authentic individual self (the heroine) into a social order and social institutions that remain fundamentally unchanged outwardly, but renovated from within by the authentic beings now inhabiting them. Meanwhile, as warnings, there are a few inauthentic courtships and marriages made for merely selfish or merely social reasons.

The alternation of linked social and psychological events informs Austen's version of the plot of romantic comedy, reconciling the Romantic culture of subjectivity to a conservative social politics of inward regeneration of gentry hegemony by the moral and intellectual characteristics of the professional middle classes. Moreover, the focus in Austen's romantic comedy is on the heroine, who must exercise the moral qualities conventionally and traditionally assigned to women, especially fortitude.[15] It is not by heroic action that Austen's heroines win in the end; it is by heroic inaction. This is especially true of the quiet and passive heroines, Elinor Dashwood, Fanny Price, and Anne Elliot. At the same time, romantic comedy is played out in a comic universe and with an order dependent on the convergence of circumstance (or coincidence, or luck) with the wise passiveness of the heroine. As important as anything about Austen's novels is that they are comic novels, for in the comic universe they construct, planning and plotting are of no avail; moral readiness is all. Thus planners and plotters are discomfited, and the active, officious heroines (Elizabeth Bennet, Emma Woodhouse) are embarrassed and learn to discipline the self and the will to patience in the face of an order that is, ultimately, benign and moral. The plot accomplishes the social recognition, in marriage, of the moral qualities of the heroine. It is worth emphasizing again that this plot form embodies a traditional (i.e., pre-Evangelical) Anglican vision or myth of cosmic order.

To focus maximum attention on this plot, characters are few in Austen's novels – not quite '3 or 4 Families in a Country Village', but near enough; and the same repertory of characters is used in each novel. Principally there is the heroine, who is silent or animated, humble or high (socially). Austen alternates the types from one novel to the next, making the other into a secondary character or 'shadow' of the heroine. Thus we have Catherine Morland and her gregarious friend Isabella Thorpe; Elinor Dashwood and her 'enthusiastic' sister, Marianne; Elizabeth Bennet and her quiet sister Jane; Fanny Price and the vivacious Mary Crawford; Emma Woodhouse and silent, suffering Jane Fairfax; the set is rather more complicated in *Persuasion*, but there are Anne Elliot and her talkative, ambitious sisters and sister-in-law. The heroines have suitors, true or false. The heroines' parents are useless – if present, foolish; if wise, dead or absent.

The heroines have rivals, though these are relatively negligible compared to the coquettish villainesses found in many 'romances' and 'modern novels'; but they may have the characteristics of coquettishness and a penchant for amorous intrigue, though there is no character in the major novels like the courtly villainess Lady Susan in the early story with that title. Nevertheless, in the published novels the heroines' enemies do show some characteristics of decadent aristocratic culture, a good example being the haughty Lady Catherine de Bourgh in *Pride and Prejudice*, who tries to prevent Elizabeth's marriage to Darcy and so helps to bring it about: intriguers in Austen's as in many other 'modern novels' often achieve the reverse of what they intrigue for. But since Austen focuses primarily on the consciousness of her heroines, she either makes the heroine into her own enemy, unwittingly intriguing against herself (as with Emma Woodhouse), or she makes the heroine's consciousness a field for exercise of self-discipline and self-control. Other characters instrumental in the plot as helpers or hinderers are siblings (though they are usually there to provide different shades of character in the same moral–intellectual 'family group'), friends, and mentors (these may include the true suitor, as in the case of Henry Tilney, Mr Darcy, and Mr Knightley).

This repertory of characters is very similar to that of the Burney novel, such as *Camilla*; but it is the Burney repertory reduced and compressed, less a social spectrum than a moral–intellectual one. The characters act less and on a smaller scale of error and folly, virtue and benevolence. Austen's novels are also shorter, less repetitive and more progressive in plot, and narrower in setting (though not much narrower) than Burney's novels. The central effects of plot, character, setting, incident, and dialogue are more concentrated, and the fictional structure as a whole is less desultory (we remember that Austen's sister hated desultory novels, though Jane thought herself more tolerant in this respect[16]) and thus, to the modern taste, more 'artistic' than most Romantic novels.

Of course, narrative method is central and centring in both Burney and Austen, and Austen's narrative method is that of Burney, with significant modifications. Like Burney, Austen wrote an epistolary novel ('First Impressions', an early version of *Pride and Prejudice*) and then, in the late 1790s, turned decisively to third-person limited omniscient narration. Like Burney's, Austen's narrator gives access almost exclusively to one character and consciousness, the heroine.[17] Like Burney's, Austen's narrator filters this consciousness or mediates it for the reader by transforming the heroine's inward speech and sentiments from the first person and present tense into the third person, past tense, a device known as 'free indirect discourse', more accurately called filtered inward speech and thought.[18] But there are major differences between the behaviour of Burney's and Austen's narrators. Burney's is more given to enunciating the brief moral essay and the maxim, more given to authoritative character portraits and moralizing; Austen's does these things less and is often what Burney's narrator is not – ironic, especially toward the heroine.[19]

More important, Austen's narrator is much more flexible, shifting, and subtle in filtering the inward speech and feelings of the heroine, so that the tone may change from unironic identification to ironic distance within the same sentence. These shifts test the reader's alertness to the subtlest change in narrative approval or reservation toward the heroine's thoughts, as the reader is led to sympathize with and yet judge the heroine's point of view and her vision, her understanding of herself and her world. Thus Austen's use of omniscient authoritative narration with filtered inward speech and feeling goes beyond the fusion of eighteenth-century third-person detached and first-person immediate modes of narration, to force on the reader an experience of the perplexities and vicissitudes of reading parallel to that being experienced by the novel's central character-consciousness. Austen's novels are 'novels of education' to a greater extent than any previous representative of that sub-genre of fiction.[20] They are novels of epistemology, the psychology of perception, the drama of consciousness played out in a comic universe with a romantic comedy plot.

This fact is confirmed by examination of the language of Austen's novels. In the first place, verbs and nouns of cognition are especially prominent in the discourse of both the narrator and the principal characters: feel, felt, feeling, and feelings occur 1711 times; know, knew, and known 2192 times; think, thought, and thinking 2621 times; seemed 600 times. By comparison, love, rather an important word in novels of romantic comedy, occurs 518 times, heart 506 times, marry 212 times, and marriage 231 times; money occurs 124 times, property 66 times, inherit 4 times, and estate 68 times.[21] Certainly verbs of interpretation, hypothesizing, supposing, and explanation are among the most common in Austen's novels, a fact supporting the argument that Austen's novels depict reading in various forms as the principal activity of the novels' central consciousnesses, the heroines.

Secondly, Austen's narrator has nothing to do and her principal characters have relatively little to do with the lyrical and expressive range of language and syntax, so important in Sentimental fiction, political and philosophical novels of rebellious selfhood, 'tales of the heart' and novels of passion, and 'romances' of all kinds. The effect for a novel reader of Austen's day must have been of implicit criticism of, guardedness toward, fending off extravagant self-expressiveness, confessional publication of one's inner self, and the politics of individualism. More important and obvious is the fact that, as in the best eighteenth-century and Romantic novels, different styles of language are related in a structure that corresponds to the structure of value in the novel. In this respect, there are two major axes of differentiation used by Jane Austen to characterize individuals within her novels and place them on a scale of moral value. First there is an axis of volubility: the greatest talkers, such as Mrs Elton in *Emma*, are the emptiest heads, though taciturnity may also indicate stupidity. Then there is a scale of conventionality: those who use the most clichés, the greatest quantities of fashionable slang, stiff formalities, modish jargon, and so on, such as Mr Collins or Lydia in *Pride and Prejudice*, are the most superficial and least morally discriminating and ethically constant characters. Often these two axes run parallel.

Finally, there is the central and centring role of the narrator's style and tone. First, this style and tone constitute the 'voice' of a model consciousness. The style is pre-eminently standard written English of a variety comparable to that of the great eighteenth-century periodical essayists, especially Austen's favourite, Samuel Johnson, and the eighteenth-century sermon writers, such as Thomas Sherlock.[22] Actually, the linguistic register, the 'diction' (in Donald Davie's sense[23]) used by the narrator is commensurate with these authors, but the syntax is on the whole relatively less formal and less hypotactic, as appropriate for a less formal kind of discourse, 'only a novel'. Yet there is gravity and dignity of a kind also appropriate; for Austen's narrator, in the famous 'only a novel' passage in *Northanger Abbey*, does assert the claims of the novel to participate in the tradition of familiar moral discourse. Nevertheless, as noticed already, Austen's narrator is far less inclined

to utter a miniature essay and far less obviously given to dropping
maxims than the narrators of, say, Burney's *Camilla* or Dr John
Moore's *Zeluco*, well-known 'serious' novels of the 1790s. Furthermore, the narrative voice of Austen's novels is far less literary and
allusive than that of many novels with pretensions to seriousness in the
Romantic period; and although Austen is celebrated for her balanced
and periodic sentences and epigrammatic phrases in pairs and triplets,
these features are more frequent or more noticeable in her earlier, more
obviously parodic and satirical novels, or they are associated with passages where she is parodying or playing off some tired novel
convention.

In all her novels the distancing formality tends to creep in where
the narrative wants to pull the reader back from his or her desire to
wallow in sympathy with the protagonist, as in the proposal scenes
that occur near the closures of the novels. The stylistic marks of a
written rather than a spoken discourse distance, as does irony, the
other principal device for that effect. Thus the narrator's style is least
formal and balanced when filtering to the minimum degree the
thoughts of the heroine, and it tends to be more formal and balanced
when ironically withdrawing and detached, and self-consciously
reminding the reader that this is 'only a novel'. The informality of
barely filtered reporting of the heroine's consciousness is descended
from the 'writing to the moment', the style of first-person immediacy
perfected by Richardson; the irony and evident literariness are
descended from the ironic, detached, patronizing (to his characters)
'voice' perfected by Fielding. To sense the relation between these styles
the reader must be alert to follow the movement from immediate
imaginative identification to detached moral reflection and judgement.
Finally, all of these features of style, in addition to the tone, assure the
reader that the world of the novel is essentially a comic universe, that
certain kinds of evil are not permissible here.[24] Nevertheless, in using
style and narrative method to test and challenge the reader, Austen
seems inclined to give less and less of this assurance with each successive novel she wrote.

Austen's first novel accepted for publication, *Northanger Abbey*, was
written as 'Susan' in the late 1790s and revised and sold in the early
1800s, though it was not published until after Austen's death. It shows
both Austen's debt to the Burney novel and all the elements of
Austen's own formal and thematic repertory. There is the put-upon
heroine, Catherine Morland – put upon by the fashionable, ambitious
Thorpes as well as by her own inexperience and lack of self-
knowledge. In her excursion into 'the World' (the fashionable spa of
Bath), Catherine learns of worldly ambition, greed, hypocrisy, and

coquetry in women, as well as of her own mind and heart. In the Thorpes, John and Isabella, she finds examples of social climbing, desire to be fashionable at all costs (moral and financial), willingness to marry for money, and petty selfishness; in the Tilneys (except for Henry), she finds examples of pride of rank and fortune. Between these extremes lie her own social territory, her family and friends, and her own moral self-awareness, encouraged and instructed by one of several lover-mentor figures in Austen's novels, Henry Tilney. Unlike his older, more glamorous brother, Capt. Frederick, he is destined for the clergy, like Catherine's own brother, James (who is jilted by Catherine's 'friend', Isabella Thorpe, when she thinks she has a chance for Capt. Tilney).

Appropriately and significantly, then, important parts of the courtship of Henry and Catherine revolve around themes of reading and writing. Henry teases Catherine on female writing (journals and letters), as well as female propensity for 'romantic' exaggeration, when he is first introduced to her by the master of ceremonies of the assembly rooms at Bath (ch. 3). When she denies having anything to do with fashionable female writing, he declares his real sentiments on intellectual relativities and gender: '"In every power, of which taste is the foundation, excellence is pretty fairly divided between the sexes"' (ch. 3). Mary Wollstonecraft would have agreed, though she would not have agreed with the implied exclusion of women from powers based on faculties other than those founded on taste. Wollstonecraft would also have agreed with Henry's censure of Catherine's Gothic-romance inspired imaginings about the General, though she would have been quick, too, to point out the connection between extravagant imaginings and the educational deprivation of women. Here books – novels – are clearly opposed to 'real life':

'Dear Miss Morland, consider the dreadful nature of the suspicions you have entertained. What have you been judging from? Remember the country and the age in which we live. Remember that we are English, that we are Christians. Consult your own understanding, your own sense of the probable, your own observation of what is passing around you – Does our education prepare us for such atrocities? Do our laws connive at them? Could they be perpetrated without being known, in a country like this, where social and literary intercourse is on such a footing; where every man is surrounded by a neighbourhood of voluntary spies, and where roads and newspapers lay every thing open? Dearest Miss Morland, what ideas have you been admitting?' (ch. 24)

Here, too, national character, religion, common sense, cultural and economic progress, the constitution, and social structure are lined up opposing the world of romance – both literary romance and the attitude of mind it engenders. More important is the language of cognition on which Henry bases his censure and the fact that, to him, accurate perception is grounded, in England, on the very nature of English society and culture. Mind is social. Not surprisingly, at the beginning of the very next chapter Catherine has one of those sudden recognitions of self and world found in most of Austen's novels: 'The visions of romance were over. Catherine was completely awakened'; and

> it had been all a voluntary, self-created delusion, each
> trifling circumstance receiving importance from an
> imagination resolved on alarm, and every thing forced to
> bend to one purpose by a mind which . . . had been
> craving to be frightened. (ch. 25)

In short, by an act of blind will, of false desire, she had misread everything around her. These last lines are in filtered inward speech, presenting Catherine's self-chastenings to us with no irony. But otherwise the narrative procedure of *Northanger Abbey* is relentlessly ironic, and playfully reflective in relation to fictional conventions, as the narrator flaunts and flouts one novelish *cliché* after another, right to the last sentence of the novel, with its mockery of conventional, moral-drawing, novel closures.

*Sense and Sensibility* is over half as long again as *Northanger Abbey*, partly because Austen doubled her material by plotting the fate of two sisters, although she still focuses her attention on only one of them. The plot of two sisters or brothers was a common form for novels of education in the late eighteenth century: parallel and diverging destinies could allow varying characters, educations, and choices to be depicted, and could allow for many morals to be drawn. It, too, was originally a novel in letters, written some time before 1796 with the title 'Elinor and Marianne', but rewritten in the third-person form some time between 1797 and 1811. *Sense and Sensibility* is far less self-conscious as a novel than *Northanger Abbey*, but it does play with a number of obvious *clichés* of Sentimental fiction, as its title suggests – 'Sensibility' being used then where we would use 'Sentimentality' now, though less pejoratively. Novels with titles from moral or mental abstractions were quite common, too, as witness Mary Brunton's widely read triple-deckers *Self-Control* (1811) and *Discipline* (1814). But Austen's novel does not so much oppose common sense in one character (Elinor Dashwood) to excessive sensibility in the other (Marianne Dashwood), as set the Dashwood sisters' moral generosity and emotional vicissitudes against the intriguing and selfishness, the stupidity, superficiality, and vulgarity of various other women characters (including their own mother) and the folly or vice of various suitors. Elinor is made the central consciousness, a self-denying and passive protagonist similar to Fanny Price in *Mansfield Park* and Anne Elliot in *Persuasion*. Nevertheless, *Sense and Sensibility* does study female passion in both Marianne and Elinor – Marianne expressing her feeling for the *galant* and impulsive Willoughby to dangerous excess, Elinor concealing her love for the erring but virtuous Edward Ferrars. Since the narrator focuses on Elinor's consciousness, right-minded as it usually is, the preferred female character is made clear; but through Elinor's sympathetic concern for her sister's misperceptions and misjudgments we have a distanced representation of the errors of a 'woman of feeling', a 'romantic' and 'enthusiastic' young woman, in the late eighteenth-century senses of those words.

The novel proceeds, in fact, in a series of blocks of major misunderstanding – of others by the Dashwood sisters, and of them by others. When everyone's character has more or less been revealed, then the marrying of true minds can begin and the novel end. In this novel, play with convention is in the form of repetition of certain kinds of incidents rather than self-conscious reflections by the narrator. Again and again, for example, Marianne expectantly awaits the appearance of the object of her desire, Willoughby, only to have another man, often Col. Brandon (whom she eventually marries), turn up in his stead. This becomes a local joke for the reader, but it makes a moral point about the power of desire and imagination, anticipates the actual upshot of the Marianne love-plot, and shifts emphasis away from parody and self-conscious narrative method to the story narrated and the moral argument it enacts. Against these episodes of false expectation are the episodes in which Elinor tries to interpret, to understand the complicated and partly hidden relationships in the world around her. These episodes, where the drama of cognition is being played out, rather than the episodes of confusing, ambiguous, and dangerous social interaction, are the chief points of thematic articulation in *Sense and Sensibility*.

In order to establish just how relative and ambiguous the social world is, Austen includes many more characters, incidents, and partial life stories than found in *Northanger Abbey*. More important, she sustains differentiation of character with highly developed characteristic speech, presented in numerous dialogues. There is the vulgar rattle and hypocritical intimacy of Lucy Steele, the vulgar candour of Mrs Jennings, the dignified pretentiousness of Fanny Dashwood, the impulsive expressiveness of Marianne (her speeches, in true sentimental-novel style, are littered with dashes and exclamations), the fervent egotism of Willoughby, the dignified taciturnity of Col. Brandon, and so on. Here, in this aspect of her art of fiction, Austen provides the socio-linguistic plenty and variety found in Burney's novels and Edgeworth's *Tales of Fashionable Life*, not merely for 'realistic' character portrayal but as a linguistic field of relativity against which to set the drama of cognition in the heroine's mind, played in a quasi-philosophical language similar to that used by the narrator when moralizing, generalizing, apothegmizing.

*Pride and Prejudice*, like *Sense and Sensibility*, may nave been cast originally as an epistolary novel, 'First Impressions' (though even that title suggests a problem of knowledge) in 1796–97, when it was offered to the publisher Cadell, but declined. Apparently, Austen cut it down considerably when it was revised and published in 1813, because she thought it to be shorter than *Sense and Sensibility*.[25] Certainly it is simpler in form and theme. Its situation, like that of *Sense and Sensibility*, rests on the displacement of the women of a family by the entailing of the family property on male heirs only, leaving the daughters well educated but almost dowerless, in a social no-man's land. But whereas the entailing of the Dashwood property in *Sense and Sensibility* has a labyrinthine complexity, in *Pride and Prejudice* it is much more straightforward. Like *Sense and Sensibility*, too, *Pride and Prejudice* deals principally with the courtship and marriage of a family of sisters, but it deals much more emphatically with the issue of marrying across social boundaries within the county gentry and the contiguous professional classes than does *Northanger Abbey* or *Sense and Sensibility*. There is a sharper sense of the conflict of love and social rank, and Elizabeth's marriage to Darcy is certainly the best match made by any of Austen's heroines. There is sharper criticism of the dependence of the professions on the gentry (in the relationship of Mr Collins to Lady Catherine de Bourgh).

At the same time, the problem of moral perception and ethical action is made more straightforward and more dramatic, and the play with fictional and romantic conventions is kept to the second half of the book, after Elizabeth Bennet's self-enlightenment. For the problem in this novel is the conflict of pride, as an excessive sense of one's own inner worth and integrity, at the expense of social conventions and traditions, against prejudice, as false notions of social rank and distinction and excessive reverence for them and for all the social proprieties. In a sense, Austen has moved Marianne Dashwood's self-centredness (not selfishness) into the centre of the action, as Elizabeth Bennet's independence and self-confidence in her own moral-intellectual discernment, and moved Elinor Dashwood's selflessness and humility to the secondary characteristic as Elizabeth's sister Jane. Austen also repeats the dramatic moment of enlightenment from *Northanger Abbey*, when Elizabeth Bennet receives Darcy's letter explaining his own motives and the character of Wickham, as well as the unsuitable aspects of Elizabeth's family's character and position, and Elizabeth realizes that Darcy is right, and she has been wrong.

> 'How despicably have I acted!' she cried. – 'I, who have
> prided myself on my discernment!. . . . How humiliating
> is this discovery! – Yet, how just a humiliation! – Had I
> been in love, I could not have been more wretchedly
> blind. But vanity, not love, has been my folly. . . . I have
> courted prepossession and ignorance, and driven reason
> away, where either were concerned. Till this moment, I
> never knew myself.' (ch. 36)

Up to this point, the reader has been inclined (indeed tempted by the unironic filtered inward speech) to accept Elizabeth's judgements of herself and others. When she recognizes her misreadings, we recognize them, and ours, too. Ironically, of course, Elizabeth then proceeds in another self-delusion, almost to the end of the novel – that Darcy will not propose a second time. That this is a self-protective delusion is increasingly obvious to the novel reader; hence there is increasing distance in judgment between reader and heroine, but also amused sympathy; both are guided by the playful, amused ironies of the narrator.

To reinforce the sense of conflict between the rights of self and the claims of society, and to guide the reader through the necessary discriminations in between, Austen adapts characteristic speech to a scale of formality and informality in this novel. Here she is less interested in sociolect and professional jargons than in idiolect as a representation of the moral and social self, differentiated according to degrees of conventional and unconventional expression. At one extreme, the excessively formal and conventional, is Mr Collins, as speaker and writer. His hackneyed language and pompous style advertise his lack of authentic self, his status as a merely dependent and imitative professional man. At the other extreme, shockingly and vulgarly unconventional, is Lydia Bennet; her prattle, larded with 'genteel' fashionable slang, advertises her lack of all discrimination in pursuit of merely public and social being (as a married woman, however shameful the marriage, she wants to take social precedence over her unmarried sisters). On the other hand, the third Bennet girl, Mary, is a mere pedant – she reads all the time, keeps a commonplace book, and studies maxims to deliver in company. In short, she speaks like a book and, like other merely bookish people in Austen's novels, has no understanding of the world, society, or herself, and no ability to apply books to life properly. Her father, too, is bookish, but he is also witty, delivering epigrams rather than maxims – an important distinction – when in society.

Nevertheless, in all Austen's novels the witty character has a special status. Wittiness advertises a good head, but rouses suspicions about the heart and the moral judgement, the willingness to participate fully in social life. Mr Bennet, closed in his library, a refugee from his stupid but once beautiful wife – the bookish man may be too swayed by mere beauty – emerges to tease and deliver *bons mots* that are above the heads of his wife and denser offspring; but his detachment has a high cost in the neglected moral and intellectual education of his daughters (Elizabeth and Jane are better educated because they have spent much time with their middle-class but virtuous, intelligent, well-informed and 'well-bred' aunt and uncle, the Gardiners – appropriate name for right cultivators of youth).

The wit in Romantic literature is often a figure of suspicion precisely because he or she seems to use language both to conceal the 'true' self and to keep the world at a distance. In her language, as in her mind, Elizabeth most resembles her father, but she feels for others and involves herself in their concerns, especially Jane's. Nevertheless, her intellectual self-sufficiency and pride lead her into near-catastrophic errors of judgment about herself, Darcy, Wickham, Lydia (and the weaker members of her family), and her strong feelings for Jane – normally a virtue – assist in promoting these errors. The narrator also gives way to sympathetic identification, especially toward Elizabeth, in the first half of the novel, and yet possesses ironic detachment, too; and thus the narrator most resembles the heroine, in language as in values. But because they 'sound' similar, Elizabeth can too easily be taken by the reader to be as authoritative a judge of herself and others as the narrator is of all the characters in the book. Only with Darcy's letter (the power of writing conveys his character to her in a way his speech did not) and Elizabeth's reflections on it, in both filtered and quoted inward speech, do we see her and our errors. As much as in a novel by Walter Scott, then, the structure of language in Austen's novels is the structure of authority, meaning, and value; but more than in a novel by Walter Scott the structure of language in Austen's novels is easy, purposively easy, to misread. Thus reading Austen is an education in the art of reading, and rereading.

In Austen's next novel, the first to have no particular ancestor in her fiction of the 1790s,[26] she pushes further in challenging the reader by the play of language and fictional conventions, and at the same time shows clearly the struggle between decadent court culture and professional values to dominate the English gentry, represented by the social, familial, economic, and cultural institution that is Mansfield Park. The shift in titling her novel, from nouns of mental abstractions to the name of a country house and estate, the focus of gentry power and culture, suggests a broader social engagement, though all of Austen's novels so far had shown the importance of the re-dedication of gentry-dominated institutions to moral purpose and the re-infusion of social-historical substance with moral-intellectual spirit.[27] Moreover, in Austen's novels these forms of social and moral renewal of gentry hegemony are carried out by women characters – not surprising, perhaps, in novels 'by a lady', but suggesting connections between Austen's ideological project and that of both professional middle-class feminists and other 'conservative' women fiction writers of the period.

In *Mansfield Park*, Austen sharpens this image of a patriarchal and paternalistic social structure not overthrown but rather renewed from its own margins and subordinate levels. For the moral and social renewal of Mansfield Park is effected not only by a young woman, but by a 'nobody' with all of the fictionally conventional physical frailties and social deficiencies of such a character. As her last name suggests, however, Fanny Price is rich in things not of this world as well as not of 'the World', or high society. Fanny is not even an immediate member of the family of the Park, but only a dependent cousin, taken in as an act of old-style gentry charity. This situation repeats the 'orphan' theme so familiar in Sentimental and Gothic novels by women such as Charlotte Smith, Elizabeth Inchbald, and Ann Radcliffe. A socially isolated young female is an ideal subject for depicting subjectivity, but Austen, as usual, uses the convention to recuperate what the convention takes for granted, and to bend the convention to new ends. It is unconventional but well within Anglican theology and social values to suggest that a great estate suffering from advanced spiritual impoverishment because of an infection of fashionable, courtly, and 'worldly' values can be enriched and regenerated by a poor cousin who has nothing but good judgment and plenitude of moral being.

In short, in *Mansfield Park* Austen sharpens into near-sentimentalist contrast the characters of inwardness and worldliness, humility and pride, good and evil. In doing so, she takes on a major artistic challenge, one usually merely fenced at by the host of moralistic and moralizing novelists of the day. A major difficulty faced by writers who wish to depict good and truth triumphing over moral error and social evil is to make evil convincing and the danger of its triumph seem real. Austen overcomes this difficulty in *Mansfield Park*, convincingly depicting moral error in the seductive shapes of the fashionable, cultivated, urbane, and morally vacuous Crawfords, Mary and Henry

– indeed, she succeeded too well for some readers, who cannot 'like' Fanny Price but 'admire' Mary Crawford, and think that Austen intended this to be so.[28] Such a view must be wrong, for, quite clearly, Mansfield Park is nearly destroyed by the invasion of all that the Crawfords represent, including seduction, adultery, and marital break-up, not to mention misplaced ambition, envy and sibling rivalry, and the familiar topics of emotional and financial extravagance.

Of course, the Park and its neighbours are all ready to receive the poison before the Crawfords arrive. Maria Bertram's fiancé, James Rushworth (not worth a rush, as his name suggests, but also impulsive and extravagant, as his name also suggests), is eager to 'improve' his estate, Sotherton Court, in all the wrong ways; Maria herself fancies Henry Crawford, and envies her unattached sister Julia's freedom to set her cap for him. Tom Bertram, the heir, is an empty and extravagant man of fashion; after the Crawfords' arrival for a visit, Tom's equally vain friend, Hon. John Yates, engages them all in a craze for amateur theatricals, a performance of Kotzebue's Lovers' Vows that will enable them to coquette and flirt, to court, without facing the consequences such courting would entail in 'real life'.

Austen is too wise a novelist, however, to have her heroine, Fanny, defeat this serried array of folly and vice by herself; rather, in a way repeated from her earlier novels, she has the courtly intriguers, especially Mary and Henry Crawford, defeat themselves. And Fanny, the young woman of fortitude and domestic heroism, is there at the end to reap the rewards of passive virtue. What is remarkable about Fanny Price is that throughout the novel she acts by refusing. Her self-denial and refusal of things not right for her, including Henry Crawford, whom all at Mansfield Park want her to marry, obtain for her a marriage of true minds with her cousin and mentor, Edmund. At the same time she obtains the Park's recognition of her moral and therefore her social worth to the Park and its now morally recentred social world. In a pattern familiar enough in late eighteenth-century fiction, authentic selfhood obscured by lowly social status endures the vicissitudes and relativities of the merely social world to achieve final recognition by that very social world, in the institution of marriage. For Fanny is the moral, spiritual, and cultural daughter of the Park, and therefore rightly marries its spiritual – in more than one sense – son, Edmund, named for the defender of 'antient chivalry' and the gentry, Edmund Burke (ch. 22), but, as a younger son, destined 'only' for a profession, the clergy, much to Mary Crawford's chagrin. Mary would have made him propose to her but for that, and she even wishes Edmund's older brother Tom dead so that Edmund may inherit the Park in his stead and thus be a suitable match for her. When Fanny's erstwhile suitor runs off with Edmund's married sister, Mary's worldly attitude to the event shocks Edmund into recognition of what she is, and of his folly in desiring her. By the next chapter he is already turning toward Fanny, who is quite happy to marry a mere country clergyman.

Henry, we remember, would have been willing to be a clergyman himself, if he had only to preach once in a while in a fashionable town to a fashionable congregation able to appreciate his artistry as a preacher. For him, the clergy could only be an aesthetic avocation suitable to a proper gentleman. As a large landowner's younger son Edmund is to be placed in a parish living at his father's nomination; but he takes his calling as a country clergyman very seriously, a fact suggesting Austen's recognition of the value of Evangelicalism in giving the Anglican clergy a new sense of moral and social purpose, free from the decadently genteel and all too worldly habits of clergymen of the older generation, such as the gourmandizing Rev. Grant in *Mansfield Park*. As Austen said, just after *Mansfield Park* had been published, 'I am by no means convinced that we ought not all to be Evangelicals.'[29] Even the name Mansfield Park suggests a re-balancing of the relationship between the landed gentleman's manor-house and its dependent manse: 'manse-field', the land supporting the minister and the church, becomes the name for a manor house, 'park' suggesting the ornamental, non-productive use of land as an aesthetic setting for the mansion.

The imagery of buildings and land and their uses is important in *Mansfield Park* – the 'improving' Sotherton Court has a disused chapel, Mansfield Park is inwardly defaced by the theatre, Sir Thomas Bertram insists his son Edmund actually occupy the rectory of Thornton Lacey (apt name for the home of a genteel servant of Christ), Mary Crawford imagines the rectory there as a pretty setting for a sentimental romance, and her brother wants to 'improve' it – Fanny only wants to live there and serve its community as Edmund's wife. At the end of the novel it is clear that she will do so, and therefore that the rectory has repossessed the Park.

Thus, in the plot of *Mansfield Park* the temptation of the morally right by the courtly, the fashionable, the worldly, and the merely social is strong, and the threat to the Park and all its best values is great. Furthermore, if Mansfield Park is taken as a figure and not merely a representation of a 'real' estate, then the novel speaks directly to national concerns and national issues of social conflict and change as the Napoleonic wars reached a climax, because claims had been made since the outbreak of war in 1793 that the aristocracy were morally, financially, and socially irresponsible and thus unfit to lead a nation in times of crisis unless rejuvenated by precisely the kind of conscious moral virtue and sense of transcendental yet social calling exhibited by

Edmund Bertram and his Fanny Price. Mary and Henry Crawford, representatives of a decadent social class no longer able to lead the nation, nevertheless have a glamour that attracts even Fanny Price; certainly, Edmund Bertram is taken in, and the other inhabitants of Mansfield Park even more so. The attraction of the Crawfords for Fanny and Edmund is like the attraction of 'the World' for virtuous middle-class heroes and heroines depicted in several decades of novels of manners and emulation; indeed, the attraction of the Crawfords for Fanny and Edmund is like the attraction of novels of emulation for several decades of readers of the 'modern novel' in Britain. Ultimately, the reader, like Edmund and Fanny, must discriminate and choose; and although *Mansfield Park* is 'only a novel', on the kind of choice it enforces rests the fate of all the Mansfield Parks in the real world. Austen wrote *for* the culture and values of those Mansfield Parks; but even if one does not accept that culture and those values, the model of moral reflection and ethical action (and refusal to act) dramatized in *Mansfield Park* was of major significance in Romantic England, and, indeed, in the mainstream of English culture for the rest of the nineteenth century.

*Emma* is the only one of Austen's published novels named after its heroine, sure sign of another and characteristic shift of emphasis, from the drama of the social institution back to the drama of moral consciousness, and self-consciousness. Emma Woodhouse is a reversion to the active, clever, outspoken heroine of *Pride and Prejudice*, the heroine *not* of accurate perception and sound judgment, and thus she is an inversion of Fanny Price. A novel about Emma Woodhouse is a novel about a self rather than an estate and its culture; but as in *Mansfield Park* there is a critical relationship between the self and the estate, at least in the sense, here, of 'estate' as station and status in society. Whereas Fanny Price was a social nobody with a rich moral self and cultivated mind, Emma is the leading lady of her neighbourhood, a rich heiress, but with a rather impoverished mind (mind as defined by Samuel Johnson, including both imagination and reason, feeling and judgment, intellectual gifts or 'temper' and intellectual acquirements). She has social power without self-knowledge and self-control; inevitably, she abuses that power. She is a woman, however, and the domain of her power is 'only' domestic and matrimonial: she undertakes to make or unmake matches according to her own ideas of individuals' suitedness to each other, which includes social status. Emma also abuses her power in small ways by embarrassing those socially inferior to or weaker than herself.

As usual in Austen's novels, the parents of the heroine are absent or ineffectual (Mr Woodhouse is a hypochondriac widower), and so she lacks normal moral guidance. But she has a mentor, Mr Knightley, who turns out to be her real suitor and who is a model of the professionalized landed gentleman, and she has a contrasting female character – here, the Fanny Price type, in the person of the virtuous, taciturn, poor, but cultivated and self-disciplined Jane Fairfax. As usual, too, the story moves forward in three blocks or groups of incidents, based on a pattern of three suitors, two false and one true. Here, the narrative blocks also involve Emma's botched attempts at match-making.

First she unmakes a match between Harriet and Robert Martin (an echo of an incident in E. S. Barrett's satiric novel *The Heroine*, 1813). Martin is a tenant farmer on Knightley's estate and of whom Knightley approves (a sure sign of a professionalized gentleman is his interest in making and keeping good tenants, even to the setting them up with suitable wives). Emma's social snobbery, however, places Martin too low for Harriet and selects instead the Rev. Mr Elton, a spruce and gentleman-like young cleric. Elton mistakes Emma's encouragement of him and proposes to Emma rather than Harriet. Emma is shocked at his presumption; he is insulted that Emma thinks he can do no better than a Miss Smith; he goes away to fetch home a suitably fashionable wife, one of Austen's great creations in the line of social climbers. Emma is shamed by her own lack of perspicacity, not by her snobbery or officiousness. The next block of narrative concerns Frank Churchill and Jane Fairfax, who are secretly engaged. Emma feels shame, again, at her lack of knowledge and cultivation compared to Jane; but she flirts with Frank Churchill, and tries to engage him with Harriet. When she learns the truth of Frank's relation to Jane, she feels some concern that she has encouraged Harriet to fall in love with Frank. But when Harriet confesses she does love and believes she is loved in return, Emma is shocked again to learn that it is Knightley whom Harriet means, Knightley whom Harriet believes Emma has been encouraging her to love. At this moment, Emma realizes that she herself loves Knightley. The self-revelation is as dramatic as in *Pride and Prejudice*, though occurring much later in the novel:

> How to understand it all! How to understand the
> deceptions she had been thus practising on herself, and
> living under! – The blunders, the blindness of her own
> head and heart! – . . . she perceived that she had acted
> most weakly; that she had been imposed on by others
> [Jane and Frank] in a most mortifying degree; that she had
> been imposing on herself in a degree yet more mortifying;
> that she was wretched, and should probably find this day
> but the beginning of wretchedness. (ch. 47)

For *Emma* has a much greater sense of accumulating evil, of progression (or decline) in its plot. The pattern of Emma's folly has moved from comedy with Elton, through the sentimental with Frank Churchill, to potential heartbreak with Knightley. The reader has been privy to her thoughts throughout; in spite of her renewed resolution to change, to improve herself, to read more, to be more circumspect, and more careful, her ethical progress has been from bad to worse. Moreover, just before Harriet's revelation, Emma has shed tears for the only time in the novel when reprimanded by Knightley for indulging her superior station and wit at the expense of poor Miss Bates. By this time the reader knows Emma Woodhouse very well, knows that she is good natured, and that the punishment she seems about to suffer – a lifetime without the marriage of true minds she has learned to imagine too late – is disproportionate to her moral character, even with all her faults. Through this part of the novel the narrator does seem rather noncommital and the narrator's tone is rather flat, allowing the reader almost to forget that this is a comic universe. It would not be enough for Emma to have to suffer in silence, as Jane Fairfax and Fanny Price have and as Anne Elliot will do. Emma is an active, too active heroine; according to the moral economy of this novel she may therefore redeem herself by active virtue.

Appropriately, her act of virtue turns out to be an act of self-denial, agony in a garden, an all-too-human and romantic imitation of Christ. When Knightley visits Emma, she thinks it is to confess his love for Harriet, which Emma thinks she has unwittingly encouraged. Afraid of the pain his confession will bring her, Emma cuts him off. His 'mortification' is evident. 'Emma could not bear to give him pain. He was wishing to confide in her – perhaps to consult her; – cost her what it would, she would listen' (ch. 49). He confesses his love not for Harriet but for Emma herself. Having brought us, by use of filtered inward thought, to experience this tremendous revolution from Emma's point of view, the narrator proceeds almost immediately to put ironic distance between us and our happy heroine, for we are not allowed in Austen's novels ever to bask in sentiment and the usual reader's rewards for sympathetic identification with the heroine. For one thing, we must be prevented from feeling that marriage solves and resolves all. Emma is still misreading – how could she (or we) imagine Knightley could fall in love with Harriet? How could she (or we) be blind to Knightley's real interest (the lover-mentor is, after all, such a *cliché* in novels of the period)? No doubt, Knightley will have much to do with his wife to keep her from her follies, just as Jane Fairfax will be kept busy with her too enthusiastic and impulsive husband; but then that is what marriages are for, among other things.

The narrator has represented Emma's thoughts and her errors fairly unironically throughout the book, allowing situation and incident to expose the extent of her self-deceptions and blindness, but balancing the reader's negative judgment of Emma's mind by intimate knowledge of Emma's moral character, and encouraging us, by relative lack of ironic distancing, as in the first part of *Pride and Prejudice*, to sympathize with Emma, to feel and judge as she does. When the closure of the novel's plot is apparent for all to see, only then must we be withdrawn from readerly implication in this story of Emma Woodhouse.

*Emma* was Austen's last completed *and* finished novel, for though *Persuasion* was completed, it was not polished and worked up to the usual stylistic finish of the previous novels. As the title suggests, Austen here swings back to the novel of consciousness of the humble heroine, the heroine of true judgment from the beginning of the story. Anne Elliot's error took place before the novel begins – rejecting a worthy man on the persuasion of her 'friends'. The irony of situation here is that Anne's error is due to her feminine and youthful ductility, a virtue in woman by conventional standards. But misfortunes caused by one feminine virtue may be made good by another – faithfulness in love, a variety of female fortitude. *Persuasion*, in other words, picks up its love-story at the point, the sentimental-pathetic point Emma had reached when it appeared she had lost Knightley forever, without realizing how much or even that she did love him.

*Persuasion* also returns to the theme of decadent gentry culture regenerated by professional culture and values, and links that theme with the love story. For mighty objections to Capt. Wentworth when he first offered his hand were his profession, his lack of social distinction, and his lack of wealth. But, Capt. Wentworth has prospered in the Napoleonic wars from his share of sales of captured French ships, and he is now looking for an estate and a wife, to convert the proceeds of the entrepreneurship of war into a 'settlement' in society. By contrast, Anne's widower father, the vain and snobbish Sir Walter Elliot, has been living beyond his estate's income and is now forced to rent his manor-house of Kellynch-hall to another returning navy man, Admiral Croft, and 'retire' to Bath. Sir Walter's favourite (and only) book, significantly, is Debrett's *Baronetage of England*, his copy of which falls open from use at the page describing Sir Walter's own family. Sir Walter, then, objects to these navy men on two grounds: their outdoor life spoils their complexions; and their profession is, as he says, '"the means of bringing persons of obscure birth into undue distinction, and raising men to honours which their fathers and grandfathers never dreamt of"' (ch. 3). Against this view is set the evident *cameraderie* and wholesome, even romantic domestic character of the navy men in the novel, and the reader's knowledge, from the world outside the novel, of just how important the navy had been in saving everything English and British from destruction. In 1815 (when the novel was begun), Sir Walter's view of navy men might seem downright unpatriotic.

With these themes of love and social class established, the novel proceeds through a central section (chs 5–21) of false and misleading courtships, including what appears to be Wentworth's interest in Louisa Musgrove. Louisa is 'romantic', enthusiastic, and impulsive – just what Anne seemed to Wentworth not to be. Yet Anne can appreciate the Romantic at the same time that she sees its place, as when she advises the grieving lover Capt. Benwick *not* to read Scott's or Byron's poems because they will only agitate his emotions rather than allaying them. Then Anne's cousin, William Walter Elliot, heir-at-law to Kellynch, appears (for, as with the Bennets in *Pride and Prejudice*, the estate is entailed to the next *male* relative, and Sir Walter has only daughters). His interest in Anne seems to make Wentworth jealous, and in the climactic chapter of this section of crossing courtships, Anne has to interpret Wentworth's conduct while at a public concert in Bath (ch. 23). This set-piece is one of the most brilliant of many outstanding passages of dialogue, incident, and filtered inward speech in Austen's novels. Indeed, what makes it the more remarkable is that, whereas in her earlier novels Austen would alternate fairly long passages of dialogue and description of incident with passages of reported inward thought as the heroine reflects on the social encounter that has just passed, here in *Persuasion* and in this chapter she combines them all in quick movement of alternation from one sentence to the next.

Three chapters later the drama of courtship shifts to writing rather than – or as well as – reading, as themes of love, gender, and profession converge. When Anne and Wentworth's friend, Capt. Harville, discuss who has more constancy in love, men or women, Anne claims that women do, precisely because of society's differentiation of the sexes:

> 'We certainly do not forget you, so soon as you forget us. It is, perhaps, our fate rather than our merit. We cannot help ourselves. We live at home, quiet, confined, and our feelings prey upon us. You are forced on exertion. You have always a profession, pursuits, business of some sort or other, to take you back into the world immediately, and continual occupation and change soon weaken impressions.' (ch. 23)

This was a commonplace of the time, but Wentworth, who is sitting nearby ostensibly writing a letter, knows Anne as Harville does not, and so he can read into Anne's argument a personal as well as a general meaning (another individual revivification of a *cliché*), and this meaning can only be enriched as the dialogue continues, always on a general plane, over the next few pages. But we do not quite know that Wentworth is so reading, and we are left to read the dialogue on its general, surface level. But by the end of the dialogue, Wentworth is obviously agitated and in haste to be gone; he returns and thrusts a letter into Anne's hand, evidently the one he was writing while Anne and Harville talked. Wentworth's letter is in effect his response to Anne's remarks to Harville, his own side of a dialogue with her. He asks her if she has not 'understood' him, 'penetrated' his feelings as he has been trying to 'read' hers, during their stay at Bath. We realize, at precisely the same moment Anne does, what Wentworth had been doing, how he had been reading her when Anne had been expressing herself but not expressing herself to Harville, and to us.

Writing, in all of Austen's novels, has a power that speech, for all its power, does not, precisely because it is silent eloquence, the 'voice' of the other 'heard' when one is alone, silently reading. This is Austen's unique contribution to the epistolary tradition, the mainstream of which she, like so many other women readers, knew so well but which she, like so many women novel writers, abandoned in the 1790s. The *éclaircissement* between Wentworth and Anne takes place soon after Anne reads his letter; here there is no irony, though the narrator does withdraw gradually, and Austen may have intended to work an ironic tone into the closure. Certainly this conclusion is superior to the earlier draft that has survived, and it may be that Austen intended to give this novel a more sombre tone, as she continued to explore and to develop, to alter and to renew the repertory of themes and formal devices that was her 'stock in trade' – to use a commercial metaphor she would not, and Walter Scott would have, used.

## Notes

1. F. R. Leavis, *The Great Tradition* (1948; Harmondsworth, 1972), pp. 13–14.

2. *Jane Austen: The Critical Heritage*, edited by B. C. Southam (London and New York, 1968), pp. 126–28.

3. *Jane Austen: The Critical Heritage*, pp. 58–69.

4. See Stuart M. Tave, *Some Words of Jane Austen* (1973), and Susan Morgan, *In the Meantime: Character and Perception in Jane Austen's Fiction* (Chicago and London, 1980).

5. See Margaret Kirkham, *Jane Austen, Feminism and Fiction* (Brighton and Totowa, New Jersey, 1983), and Mary Poovey, *The Proper Lady and the Woman Writer: Ideology as Style in the Works of Mary Wollstonecraft, Mary Shelley, and Jane Austen* (Chicago and London, 1984), ch. 6.

6. See David Monaghan, 'Jane Austen and the Position of Women', in *Jane Austen in a Social Context*, edited by David Monaghan (London and Totowa, New Jersey, 1981), pp. 105–21, and Gilbert Ryle, 'Jane Austen and the Moralists', in *Critical Essays on Jane Austen*, edited by B. C. Southam (1986), pp. 106–22.

7. *Jane Austen's Letters to her Sister Cassandra and Others*, edited by R. W. Chapman, 2nd corrected edition (Oxford, 1959), p. 38; to Cassandra Austen, 18 Dec. 1798.

8. See Mary Lascelles, *Jane Austen and Her Art* (Oxford, 1939), p. 41; see also Kenneth L. Moler, *Jane Austen's Art of Allusion* (Lincoln Nebraska, 1968), and Frank W. Bradbrook, *Jane Austen and Her Predecessors* (Cambridge, 1966).

9. See Donald Greene, 'The Myth of Limitation', in *Jane Austen Today*, edited by Joel Weinsheimer (Athens Georgia, 1975), pp. 142–75.

10. *Letters*, edited by R. W. Chapman, pp. 468–69; 16 Dec. 1816.

11. *Letters*, edited by R. W. Chapman, p. 452; to James Stanier Clarke, 1 Apr. 1816.

12. *Letters*, edited by R. W. Chapman, p. 401; 19 Sept. 1814.

13. See Howard S. Babb, *Jane Austen's Novels: The Fabric of Dialogue* (Columbus Ohio, 1962).

14. John Odmark, *An Understanding of Jane Austen's Novels: Character, Value and Ironic Perspective* (Oxford, 1981), p. 90. See also Daniel Cottom, *The Civilized Imagination: A Study of Ann Radcliffe, Jane Austen, and Sir Walter Scott* (Cambridge, 1985), p. 86, where Austen is seen as depicting her heroines in an impossible situation, epistemologically and socially.

15. See J. P. Hardy, *Jane Austen's Heroines: Intimacy in Human Relationships*, (1984).

16. *Letters*, edited by R. W. Chapman, pp. 299–300, 395–96.

17. See Patricia Voss-Clesly, *Tendencies of Character Depiction in the Domestic Novels of Burney, Edgeworth, and Austen: A Consideration of Subjective and Objective World*, 3 vols (Salzburg, 1979).

18. Norman Page, *The Language of Jane Austen* (Oxford, 1972), pp. 123–36.

19. See Marvin Mudrick, *Jane Austen: Irony as Defense and Discovery* (Princeton New Jersey, 1952).

20. See D. D. Devlin, *Jane Austen and Education* (1975).

21. See Peter L. de Rose and S. W. McGuire, *A Concordance to the Works of Jane Austen*, 3 vols (New York and London, 1982).

22. On her preference for Johnson, see the 'Biographical Notice' of her by Henry Austen (*Northanger Abbey* and *Persuasion*, edited by John Davie and James

Kinsley (1971), p. 5). See also *Letters*, edited by R. W. Chapman, p. 406; 28 Sept. 1814; and D. D. Devlin, *Jane Austen and Education*, chs 1 and 3.

23. Donald Davie, *The Purity of Diction in English Verse* (1952, 1967), p. 5.

24. Martin Price, *Forms of Life: Character and Moral Imagination in the Novel* (New Haven and London, 1983), p. 67, somewhat overstating the case.

25. *Letters*, edited by R. W. Chapman, p. 298; to Cassandra Austen, 29 Jan. 1813.

26. Q. D. Leavis and B. C. Southam disagree on this; see 'A Critical Theory of Jane Austen's Writings', in Q. D. Leavis, *Collected Essays*, vol. I (Cambridge, 1983), pp. 61–146 (originally published in *Scrutiny*, vols x and xII); B. C. Southam, *Jane Austen's Literary Manuscripts: A Study of the Novelist's Development* (1964), pp. 136–48.

27. See A. M. Duckworth, *The Improvement of the Estate* (Baltimore, 1971).

28. See Lionel Trilling, 'Mansfield Park', in *The Opposing Self*, and reprinted in *Jane Austen: Sense and Sensibility, Pride and Prejudice, and Mansfield Park: A Casebook*, edited by B. C. Southam (London and Basingstoke, 1976); see also the essays by D. W. Harding and Kingsley Amis in the same collection for other examples of misreading Fanny Price.

29. *Letters*, edited by R. W. Chapman, p. 410; to Fanny Knight, 18 Nov. 1814.

# Chapter 5
# History and Romance: Sir Walter Scott

## 'A Castle-Building Romance Writer & Poet'

When in 1823 Maria Edgeworth visited Abbotsford, the fake castle which Scott was building with the profits of his novel writing, she wrote admiringly if somewhat ambiguously, 'All the work is so solid you would never guess it was by a castle-building romance writer & poet.'[1] To the privacy of his journal, Scott confessed pride in his prose romances, and in their success. On one occasion he imagines his 'genie' recommending regular exercise in 'castle building', for 'Life were not life without it', to which Scott replies, complacently, 'I reckon myself one of the best aerial architects now living'.[2] Yet he was puzzled at the enormous success of his novels and by the nature and apparently inexhaustible resources of his creative imagination. He compared the latter to the magical powers possessed by heroes of the chapbooks he had devoured as a boy, or, more like an Enlightenment 'philosopher', he tried to account for them in terms of some as yet ill-understood physiological process.[3] Publicly, Scott adopted an attitude at once slightly self-mocking yet at the same time aware of the reality of literature as part of a market economy.

For example, in the preface to *The Fortunes of Nigel* (1822) he has 'the Author' discourse on the art of the novel with one of his creatures, Capt. Clutterbuck, in the language of 'political economy', manufacture, and the industrial revolution. In the preface to *The Betrothed* (1825), Scott as the 'image' of the author even proposes to build a novel-manufacturing machine and to incorporate all his fictional personæ into a company 'to carry on a joint-stock trade in fictitious narrative, in prose and verse'. When they refuse, he threatens to turn to more solid productions:

'  – I will leave you and your whole hacked stock in trade
   – your caverns and your castles – your modern antiques,
   and your antiquated moderns – your confusion of times,

> manners, and circumstances – your properties, as player-
> folk say of scenery and dresses . . . . in a word, I will
> write HISTORY!'

For Scott, as for Austen, the phrase 'only a novel' had ironic significance. Whereas Austen met the problem of the low moral and artistic status of the 'modern novel' by a critical use of certain fictional conventions, Scott met the problem by appropriating elements of the major narrative, descriptive, and critical discourse of the late Enlightenment – historiography. What is more important, and as he knew very well, during his career as a novelist Scott demonstrated to more people than ever before – in Europe and America as well as in Britain – that the novel had literary potential of the highest order and that it was an ideological discourse of the first importance in constructing a new kind of national culture, one that comprised both 'national' history and 'national' literature and one that Scott himself wished to make the basis for the education of Britain's leaders of the future.[4] Thus Scott, like Austen, but in a different way, also responded to the social crises of the Romantic period by turning the novel into literature made and fit for a coalition of gentry and professional middle classes.

In a sense, Scott was a novel-making machine, unwittingly designed by half a lifetime's reading, professional activity, social experience and observation, and by considerable experience and success as a poet, to build the new literary institution of the novel as the main element of a new kind of national culture based on print. His mind was well stocked with Scottish Enlightenment history and sociology, Enlightenment ideas of progress, the social construction of reality, criticism of court culture, criticism of 'superstition' and 'prejudice', and cultural, political, and economic 'modernization'. He was well read in the Bible, popular chapbook literature, and 'classic' English literature. He was well versed in oral popular culture – folk poetry, folk tale, proverbial lore, popular traditions, and what were then called 'popular antiquities'. He was well enough trained in Scottish law, with its common law tradition of communal values, standards, and responsibilities; he was well-informed about the literature of the day, including the manufacture and marketing of literature, the public taste, and so on. He was well-informed, well-connected, and deeply interested in the politics and related issues of his time. And he was an inveterate, skilled, and habitual anecdotalist and storyteller. It would seem Scott had little to do but let his imagination combine and re-combine these elements, every now and again by an effort of will shifting emphasis one way or another, to produce novel after novel that spoke forcefully and directly to the interests, in several senses, of the novel-reading classes, especially men in professional, intellectual, and political life.[5]

For whereas Austen focused on the realm of the domestic, the familial, and the local – by no means, as we have seen, peripheral issues in Romantic culture and ideology, whether conservative or liberal – Scott emphasized the public and wider social roles and involvements of individual men and women. More particularly, Scott achieved an ideologically motivated but especially effective combination of language, literature, and history in the form of the Waverley Novels – the English language in its many but hierarchically structured varieties, under the recently standardized written language; literature as the continuing yet stable form of the 'national' language, embodied in texts ranging from the 'classics' of the past to the 'modern novel' of the present; and history as the central discourse of professional, Enlightenment culture, attacking unreason and the *ancien régime* and constructing a narrative of 'national' origins, the historical vicissitudes of an entire, 'national' society, and the grand historical plot of 'progress'.[6]

Thus Scott's novels, in the way they treat the past, are about the immediate present and future of Scotland, of Britain, and the Christian West – largely as imagined by Edmund Burke in his French Revolution tracts. Scott's principal subject in his first eight novels is the 'modernization' of Scottish society, that is, its transformation, through a series of historical crises, from a society that was agrarian, aristocratic, court-dominated, feudal, often fanatically religious, mainly oral, lacking in effective public institutions, and based on personal loyalties, to a society that is open, urban as well as rural, gentry-dominated, capitalist, professionalized, rational, literate, with more effective public institutions (especially the law), and with a strong sense of 'national' identity and interest transcending class differences. For Scott, the key points in this history were the seventeenth-century Civil War, the Restoration of the monarchy, the breakdown of order during the 'killing time', the restoration of social harmony with the Glorious Revolution of 1688, the Union of England and Scotland in 1707 (the necessary basis for Scottish economic development and modernization, but also the precondition for the professionalization of Scottish society), the 1715 Jacobite rebellion (attempting to reverse developments since 1688), the Porteous Riots (a symbol of the persistence of old loyalties), the 1745 Jacobite rebellion, the gradual modernization of Scotland, the threat of disorder again with the 1790s and the Napoleonic wars, and finally the future development of social reconciliation under the social leadership of an enlightened, professional, responsible landed gentry working with cultivated professional men. Most of Scott's Scottish novels are set in these significant turning-points:

The 'Killing Time': *Old Mortality* (1816)
The Union: *The Bride of Lammermoor* (1819)
The 'Fifteen': *Rob Roy* (1817)
The Porteous Riots: *The Heart of Midlothian* (1818)
The 'Forty-Five': *Waverley* (1814)
The Period of 'Modernization': *Redgauntlet* (1824);
  *Guy Mannering* (1815); possibly *The Pirate* (1821)
The Threat to Stability: *The Antiquary* (1816); possibly
  *St. Ronan's Well* (1823)

Most of these novels are also, significantly, among Scott's best, and most were produced during the first five years of his career as a novelist.

Even though Scott's first eight novels were about Scotland, however, they could be taken by readers in other parts of Britain, as Maria Edgeworth's Irish tales had been, to apply to British society in general. In 1819, moreover, Scott turned away from the matter of Scotland, to treat issues of social and cultural conflict in Medieval England and Christendom, and most of the novels he wrote during the remainder of his life were set neither in Scotland nor in the period of living memory and oral transmission. Scott's novels of the 1820s are partly responses to the popularity and the innovations of other novelists, particularly novelists of passion or extreme individualism, novelists of 'historical romance', and novelists of the exotic and alien. Nevertheless, his own subject continued to be social conflict and compromise, the relation of the individual to historical change, and – increasingly in the 1820s – the dangers of excessive individualism yet the need for heroism and leadership on both the domestic and the public planes in order to achieve a stable, just, and secure society. For in all of his novels Scott's first point of reference, explicit or implicit, is his own present and the immediate future of Britain. There could be no more 'solid' work for 'a castle-building romance writer and poet', no more interesting subject for his many readers.

## History and Romance

How did Scott build his castles? Like Abbotsford, they are composed of diverse elements. On one hand there is an intellectual and scholarly conception of history, rendered through authoritative narration, with footnotes and documents, and on the other dramatically and energetically presented descriptions, episodes, characters, and details, rich in symbolic or emblematic resonance, but often only loosely strung together in a plotted sequence. On one hand there is this poetic, figural mode of representation, and on the other a detailed, descriptive mode of 'realistic' representation relying on the convention that realism is achieved by superfluous detail and particularity. Such realism, Scott thought, was the special achievement of Defoe and Richardson, and essential to the successful historical romance.[7] Yet Scott declared that 'Every successful novelist must be more or less a poet, even although he may never have written a line of verse', and he argued that the two requisites for the highest form of historical romance were a 'poetical imagination, and a strict attention to the character and manners' of the age depicted,[8] that is, historical realism. The conclusion – supported by Scott's own remarks on the novels of others – is that for a reader both to perceive the full significance of any part of a Waverley Novel and grasp the overall unity of its structure he or she should have familiarity with the two most prestigious discourses of literary culture during the Romantic period, that is, poetry and historiography.

Scott's plots also fuse literary and historical discourse. He usually turned to romance or tragicomedy for his plot forms. He was familiar with Medieval and Renaissance verse romance – the knight's excursion into a more or less alien world in quest of something or other, and in the process of which he is 'proven', that is, his moral character is tested and shown to accord more or less with his knightly social status.[9] Scott also knew the later romances or novels that varied this pattern with the revelation of true parentage at the end so that social status is finally shown to conform to demonstrated nobility of mind and soul, as in novels by Fielding and Smollett. Fanny Burney and Jane Austen, both of whom Scott admired greatly, wrote female versions of this romance. Furthermore, Scott was well acquainted with the dramatic counterparts of the romance, Renaissance tragicomedy and Restoration Heroic Drama, which deal with noble characters and the intermingling of court politics and domestic relations, which display strong passions, especially ambition on one hand and self-sacrifice on the other, which emphasize fortitude and endurance and long suffering, and which have a more or less happy ending. For what the Scott protagonist learns or what the world in the novel recognizes in the protagonist is a fusion of gentry and middle-class values, the gentry elements being distributed to the social standing of the protagonist, the middle-class elements going to his or her inward, moral and intellectual character.

This 'lesson' of the romance journey is then inserted into the novel's second, implicit plot, the plot of progress in history. Whereas the protagonist's plot is usually a journey and a return, the plot of history is one of dialectical resolution and progress, rather resembling the grand design of history proposed by Scottish Enlightenment 'philosophical historians'. Nevertheless, tensions between romance and history remain. Scott often registers a sense of nostalgia or incorporates an elegy for values, ways of life, and individuals necessarily lost in the historical plot of progress from savagery to civilization. Like so many professional men of his time, Scott, the greatest inventor of 'tradition' of the Romantic period, perhaps of the nineteenth century, felt the glamour of 'antient chivalry' and the charm of the oral community that he was arguing against in his fictions. There is another ambiguity in his romance plots, too. The romance journey often takes the form of a departure from home, an excursion into the public, social, and historical planes of experience, and a return to a home, often with a new wife or husband. But the returner is often sadder but wiser, and there remains the feeling that though the protagonist's re-entry into the normal social structure of quotidian and domestic 'reality' is desirable and necessary, the excursion into history was a heroic and more intense, a 'romantic' experience never to be equalled. The question then is, which is the fundamental, the determining reality – home or the journey, domesticity or romance? Or are both somehow necessary to the fully developed, historically conscious mind able to make out its own, and its society's destiny?

For, significantly, the protagonist in Scott's novels (hero or heroine) seems to have little idea where history is taking him or her, and the novels are full of episodes in which the protagonist gets lost, is benighted, has a concealed identity, is abducted, confined, or used as a tool by others, or has to rely upon the superior knowledge and power of others. The protagonist is certainly no source of authoritative understanding of the history being made around and through him or her. History is fully accessible only to the authoritative narrator and his peer, the reader. Thus there are two separate planes of historical experience and knowledge in the Waverley Novels – that of the protagonist, floundering in darkness and ignorance, and that of the omniscient narrator, explaining what no single character in the novel, nor all the characters collectively, could possibly know.

Yet the narrator in the Waverley Novels, especially in the Scottish novels, frequently compares the past in the novel with the present of the novel and its readers. This device suggests a continuity between historical hindsight and contemporary overview, the possibility that one such as the narrator may know his own present the way he knows the past. Somehow the present, which engulfs almost all the characters within each novel, cannot reach the narrator, even as his own present. There are, it is true, would-be overviewers within the novels; but these are plotters and intriguers, such as Fergus Mac-Ivor in *Waverley*, Rashleigh Osbaldistone in *Rob Roy*, Redgauntlet in the novel of that title, or Cromwell or Rochecliffe in *Woodstock*; or they are benevolent and forward-looking *dei ex machina*, such as Argyle in *The Heart of Midlothian* or Anne of Geierstein in the novel of that title; or they are actual visionaries and prophets, witches or astrologers such as Meg Merrilies and Guy Mannering in *Guy Mannering* or 'wise women' such as blind Alice in *The Bride of Lammermoor*. The intriguers and the wizards are, on the whole, discredited; only the historically conscious progressives receive the approval of the narrator; yet, paradoxically, their instrumentality in the destiny of the protagonist and the plot of history is often accidental or fortuitous or too good to be plausible. Moreover, the importance of these transcendental characters in breaking through the impasse in the plot only serves to emphasize further the helplessness of the protagonist in the face of history.

In short, the progressive plot of history and its authoritative, historically conscious narrator seem to be resisted by a number of other elements in the Waverley Novels – the plot of romance, the play with narrative personæ, the evident energy of those things which 'modernization' abolishes (such as oral culture, 'antient chivalry', superstition, strong belief, and feudal loyalty), the subjection of the protagonist to forces or powers beyond his or her control, the failure of plotters, the irrationality and obscurity of prophecy, and, frequently, the victimization or relative powerlessness of those within the novel who do have some idea of where the future does or should lie. Significantly, these anticipators of the future are often women characters and they seem to act on an innately if conventionally female principle of reconciliation rather than on a conventionally masculine informed and thoughtful historical awareness. On the other hand, as we have seen, the world of romance adventure and the world of domesticity often seem far apart or even at odds in the Waverley Novels, and women who do venture into the realm of politics and the romance of history, such as Flora Mac-Ivor in *Waverley*, Lady Ashton in *The Bride of Lammermoor*, or Margaret of Anjou in *Anne of Geierstein*, suffer for it or cause suffering for others. The good women stay at home, or venture on the romance journey as a last resort and for limited, domestic reasons, as does Jeanie Deans in *The Heart of Midlothian*. Even if they stay at home, however, the good women such as Lucy Ashton in *The Bride of Lammermoor* or Amy Robsart in *Kenilworth* may become victims of political women and ambitious men. Problems of the relation of history and romance thus draw in not only aspects of narrative method, character repertory, and characterization, but also issues of gender in relation to society, social change, and historical progress.

The problematic nature of the relationship of history and romance is increased, not lessened by Scott's celebrated mastery of the episode and his deployment of description. Certainly the widespread perception in Scott's own day that he was a revolutionary novelist, and not just a˙ rearranger of the achievements of his predecessors, centred on two aspects of the Waverley Novels – their powerful and memorable episodes, characters, and details, and their handling of historical realism through description. Scott aimed at the vivacity of episode and characterization achieved, he thought, by Le Sage, Fielding, and Smollett; but his handling of these things is different from theirs and anticipates that of major Victorian novelists, such as Dickens and the Brontës, and that of Scott's own greatest admirer, George Eliot. Like those novelists and the Romantic narrative poets – of whom Scott himself was one, and the most successful in his lifetime, next to Byron – Scott can give his episodes a kind of symbolic resonance or emblematic significance that one associates with Richardson rather than Fielding among the earlier novelists, with the long tradition of English narrative poetry, which Scott knew well, and with the Romantic art-ballad, with which Scott had toyed in the 1790s and which he developed into his own enormously successful narrative poems after 1800.[10] In his descriptive set-pieces Scott does combine authoritative, historically conscious narrative with symbolic representation of persons, places, objects, gestures, and actions, sharp characterization and dialogue, and dramatic incident. He manages to combine realistic description with figural suggestiveness, representing a whole set of values or social practices in a setting, action, or character. The very energy and vitality of representation and richness of suggestion in such episodes and details could, however, make much of the rest of the particular novel seem slack and, worse still, make the novel seem merely a loose sequence of episodes.

There can be little doubt that Scott was both a major poet and major novelist of description in the Romantic period, and he himself saw 'description and narration' as 'the essence of the novel'.[11] As he said (after reading a novel by James Fenimore Cooper), 'so people once take an interest in a description they will swallow a great deal which they do not understand'.[12] But description is used scrupulously by Scott, and only seldom as filler or mere spectacle, at least in the Scottish novels and the better medieval novels. In common with his time, Scott had a profoundly political and moral attitude to the material objects of life, state or domestic, and to the shape of the physical environment in which people lived. He had an acute interest in and good practical knowledge of such major aspects of gentry culture as landscape, architecture, and rural 'improvement', and he also shared the Enlightenment interest in the relation of topography and climate to 'national character' and economic life. Those novels set in remoter times and foreign climes required more description than some of the earlier novels, and seem to many critics to be not much more than costume melodramas in prose, counterparts to the costume melodramas so popular in the theatres in the 1810s and 1820s. In fact, some of Scott's novels, particularly *Guy Mannering, Rob Roy*, and *Ivanhoe*, were quickly made into highly successful theatrical pieces – Scott referred to them as his 'literary grandchildren' – and later, of course, into grand operas such as *I Puritani* (from *Woodstock*) and *Lucia di Lammermoor* (from *The Bride of Lammermoor*). Scott proved himself to be an able manager of spectacle in real life, and spectacle was always an important element in the popularity of the Waverly Novels and their offshoots.

The descriptive material deployed by Scott is of several types, much of it found already in 'Gothic romance' of the 1790s and 1800s and 'national tales' of the 1800s and 1810s: topographical description, historical background, local and antiquarian description, and various kinds of furniture and costume. This kind of fictionalized encyclopaedia of past times Scott knew already from his work completing the antiquarian Joseph Strutt's novel *Queenhoo-Hall* (1808). Scott didn't care much for this kind of animated–museum work, thought it for 'men more desirous of information than mere amusement', and resolved not to practise it himself.[13] Nor was he particularly charmed by description and atmospherics for subjective consciousness of the kind practised by Ann Radcliffe and Charlotte Smith. Scott's intellectual inheritance in deployment of description was that of Scottish Enlightenment social history and sociological explanation, a ground of historiography he shared to some extent with the English Jacobin novelist William Godwin. If Scott did not go quite as far as Godwin in arguing that social circumstances and institutions determine individual character, he at least believed that growth and exercise of individuality was always constrained by social circumstances and institutions, including institutions of belief and value. This attitude left him closer to the position of Burke than of Godwin.

So prominent is description in Scott's novels that it displaces plot and absorbs character (including dialogue). In the first place, history in Scott's novels is largely constituted as dense descriptive material which is apparently, for the historical moment in which the novel is set, relatively fixed and unchanging, and the plot of historical change lies outside the framework of the individual novel, only intimated by the authoritative and omniscient narrator. Within the novel, the plot concerns significant change only in the destiny, the turning point of the biography of one individual or group of individuals, who, as we have seen, usually do not or cannot see the larger plot of history, immersed as they are (and as the reader partly is) in the richly described and represented setting of the novel. Jeanie Deans in *The Heart of Midlothian* does not know or knows only dimly that she is contributing to the 'modernization' of Scotland, through the agency of the Duke of Argyle; Henry Gow in *The Fair Maid of Perth* does not know that he is participating in the transition from a martial to a mercantile society. But the reader does know, and thus the point of view from which understanding of the descriptive material and its relation to plot and character takes place is the implicitly transcendental, extra-historical vantage point of the reader and the narrator. In the second place, the absorption of character and dialogue by description results in a significant distribution of meaning and value amongst the characters in the novel. Most characters are part of the setting; as such they are socially (and historically) representative, and thus they are not individuals with individuality that extends beyond 'merely' social and external attributes of class, region, and speech; and their personal idiosyncracies (often brilliantly realized and memorable) are presented as the result of their particular social and historical location.

Language is particularly important here because dialogue, including dialect, sociolect, and idiolect, as well as characteristic speech, is one of Scott's chief methods of characterization, as he points out in the first chapter of *The Bride of Lammermoor*. There were problems when Scott went back in time or out in geographical space beyond societies roughly similar or plausibly related to those of the majority of his readers, for in these cases Scott did not know what linguistic relativities existed in the past and had to rely on his reader's ability to recognize transcribed 'speech' from the historical fictions that preceded him, principally dramatic literature, and the result was a great deal of what the later nineteenth-century Scottish writer Robert Louis Stevenson called 'tushery' – versions of 'speech' heavily laced with such bookish expressions as 'tush', 'forsooth', and so on.[14] Furthermore, even subjectivity, that master-theme of Romantic fiction, especially in the 1810s and 1820s when Scott was publishing the Waverley Novels, is absorbed into the historical descriptive terrain by means of the distribution of language, but in a paradoxical way. Only characters who 'speak' in standard English are allowed much subjectivity, and of such speakers the ones who use bombast or excessively literary language usually have little or no subjective self. And yet the most self-expressive characters, the ones with the most 'character', seem usually to be dialect speakers. Scott himself was wary of subjectivity and cured himself of too much of it by large doses of socializing. He also believed that Byron was far better than he was at representing subjectivity – 'he *bet* [i.e., beat] me out of the field in the description of the passions, and in deep-seated knowledge of the human heart', Scott told an acquaintance just before he died.[15] The problem is, how can the historical novel of description make characters seem both socially representative and richly, autonomously subjective?

Scott's representation of society accords with the understanding of society and especially class relations common in his time. If he was suspicious of mere subjectivity he was also suspicious of the merely social, be it the world of fashion and courtly surface or the world of unindividuated or deindividualized social action, especially the 'mob'. One of the noticeably 'progressive' elements in Scott is his critical treatment of court culture and politics, especially court intrigue, the 'mistress system' or 'backstairs politics', the selfishness and damaging competitiveness of courtiers, and the way these negative social values and practices filter down through the rest of society. In spite of his evident admiration for certain aspects of feudal culture, most of Scott's novels display the negative aspects of the decadent feudalism of court politics – perhaps a link between Scott's work and that of the English author he admired most, Shakespeare, from whose plays, especially the English histories and Roman plays, he quotes often and usually with rich political allusiveness.

At the same time, in spite of his evident sympathy for the hardships of the common people and his admiration for the vitality and solidarity of traditional popular culture, Scott, like Shakespeare, tends to depict the lower classes as individually comical and collectively menacing. Like most middle- and upper-class men of his time he did not fully understand the 'moral economy' of the common people, much less the psychology of the individual still within such a collective, 'pre-modern' social order. Yet Scott was one of the most astute and comprehensive recorders of action based on such a 'moral economy' (though he does fall back on the outside agitator explanation for collective action such as the Porteous riots, in common with many Anti-Jacobin writers of his day), just as he was, for his time, an astute and perceptive recorder of popular oral culture in his *Minstrelsy of the Scottish Border* (1802–03) and elsewhere. Indeed, a major element in Scott's fiction and in his 'realism' is his use of popular culture, superstition, folklore, folksay, and the rootedness of lower-class individuals, even when socially marginal (beggars, village 'wise women', wanderers of various kinds), in a communal culture, even though his attitude to this 'pre-modern' culture is that of the progressive and rational man of the Scottish Enlightenment.

## The 'Scotch Novels': *Waverley* to *The Bride of Lammermoor*

*Waverley; or, 'Tis Sixty Years Since* (1814), the first of the Waverley Novels and the one that gave them their collective name, displays clearly the conflict of romance and reality-as-history. It also contains the major themes, the character repertory, the deployment of language, the narrative method, the use of description, the kind of strengths and weaknesses found in the serried array that followed through the next eighteen years. The novel is dedicated to Henry Mackenzie, one of the masters of Sentimental fiction, and the hero of Scott's novel is perhaps a cross between Mackenzie's too-susceptible men of feeling and Fielding's Tom Jones, with elements of the too-trusting idealistic heroes of Anti-Jacobin novels. Like *Tom Jones, Waverley* is in some ways a picaresque romance: it sets a naive, good-natured protagonist on a journey of misadventures; it displays a wide range of social classes and professions; it has an authoritative, omniscient, and somewhat intrusive narrator; it has the hero's spontaneous acts of charity play a role in his eventual redemption; it exposes the nature of courtly intrigue; it depicts the landed gentry as in need of some reform and reorganization if they are properly to fulfil their social responsibilities, and it is set in the turmoil of the 1745 Jacobite rebellion in favour of 'Bonnie Prince Charlie', or the 'Young Pretender', Charles Edward Stuart. Scott also takes advantage, however, of the work of writers of 'national tales' in the 1800s and early 1810s: he re-organizes Fielding's and Mackenzie's character repertories and the romance plot to fit in with greater emphasis on the national historical event; he adds great quantities of historical, social, and topographical descriptive material; he adds the historical perspective of past, present, and future; and he concentrates on the collision of different cultures and 'mentalities'.[16]

In short, he thoroughly historicizes, according to his own version of Scottish Enlightenment 'philosophical history', the fictional elements he chose to take over from others. As Scott himself admitted, the descriptive material at times deflects the plot, which is in any case heavily dependent on circumstance and coincidence. This would be all right if Scott were offering a circumstantial, sceptical, and ironic view of history and social change, but he is not. Rather, his aim is to depict the play of contending social-historical forces and values – feudalism and 'modernization'; court culture and an independent, socially self-conscious gentry; Catholicism and Protestantism; religious zeal and a secular order of toleration and pluralism; Highland and Lowland Scotland; English and Scottish attitudes and ways of life; 'romance' and 'realism'; selfless heroism and worldly self-interest; decadent gentry and 'pushing' middle class; masculine and feminine social roles – the list could go on. What makes *Waverley* such a richly textured novel for its time, and superior to most 'national tales', is the interplay of these different forces throughout the narrative.

His next novel, *Guy Mannering; or, The Astrologer* (1815), is not really a historical novel, but rather a study of the old-style Scottish gentry trying, in the late eighteenth century, to apply 'modern' policies of 'improvement' and consequently breaking up the old ideological and cultural solidarity of the different ranks and classes in 'pre-modern' rural society. The estate is almost taken over by a grasping, conniving professional man (another echo of *Castle Rackrent*) before timely revelations and the work of benevolent mediators set the situation to rights. In *The Antiquary* (1816), Scott brought these same themes down to the 1790s and replaced the conniving professional man with a German Jacobin and spurious alchemist, Dousterswivel, based on the villains of Anti-Jacobin novels of the late 1790s. This villain, too, preys on the foolish aristocracy and gentry, just as Burke had warned in his *Letter to a Noble Lord* (1796). Again, timely revelations overturn the villain's plans, effect social reconciliations and restorations, and conclude in a marriage of the hero and heroine. The 'hero' and 'heroine' here are, as often in Scott's novels, rather secondary and uninteresting characters, as they are in Shakespeare's late romances, which furnished Scott with important formal models at this period of his career as a novelist.

Scott's next publication comprises two novels together, *The Black Dwarf* and *Old Mortality*, as the first set of four series of 'Tales of My Landlord' (1816), for here Scott began experimenting with a variety of more or less pedantic and comic frame narrators or 'editors', as if to distance the romantic fictions one more remove. In 'Tales of My Landlord' the text is supposed to be assembled by Peter Pattieson, village antiquarian, and edited by Jedediah Cleishbotham, village schoolmaster of Gandercleugh (Jedediah: one of the names of Solomon, wisdom of the ages; Cleishbotham: Scots for flog-bottom, apt name for a schoolmaster[17]). Certainly one of Scott's best novels, *Old Mortality* goes back to the late seventeenth century to examine the conflict of religious and political fanaticisms remaining from the Civil War period of the 1640s and 1650s, between Presbyterian Coven-anters and aristocratic Royalists, a conflict in which, as often in Scott, class conflict is subsumed under religious or cultural clashes, while various mediating forces try to establish a civil order that will reconcile such divisions or hold them in a larger framework of socially progressive pluralism and national interest. But since the seventeenth-century conflicts were seen throughout the Romantic period as an analogy to and warning about contemporary conflicts, *Old Mortality* in a sense develops the social study embodied in *The Antiquary*; not surprisingly, those who did not share Scott's conservative views of past and present were offended at the depiction of those seventeenth-century Jacobins, the Covenanters, and several fictional ripostes were published, including James Hogg's *The Brownie of Bodsbeck* (1818).

In *Rob Roy* (1817; dated 1818) Scott returned to Scotland and the

Stuarts, setting his novel in the period of the rebellion of 1715, and focusing on the collision of three different sets of values: those of 'traditional' society (represented by Rob Roy and the Highlanders), those of court society (represented by Rashleigh Osbaldistone, the pro-Stuart courtly intriguer), and those of the urban mercantile spirit (represented by the father of the novel's hero Frank Osbaldistone, and, in a more comic vein, by Bailie Nicol Jarvie, the Glasgow merchant who is yet a cousin of Rob Roy). Here, too, Scott shifted narrative mode, to the first-person autobiographical mode of the Waverley-character, Frank, who ranges the margin between the mercantile class and the gentry as well as the wilds of the Highlands and the secret passages of courtly intrigue, and who finally settles down, as Waverley did, a landed gentleman with a suitable wife. *Rob Roy* was also one of many but one of the most successful of Scott's novels to be dramatized or melodramatized, in a process Scott called 'Terry-fying', after his long-time friend, the theatre manager Daniel Terry.

The second series of 'Tales of My Landlord', and perhaps Scott's finest novel, *The Heart of Midlothian* (1818), depicts Scotland in the decades after the Act of Union and before the 'Forty-Five'. It plots the relation of a public event to individual and common lives within the larger historical plot of the 'modernization' of Scotland, set in three historical layers: the 'killing time' or persecution of the Presbyterian Covenanters during the 1680s (the youth of Davie Deans), the Porteous riots of 1736 and their aftermath (the actions of Jeanie Deans and her sister Effie), and the present of the novel and its readers. The point of view is that of the present, but the fanaticism of Covenanters and Royalists in the 1680s is threatening to revive in the 1730s and is implicitly to be compared to the renewed threats to social order in the post-Napoleonic period of economic depression in Britain. The larger historical matrix in which the Porteous riots are set again brings into play a historical commonplace of the 1790s and early 1800s – a parallel between the civil disorders of these decades and the period of the Civil War in the seventeenth century, as seen already, for example, in Godwin's *Caleb Williams* and Scott's *Old Mortality*.

But Scott enriches this historical framework with many other themes of social conflict and reconciliation – monarchists (old Dumbiedikes) versus Covenanters (Davie Deans), town (the Edinburgh 'chorus') versus country (St Leonard's), metropolis (London) versus provinces (Scotland), court (Queen Caroline) versus public opinion (the people of Edinburgh), law (the trial scene, the Tolbooth) versus revenge (Meg Murdockson), social community (Knocktarlitie) versus individualism (Robertson/Staunton), moderates (Bailie Middleburgh, Reuben Butler) versus fanatics (Davie Deans), 'folk' culture (including superstition) versus rationalism, old-style gentry (Dumbiedikes) versus the progressive (the Duke of Argyle), the civilized (Knocktarlitie) versus the savage (the Whistler), the public (the riot, royal policy) versus the domestic (the Deans family, intrigues in the royal family), court life (Effie and Staunton) versus middle-class life (Jeanie and Reuben), and so on. It is important to note, then, that these contrasting or conflicting pairs do not always represent a positive and negative value, but rather values relative to one another and partly validated or appraised by the story as well as by the authoritative narrator. There is, in fact, much social and historical relativism in the Waverley Novels, though Scott's historical vision is not a sceptical or relativist one.

The framework of the narration, in the preamble by Jedediah Cleishbotham, also has considerable interest in contrasting yet linking law and fiction in the dialogue of the gentleman-like young lawyers, Halkit and Hardie, as they discuss 'the Heart of Midlothian' – the Tolbooth prison in Edinburgh – as a suitable subject for study of human passions and motives (if only the walls could speak. . .). Halkit claims that Hardie hides novels of the day among the law books on his desk. Interest in humanity breaks in on their professional pursuits; since the Scottish law tradition is one of precedent and common law (community standards codified) and places the individual in relation to social and community values, and since a novel worth reading would also study the individual in society, then law and novels could have much in common after all. Furthermore, novels and 'the Heart of Midlothian' represent, as it were, different ends of the spectrum of social institutions that bear upon individual lives and destinies: novels usually depict the individual in relation to a variety of social conventions and ideological forces; the prison represents social convention codified into law and solidified into stone walls, society's exercise of main force on the individual.

Finally, the Tolbooth itself is depicted as a historical institution; its history is the history of Scotland, for it was once the meeting place of the Scottish parliament, once held the law courts, was once King James's place of refuge during a religious uprising, and it is now to be demolished and replaced by a modern prison – in fact it was demolished the year before Scott's novel was published. (The new prison, finally built in the 1820s, was designed with a modern interior but an exterior in a fake-gothic style inspired by, of all things, the Waverley Novels.)

If the Tolbooth is the dominating social and historical symbol in *The Heart of Midlothian*, the centre of the action is a woman who represents not the public, the legal, and the historical, but the domestic, the personal, the immediately affective – Jeanie Deans. Like many Gothic novels, *The Heart of Midlothian* depicts the male sphere and male actions as dangerous, confusing, violent, and socially disruptive, whereas women, or at least the feminine women, represent reconciliation, harmony, nurturing, and, most important, progress beyond the divisions and hostilities instigated by men. Robertson/Staunton may pursue his personal passions to the destruction of his friends and the near destruction of himself, the disgrace of his family, and the ruin of Effie; Davie Deans may cling to his Cameronian self-righteousness almost to the ruin of one daughter, the blasted marriage hopes of the other, and the financial ruin of his household; the virago Meg Murdockson may pursue her personal and social vendettas to her own execution and the social ostracism of her daughter; the domineering Queen Caroline may pursue her personal power and authority to the detriment of the peace of the kingdom. Jeanie redeems her sister from the law, something Robertson cannot do, though he raises a public riot to attempt it; she moves her father to some moderation, not by words or persuasion, but by quiet domestic perseverance; she eludes Meg Murdockson's machinations; and, quieted by the Duke of Argyle, she brings out the Queen's best impulses. She does these things not by defying the public, the legal, and the historical, but by modifying them in terms of her feminine and domestic virtues and values.

In order to achieve these ends, however, she must exercise her virtues perseveringly, with fortitude, through trials in space and time, in her romance journey from Scotland to Hampton Court palace; passing through the hands of devilish *banditti* (chs 29–30) and an encounter with the tempter in the seductive shape of the Anglican church and its liturgy (ch. 31), Jeanie remains undaunted, her Presbyterian and Cameronian faith somewhat broadened. True to her largely oral and communal culture and her domestic habits of frank, face-to-face communication, Jeanie insists on making her journey in quest of forgiveness because she believes speech has a power writing cannot have. As she tells Reuben Butler, who, as a clergyman and a scholar, believes in the power of the written word, '"writing winna do it – a letter canna look, and pray, and beg, and beseech, as the human voice can do to the human heart. . . . It's word of mouth maun do it, or naething, Reuben"' (ch. 27). Yet her way is smoothed by a scrap of writing from Ratcliffe, the sometime thief, sometime jailer, and Reuben's letter to the Duke of Argyle, recalling a generation-old debt of loyalty from the 'killing time'. These writings arm Jeanie with protection from above and below, rather like magic tokens in old romance. Furthermore, in the brilliant last chapter of volume 3, describing Jeanie's interview with the Queen in Hampton Court palace garden, it is Argyle who silently directs Jeanie's eloquence to the desired end, with pre-arranged signals (ch. 37).

For Argyle is the wizard of this romance, the *deus ex machina* who
descends from above to help Jeanie obtain her miracle, and who then,
seeing what Jeanie is made of, transports her and hers to his pastoral,
utopian microcosm of rural Scotland, where the Deanses and the
Butlers become part of Argyle's project for the modernization of Scottish society, culture, religion, and economics, described in the controversial, and to some critics anti-climactic fourth volume of *The Heart
of Midlothian*. Before the climactic interview, Argyle instructs Jeanie
in how to conduct herself and follow his signals. Jeanie, who has
declared the superiority of speech over writing several chapters earlier,
now wonders if it were not better for Argyle to give her a speech to
learn by heart; but Argyle, too, knows the power of authentic
utterance:

> 'No, Jeanie, that would not have the same effect – that
> would be like reading a sermon, you know, which we
> good presbyterians think has less unction than when
> spoken without book,' replied the Duke. 'Just speak as
> plainly and boldly to this lady, as you did to me the day
> before yesterday; and if you can gain her consent, I'll wad
> ye a plack, as we say in the north, that you get the
> pardon from the king.' (ch. 36)

Here we are made aware that Argyle normally speaks standard written
English, though he can descend to Scots dialect and a Scottish proverb
to show his solidarity with his countrywoman.

The chapter ends with Argyle, who is also the Duke of Richmond
and thus a truly British nobleman, pausing on an eminence to admire
the lush Thames valley countryside just before conducting Jeanie to the
interview with the Queen. When he asks Jeanie her opinion of the
view, she replies as a Scotswoman and a skilled dairywoman that she
sees plenty of good pasturage for cows but in point of taste rather
prefers the sights of Midlothian: 'The Duke smiled at a reply equally
professional and national' (ch. 36). Here is succinctly represented a
hierarchical relationship drawing on a number of codes of value; but
clearly the reader is invited to share the aristocratic and British point
of view of Argyle – in short, to regard Jeanie and all she stands for
fondly but patronizingly. Through the complex narrative and dialogue
of the next chapter, 37, we realize further that the one character in the
novel who is closest to the narrator, in terms of the novel's linguistic
structure, is Argyle; with the first few chapters of volume 4 and
Jeanie's translation to Argyle's Scottish estate in the function of a
professional dairywoman, we realize that Argyle is the author's representative within the novel, as much an artistic recreator of a society

as the author is. In short, Argyle is the *British* statesman Scott felt that the new United Kingdom (Britain united with Ireland in 1800) needed in the deepening crisis of the late 1810s.

Thus volume 4 may be anti-climactic in some ways, but it is very important to the project Scott has in hand in this novel. It is also rich in thematic materials. It contains one of the finest moments of pathos in all of Scott, the execution of Meg Murdockson at Carlisle and the pitiful grief and brutal persecution of her daughter Madge Wildfire (ch. 40). Then there is the utopian world of Knocktarlitie, a microcosm of the Scotland of the future as the Tolbooth was of the Scotland of the past; and as the Tolbooth dominates volume 1, so Knocktarlitie dominates volume 4, just as volume 2 with its scenes of flight and pursuit culminating in Effie's trial in court is balanced by volume 3 with Jeanie's journey and her trial at a court of a different kind. But if volume 4 holds Jeanie's (and Reuben's) reward, it also holds Effie's (and Robertson's) punishment. This is of two kinds. First, we learn that Effie and Robertson have married but are, ironically, childless (while Jeanie's family increases), and that their new life in court circles under assumed characters is one of constant pretense and fear of discovery. Secondly, their one child, the occasion of the entire story, who was secreted away by Meg Murdockson in revenge for Robertson's seduction and abandonment of Madge, has become a Highland bandit, under the name of the Whistler. Effie's and Staunton's extra-legal act of passion has produced an outlaw. At the end of the novel, the Whistler unwittingly kills his own father, and then escapes, apparently to live with the Indians in North America; he thus becomes a symbol of the foundering of false gallantry, egotism, and illicit passion into savagery, a movement precisely the opposite to the continual rise of Jeanie's family. Reservations do remain about Scott's management of volume 4, but its importance to the argument and the formal balance of the novel is obvious.

The third series of 'Tales of My Landlord' (1819) includes *A Legend of Montrose* and *The Bride of Lammermoor*. The latter is set during the period immediately after the intense intriguing and negotiating for the Act of Union of England and Scotland, an event Scott considered to be decisive in shaping 'modern' Scotland, including the residual hostilities and suspicions depicted in *The Heart of Midlothian*.[18] In *The Bride of Lammermoor*, past and present, feudal gentry and courtly intriguers, oral culture and the culture of writing, noble chivalry and mean self-interest, and conflicting wills collide once again; but here there is no statesmanlike Argyle to reconcile and mediate: a noble house and its chief are extinguished, love is destroyed, and ambition undermines itself. Like *Castle Rackrent*, again (*The Bride of Lammermoor* includes a comical but faithful family retainer on the pattern of Thady Quirk), the broad and enlightened attitude necessary to halt the decline of the Ravenswood family is simply missing, and thus *The Bride of Lammermoor* teaches the same lessons as *The Heart of Midlothian*, but by negative example, as it were.

## The Romance of History: *Ivanhoe* to *Redgauntlet*

With his next novel, the author of Waverley turned to the matter of England and the Middle Ages; only 6 of his remaining seventeen novels would return to Scotland, only 3 would be set after 1660, and 5 would be set outside Britain altogether.[19] On the other hand, though his novels continued to sell well, the first series of Scottish novels, published in only six years, is still considered his characteristic and most important work. Nevertheless, Scott's willingness to try new 'lines' indicates his continuing interest in and enthusiasm for the 'romance' in prose, and he retained his former thematic interests – social and ideological conflict, the clash of cultures, mediation, reconciliation, progress – but he altered and variegated the decor, the costumes, furniture, and properties by which he presented them. Thus *Ivanhoe; A Romance* (1819; dated 1820) – the generic distinction is important – goes back to a period of considerable and continuing interest to the Romantic antiquarian, folklorist, and historiographical movements and to political theorists and speculators – the age of Robin Hood, Richard Cœur de Lion and his brother John, the Crusades (a reckless if glorious extravagance of chivalric culture, to which Scott would return in three more novels), and, to Scott, the beginning of the amalgamation of Normans and Anglo-Saxons into one people. During Scott's lifetime it was thought of very highly by some critics, and condemned with equal enthusiasm by others who saw in it very clearly the problem of 'historical romance' inherent in all of the Waverley Novels but now made more obvious by the remoteness of the historical period represented, its customs, culture, and above all its language.

More particularly, *Ivanhoe*, the Waverley Novels, and other historical romances of the period perhaps reveal a contradiction in the late Enlightenment models of historiography that dominate these fictions. On one hand is the idea that the historian should investigate historical and cultural relativities objectively and refuse to judge one culture or society in terms of another (even if the other is the historian's own), and on the other hand is the assumption that the historian should use rational models of explanation and cause and effect and some kind of plot (of progress or decline) if historiography is to be permanent and useful knowledge – useful in the present and future.

*Ivanhoe* is very clearly a novel of description, and Scott invents another frame antiquarian editor figure to mediate the fictitious narrative – Laurence Templeton, addressing himself in a laboured and pedantic 'Dedicatory Epistle' to the Rev. Dr Dryasdust, Fellow of the Antiquarian Society. This pose and this language are, as in the case of Jedediah Cleishbotham, dropped in the novel itself, however. The descriptive and narrative materials are arranged around three different places in the three volumes – Ashby and its tournament, Torquilstone castle under seige, and Templestowe and Coningsburgh castles. Associated settings are the parts of the forest inhabited by Robin of Locksley and his band of outlaws. The characters, as usual, are socially representative types, and there is no transcendental historical figure such as the Duke of Argyle in *The Heart of Midlothian*. Nevertheless, unlike *The Bride of Lammermoor, Ivanhoe* has a happy ending of a kind. It attempts, with limited success, to join a plot of romantic comedy to a larger plot of social progress by having the separation and eventual marriage of Ivanhoe and Rowena represent the abandonment of narrow cultural and social values of the past in favour of a 'modern' acceptance of change and a new national identity.

This depiction of an incipient national identity is reinforced by the presence of self-interested outsiders – the Templars, who represent chivalric and Christian ideals in an advanced state of corruption, and who are, moreover, foreign elements. Like the Jacobin Dousterswivel in *The Antiquary*, they profess high ideals but are in fact merely selfish or else blindly and uncompromisingly fanatical. The Templars, in fact, bear a striking resemblance to the Illuminati of the eighteenth century, supposed by various Anti-Jacobin writers to be the secret international brotherhood that instigated the French Revolution. King Richard merely reveals himself, however, and the Templars depart the land, rather as the Jacobin villains in Anti-Jacobin novels of the 1790s are suddenly discomfited and banished by the descent of a *deus ex machina*. Thus King Richard's presiding over this representative national purification, the reconciliation of Saxon and Norman values, and the reintegration of the outlaw, Locksley, into society, however temporarily, represents once again Scott's vision of social leadership and authority of almost magical transformative power.

There are, however, powerful ambivalences working against this visionary ideal, ambivalences which reflect the renewed social unrest of the late 1810s. In the first place, the common people are depicted as an ignorant and irrational mob, beneath the redemptive social reconciliations animating their betters. Whereas revolutionaries and even liberals argued that the nation was 'the people', Scott seems to suggest here that the people remained outsiders in the new nation forming above them, among the upper and middle classes. Secondly, the Jews, representing the narrowly commercial middle classes but instrumental in helping the defeat of courtly and aristocratic evil in the novel, remain outside the pattern of social integration and reconciliation, a fact represented sentimentally in the fate of Rebecca, condemned as a witch for healing the sick with her science and redeemed in trial of combat by Ivanhoe and by his foe's sudden death from contending passions (the Norman aristocrats and King John resemble villains of Gothic romance in their tendency to self-destructive psychomachia). But Rebecca's redemption ends there; she is left to live on alone, devoting her life to good works, probably harbouring an undying love for the noble and heroic Ivanhoe. Rebecca and her father remain the representatives of all the unassimilable though worthy and useful elements in society, past and present, excluded because of irrational superstition and prejudice (a version of class hostility); and yet Scott does not really challenge that irrationality, in regard to Jews or to their counterparts in early nineteenth-century Britain.

Thirdly, there is nothing in the novel to compensate for the dreadful inset narrative of the Saxon woman Ulrica, raped by the Norman Sir Reginald Front-de-Bœuf after he had killed her father and brothers, kept as his mistress, and then discarded. She sets fire to Torquilstone in an act of revenge and herself dies amidst the flames. This terrible exposure of chivalry's glamour resembles that in *Ran*, the revision of *King Lear* by the great Japanese film director, Akira Kurosawa. Moreover, Ulrica in *Ivanhoe* is a dark version of the fate that could befall Rebecca, abducted by the corrupt Templar, Bois-Guilbert, or even the fate of Lady Rowena, if forced to marry the Saxon oaf Athelstane out of her guardian's desire to use her marriage to reunite the Saxons in a common cause. Scott exposes the supposedly chivalric culture of Medieval England as in fact routinely brutal in its treatment of women. If true chivalry and true love triumph in the end, the triumph means nothing to Ulrica, very little to Rebecca, and barely seems to do justice to Rowena. Certainly Scott felt that he had to go on, in novels such as *The Betrothed* and *The Talisman* (*Tales of the Crusaders*, 1825), to depict again and more amply both the 'romantic' extravagances of and the brutal reality behind what Burke called 'antient chivalry' and which he defended as the animating spirit of the best of modern civilization.

Finally, the great hope and agent of social redemption, King Richard, proves unwilling and unable to sustain his magical powers, for we are told at the end of the novel that he goes off on yet another crusade, only to die ignominiously. The narrator declares on the novel's last page, 'With the life of a generous, but rash and romantic, monarch, perished all the projects which his ambition and his generosity had formed. . .'. The novel closes with a slightly modified quotation from Samuel Johnson's poem 'The Vanity of Human Wishes', referring to the pointless death of Charles XII of Sweden, a byword in polemical Enlightenment historiography attacking the aristocratic and monarchical tradition of military glory. Yet *Ivanhoe* obviously does celebrate 'antient chivalry' in many respects, glamorizes it, and contributed greatly to the rapidly swelling tide of Romantic medievalism. In short, *Ivanhoe* is, like all of the Waverley Novels and like the Romantic novel in general, only more obviously so, profoundly ambivalent about the relation of aristocratic and middle-class cultures, about the relations of different classes, about the past it criticizes and celebrates, and about the plot of progress it attempts to embody.

Scott's next three novels, *The Monastery* (1820), its sequel *The Abbot* (1820), and *Kenilworth* (1821), move through the religious and political conflicts of Scotland during the Protestant Reformation and the reign of Mary, Queen of Scots, (a favourite heroine of Sentimental and Romantic poems and tales,) to the amorous and political intrigues of the English court under Elizabeth I. In the Queen of Scots and the ill-starred heroine of Kenilworth, Amy Robsart, as in the desperate heroine of *St. Ronan's Well*, Scott was perhaps acknowledging the vogue of the novel of female passion of the 1810s, such as Lady Caroline Lamb's *Glenarvon* (1816), discussed in the next chapter. He may also have been commenting obliquely on the irresponsibility, selfishness, and frivolity of Georgian 'silver-fork society'. But such topical themes are overshadowed by Scott's attempt, true to Enlightenment historiography as well as to the historical analogies thrown up by the French Revolution debate, to broaden the range of analogy in the Waverley Novels. Yet Scott continued to play with narrative personæ incapable of such broad, statesmanlike historical vision, and in these novels of Medieval and Renaissance England and Scotland, Scott also introduced a new frame narrator and 'editor' in the person of Captain Clutterbuck, another retired professional man who turns to narrow antiquarianism merely as relief for an inactive mind.

*The Pirate* (1821; dated 1822) considers a different clash of cultures, of passing and developing world-views or 'mentalities', of excessive individualism and the claims of community, in the Orkney and Zetland Islands in the late seventeenth century. These thematic interests of Scott's continue to put a stress on characterization in his novels, the conflict between complex individualism in character and mere social representativeness; but, as *The Pirate* aims to show, this conflict was also inherent in the transition from the community-based values of a traditional, 'pre-modern' society to the autonomous inward-based values of the new culture of reason, individualism, social mobility, personal merit, and entrepreneurship. Like most conservative Romantic novelists, Scott was concerned in *The Pirate* (the pirate being a classic type of the egotist as adventurer) to warn against the excessive individualism that could tear a society apart before most of its individual members could stand on their own, especially when such individualism brought into the society 'outside' values. Typically, too, it is women who are among the victims of male anti-social conduct. Significantly, the glamorous pirate Cleveland takes the same name as the hero of an eighteenth-century Sentimental romance by the French novelist Prévost. Scott's Cleveland eventually redeems himself but he remains an ambiguous representative of the extra- or anti-social values the novel aims, in part, to depict and to condemn.

Scott's next three novels continue his restless search for historical themes and formal devices to bring his own vision of society, and especially politics, to bear on the crises of Britain in the 1820s. *The Fortunes of Nigel* (1822) is clearly one of Scott's novels of education, set in and around the court of James VI of Scotland and I of England and depicting the misadventures of a good-natured but inexperienced young man in the face of courtly intrigue and machiavellian plots. Like Scott's other novels of this type, such as *Waverley, Rob Roy*, and *Redgauntlet, The Fortunes of Nigel* draws on the picaresque tradition in fiction and on Fielding's *Tom Jones* and Mackenzie's *The Man of the World*. The scenes depicting London low life in *The Fortunes of Nigel* and particularly the use of underworld slang probably owe more than a little to the example of Pierce Egan's great success of 1820–21, *Life in London*, discussed in the next Chapter. In *The Fortunes of Nigel*, too, Scott reveals again his predilection for the doctrine of the Church of England (in Scotland, Episcopalian Church) that free will and good works as well as true faith are the grounds for salvation hereafter and happiness here-below.

*Peveril of the Peak* (1823; dated 1822) remains in England but the action moves to the time of Charles II and the so-called Popish Plot, when old wounds from the Civil War were being re-opened. Focusing on fanaticism in politics, its consequences on domestic relations and the younger generation, and the slide into fanaticism of Major Bridgeworth, *Peveril* shows signs that Scott had read with attention his protégé Charles Maturin's highly successful Gothic extravaganza, *Melmoth the Wanderer* (1820), especially the story of 'The Lovers' (see next Chapter). But in *Peveril* Scott was also registering concern over important religious divisions in British society in the 1820s.

*Quentin Durward* (1823), like *The Fortunes of Nigel*, follows the involvement of an inexperienced and idealistic young man through another phase in the long transformation of court culture, the struggles between the cunning and politically sophisticated Louis XI of France, founder of the Bourbon dynasty, and the impulsive and ambitious Charles, Duke of Burgundy. Quentin's adventures and his social rise through personal qualities and martial valour have something in them of the career of the hero of a chapbook romance. But they also embody the Renaissance themes of the relationship of *Fortuna* (or chance and opportunity) and *Virtù* (or manliness, moral and physical), made famous in political theory by Machiavelli and in literature by the Renaissance verse romances – Scott, of course, was well read in both chapbook and verse romances.

With his next novel, however, Scott apparently turned to the 'modern novel' of manners and emulation, set in a semi-fashionable Scottish spa-town, in the contemporary line of fiction of which Scott was a great admirer and astute critic, including Fanny Burney, Maria Edgeworth, and Jane Austen, all singled out for praise in the preface to *St. Ronan's Well* (1823; dated 1824). The character repertory used by Scott here has a general resemblance to that of Burney's *Camilla*; but the social satire in Scott's novel has more of the broadness and humour of Fielding and Smollett than the sentiment and irony of Burney and Austen, and the love-plot has the dark colouring of *The Bride of Lammermoor* and novels of passion of the 1810s and 1820s, with suggestions of incest and the emotional and mental derangement of the heroine, Clara Mowbray. *St. Ronan's Well* is also the only one of Scott's novels set in the nineteenth century; its peculiar tension, greater than in any novel of manners and sentiment, is caused by the distance between social surface and the superficialities of pseudo-genteel social life on one hand and the 'real' selfishness, egotism, and passions of the major characters on the other.

In *Redgauntlet* (1824), considered by many to be Scott's best novel of the 1820s, he returned to the matter of Scotland and the Stuarts (though much of the action takes place in the north of England) as Stuart loyalists continue plotting another uprising after the failure of the 'Forty-Five', and the now middle-aged Young Pretender returns in disguise from exile to assess the strength of Stuart following. To this public theme is added another version of the plot of the young man, the Tom Jones character, in search of his moral and social identity; he is drawn from one familiar world, Scotland, where he is yet an exile, across a border (which he has been forbidden to cross) into another world, England, which is, however, his land by birth. Here the plot is doubled, with Alan Fairford (supposed to be a portrait of Scott himself as a young man) and his friend Darsie Latimer in quest of identity of different kinds in different social worlds and in different ways, the former seeking his autonomy and distinctive selfhood within a professional middle-class context and the latter in the glamorous and risky world of the upper-classes and court society, their high ideals and low politics.

*Redgauntlet* is, moreover, another experiment in narrative technique, for part of the novel is in letter-journal form, and it includes the famous inset tale in dialect, Wandering Willie's Tale. Certainly there are inset first-person narratives in other Waverley Novels, and in *Rob Roy* Scott did use first-person narration throughout. But in *Redgauntlet* as nowhere else in his fiction Scott attempted to juxtapose different modes of narrative, not to expose the relativity of cultures, with their own registers of language and conventions of representation, but to suggest the rich resources and pluralities of language within a culture which yet remains one 'national' culture. *Redgauntlet* is about crossing borders, transgressing in more ways than one, for good as well as ill, and it is about the risks to personal and social identity in doing so. To that extent *Redgauntlet* is perhaps Scott's most searching reflection on the relation of language, culture, and identity.

## Heroism and the Abyss: *The Betrothed* to *Castle Dangerous*

In the nineteenth century, and even in the twentieth, Scott's later novels such as the *Tales of the Crusaders* (1825) were sometimes dismissed as 'mere' adventure stories, fit for childhood reading but not much else. It is true that in the novels that came after *Redgauntlet* Scott seems to turn more decidedly to far-off times and places, to indulge his partly escapist wish to fuse antiquarian lore with prose romance. Of his remaining seven novels, four have medieval settings, three are set outside Britain, only one takes place in Scotland, and the closest Scott comes to his own time and place is seventeenth-century England. But Scott realized that boys and men (women he was less concerned about) could read the same novel with equally deep feeling, if different (though not necessarily better) understanding.[20] At the height of his fame in the 1820s, he was also very aware of his rivals in the novel market, and perhaps he was also responding to the success of novels of exotic places (discussed in the next chapter). More important, in the 1820s Scott was increasingly concerned over the growing political and social crisis that dominated the period before the Great Reform Bill of 1832. Images of the hero lost, wandering, or benighted, which recur often in the earlier novels as representations of heroism's doubtful enterprise, seem to acquire in the later novels more menace, and images of the hero poised over a precipice or abyss become prominent.

Heroism of various kinds, public and domestic, is a continuing theme in the Waverley Novels; and it is inseparable from adventure, as it is strongly associated with the chivalric culture that had been made such a vital political topic by Burke and the entire French Revolution debate, as well as by the career of Napoleon, whose biography Scott now in the mid-1820s undertook to write. But in the accelerating political and social crisis of the late 1820s and early 1830s Scott may have felt heroism's relevance to contemporary life even more strongly, and his own sense of the personal and public significance of heroism may have been sharpened by his private trials. It is no accident that in resolving to discharge honourably every penny of the enormous debts left by his bankruptcy in 1826 he should several times have used the chivalric slogan, 'My own right hand shall do it.'[21] At the same time, Scott continued to reveal deep scepticism about the sentimental versions of chivalry, adventure, and the heroic, rapidly becoming major elements of nineteenth-century professional middle-class ideology and national imperialism. Thus Scott's later novels reveal a deep yearning for heroism alongside a painful awareness that heroism could lead to the abyss; and, as in his earlier novels, it is again the image of the woman as mediator, civilizer, and domesticator which stands against the perilous heroics and adventuring of men, expecially in 'pre-modern' times.

*Tales of the Crusaders* (1825) focuses specifically on the male culture of 'antient chivalry' which meant so much to the Victorian 'return to Camelot', but Scott the historian could never perpetrate a narrowly romantic celebration of that culture. The first of the *Tales, The Betrothed*, is set in the Welsh Marches in the twelfth century; it opposes things medieval of the kind that entered the Victorian world of public school heroics to the practical interests and well-being of twelfth-century society at large. *The Betrothed* affirms the value of heroism, martial, civil, and domestic, but it also warns the upper classes and their emulators to beware of pursuing their own values at the expense of their 'natural' social responsibilities. *The Talisman* shifts the scene and these conflicts to Palestine during the Crusades, the place where the noblemen supposed to lead society in *The Betrothed* have gone in pursuit of their high chivalric ideals, as well as indulging in the traditional aristocratic appetite for 'glory', a positive value in Scott's eyes but also one with possibly disastrous consequences for the aristocracy themselves and for society at large, as Scott had shown in his earlier novels, too. The *noblesse d'épée* Scott always preferred to the *noblesse de robe*, the titled lawyers who played such an important role in the Scottish Enlightenment and the professionalization of the gentry in

Scotland in Scott's own day. The wild, useless, and destructive project of the Third Crusade, the event that provides the setting for *The Talisman*, involves all of the contradictory elements of 'antient chivalry'.

Set against this glorious and sinister folly is the character of Saladin, an enlightened, cultivated, rational, responsible, mediating monarch, a model of the professionalized gentleman that was Scott's principal recommendation to his own time for the cure of his society's ills. Saladin's disguise as a physician and his possession of a healing stone resonate down the centuries into the 1820s. As Saladin tells Richard Cœur de Lion, '"The master places the shepherd over the flock, not for the shepherd's own sake, but for the sake of the sheep"' (ch. 28). Significantly, too, the powers of the talisman grow weaker through time.

As we have seen, after Scott's bankruptcy he resolved to heave off the huge debt himself, almost as a knight of chivalry determined to fight on against all but hopeless odds. A grand project of serial republication of all the Waverley Novels, with notes by Scott as a marketing device – what Scott called the 'Magnum Opus' edition – was to clear off some of the debt; new Waverleys were to do the rest. And in the midst of this heroic effort in defence of his honour and his estate, Scott produced perhaps the best of the later Waverley Novels, *Woodstock; or, The Cavalier: A Tale of the Year Sixteen Hundred and Fifty-One* (1826). It presents Scott's mature deliberations on politics, language, and power, subjectivity, authority, and literature, with particular reference to British society in a post-revolutionary, or perhaps pre-revolutionary age. In order to do so, the novel is set once again in the seventeenth century, in the aftermath of an explosion of revolutionary excess and transgression – the Civil War and the execution of Charles I – and it returns once again to a late Enlightenment analysis of court society and its influence on society at large, but it also turns to one of the preoccupations of the Romantic novel, especially in the 1820s – Romantic individualism. Court culture is represented by the young Charles II, fleeing from the Royalist defeat at the battle of Worcester. The gentry, torn between quasi-feudal loyalty to the monarchy, proud and selfless independence, and risky opportunism and ambition, are clearly in the kind of situation Scott – and Burke – felt that the British gentry had reached in the 1790s and the 1820s: divided between loyalty to the old order and determination to reform that order so as to prevent a total revolution. Sir Henry Lee represents the loyalist; Markham Everard is the selfless, disciplined, socially responsible gentleman, drawn to the Parliamentary side by the King's excessive claims; Wildrake represents the extravagant, doomed, decadently chivalric gentry; and Cromwell, a real historical character, represents the wily, ambitious, but at least partly principled gentry aiming both to reform the old order and serve their own interests.

The bourgeoisie, who, significantly, play very little part· in the novel, are represented by the burghers of the town of Woodstock; and the lower classes, who play a much more prominent role, are again divided between loyalists, self-servers, and (deluded) reformers of state and religion – a mirror image of the gentry, as the common people were usually seen by the middle classes in the late eighteenth and early nineteenth century. The professionals are represented mainly by the clergymen, Rochecliffe the Anglican and Nehemiah Holdenough the Presbyterian; but the conflict between them and with the Independents is a major thematic focus in *Woodstock*. This conflict is made emblematic of the larger divisions in society. The Anglicans stand for monarchy, aristocracy, and part of the gentry, and are implicated in court culture and court politics. The Presbyterian Holdenough stands for the Parliamentary party, led by some gentry. The Independents stand for the army and the common people, used as political instruments to advance the interests of selfish individualists such as their leaders Tomkins and Cromwell. Thus Scott again uses individual characters along with choruses or groups of social representatives to show the major elements of an entire historical society in a period of crisis.

As readers in the 1820s would know, the events described or referred to in the novel would be overshadowed by the restoration of Charles II in 1660, and many of these readers would be inclined to see a parallel between the 1650s and 1660s and the 1790s and 1820s. For after the fall of Napoleon, monarchy had also been restored in France and other parts of Europe. As Scott himself wrote to the Poet Laureate and his fellow Tory, Robert Southey, in September 1824:

> did you ever observe how easy it would be for a good
> historian to run a parallel betwixt the great Rebellion [i.e.,
> the English Civil War] and the French Revolution, just
> substituting the spirit of [religious] fanaticism for that of
> soi-disant philosophy [i.e., Revolutionary political
> philosophy]. ... . I sometimes think an instructive
> comparative view might be made out, and it would afford
> a comfortable augury that the Restoration in either case
> was followed by many amendments in the Constitution.[22]

Scott has in mind the Glorious Revolution of 1688, the final fall of the too-courtly, too-cavalier Stuarts. In the 1820s, then, he seems to have accepted that constitutional reform of some minimal kind was necessary to prevent another revolution in Britain. Thus the last scene of *Woodstock*, the restored Charles II's grateful acknowledgement of Sir Henry Lee and his family during the triumphal royal procession into London in 1660, has the kind of nostalgic sentiment mixed with historical irony found in the arrival of King Richard in Scott's *Ivanhoe*. The ambivalences are a measure of Scott's concern for the fate of Britain in the 1820s, as in the 1790s.

The major thematic focus of *Woodstock*, then, is in its familiar Enlightenment sociology of court culture, as Scott meditates on the worthiness of court and aristocracy to rule, in the last years of the reign of the decadent George IV. In order to do so, Scott combines plots of love intrigue and political intrigue in *Woodstock*, touching once again the commonplace late Enlightenment image of court society based on 'backstairs politics' and the 'mistress system'. Not only does the King, disguised as a gypsy and then as master Kerneguy, a young nobleman, pursue an amour with the virtuous Alice Lee, the beloved of Markham Everard, but the setting for these intrigues is the Woodstock that was the scene of the amours of Henry II and Rosamond Clifford in the most popular chapbook tale of illicit if courtly love, and one of the most reprinted chapbooks over two centuries, *The Fair Rosamond*. The hidden passageways of Woodstock Lodge are instrumental in the political plot of *Woodstock*, are a parallel to the maze in which Henry II concealed his mistress, and serve, along with Charles II's bizarre disguises, as apt emblem of the intricacies, mysteries, and false-seeming of court culture and politics. Furthermore, the allusions to Rosamond are reinforced by references to another great king whose political achievement was undermined by his courtly amorousness, Charles II's grandfather, Henry IV of France. Since this Henry was often mentioned in the French Revolution debate, the reference brings in a general theme of the decadent culture of the *ancien régime*, supposed by many to be a cause of the French Revolution. Burke had attempted to exculpate this decadence in his *Reflections on the Revolution in France*, in a notorious phrase, to the effect that the chivalry of court culture 'ennobled whatever it touched, and under [it] vice itself lost half its evil, by losing all its grossness'.[23]

Scott's intertwining of amorous and political intrigue, love and loyalty in *Woodstock* has a precise political point to make, one that was derived from Enlightenment historiography but applied to the particular circumstances of the 1820s, as Scott saw them. It is signifi-cant that Alice Lee, the object of the King's desire, should not only fend off his passion and thus avoid the fate of Rosamond, but also paint a portrait of the ideal king (ch. 22). But it is Alice's suitor, Everard, who makes clear the dangerous effects of courtly amorous culture. He himself is prepared to tolerate the defeated monarchist party,

'But if those who have brought civil war and disturbance
into their native country, proceed to carry dishonour and
disgrace into the bosom of families – if they attempt to
carry on their private debaucheries to the injury of the
hospitable roofs which afford them refuge from the
consequences of their public crimes, do you think, my
lord, that we shall bear it with patience?' (ch. 24)

The 'lord' he is addressing is, unknown to him, the King, and
Everard's moral indignation leads to a duel between them – yet a
further example of Charles's failure to govern his private character
according to the requirements of his public position and responsibilities. It was a commonplace of Enlightenment sociological history that
the vices of court government filter down through the rest of society
by the processes of emulation, so that the whole social fabric is
vitiated. As we saw in Chapter 3, in late-eighteenth- and early-
nineteenth-century Britain there were many who thought that the vices
of the court and aristocracy were the cause of Britain's moral decline
and therefore her political and international difficulties, especially in the
last years of George IV. Thus there is contemporary pointedness in
Scott's mingling of the amorous and political intrigues in *Woodstock*.

These themes of Enlightenment sociology of court-dominated
societies and the revolutions to which they gave rise were reinforced
by Scott's meditations on a subject directly related to them, the self-
professed embodiment of the French Revolution, as well as the embodiment for many of Romantic genius and individualism, Napoleon
Bonaparte. For as he wrote *Woodstock* Scott was also toiling on a
massive biography of the man who loomed over Europe in Scott's lifetime as Cromwell loomed over Britain during the time of the novel.
The character of Cromwell in *Woodstock* enables Scott to deal figu-
ratively, yet historically, too, with issues of selfhood, power, and
language that he could not deal with as fully within the conventions
of historiography, but that lay at the heart of Romantic fiction,
especially of the 1820s, and that Scott had himself experienced as man
and author. Furthermore, co-ordinated with these issues in *Woodstock*
is the question of the nature and function of the kind of powerful,
'national' discourse Scott was by now acknowledged to be writing
whenever he undertook a new Waverley Novel – literature. The
character of Cromwell enables Scott to explore again the relationship
of subjectivity to the social and historical, and, through language, to
authority. Clearly, these relationships are central to Scott's own
activity as an imaginative writer on public issues. Significantly, Cromwell is associated, by the ignorant and superstitious characters in the
novel, with the devil.

The theme of dangerous subjectivity is focused in the character of Cromwell. In a way, all the characters in the novel are manipulated directly or indirectly by him; he is the *diabolus ex machina*, a real counterpart to the imagined and faked devil-work conducted at Woodstock Lodge to frighten off the Parliamentary commissioners and allow Charles to seek temporary refuge there. Indeed, after his private interview with Cromwell, Wildrake tells his friend Everard, "'I have seen the devil'" (ch. 9). The cavalier is shaken not because he has met the murderer of his liege lord, Charles I, but because Cromwell has involuntarily revealed to Wildrake his own deepest passions – his desire for greatness but also his inward suffering, when he mistakenly draws forth a portrait of Charles I. Scott was wary of passion and subjectivity; here, in *Woodstock*, he seems to associate it with what Burke, in his treatise on the sublime, defined as the dark sublime of power, at once awesome, frightening, and unknowable. For Cromwell remains known only to himself. Just as he wears a coat of mail hidden under his clothes to ward off such assassination attempts as Wildrake is at first moved to, so he wears mental and emotional armour against his mind and his self being penetrated by others. Moreover, like his agent Tomkins, he, too, has undergone a complete reversal of character in his lifetime. His real self, if he has one, is as obscure and maze-like as the secret interior of Woodstock Lodge.

Cromwell's sublime obscurity and his self-contradictions are exhibited, however, in his language. *Woodstock* displays Scott's usual skill and usual practice in use of language for characterization, as well as his structuring of different varieties of sociolect under the aegis of standard written English to suggest an ordered, hierarchical society dominated by an authoritative variety of English not specific to class or region. Sir Henry Lee's old-fashioned gentry values are indicated by his fondness for 'tushery' and quoting Shakespeare; the character of Charles/Kerneguy is suggested by his fondness for wit, and inability to refrain from taking an authoritative tone toward others; Cromwell is alternately blunt in a very uncourtly way and obscure in a hypocritically religious and political (but just as uncourtly) way; Wildrake is, judging from his style of language alone, a man of excess; Everard, however, is always simple, direct, and candid – somewhat like the narrator; Holdenough speaks in exaggerated Biblical phrase, but is clearly dangerous in this rhetorical mode, judging by his ability to rouse the Parliamentary troops to battle fury; Rochecliffe – Anglican, antiquarian, and intriguer – speaks in high sentence; Joliffe the gamekeeper and outdoorsman speaks with colloquial vigour and plainness, his Phoebe with honest plainness, but Tomkins with alternating religious extravagance and insinuating amorousness (to Phoebe).

The different kinds of language also have different, contrasting uses, again related to characterization, including self-expression or self-concealment, communication or obfuscation, persuasion or command. For example, Charles and Cromwell are similar in that both shift tone from persuasion to command (though 'naturally' tending to the latter). Charles tries to persuade or seduce Alice Lee to his own desire, Cromwell to seduce men to desire and service of a different kind. Charles uses the language and, imperfectly, the dialect of an assumed character to conceal his real identity; Cromwell uses language of piety and patriotism to conceal his real ambition. Charles involuntarily reveals his character in slipping into a tone of authority; Cromwell involuntarily reveals his authoritarian character in moments of blunt command and reveals his passions in powerful expressiveness. In contrast to these different characters and uses of language are the character of Everard and his language – candid, temperate, and self-expressive without being extravagant (unlike his friend Wildrake). Of all the characters in the novel, Everard is the one whose language is most like that of the narrator, though his language is naturally more individual and personal than the detached and general language of the narrator. As in all of the Waverley Novels, it was one of Scott's major formal achievements to illustrate the familiar quotation, 'the style is the man (or woman)'; but the different individual languages and characters are also related to one another in a framework of moral and social values advanced by the novel as a whole.

Thus language, its styles, and its personal and social uses are not only techniques of characterization, but major ways of unfolding the themes and developing the arguments of *Woodstock*, as exemplified in the opening scene of the novel, in which the soldier and Independent Tomkins forcibly usurps from the Presbyterian minister Holdenough the pulpit formerly occupied by the Anglican and monarchist Rochecliffe. The pulpit: constitutionally appointed place of public religious and civic instruction, instruction 'properly' carried out by reading aloud a written discourse (sermon and Bible) unless, of course, the preacher is Tomkins, who, though unordained, claims equal or prior right '"to shake forth the crumbs of comfortable doctrine"'. His claim is enforced by his fellow troopers, who see in him a man of 'gifts', that is, one ordained by God and his own inner conviction and therefore superior to those qualified merely as 'men of the cloth' – as they say, '"we see not why men of gifts should not be heard within these citadels of superstition [the parish church of Woodstock], as well as the voice of the men of crape of old [the Anglicans], and the men of cloak now [the Presbyterians]"' (ch. 1). This scene, emblematic of the social, religious, and political divisions of the Civil War and its aftermath, which it is a major task of *Woodstock* to describe, also initiates a major theme of the novel, the relationship between language and authority.

Scott's use of style, quotation, and allusion to create an authoritative narrative 'voice' subordinating all other voices in the novel has already been described earlier in this chapter, and that description applies with full force to *Woodstock*; but in this novel Scott also more systematically aligns the various contenders for authentic and authoritative language with the political and social themes at hand. Scott does this partly through use of language for characterization, just described. He also does it by showing the rhetorical effect of language, as in Holdenough's exhortation to his troops in chapter 17; or Gilbert Pearson's insinuating addressing of his captain, Cromwell, as 'your Highness', in chapter 34; or the various incidents of the steadying effect on others of Everard's calm candour; or the various incidents in which Charles and Cromwell exert their will on others simply by speaking in their known public characters and in an authoritative tone of voice. Significantly, when Charles speaks regally but in the character of Kerneguy he is taken for impertinent, presumptuous, or ignorant of the social decorums of language. Significantly, too, when Pearson tries to emulate Cromwell's language and nasal snuffling tone (supposed to be the tone adopted by the religiose) his master rebukes him; later Pearson confesses to Cromwell, "'You made a jest of me yesterday, when I tried to speak your language; and I am no more able to fulfil your designs than to use your mode of speech'", and later still, when rebuked by Cromwell for swearing, he complains, "'Zooks, sir, I must speak either in your way or in my own'" (ch. 34). Authentic language, then, is a matter of both personal identity and social authority.

This theme is treated another way through Scott's deployment of three different kinds of language: speech as proverbial language, or 'folksay', as folklorists call it; speech which falsely imitates writing; and writing as literature. If one kind of would-be authentic speech is that of divinely inspired religious expostulation, another could be the wisdom of the people embodied in those pithy 'sayings' known as proverbs. Proverbs are rooted in oral culture but have a long literary history as well, and are used to effect in popular chapbooks as well as by such great literary artists as Shakespeare; they also constitute one of the books of the Bible, and have their learned and courtly counterparts in the maxim and epigram, collections of which, by masters such as La Rochefoucauld, were widely known in the eighteenth century. In *Woodstock*, proverbs are used principally by Cromwell when in his blunt, down-to-earth character of man of the people, an alternative and supplement to his Bible-quoting character as chosen man of God. Sir

Henry Lee also uses proverbs and proverbial expressions, but his doing so indicates his self-appointed inheritance of the culture of 'merry England', when masters and people supposedly shared the same culture. Against this supposedly authentic language of the people is speech fashioned after different kinds of writing – on one hand the Biblical language used by the religious hypocrites Tomkins and Cromwell (and for using which, as we have seen, Cromwell rebukes his soldier Pearson), and on the other hand the sententious and elaborate language of the two egregious professional men of the cloth, Holdenough and Rochecliffe.

Finally, there is direct reference to different forms of literary discourse in *Woodstock*, partly for purposes of characterization but partly, too, for purposes of plot and historical argument. Use of the popular chapbooks and broadside literature of the Fair Rosamond has already been mentioned; almost as significant to the novel's themes is the debate between Sir Henry Lee and his would-be son-in-law, Everard, on English literature. Sir Henry is a devotee of Shakespeare, for reasons already mentioned; and his preference has dramatic point several times in the novel, as, for example, when he offers to divert young master Kerneguy by reading aloud Shakespeare's *Richard II*, a play about a weak king and his old-fashioned advisor, John of Gaunt – a historical character also intimately connected with Woodstock. Kerneguy feigns cramp to escape Sir Henry's entertainment – a ploy that says a great deal about Charles II's future character as a man and as a patron of letters. In a more significant episode in chapter 25, Sir Henry also defends Shakespeare against Kerneguy's preference for the contemporary writer of bombastic, stylized Heroic Drama, William D'Avenant (one of the leaders of the Restoration royalist theatre), because D'Avenant claims to be Shakespeare's illegitimate son – just the sort of escapade of 'gallantry' to please the rakish King. Everard the Puritan is shocked at this levity, and admits, '"I cannot, even in Shakespeare, but see many things both scandalous to decency and prejudicial to good manners – many things which tend to ridicule virtue, or to recommend vice, – at least to mitigate the hideousness of its features."' Bowdler's notorious expurgated *Family Shakespeare* had been in circulation for some years when Scott had Everard say this.

More important, here again is a criticism of court culture very pertinent to the French Revolution debate, and raised many times in criticism of literature of Scott's own time. Sir Henry then sarcastically demands of Everard '"whether the convulsion which has sent us saints and prophets without end, has not also afforded us a poet with enough both of gifts and grace to outshine poor old Will, the oracle and idol of us blinded and carnal cavaliers"'. With this thrust he expects to have his opponent down because of the Puritans' well-known antipathy to drama and to 'mere' art in general; but Everard asserts he knows '"a friend of the Commonwealth"' who has written verses not only dramatic and equal to Shakespeare, but '"free from the fustian and indelicacy with which that great bard was sometimes content to feed the coarse appetites of his barbarous audience"'. When Everard quotes some of the verses, Sir Henry admits their beauty; but he cannot hold a purely literary opinion, for when Everard reveals the lines to be by the Puritan polemicist and Commonwealth's public servant, John Milton, Sir Henry feels he has been tricked into praising treason. Everard mildly replies, '"You pressed me – you defied me to produce poetry as good as Shakespeare's. I only thought of the verses, not of the politics of Milton."'

Ironically, as readers who recognized the lines from *Comus* would know, Everard is not being quite so disinterested, for the lines he quotes could well apply to Alice Lee's dangerous situation, courted as she is by another Comus the enchanter in the form of Kerneguy. The reference to *Comus* is ironical, too, in that the literary debate produces heated passions that ignore the lessons of Milton's masque and lead directly to the nearly fatal duel between Everard and Kerneguy – nearly fatal to the monarchy in more ways than one. But for the reader of the novel, the debate has a resonance beyond the plot of *Woodstock* and beyond the seventeenth century, for by the time *Woodstock* was published *both* Shakespeare and Milton were firmly established as 'classics' of the national literature, supposedly transcending their own social situations and the social and political uses to which earlier, less enlightened and cultivated times (such as the Civil War and Commonwealth) might have put them. This transcendence of politics by possessing evident signs of being literature was, appropriately, exactly the aim of *Woodstock*, the Waverley Novels, and much Romantic literature in its own time. As we have seen, however, this transcendence was really another way of being political.

Scott's next publications were two series of *Chronicles of the Canongate*. The first (1827) comprises three short stories, two of which, 'The Highland Widow' and 'The Two Drovers', are classics of the early short story. The second series (1828) is one novel, *The Fair Maid of Perth*, set in late fourteenth-century Scotland, at another turning point in Scottish history, and it continues the themes of Woodstock, but with a shift of interest towards the bourgeoisie, who were neglected in *Woodstock*. Here the relations of the aristocracy and the middle classes are played out in a plot of courtship and amorous intrigue circling around the 'fair maid of Perth', the daughter of a guild artisan of that town. Connected to this plot are, on one hand, the theme of the transition from codes of Highland clan loyalty and personal vengeance to more 'civilized' principles of social order, and, on the other hand, the theme of self-destructive and socially harmful intrigues and rivalries of court politics and the social irresponsibility and self-indulgences of aristocratic culture. The omniscient narrator (for the 'Chronicles of the Canongate', the new persona of Chrystal Croftangry) deals evenly with these diverse, colliding worlds, but merchants and artisans of Perth have the future on their side, as Scott's readers would know; and, besides, the novel does seem to view the aristocratic and courtly worlds, as well as their part-mirror, the world of Highland clan honour, from the burghers' point of view.

*Anne of Geierstein* (1829), the last of the Waverley Novels before Scott suffered a series of crippling strokes, returns to the conflicts of Burgundy with its neighbouring states in the fifteenth century, first treated in *Quentin Durward*; but it represents yet again Scott's vision of the transition from a society dominated by chivalric court culture to one dominated by the values of a professionalized gentry. To negotiate this crisis, both public and private, chivalric and professional, heroic and domestic virtues will be necessary; the only alternative is the abyss of social anarchy and historical oblivion and the path to this abyss lies within each individual, in giving way to the merely personal and subjective and failing to respond to inherited social codes and larger social duties, particularly duty to the 'national' community.

Scott sets his fable within the matter of Switzerland, well-known Romantic symbol of national independence, but links to it the fate of England near the end of the national disaster of the Wars of the Roses. The novel intertwines in a European theatre the struggles of the defeated English Lancastrians, led by Margaret of Anjou, to return to power, and the confrontation of the Swiss cantons and Charles the Bold of Burgundy. Charles, like many an autocratic monarch before him in Scott's novels, undermines his own power as well as the very existence of his state through his excessive commitment to chivalric honour on one hand and his excessive individualism on the other, both suggested by his nickname. These qualities blind him to the moral and social strength of the Swiss, who destroy his armies, deliver him to his enemies, and cause the break-up of Burgundy. But Charles's martial chivalrousness seems preferable to the merely courtly and aesthetic chivalric culture of Margaret of Anjou's effete father, King René of Provence, who writes courtly love songs and devises court entertainments while his kingdom dwindles away. Charles and René represent the two aspects of court culture, useless without one another, and perhaps useless in any case. For the future is represented by the Swiss, and particularly their leader, Arnold Biederman. As his name suggests, Biederman, like Everard in *Woodstock*, represents the fusion of middle-class moral virtue and self-discipline with noble blood and ideals – a 'peasant count' as Charles of Burgundy sneeringly calls him

– placed in rural independence on his Swiss farm, symbolically built under the ruins of his family's feudal castle, Geierstein. For just as Biederman has laid aside his title by birth and acquired the title of landamman of the canton of Unterwalden by merit and election, so he has abandoned his feudal castle for a farmhouse in a 'mountain-paradise' (ch. 3). Significantly, Biederman is a staunch nationalist, harking back to the Swiss patriot Wilhelm Tell, but he is also an advocate of peace, attempting to restrain the hot-blooded youth of his own nation in their thirst for martial glory (a vice of aristocracy) on one hand and their increasing appetite for luxuries (another aristocratic vice) on the other.

Once again the novel opens with a theme-setting episode, with travellers passing through a landscape, the Swiss Alps, that diminishes them. When Philipson and his son Arthur are then cut off by an avalanche on the road, Arthur insists on searching for a way through. A beautiful young woman appears to lead him to safety, but he finds himself unable to take a step 'which must cross a dark abyss, at the bottom of which a torrent surged and boiled with incredible fury' (ch. 2). Arthur is paralysed by 'his too active imagination', the mirror of the abyss, or the subjective faculty within him that gives the abyss its power; but the young woman shows him how to cross, and 'shame now overcame terror'. Once more Anne of Geierstein rescues Arthur from a perilous abyss, when he and his father are imprisoned by a brutal agent of Charles the Bold. For in the floor of Arthur's cell is a cleft that drops away into a seemingly bottomless abyss, 'of Nature's conformation, slightly assisted by the labour of human art' (ch. 15). Again Arthur's too vivid imagination paralyses him with horror, and when Anne and an assistant mysteriously appear in his cell and cut his bonds, he is still unable to move or act; but

> a second time it was the hand of Anne of Geierstein – a
> living hand, sensible to touch as to sight – which aided to
> raise and to support him, as it had formerly done when
> the tormented waters of the river thundered at their feet.
> Her touch produced an effect far beyond that of the slight
> personal aid which the maiden's strength could have
> rendered. Courage was restored to his heart, vigour and
> animation to his benumbed and bruised limbs; such
> influence does the human mind, when excited to energy,
> possess over the infirmities of the human body.

Anne represents both the spirit of intellectual inquiry ('the human mind excited to energy') and female domestication of male chivalry, represented by Arthur Philipson. She is descended from the Barons of Arnheim, unusual aristocrats, for they

'did not restrict their lives within the limits of sinning and
repenting, – of plundering harmless peasants, and
pampering fat monks; but were distinguished for
something more than building castles with dungeons and
folter-kammers, or torture-chambers, and founding
monasteries with Galilees and Refectories. . . . [They] strove
to enlarge the boundaries of human knowledge, and
converted their castles into a species of college'. . . . (ch. 10)

They also attacked priest-craft and supported challenges to the Papacy
– in short, they were supporters of a kind of fifteenth-century Enlightenment. For these reasons, they were suspected by the ignorant and
superstitious of traffic with the devil. Like the eighteenth-century
Enlightenment their progressive work has a dark and degenerate counterpart, represented by Anne's father, Biederman's younger brother.
He has become a leader in a secret society, the Vehme-gericht, which
judges and punishes evil-doers and those who challenge its power, such
as Charles the Bold. Thus the Vehme resembles the European secret
societies such as the Illuminati, along with the Enlightenment philosophers widely supposed to have instigated the French Revolution.
Anne's mysterious ability to know of secret plots and secret exits from
places of confinement and to free Philipson and restore his manly
courage is in fact a positive counterpart to her father's darker purposes,
which lead to his own end and contribute to the disappearance of a
European state, rather than the building of one. Philipson, by contrast,
is revealed to be son of the Earl of Oxford, who has come to Switzerland and Burgundy to seek help for the supporters of Margaret of
Anjou and the house of Lancaster; supported by Anne as his wife, he
returns to England, we are told on the last page of the novel, to assist
in the triumph of Henry Tudor at Bosworth field – the end of the
medieval baronial wars and the beginning of the modern English state,
according to Scott. By this rather tortuous route does Scott again
retrace the moral and intellectual origins of modern Britain and recommend again the fusion of Enlightenment intellectual culture, largely a
professional middle-class movement, with the best of Burke's beloved
'antient chivalry'.

The novel is aptly titled, then, even though Anne does not appear
much in it. In one sense she is a female counterpart to Biederman
(her moral father) and a contrast to her father by blood. Like Biederman and unlike her father, Charles the Bold, and King René, she
is, however indirectly, a state-builder rather than a state-destroyer.
This meaning of her character is reinforced by the epigraph on the title
page from Shakespeare's play of the Wars of the Roses, *Henry VI Part
III*, 'What! will the aspiring blood of Lancaster Sink in the ground?'

– and by numerous quotations from this and related Shakespeare plays in the text of the novel. In this epigraph, too, there is an opposition between aspiration and oblivion, making history and disappearing into the abyss of time. A related contrast is that between Anne and the desperate and embittered Margaret of Anjou, who dies before her schemes reach fruition (ironically, it is a piece of Margaret's feminine ornament, a necklace, which is sold to raise troops to fight the battle of Bosworth). For Anne retains her entirely domestic character and supports heroic and public enterprise from there, rather than venturing into public and political life herself; where she does intervene, she does so secretly, obliquely, in disguise, and on the individual level, partly out of romantic love for Philipson. Anne of Geierstein, as much as personal courage and heroism, is the opposite of the abyss that terrifies Philipson, an abyss in nature but given its power by his own imagination and subjectivity – or rather, Scott's novel argues that both manly courage and what Anne represents are necessary to make the man who helps to make history.

On the other hand readers might feel that the significance of Anne is argued with a degree of tortuousness and indirectness that undermines the rhetorical effect of this linking of character with plots of romance and history. She is, for example, of undecidable social character, on one hand Countess of Arnheim, on the other the ward of a simple Swiss farmer. Throughout the novel she remains idealized and goddess-like, compared to Minerva (ch. 3), a symbol and an icon, and often in disguise. At her own castle of Arnheim, as hostess to Arthur, she seems unable to find the right way of comporting herself to him, and in general the significance of their romance seems overshadowed for much of the novel by the blind and bloody wilfulness of the other major figures. Furthermore, the full historical significance of her character is revealed only in the last, hastily narrated page of the novel. Thus to some extent she remains to the reader, as to Philipson, what she is defined as in the novel's subtitle – 'The Maiden of the Mist' – an ideal of salvation to be hoped for, but of uncertain provenance and reality.

Scott's last two novels, *Count Robert of Paris* and *Castle Dangerous*, were published together in 1831 (dated 1832) as the fourth series of *Tales of My Landlord*. By then Scott had suffered a series of paralytic strokes; his mind, his body, even his ability to write coherently were fading fast as he faced continuing pressure from his publisher, Robert Cadell, to finish annotating the 'Magnum Opus' edition of the Waverley Novels and to churn out yet more 'Romances'. *Count Robert of Paris* returns to the Crusaders and the study of decadent court culture in eleventh-century Byzantium, as the remains of ancient eastern Mediterranean civilization meet the challenge of the 'new' culture of chivalry and feudalism from western Europe; as usual, the two cultures, exemplified in the leading characters, the emperor Alexius Comnenus and Count Robert, seem to acquire at least a glimmering of respect for one another's differences, helped by the mediation of the Saxon mercenary, Hereward, but only after the failure of a plot led by the pseudo-philosopher Agelastes – yet another Jacobin-like self-interested schemer. In conception *Count Robert* is an interesting expression of Romantic orientalism, relating themes of national division to demands of empire at an important turning point in European political history and imperial expansion. The ideas, if not the artistic execution of *Count Robert*, show Scott's mind as keenly interested as ever in discoursing on the present through imaginative re-presentation of 'the past'.

*Castle Dangerous* shows the medieval conflict of England and Scotland, again criticizes chivalric culture (especially courtly love), and in doing so shows signs that Scott remembered James Hogg's similar project in his novel *The Three Perils of Man* (1822), which is, in fact, an antidote to Scott's tendency to glamorize feudalism and chivalry in spite of his criticism of them and his repeated argument in his novels that such values had to be combined with 'modern' ones if society were to progress. Scott himself warned his acquaintances not to read the last of the *Tales of My Landlord*. By the time they were completed he was on his way to the Mediterranean in a desperate voyage for health. While at Malta he began another medieval romance to be set there; but he could no longer sustain coherence, even in sentence structure or spelling of individual words, let alone through yet another romance.[24] Before he had returned to Scotland in July 1832 he was shattered in mind and body and, though he tried till the tears ran down his face, could never manage to hold a pen again.

Within a few months of his death, an anonymous writer in the *Monthly Repository* had already put together the two sides of Scott's career as a castle-builder. The 'distinguishing quality of Scott's mind', the writer declared, 'was the faculty which has been termed *conception*'. 'His forte was description' and 'he occupied a midway station between the man of memory who merely reproduces what he found *as* he found it; and the man of poetical imagination, or of creative power'. Thus much for Scott's mind – the inward, subjective space of literary castle-building. But to the *Repository* critic, this self was vitiated by the other castle-builder.

> The king's evil of aristocracy was hereditary in his moral
> constitution, and the disease was incurable; in fact, he died
> of it. . . . He more gloried in being the laird of
> Abbotsford than the author of *Waverley*. His passion for

becoming the connecting link of a broken feudal chain was
his ruin. The purchase and improvement of his 'policy'
[i.e., his estate] outran even the unprecedented profits of
his publications. . . . The laird destroyed the novelist.

Yet this, though harsh, was not the last word; the literary castle-
builder triumphed after all:

In theory he was no disciple of Bentham; no advocate of
the 'greatest happiness principle'; but practically, and
considering only the immediate result, who is there of our
times, either among the living or the dead, that has
generated a greater amount of human enjoyment?[25]

In the last few decades criticism has begun to show the extent to
which that enjoyment was and is not merely the thrill of adventure or
romantic escapism, but rich and varied in its literary means, its intellectual reference, and its contemporary relevance, speaking to Scott's
readers in his own day of their most pressing interests, and to
professional middle-class readers in the Victorian age as the prophet
of their social triumph. To those nineteenth-century readers, such as
Tolstoy, Manzoni, Balzac, and George Eliot, who were also novel
writers, Scott showed the artistic and rhetorical potential of the novel
and thus, in spite of Scott's own limitations, the power of the novel
as designed by him to disseminate a particular vision of social structure, 'national' culture, 'national' language, and historical change.
More recently, criticism has begun to show how Scott, because –
rather than in spite – of his contribution to nineteenth-century culture
and ideology, can be considered a modern classic as well.[26]

# Notes

1. Edgar Johnson, *Sir Walter Scott: The Great Unknown*, 2 vols (New York, 1970), p. 841.

2. *The Journal of Sir Walter Scott*, edited by W. E. K. Anderson (Oxford, 1972), 18 Mar. 1829, pp. 535–36.

3. *Journal*, 24 Feb. 1828, p. 433.

4. Johnson, *Scott*, p. 878; Thomas Crawford, *Walter Scott* (Edinburgh, 1982), pp. 117–18.

5. See Duncan Forbes, 'The Rationalism of Sir Walter Scott', *Cambridge Journal*,

7 (Oct. 1953), 20–35; Peter Garside, 'Scott and the "Philosophical Historians"', *Journal of the History of Ideas*, 36 (1975), 497–512; Nicholas Dickson, *The Bible in Waverley* (Edinburgh, 1884); Crawford, *Scott*, p. 87; J. G. Lockhart, *The Life of Sir Walter Scott, Bart.* (1893), ch. 1 (Scott's fragment of autobiography); Richard M. Dorson, *The British Folklorists: A History* (1968), pp. 108–18; David Lieberman, 'The Legal Needs of a Commercial Society: The Jurisprudence of Lord Kames', in *Wealth and Virtue: The Shaping of Political Economy in the Scottish Enlightenment*, edited by Istvan Hont and Michael Ignatieff (Cambridge, 1983), pp. 203–34; and Lockhart, *Scott*, pp. 532, 534.

6.  Anand Chitnis, *The Scottish Enlightenment: A Social History* (London and Totowa, New Jersey, 1976), pp. 95–99.

7.  Walter Scott, *The Lives of the Novelists* (London and New York, n.d.), pp. 208–9.

8.  Scott, *Lives of the Novelists*, p. 109 repeated p. 295; p. 209.

9.  See Francis R. Hart, *Scott's Novels: The Plotting of Historic Survival* (Charlottesville, 1966), p. 30.

10. Jane Millgate, *Walter Scott: The Making of the Novelist* (Toronto, 1984), p. 34.

11. Scott, *Lives of the Novelists*, p. 50.

12. *Journal*, 14 Jan. 1828, p. 415.

13. Johnson, *Scott*, p. 680.

14. See Graham Tulloch, *The Language of Sir Walter Scott: A Study of His Scottish and Period Language* (1980); and 'The Use of Scots in Scott and Other Nineteenth-Century Scottish Novelists', in *Scott and His Influence*, edited by J. H. Alexander and D. Hewitt (Aberdeen, 1983), pp. 341–50; and J. Derrick McClure, 'Linguistic Characterisation in Rob Roy', in *Scott and His Influence*, pp. 129–39; David Murison, 'The Two Languages in Scott', in *Scott's Mind and Art*, edited by A. Norman Jeffares (Edinburgh, 1969), pp. 206–29; and Mary Lascelles, *The Story-Teller Retrieves the Past: Historical Fiction and Fictitious History in the Art of Scott, Stevenson, Kipling, and Some Others* (Oxford, 1980), ch. 6. Tushery: 'used by R. L. Stevenson for a conventional style of romance characterized by excessive use of affected archaisms such as "tush!"'; see *Oxford English Dictionary*, 'tush'.

15. Quoted in Johnson, *Scott*, p. 1232.

16. 'Mentality' is a term borrowed from French cultural historians and refers to the totality of habitual ways of thinking and moral and emotional attitudes of a community and shared by each of the community's members.

17. See Coleman O. Parsons, 'Character Names in the Waverley Novels', *PMLA*, 49 (1934), 276–94.

18. Peter D. Garside, 'Union and *The Bride of Lammermoor*', *Studies in Scottish Literature*, 19 (1984), 72–93.

19. See Alice Chandler, 'Chivalry and Romance: Scott's Medieval Novels', *Studies in Romanticism*, 14 (1975), 185–200.

20. See Scott, *Lives of the Novelists*, p. 256.

21. *Journal*, 22 Jan. 1826, p. 65.

22. J. G. Lockhart, *Life of Scott*, p. 525.

23. Edmund Burke, *Reflections on the Revolution in France*, edited by C. C. O'Brien (Harmondsworth, 1968), p. 170.

24. See Jane Millgate, 'The Limits of Editing: The Problems of Scott's *The Siege of Malta*', *Bulletin of Research in the Humanities*, 87 (1979), 190–212.

25. *Scott: The Critical Heritage*, pp. 332–35.

26. See Richard Waswo, 'Scott and the Really Great Tradition', in *Scott and His Influence*, pp. 1–12.

# Chapter 6
# 1815–1830: Romance, Realism, and Satire – The Limits of Romantic Culture

In the last four chapters we have seen how the novel was used as part of the struggle for self-definition as well as leadership of those who wrote and read novels – the professional and middle classes. We have also seen how fiction was used by some elements of those classes, principally the Evangelicals, in an attempt to suppress genuinely popular cheap fiction and to remake the lower classes in the image of the professionalized middle classes. Meanwhile, of course, commercial cheap fiction developed in its own way into a culture of fashionable consumption by taking over Sentimental and Gothic stories from the circulating-library novel market. Furthermore, we saw how fiction was used as an important form of social reproduction, in tales for children and youth, and we saw continuing concern over the role of fiction in the moral and intellectual 'miseducation' of women. These various projects in fiction worked from a common repertory of themes – the subjective self; the 'domestic affections'; society (dominated by court culture and aristocratic patronage) as unnatural and oppressive to the authentic self; the dangers of social emulation through the fashion system; various models of authentic community based on professional middle-class values, from the remade rural community to the nation; and language and literature.

Finally, we have seen how these themes were developed through new formal devices or old formal devices given new tasks, including the plots of romance and romantic comedy; shift to authoritative narration, often used with free indirect discourse, focusing on a central subject consciousness; domestic realism; factual, historical, topical, or folkloric descriptive material, supported by footnotes and other 'editorial' apparatus; quotation, and allusion; reflexivity, or formal self-consciousness; a hierarchical structure of language, or linguistic universe, including dialect as a major element; and irony and satire of various kinds. Through all of this we glimpsed a continuing ambivalence about the desired and feared 'Other' of the professional middle-class fiction writer or novel reader – court and aristocratic culture, sometimes extending to the late eighteenth-century professional middle-class culture of inward 'nobility of soul', Sensibility, and some-times embodied in the 'not British', the alien, and the exotic.

After the final defeat of Napoleon, and the economic and social dislocations of a post-war era, and as population increase, urbanization, industrialization, and increased if spasmodic social conflict presented new problems, ideological competition and conflict intensified, and the struggle for power and leadership in British society, and leadership of the increasingly powerful professional middle classes, also intensified. The nature and value of emergent Romantic art, literature, and culture in relation to these struggles were hotly debated; the Evangelicals and other social reformers became more organized and more militant; lower-class protest re-emerged with renewed vigour and articulateness; and essentially professional middle-class ideological and social move-ments, such as Utilitarianism, became prominent.[1] Throughout the later 1810s and the 1820s social, administrative, and cultural institutions came under greater stress and greater scrutiny. In all of these areas fiction, though in many ways implicated in the controversial Romantic movement, was used to depict, work out, or argue contending values, ideologies, and visions, and something of the variety of these fictional depictions, negotiations, and arguments will be examined in this chapter.

There is no master-key to this variety; but a major complex of issues and themes centred around one sense of the word 'romantic', much used in the literature and criticism of the late eighteenth and early nineteenth century, but not yet applied to the period as a whole.[2] The word 'romantic' derives from the French word for literary romance, *roman* (which, interestingly enough, also means 'novel'), and in the seventeenth century 'romantic' meant 'of the nature of, having the quality of romance in respect of form or content' (*OED*). To some people such a quality was bad, as it meant 'of a fabulous or fictitious character; having no foundation in fact', or 'fantastic, extravagant, quixotic; going beyond what is customary or practical' – again, by association with elements of the fantastic, supernatural, fabulous, or marvellous in Medieval and Renaissance verse romances. But in the eighteenth century such qualities began to be viewed more positively, and associated with the imagination and inward moral or aesthetic sensibility, which were supposed to be faculties capable of perceiving the 'romantic' in anything. The romantic rose in prestige with the rise of subjectivity, and the rise of those literary or artistic forms which were used to represent or express subjectivity, especially lyric verse and music. The 'extravagant' and 'quixotic', or 'going beyond what is customary or practical' or even legal, could be seen as signs of a rich subjectivity or plenitude of self, especially in the face of social insti-tutions or practices thought to be unnatural, artificial, and hostile to the authentic self, i.e., court cultures characteristic of the *ancien régime*.

Excess and transgression, the extravagant and quixotic, became familiar in the literature and culture of Sensibility; they became obvious in the French Revolution and the debate over it in Britain during the 1790s. The crises of the Napoleonic period – indeed, the career of Napoleon himself – only reinforced these associations. Not surprisingly, English Romantic fiction in the post-Napoleonic era frequently turned with fascination and horror to themes of excess and transgression, margins and limits of self and society, along with other forms of intellectual inquiry and artistic activity. Moreover, this questioning and exploration of limits was extended to the very means of questioning and exploration – literature, writing, the novel, and even language itself.

## The Limits of Self and the Domestic Affections: Later Romantic Novels of Passion and Gothic Romance

Certainly by the later 1810s Romantic culture, literature, and fiction seemed preoccupied with themes of excess and transgression – excess of self and individualism; transgression of limits personal, familial, and cultural, of limits moral, ethical, and existential. The late 1810s and the 1820s seem to be the period of Romantic fiction, and Romantic literature in general, that is most 'romantic' in the usual sense of that word in that time – 'fantastic, extravagant, irrational' – rejecting the domestic, the familiar, the rational, and the realistic that we have noted as a major strain of fiction in the 1790s and 1800s. The exploration of excessive selfhood marked a deep ambivalence, a revulsion against yet a fascination with this central theme of Romantic culture, for excessive selfhood could be seen as a transcendence of merely social categories and values, yet still somehow associated with courtly and aristocratic egotism and, paradoxically, with the self-righteous individualism of revolutionary transgression against traditions and laws.

This ambivalence about Romantic individualism is seen most clearly in the novel of passion that was one of the most widely read forms of the novel in the 1810s and 1820s. Of course, as we saw in Chapters 2 and 3, there were novels of passion before 1814, and even before 1789, for novels of Sensibility, particularly novels in letters, also foreground passion. But novels of passion seem to become more prominent in the age of Byron. Furthermore, the novel of passion was particularly associated with women writers and readers, and some use passion as a subversive feminist theme, overtly as in Wollstonecraft's *The Wrongs of Woman* or covertly as in the tales of Amelia Opie. This association was reinforced by the European success of Mme de Staël's *Corinne* (1807) and the British success of novels partly influenced by de Staël, such as Lady Morgan's *Woman; or, Ida of Athens* (1809), which join nationalist ideals and politics to the theme of passion. Other women novelists, such as Maria Edgeworth in *Belinda* (1801) and Mary Brunton in her two novels, significantly titled *Self-Control* (1810) and *Discipline* (1814), opposed the novel of passion and the heroine burdened with excess of self, in novels that promote reason and 'self-control' and try to depict heroines who are rational and self-contained yet still interesting as subjects.

Moreover, many other fiction writers, such as Opie, who display heroines who are passionate and desiring subjects, insist on expressing an official morality of disapproval and disavowal of what they describe so luxuriantly. Nevertheless, such moralizing, often tidily kept to the last page of the novel, could easily be ignored by women readers interested (in more ways than one) in representations of female subjectivity. It may well be that the novel of passion was, for women readers and writers, the counterpart to the richly and complexly expressive Romantic lyric and the Romantic epic of subjectivity written by men, such as Wordsworth's *Prelude* or Byron's *Childe Harold's Pilgrimage*. Poetry and prose fiction were – except as merely decorative pastimes – still largely divided according to distinctions of gender.[3]

These issues and associations are seen clearly in one of the most spectacular and successful novels of passion of the later 1810s, Lady Caroline Lamb's *Glenarvon* (1816). It created a sensation when it was published, for it was widely supposed to be a quasi-novel, a *roman à clef* depicting Lamb's adulterous, tempestuous, and too-public affair with Byron in 1814. This affair had itself become a public spectacle of excess and transgression on Lamb's part. But this can have been only part of the reason for the novel's enthusiastic reception. Even readers unable to identify the fictional characters with people in real life could respond to *Glenarvon*'s lavish and particular descriptions of the transports and torments of love and its depiction of the conflict of love, as a personal imperative, against the laws and conventions of society. For Lamb takes the excess of passion over social limits found in Opie's 'tales of the heart' and gives the passion an explicitly amorous and erotic definition, one more in keeping with the aristocratic birth and breeding of her characters and herself.

But Lamb also tries to give her fable a public and political dimension, too, as she adds elements of the 'national tales' of Lady Morgan,

Jane Porter, and 'the Great Unknown', with some elements from Mme de Staël – particularly the character of the female 'national' poet and prophet, the character 'constructed' by 'national' topography, historical elements (the Irish uprising of 1798), and the polarization of values between the individual, national, rural, and authentic, and the merely social, fashionable, metropolitan (and cosmopolitan), and relative. All of this is purveyed in a novel with such formal excess – so many characters (several of them having more than one identity), so much intrigue, such complicated family relations, and so tortuous a plot (concealed, moreover, for long passages by extravagant descriptions of passion) – that many readers must have been baffled by it. In fact, the repertory of characters, their relationships, and the plot are so complex that the passages of description of passion become the dominant element in the composition.

Thus the moral and formal contradiction in *Glenarvon* is that passion is officially condemned and disavowed by the omniscient narrator, throughout the novel and in the moral at the end, as well as in the author's preface – much strengthened and reinforced in the second edition, after the novel's extravagance of feeling and action, furniture and plot, had been widely condemned by critics and readers; but passion dominates the narrative, the descriptive material, the structure of the plot, and the structure of the text. What is condemned fascinates. This excess in the text was seen as commensurate with Lamb's excesses in life and love and thus offered another way of reading autobiography into the novel.

Yet the excess and the extravagance also offered readers, especially women readers, an example of transcendent female selfhood – transcendent over merely social codes (including the sexual double standard) instituted and operated largely for the benefit of men in a society still patriarchal through and through. For the heroine, Calantha, manages to elude the control of her father, so that she grows up too free in spirit, too sensitive within, too idealistic, too ignorant of what society demands of women; she is limited as a social being by her excess of sensibility. She also eludes her father's choice of a mate for her, the libertine William Buchanan, and manages to marry, for love, Henry Mowbray, Earl of Avondale. She then transcends fashion and the hypocritical moral values operated as a system of power by wealthy women in London and their emulators in the provinces. Later she eludes her husband to pursue her amour with Glenarvon, all the while defying the disapproval of her more prudish female relatives and the intention of her father-in-law to crush her independent spirit. This transgression only leads again to bondage, however, as she becomes Glenarvon's victim, even his slave: symbolically, he dresses her in jewelled golden chains. But she eludes him, too; for though she is no more than a vessel of passion, her passion, unlike his, is selfless, disinterested, and so sublime it transcends even his wish to command it as a sign of his own power. Extravagance and transgression, officially condemned, become signs of superiority, in both the novel's heroine and its author.

Calantha even transcends the Irish rebellion (another form of transgression), partly led by Glenarvon and partly inspired by another of his mistresses, the 'wild Irish girl' Elinor St Clare. The rebellion is also to be assisted by a French invasion (as actually happened in 1798), so that the Revolution is brought into the novel, too. Unlike Scott, who denies the possibility of transcendence to historical man and woman, Lamb requires her heroine to rise above history. Through extravagant passion, inspiring transgression of social codes and even laws, a woman (or anyone) may be free, free absolutely. But limits are finally reasserted, limits human, social, and supernatural: Calantha dies; the rebellion is suppressed; Glenarvon dies pursuing a ghost-ship; the novel ends with his declaration, '"God is just; and the spirit of evil infatuates before he destroys"'. How many of Lamb's readers would have felt that this moral and Calantha's death cancelled her passion, which is to say her paradoxical and ironical experience of freedom from the relativities, be they marriage, fashion, nationalist politics, or revolution, of the merely social world dominated by the values of men?

A far more successful novel of passion and transgression on the personal and public planes is Mary Shelley's *Frankenstein* (1818), one of the few Romantic novels to have become a modern classic. But whereas *Glenarvon* is a novel of erotic passion and transgression, *Frankenstein* excludes the erotic; rather, it is a novel of intellectual passion and transgression. In this, Shelley, though a woman author like Lamb, lays claim to men's domain of culture and experience, without relinquishing women's. In this, Shelley was taking up the intellectual legacy of both her parents, William Godwin and Mary Wollstonecraft. *Frankenstein*'s resemblance to her father's *Caleb Williams* is obvious, and signalled in the novel's dedication, 'To William Godwin, Author of Political Justice, Caleb Williams, &c . . . .' Not only does *Frankenstein* exhibit the circumstances forming its protagonists' characters, it also takes the form of 'adventures of flight and pursuit' (Godwin's description of the form of *Caleb Williams*), shows the nature of social injustice, illustrates the mutual interdependence of beings, makes use of historical analogies to comment on contemporary political issues, and presents a critique of excessive individualism, however high-minded. Like *Caleb Williams*, *Frankenstein* also exploits to the full the first-person confessional narrative form in order to foreground the vicissitudes of the self in a material and social world unfit for it, but also in order to argue for the power of self-narrative. The narrative structure of the novel is in fact a chain or series of confessional narratives, each contained in the other, and each with a similar moral: passion, that inward imperative and sign of authentic selfhood in Romantic fiction, isolates the individual from society, destroys the domestic affections, and brings the individual to the edge of self-obliteration.

But in emphasizing the domestic affections, *Frankenstein* also resembles Wollstonecraft's *The Wrongs of Woman* and Godwin's novels *St. Leon* and *Fleetwood*. For example, outside Frankenstein's story is Mrs Margaret Saville in England, a symbol of the 'domestic affections' that must be left behind when men pursue their passions of curiosity, love of fame, and general philanthropy. At the core of the narrative is the dæmon's tale of the De Laceys, an illustration of the beauty of the domestic affections, the nobility of self-sacrifice, and the injustice of a society (clearly pre-Revolutionary France) that makes such virtues fly to a wilderness in order to survive. Thematically and formally the novel seems designed to be what Percy Shelley said it was in the Preface he wrote for the first edition – an 'exhibition of the amiableness of domestic affection, and the excellence of universal virtue'. The novel seems to illustrate this moral negatively, however, for once again we have a novel that seems to set excessive selfhood against social relations and that argues, if not for the priority of society to self, then for the claims of the domestic affections in one's immediate social sphere of family and friends.

*Frankenstein* treats this theme in terms of romantic irony – aspiration thwarted, unfulfilled, or failed because of inherent or socially imposed human limitations. The novel's use of romantic irony is parallel to other Romantic versions of this irony, such as Goethe's *Faust*; and other novelists, such as Maturin in *Melmoth the Wanderer*, also deal with the theme. Moreover, as in the Anti-Jacobin novels, romance, as the projecting, theorizing, speculative imagination, is crossed and contradicted by reality in the form of social or natural limitations on the aspiring, reformative, or even revolutionary individual. For, as in Godwin's novels of the 1790s, there is a revolutionary dimension to the romantic irony: the hero's quest is not just to satisfy his personal desire for transcendental knowledge (the secret of life), but to benefit society at large, in the spirit of 'philanthropy' that was one of the Revolution's slogans. Furthermore, Frankenstein's passions of curiosity, desire for fame, and philanthropy are those recognized by major Enlightenment philosophers as causes of social progress.

Paradoxically, *Frankenstein* shows that these passions force the inquiring individual to be anti-social in order to achieve his ambition. But it is precisely the failure of reality to match desire, of practice to match theory, of Frankenstein's vision of a 'new man', a super-man, to be made beautifully incarnate, that shocks and revolts him. Frankenstein fails to be a New Enlightenment Pygmalion. His creature is a 'monster', an 'abortion', but only in relation to Frankenstein's sublime imaginings. This is at once a philosophical, moral, and aesthetic reaction. It is also, as the epigraph on the title page suggests, *a re-reading (or re-writing) of Milton's cosmographical epic, Paradise Lost.* Later in the novel, the social dimensions of the failure of Frankenstein's romantic project in the face of reality become apparent, as the real and actual version of Frankenstein's theories turns out to be harmful to society at large, to the smaller society of the philanthropic inquirer's family and friends, and to the inquirer himself. Finally, the inquirer may find himself, as Shelley's parents did, execrated by and expelled from society rather than recognized as a prophet of truth and social progress. Thus the inquirer is left alone, without relations, familial or social, and with only one social act to perform: to relate his 'tale' to another. Appropriately, in *Frankenstein* this relating takes place in an asocial space, sublime nature in the Alps or Arctic wastes; sublime: beyond normal limits. This pattern of transgression from society into the terrible sublime of self-narration was seen already in Mary Shelley's parents' novels and in Coleridge's 'Rime of the Ancient Mariner' and the third canto of Byron's *Childe Harold* (both are quoted in *Frankenstein*).

Yet *Frankenstein*, like *Glenarvon, Melmoth the Wanderer,* and other quasi-Gothic novels of passion of these years, seems to centre on the extravagant selfhood it disavows, and it seems pessimistic about the authenticity of the social and the power of the domestic. There are four ways in which this contradiction appears. In the first place, as in *Caleb Williams*, social institutions are seen to be unresponsive to the needs of the individual, less satisfying than domestic life, or unable to establish the moral identity of the individual. Frankenstein finds that the university does not serve intellectual inquiry as he sees it; Justine Moritz is wrongly condemned by the legal system; the De Laceys are victims of the institutional self-interest and tyranny associated with court governments; and the common people are shown to be ignorant, prejudiced, irrational, impulsive, and wrong in their perception of the real moral character of Justine, Frankenstein, and the dæmon. Worse still, as the dæmon discovers, other virtuous and enlightened individuals, such as Frankenstein and Felix De Lacey, are unable to recognize his inner worth because of his merely outward monstrousness. The relationship between Frankenstein and his creature degenerates into one of revenge, a private code of justice.

Secondly, throughout *Frankenstein* the domestic affections seem fragile in the face of social injustice on one hand and excessive selfhood on the other. Pursuit of the domestic affections seems to require withdrawal from public social life, in the case of Frankenstein's parents, or may result in social ostracism or persecution, in the case of the De Laceys. The result of the mutual code of individualistic revenge between Frankenstein and his creature is to deny both of them the domestic affections. Thirdly, society and the family seem to deal particularly harshly with women in this novel, though *Frankenstein* is not as overtly feminist in its critique of the patriarchal family and social institutions as Wollstonecraft's *The Wrongs of Woman* is. Nevertheless, as in Radcliffe's Gothic novels, though more disastrously, women in *Frankenstein* are caught between men's ambitions and society's conventions, between male aspiring and social limiting.

Finally, the dimension of desire as erotic love is either rejected or strangely absent in *Frankenstein*. Walton's closest relations are with his sister and his belated soul-mate, Frankenstein; Frankenstein decides not to make a mate for the dæmon because they might engender a race of monsters to war against mankind (a revision of the Greek myth of the successive races of giants and gods); Elizabeth Lavenza is raised as Frankenstein's sister and their marriage remains unconsummated when she is murdered by the dæmon. On the other hand, the novel insists on the spiritual and intellectual sympathies between Walton and Frankenstein and between Frankenstein and the dæmon, and these relationships are ones of mutuality of suffering, alienation, and, of course, narration (like Mary Shelley's relationship with her dead mother, whose largely autobiographical books she continued to read and re-read). The death of Frankenstein leaves Walton and the dæmon alone once more. (Frankenstein does have a close friend, Henry Clerval, who is killed by the dæmon; but this relationship is not presented in much detail.) Again, the relationship of relating, of confessional self-narration, between three male characters is foregrounded by the treatment of other relationships in the novel. In short, the domestic affections which the novel purports to promote over broader social or intensely individual values are shown to be precarious, marginal, and problematic.

These facts may, as some critics argue, reflect Mary Shelley's resentment of her parents' relationship, her criticism of their and Percy Shelley's grand intellectual and philanthropic schemes, her reservations about Percy Shelley as a husband, or her own emotional and psychological ambivalence about her situation as a daughter, woman, wife, or mother.[4] Yet Mary Shelley generalizes and broadens what might be personal experience into larger, indeed very ambitious public and social-historical themes, just as her parents did in their novels of the 1790s. The plot of the creature becoming the master of its creator was quickly picked up by political satirists, who liked to show the common people as a giant controlling its creator, the political reformists and liberals.[5] More important, the relationship between Frankenstein and his creature could be seen as an analogy to the plot of the French Revolution, in which the Revolution's creators, the Girondins (those moderate reformers with whom Wollstonecraft and Godwin had closest ties), were swept away in the *coups d'état* of 1793–95 by their creatures, the Jacobins and their successors.

Out of this conflict arose a titan, a 'modern Prometheus', a heroic transgressor in the name of humanity, the self-proclaimed embodiment of the Revolution, Napoleon Bonaparte, whose career had only just been halted when Mary Shelley began her novel in 1816. These associations are reinforced by Shelley's denomination of the creature as a 'dæmon', in Greek mythology a being partly human, partly divine. This denomination is doubly ironical. Frankenstein intends to create a 'new man' better than any man before – in sum, a dæmon in the original sense; instead he creates a monstrosity, a 'modern' (i.e., degenerate) dæmon, just like the Revolutionaries who intended to create a 'new man' by changing the institutions that make man what he is.

There is another revolutionary analogy here, too; for the site of origin of both the novel and the novel's story is Geneva, and one of the Revolution's adopted fathers was the man who signed himself 'Citizen of Geneva' – Jean-Jacques Rousseau. Here was another 'modern Prometheus' who brought the fire of 'enthusiasm' to Enlightenment thought and who paid the price of social ostracism, alienation, and solitude for the truths/transgressions he advanced. Furthermore, Rousseau's and the Revolution's professions of general philanthropy had often been set against Rousseau's confession of having abandoned his own children and the Revolution's disregard for individual and family in the name of 'the people'. Moreover, Godwin's *Enquiry Concerning Political Justice* declared that the general benefit of mankind was a higher claim than love for one's family and friends, and in the name of general truth Godwin had even revealed his late wife Mary Wollstonecraft's sexual 'indiscretions' and transgressions, in his biography of her, published just after her death and Mary's birth in 1797. Both Godwin and the memory of Wollstonecraft suffered publicly in consequence. The fate of the Godwin–Wollstonecraft family was implicated at several points with that of the Revolution and with the politics, personal and public, of excess and transgression.[6]

Mary Shelley's fictional analogy, however, is more public than private, and is not merely a case of the 'female Gothic', dealing only with women's concerns and culture. The very name Frankenstein, possibly a combination of pidgin-German for Franks (Franken) and the German for domain or realm (stein), suggests a parallel between the fate of Victor (ironic Christian name) Frankenstein and the fates of the

Revolution, the Revolution's 'father', its son, Wollstonecraft, and Godwin. Read in this way, *Frankenstein* is a critique of revolutionary optimism of the 1790s, which was inherited from the eighteenth-century Enlightenment and such writers as Rousseau, developed by Godwin, Wollstonecraft, and others, and now discussed and meditated on by those in the Shelley circle, genuinely interested in the possibility but painfully aware of the social obstacles to human 'perfectibility' – a term associated with Godwinian philosophy – including progress through science.[7]

These are historical analogies that could be read into the novel by well-informed readers in 1818; the mythological analogy is more obvious, declared in the novel's subtitle and reinforced by literary-historical references and allusions within the text. In this respect, *Frankenstein; or, The Modern Prometheus* claims to participate in the repertory of Romantic poetry from the 1790s to the 1810s, and to require a symbolic, poetic reading rather than a historical, prosaic, and 'realist' one. The myth of Prometheus used in the novel was something of a commonplace by the 1810s, but Mary Shelley uses it well. Both Prometheus and his modern counterpart transgress out of desire to benefit mankind, and both are punished for doing so. Furthermore, the intentions of both are not exactly fulfilled: Prometheus's theft of fire from the gods proves to have harmful as well as beneficial effects for mankind, and Frankenstein's discovery of the 'spark of life' turns out to be a curse to himself, his family, and other innocent people. Nevertheless, Prometheus's transgression is heroic and mythic and does lead to many benefits – the advanced civilization that fire makes possible – whereas Frankenstein's crime is wholly negative in its effects, except as a moral lesson to readers. The myth of Prometheus would inspire emulation; the story of the 'modern Prometheus' would inspire revulsion.

'Modern' here, then, means not only 'contemporary' but something like 'fallen from the mythic and heroic past', that is, from a past beyond or above history. If Prometheus was heroic or superhuman, the 'modern Prometheus' is, and by the logic of romantic irony must be, all too human – historical rather than mythical man. Failed heroism might even lead to the demonic, as Frankenstein's 'dæmon' (his usual denomination in the novel) suggests when he compares himself several times to Satan (another allusion to *Paradise Lost*). The implication of the subtitle and associated allusions is anti-historical: only in myth (or epic literature?) is effective and fruitful heroic action (transgression) possible. The implication is reinforced by the range of quotation in the novel – Canto III of Byron's *Childe Harold's Pilgrimage*, Coleridge's 'Rime of the Ancient Mariner', Wordsworth's 'Tintern Abbey', Percy Shelley's 'Mutability' – and allusion – Ariosto's Renaissance chivalric romance, *Orlando Furioso*, Dante's great Medieval allegorical romance, *The Divine Comedy* – as well as by the dæmon's bookshelf of classics, through which he learns of the 'domestic affections', civic heroism, the cycle of historical decline, and the fall from the sublime into history.

These classics are Goethe's *The Sorrows of Werther*, Plutarch's *Lives*, Volney's *Ruins of Empire*, and *Paradise Lost*. This canon is very much a list of key texts for Wollstonecraft and Godwin; but for a reader of the 1810s the principle that would run through all of them, as well as through the texts quoted or alluded to, would be the conflict between the social and historical on one hand and the transcendental and subjective on the other. History and the social recapture the individual who expresses his (for this is a male domain of action) individuality by sublime and heroic, historically and socially transcendental aspiration, ambition, or transgression. For the sublime visions the dæmon receives from his study of the De Laceys and the books prove to be only visions, not realities for him, just as Frankenstein's sublime vision of a superhuman being turns out in reality to be inhuman or subhuman, though the dæmon is made that way by society and the prejudice and ignorance of others.

The dæmon is also made that way by reading Frankenstein's own journal account of the creation of the monster and revulsion from what he had made. The journal reveals to the dæmon his real identity, and he exclaims: '"Accursed creator! Why did you form a monster so hideous that even *you* turned from me in disgust? . . . Satan had his companions, fellow-devils, to admire and encourage him; but I am solitary and abhorred"' (ch. 15). Like Caleb Williams, the dæmon finds that the surface is mistaken for the authentic self, which remains forever beyond domestication and social knowledge. Furthermore, the shift of transgression to an original sin of ugliness could be seen to reflect in particular a woman's perception of the problematic relation of self, appearance, and society in Romantic fiction, although the parallel between aesthetic and moral perception was a commonplace in eighteenth-century thought since the work of Francis Hutcheson (1694–1746). Nevertheless, ugliness or monstrosity can hardly be compared to Caleb's transgression of social-political codes in Godwin's *Caleb Williams*, or Satan's transgression of moral codes in *Paradise Lost*, or even Prometheus's moral-political transgression in Percy Shelley's 'lyrical drama' *Prometheus Unbound*, begun just a few months after *Frankenstein* was published.

In a sense, *Frankenstein*, too, is lyrical – expressive, personal, and dealing with passion – as well as poetic – symbolic, allusive, figural, mythic, and literary. It transforms history, and the pointed if covert social-historical critique it contains, into myth, and into the kind of novel fit to be read by those in the Shelley circle. To this extent, it abandons the fictional project of Mary Shelley's parents during the 1790s – to remake the 'modern novel' into a vehicle for intervention in history rather than for escape from it. The social-historical plane of being is shown in *Frankenstein* to be hopelessly relative and inauthentic, in short, unreformable and irredeemable, as it is shown to be in Romantic poetry, especially Byron's and Shelley's poems of the years 1816–18, when *Frankenstein* was composed. There remain only the sublime and the subjective – also major themes of Romantic poetry – and, of course, the self-expressive act of relating, in a literary rather than a social or historical sense.

Thus language, as Peter Brooks has shown, is a major theme in the novel.[8] It is mastery of this 'godlike science', as the dæmon calls it, that enables him to understand what it is to be human and to communicate his full and complete inward humanity, in spite of his outward monstrosity, to his creator, in the central narrative of the book. Here, in the midst of sublime, unspeakable nature of the Alpine glacier (the dæmon's refuge from human society, which rejects him), the dæmon persuades Frankenstein to create a mate so that the dæmon's incompleteness, his lack of society (specifically the domestic affections), may be remedied. So well has the dæmon mastered language, that, like Caleb Williams, he persuades his creator/would-be destroyer to relent, to sympathize, to 'compassionate', to admit his own guilt and responsibility. But this is not a terminal act in *Frankenstein*, as it is in *Caleb Williams*. Frankenstein changes his mind, and in another doubling the dæmon strips Frankenstein of all his domestic relations, and of human society in general, leaving the creator only his creation (until Walton comes along).

Mary Shelley's novel, then, has the pessimistic conclusion about language, self-expressivity, the rhetoric of self-disclosure, that was implicit in Godwin's original, pessimistic conclusion to *Caleb Williams* – Caleb fails to move Falkland, and dies. Language, even language formed on the model of the candid speech of the virtuous De Laceys and the writing of Plutarch, Milton, and Goethe, cannot surpass the limits of moral, aesthetic, and social prejudice. Perhaps that is also why the women in this novel are either strangely silent, or ineffectual in their acts of persuasion (such as Elizabeth's letter to Frankenstein early in his tale). The only relationship possible is through language, but that relationship remains mere relating, a self-narrative without issue. This, again, may be viewed as Mary Shelley's pessimistic reflection on the public career of her parents, of such figures as Rousseau, or of her own husband as revolutionary but largely unread poet. It may be that she meant to celebrate relating through language, to transcend political discourse by acts of self-narration, to 'go beyond ideology, from the world at large to the quarrel within'.[9] It may be that she models in

*Frankenstein* a woman's experience of the failure of language to do any more than express the self, the failure of language to change the world, dominated as it is by men and *their* passions and prejudices. Para-doxically, of course, *Frankenstein*, however misread, has entered into modern mythology and culture, and to that extent did become a form of effective action in the social and public spheres of men rather than the merely personal, domestic, or literary spheres (the despised Gothic romance) relegated to women.

*Frankenstein* is a novel about excess and transgression, but formally it is symmetrical, shapely, obviously ordered to a purpose. As with Austen's novels, this sense of control communicates to the reader an aesthetic experience that may, after all, balance the spectacle of excess and transgression in a way that is not visible in a mere summary of *Frankenstein*; perhaps that is why many readers familiar with other, disturbing versions of the story find the experience of reading the novel to be strangely undisturbing. A novel that combines a powerful story of excess and transgression with formal excess is the Rev. Charles Robert Maturin's *Melmoth the Wanderer* (1820). Maturin was a socially marginal character in several ways, and it seems appropriate that *Melmoth* should represent the extreme, the limits of Gothic romance during the Romantic period. But like *Frankenstein*, *Melmoth* is not so much a Gothic romance as a novel of passion that uses elements of the Gothic to exhibit the authenticity yet the dangers of extravagant self-hood in an inauthentic social-historical world. Like *Frankenstein*, *Melmoth* also uses the scheme of romantic irony to develop the theme of limits and transgression, and Maturin, like Shelley, draws on both the legend of the Wandering Jew, cursed with extended life, and the story of Faust, who sold his soul for transcendental knowledge.

Melmoth's Wanderer, like Shelley's Frankenstein and Godwin's St Leon, learns that the possession of superhuman power or knowledge (or power-knowledge) is a transgression of 'natural' human limitations that cuts him off from society in general and the domestic affections, leaving him a wanderer. Furthermore, the transgression has only bound him in a contract with the Devil, and in fact most of the charac-ters in *Melmoth*'s many inset tales are subject to a binding, limiting document of some kind, usually a will. Thus the Wanderer seeks to break the limits of his contract by persuading one or other of the victims of these other contracts to take his place with the Devil, so that Melmoth can re-enter the limitations of the normal human condition, and enjoy both the limits of domestic affection and social rootedness, and the final human limitation of death that alone seems to give meaning and value to life.

For the most part, however, the novel's inset tales display the agony and passion of victims of society's various oppressive relationships, conventions, laws, and institutions. Thus the connections between these tales are thematic and tonal rather than plotted. The organizing thematic principles are, first, that society is irredeemably relative, artificial, and conflicted, such that authenticity of being in the individual or the domestic affections is rendered precarious, perhaps impossible; and, second, that extravagant selfhood also destroys authentic inward being and domestic affections. Each tale in *Melmoth* shows how both social institutions, such as religion, government, and law, and excessive individualism or self-interest threaten to break up families or prevent true romantic love between two people from being realized in a stable, happy marriage. Each tale seems to depict the destructive effect of the will to power and the way the circuit of power dehumanizes the powerful and reduces the oppressed to the sub- or non-human. In *Melmoth*, society and its oppressive institutions, or extreme forms of egotism, desire for power, and passion, drive other individuals beyond their human limits, to apathy or emptiness of self, to madness or self-disintegration, to suicide or self-destruction, to self-alienation through disguise or playing a false self, or finally – and this is the plotted link between the tales – to seeking relief from oppression by transgressing of both human and natural limits and exchanging places with the Wanderer in his contract with the Devil.

As in *Frankenstein*, important historical patterns and parallels as well as major thematic concerns are also suggested in *Melmoth*'s patterning of tales within tales. Each tale also contrasts the simple, natural, authentic, selfless, and independent with the sophisticated, artful, artificial, self-interested, and confining (scenes of imprisonment and confinement, self- or institutionally-imposed, abound). Every tale has its courtly intriguer and hypocrite: and the novel as a whole is yet another representation of the evils of decadent court culture and social emulation, another representation of the ways this culture deforms and denatures the authentic inward self, within the historical span from one age of revolution and restoration – the seventeenth century – to another – the age of the French Revolution and the post-Napoleonic restoration of monarchy and Catholicism. The frame narrative is set in Ireland in the late 1810s and owes a good deal to Maria Edgeworth's 'Irish tales' of old-fashioned Irish gentry running down their estates in pursuit of short-sighted passions – in this case, old Melmoth's passion for accumulation at the expense of 'improvement'. The first and last inset narratives depict late seventeenth-century England for the most part, the period when the Wanderer's career began and when Ireland's – indeed, Britain's – social structure of Protestant gentry hegemony was established for the next 150 years (the term of the Wanderer's contract with the Devil). The second and second to last inset tales depict Spain under the Inquisition and court government – the kind of state power structure done away with by the English Civil War and its aftermath, the Restoration and Glorious Revolution of 1688, but also the kind of power structure restored in most of Europe after the final fall of Napoleon in 1815.

There are other, short inset tales, especially in Alonzo's tale (the second major inset tale), but the major tale at the centre of the novel is the 'Tale of the Indians', set into Alonzo's tale, and its central description is of the paradisal world of the beautiful castaway and child of nature, Immalee. This world is set in obvious contrast to the thoroughly divided and conflicted social world on the Indian mainland, and the similarly divided societies of Spain and Restoration England. Thus 'nature' is opposed to both Oriental superstition and European court culture – both disastrously divided societies. If Ireland, the setting of the frame narrative, is seen to be less viciously divided, it is divided nevertheless, and, after all, the 'home' of the Wanderer, to which he returns at the end of the novel to pay his debt to the Devil. The connection between the public and private themes in *Melmoth* is that all the tales relate the Wanderer's attempts to exploit the misery of an individual so reduced by some kind of social conflict and oppression that he or she might be willing to take over the Wanderer's contract in return for release from whatever it is that binds and oppresses. But this is merely to exchange one kind of limiting for another: freedom is an illusion, in time or out of it.

The major argument of *Melmoth*, then, is the oppression of the individual by a social institution of some form, especially organized religion and property. The main device for illustrating this argument is organized religion, including Catholicism, Judaism, the religions of India, Islam, and Calvinist or Puritan Protestantism; left out is the Church of England, the Rev. Maturin's own church. Nevertheless, Maturin's treatment of religion could easily stand for the place of ideology, or general, secular world-views and systems of belief as these operate in society; for religion is, perhaps, only a particularly clear example of the reproduction of ideology by means of various institutions, secular and ecclesiastical, in any historical society. Furthermore, Maturin clearly suggests that oppressive, confining religion is a metonym for the whole of society, denaturing and disintegrating the individual in ways that anticipate the fiction of Franz Kafka.

The use of the Catholic monastery as a metaphor for the interconnected social conventions and institutions that confine and shape the individual is seen already in *The Monk* and other earlier Gothic fictions, but Maturin gives the figure full development, especially in Alonzo's tale. When Alonzo is denied converse with the other monks in the monastery (which he has been forced to enter for reasons of family 'honour') Alonzo realizes that his cries 'would be echoed by no friendly answering tones in a community of sixty persons, – such is the sterility of humanity in a convent' (vol. 2, ch. 6) – in other words, the convent is a false community, and Alonzo experiences near-maddening anomie surrounded by 'brothers'. Later, when he considers escape, he realizes with despair that 'All Spain is but one great monastery' (vol. 2, ch. 8), a realization similar to Caleb's recognition that all of society is a prison, in Godwin's *Caleb Williams*. Another aspect of the dehumanizing effect of the monastery is that it reduces individuals to their outward shells, either play-acting hypocrites or empty, apathetic machines. Metaphors of theatre and theatricality also occur throughout *Melmoth*, and are used to describe the all-pervasive hypocrisy and artifice in social relations.

In the second place, society is depicted as a scene of brutal conflict, amounting almost to warfare. In India, Spain, and seventeenth-century England, the settings for the various tales, religions vie with each other for influence and power while the religions' priests strive for absolute power over their adherents. Civil war may threaten, or actually break out. At the least, there may be mob violence. This was another of Maturin's preoccupations that came from his position in the Anglo-Irish Protestant minority, and though again he generalizes it, he cannot resist revealing the connection. In an episode reminiscent of the scenes of popular disturbance in Lewis's *The Monk*, Alonzo hears how a criminal monk is lynched by the people of Madrid – a scene to disturb any member of the novel-reading classes, in 1796 or in 1820.

Alonzo learns how the monk is beaten to a pulp by the angry mob; a footnote then establishes the plausibility of such an episode by drawing attention to a similar incident in Ireland during the political violence of the late 1790s (vol. 3, ch. 12). The historical parallel is clear, and is, as it were, brought home to the novel's readers. The exercise of power can even destroy the most authentic of human relationships – romantic love – in a maddening and selfish passion that erases all human and humane ones. The obvious example is the story of the two lovers who are betrayed to the monastery's ruthless Superior by the parricide monk and left to starve in a dungeon. Maddened by hunger, the man tries to bite a piece of flesh from his mistress's shoulder – '"that bosom on which he had so often luxuriated, became a meal to him now"' (vol. 2, ch. 9). *Melmoth* as a whole shows how social conflict can reduce the individual to something non-human – an apathetic automaton, a hypocrite, a madman, a cannibal, or a physically unrecognizable object.

*Melmoth* represents social relativity, conflict, and oppression of the individual in several ways, then, but in the 'Tale of the Indians' in Adonijah's manuscript it also represents powerfully an ideal, whole, and authentic world of value. Immalee, a Spanish girl lost on an uninhabited island off the coast of India, grows up without human contact and so is innocent, pure, and natural. The isle had formerly been the site of a temple of one of the harsh Indian religions, but it was abandoned after an earthquake and violent storms. Immalee appears to a few visitors from the mainland, and popular superstition rapidly makes her a goddess and the isle sacred to the worship of love and happiness. The Wanderer then appears, fascinated by this rarity of human nature, a natural being. In scenes reminiscent of the education of the dæmon in *Frankenstein*, the Wanderer introduces Immalee to the social and relativist rather than natural use of language, and to the 'realities' of life outside her whole and harmonious, because hitherto solitary paradise.

Thus begins Immalee's fall. Through his telescope the Wanderer shows her life on the mainland, a scene of human misery dominated by the temples and cruel and bloody ceremonies of various religions united only by their imposition of suffering on their followers. Immalee's fall into knowledge of society is completed when she begins to discover that she is not sufficient unto herself – she, too, experiences desire, for the Wanderer, and is willing to leave her paradise for him. But she is recovered by her family, and taken back to Spain, which, like the Indian shore viewed through the telescope, is opposite in every way to the unfallen, undivided world she left behind, and where she is renamed Isidora. In Spain, her greedy parents prepare to sell her on the marriage market, but the Wanderer persuades her to a secret marriage. Now the object of her family's and the Church's suspicions, she ends in the hands of the Inquisition, her dead infant at her breast. After much suffering, she dies, calling death, the final limitation of humanity, her 'liberation' (vol. 4, ch. 37). She has traversed the full range of human experience from the wholeness of paradise to the social hell of social division, artifice, hypocrisy, and confinement of every kind. She is not, after all, a goddess, and like the Wanderer and all the other victims in all the other tales, she, too, is a victim of her humanity in being the victim of her desire.

The emphasis of *Melmoth*, then, is not so much on desire as on its consequences. This emphasis is reinforced by the narrative form of the novel, which requires complexity, considerable length, and immediacy in order to have full effect. In each tale, as well as in the frame narra-tive, Maturin establishes a situation of conflict or unfulfilled desire and prolongs that situation with one delay or another, just as the inset tales, one after the other, defer the conclusion of the frame narrative's tale of the Wanderer's return and the settling of his contract. As in Radcliffe's 'Gothic romances' this deferral allows full scope to the representation of inward subjectivity, though the subjectivity Maturin fixes on is passion in the original sense of suffering, and perhaps especially the sufferings of Christ on the cross, a combined physical and moral agony in which one's individuality and humanity are most exposed and most tempted to transgress limits human or divine. The pattern of bondage, agony, and temptation is repeated again and again in the inset tales as well as in the story of the Wanderer.

This pattern is about transcendence of the world. In many religious tracts and 'tales for youth', for example, suffering for virtue and withstanding the lure of the world were held out as transcendental acts for young people and the poor, and in *Melmoth* passion as suffering seems to have a related purpose. Besides foregrounding subjectivity, as in Radcliffe's or Lewis's novels, it sublimates the self, raises it above the social relativities, conflicts, and obstacles which, paradoxically, repress the self as desire. Passion of any kind transcendentalizes the subject. Furthermore, the style of narration in each tale, whether narrated by the tale's protagonist (as in Alonzo's tale) or by an informed outsider (as in most of the tales), has considerable energy and immediacy, so that the reader of the novel easily takes the place of the reader or hearer within the novel and is drawn in to share and sympathize with the passions described and represented. The rhetorical strategy of narration in *Melmoth* is to engage the reader in sympathetic relationship with a succession of victims of passion, just as the novel as a whole is structured internally as a succession of such relationships. The notable exception is the Wanderer, whose feelings are described in detail only in the 'Tale of the Indians', in which he suffers conflicting desires – for Immalee as partner and bride, for Isidora as victim and substitute in his hellish contract. As a result, the Wanderer is, for much of the novel, a remote and menacing figure, the double of each sufferer in his extremity of approaching self-alienation.

Finally, then, the formal structure of *Melmoth The Wanderer: A Tale* is interestingly similar to that of *Frankenstein* in its emphasis on relating or tale-telling, both as a way of expressing the self, of leaving a record of the self's traversal of passion, and as a way of creating a relationship with another. Of course the tales in *Melmoth* and the tale of the Wanderer, like the tales in *Caleb Williams, The Wrongs of Woman*, and *Frankenstein*, also have a didactic function: individual experience produces general conclusions about 'things as they are', the interlocked, historically specific structures of ideology, value, and social institutions which bear upon the authentic individual. But, like *Frankenstein* and unlike *Caleb Williams, Melmoth* seems less interested in changing the world than in representing it and, in the nature of the representing-in-relating, transcending it. Furthermore, in its revelling in fictionality and narration *Melmoth* clearly represents one reason why Evangelical Christians, moral and social conservatives, and radical political reformers alike could be suspicious of novels that created a taste for narratives of excess and transgression, of the strange, the 'unreal', the unhomely, the alien, and the hellish or sublime – in short, a taste for reading as excess, as other than 'solid' or 'useful' reading, as an end in itself.

# Centres, Margins and Limits of British Society: Novels of Country, Town, Region and the Exotic

As the novel of passion and the Gothic romance were reaching a climax of extravagant subjectivity and formal complexity other fictions rooted in familiar, homely, social, everyday 'reality' were also achieving a wide readership. Just as 'village anecdotes' and quotidian reality were used to criticize forms of excessive individualism and artificial forms of social life in the 1800s, so in the later 1810s and the 1820s domestic realism could form an alternative to egotistical and neo-Sentimental fictions in prose and verse: Byron could be offset by George Crabbe; Maturin by Mary Mitford. For while growing appreciation of the art of the novel could not silence a continuing chorus of criticism of the extravagant, the 'romantic' aspects of the novel, particularly the novel of passion, most conservative and anti-'romantic' critics were by now willing to allow that certain types of novel, especially novels of common life and domestic realism, could be eminently 'useful'. As a writer in the *Scots Magazine* put it, in 1822,

> the familiarity of [realist novels'] descriptions domesticates us, as it were, more completely than poetry can do, in the most touching scenes of humble life, and brings them directly to our hearts, by a homeliness of detail, which could not be attempted, according to received notions of poetry.[10]

The writer claimed that certain novels had depicted humble life better even than the poems of Crabbe or those of the 'Lake School' of the Wordsworth circle. This kind of fiction, which tended to associate domesticity and 'realism' with rural life, simplicity, and virtue, developed from the Sentimental tale of the two or three decades before the 1790s, anti-Jacobin novels by the likes of Jane West during the 1790s, and novels of rural life and 'national tales' of the 1800s by writers such as Elizabeth Le Noir, Maria Edgeworth, and Elizabeth Hamilton. Jane Austen's novels, to some extent, reinforced the image of authentic life, love, and domestic virtues residing in the well-run country estate, and the 'Wizard of the North' added rich materials to the theme, as in the depiction of the rural Eden on the Duke of Argyle's estate in volume 4 of *The Heart of Midlothian*. In the late 1810s and 1820s several highly successful fiction writers rapidly developed these themes of rural life, the opposition of town and country, and regional, provincial culture. Nevertheless, readers of 'village anecdotes' probably indulged in reading novels of passion and Gothic romances, too, for both dealt with the same complex of issues and interests, though in apparently quite different ways.

For example, the most successful writer of 'sketches of rural character and scenery' in the 1820s – indeed, of the nineteenth century – Mary Mitford, also wrote potboiler stage tragedies. Her widely read quasi-novel, *Our Village: Sketches of Rural Character and Scenery*, was first published in the *Lady's Magazine* in the early 1820s and helped to define further for the reading public an emergent vision of rural England as the 'real' England, the essential England, but a rural England relatively free from the class conflict, mass economic hardships, and brutalizing labour increasingly seen as typical of the industrial towns. Thus *Our Village* is another attempt to redefine rural England, the 'real' England, in terms of gentrified middle-class values and culture, rather than historical gentry hegemony. It remained influential and widely read throughout the nineteenth century, and its mark can be traced in the work of Victorian novelists from Elizabeth Gaskell to George Eliot. *Our Village* played a decisive role in inventing a unified and harmonious 'national' culture – whether English or British – as essentially a rural and traditional culture, a culture in which the realities of social conflict and exploitation have been marginalized, or removed altogether. The texts that embodied this invented tradition thus became central to the emerging literary institution of the novel.

The method by which Mary Mitford made her important contribution to fiction, to literature, and to the national culture is the 'sketch' promised in the subtitle of *Our Village*. This literary genre is related to the tale in its claims to realism, unpretentiousness, and authenticity of a certain kind, to be distinguished from full-dress literature of elite or learned cultures – upper-class, professional, and male cultures. The sketch aims to seize the 'essence' or 'spirit' of a thing rather than to present a finished version of its object. It is associated with the artistic 'accomplishments' of well-bred, leisured young ladies (several of these appear in the book to do sketching with pencil and paper), and so the sketch also claims to be art for one's own sake, rather than for commercial or professional artistic production. The genre of the country sketch in prose still survives in 'better' sorts of newspapers and magazines, and is often written by educated, cultivated, and leisured people living in the country. Above all, the sketch, whether pictorial or verbal, lays claim to a certain essential realism but is in fact already, by its nature, an aestheticization of what it represents. This is the consistent formal characteristic of Mitford's 'Sketches of Rural Character and Scenery', or rather, it is the consistent thematic *and* formal characteristic of these sketches. For in making rural characters and scenes subjects of sketching in the way that she does, Mitford both represents them and evaluates them.

Mitford admits that her work is a quasi-novel, for at the end of *Our Village* she refers to her text as a 'history, half real and half imaginary, of a half imaginary and half real little spot on the sunny side of Berkshire'. There is a rhetorical point to this admission, for the 'reality' of rural life is softened or even transformed by the sketcher's hand, while the depiction of rural life and its importance in the national culture is authenticated by the basis in 'real' life. For like Hannah More's treatment of the common people in Cheap Repository, Legh Richmond's treatment of the common people and natural scenery in *Annals of the Poor*, and Scott's treatment of the people and places of Scotland, Mitford's treatment of 'rural characters and scenery' claims close kinship with real life and nature. Like Legh Richmond and Walter Scott, too, she created a tourist industry for the 'little spot' she sketched, as hundreds of visitors took the road from London to the real village of Three Mile Cross where Mitford lived, wishing to find the imaginary real. This, after all, is what the sketch is: a form of personal rather than public art, combining 'realism' with expressiveness, but in which the 'real' is not the text but the pre-text. Quite clearly, however, Mitford's England is not the real England of her day. It is not the rural England of gentry hegemony and rural labour, but rather the rural England of John Claudius Loudon, the cottage *ornée* (or at least the suburban villa), the flower garden, watercolours, nature notebooks, and the 'country life' column in local newspapers and magazines – in short, a thoroughly middle-class rural England.

This *embourgeoisement* of rural England is represented both thematically and formally. First there is the pattern of reassuring recurrence. Certain individuals and families recur in several sketches, and the character or family history is a recurring formal element. Certain temporal patterns recur, as well, particularly the reconciliation of petty local conflicts, the rewarding of virtue and fortitude, the discomfiture of vanity or social climbing, the occasional local 'tragedy' (due to chance, it seems), and the operation of benevolence and good will to resolve social impasses, bridge social gaps, relieve misery and suffering. There are many recurring thematic elements, of course, especially the opposition of town and country and foreign and English values, and the Englishness of 'our village' and its people and places. Then there are larger patterns, that flow through the life of 'our village'. One of these is 'improvement', *viz.*, agricultural revolution, architectural and gardening fashions, and social amelioration through education and 'civilizing' forces. Another is the pattern of life – birth, childhood, marriage, the founding of families, old age, and death – though the optimistic tone of *Our Village* is suggested in the predominance of marrying over all the other events and stages of life. Allied to these patterns are those of rise and fall in individuals' and families' fortunes, due to certain natural traits of character or, less often, to circumstance.

Larger patterns of national destiny loom distantly in these sketches, though references to economic and social change, to war, and political events are brought in from time to time. The most frequent references to life outside 'our village', however, have to do with fashion of some kind or another, and these references collaborate with references to larger national events and the patterns referred to earlier to suggest that whatever happens outside 'our village' is not recurrent but merely superficial, occasional, and ephemeral, whereas the perduring social and moral realities and perduring human nature are found here, in 'our village'. This argument is reinforced by the various natural calendars, including the annual life cycle of the earth, of animals, of trees and flowers, of social festivals (such as Christmas and Maytime), and – though far less prominent – of work and harvest. The rhythms of nature, including the weather, seem to operate independently of human social change, to subordinate both the rise and fall of individuals and families and the patterns of national events and movements. At the same time, the economic realities of rural life, of work, property, and production, are also subordinated to the aesthetic function of flowers, trees, animals, wild and domesticated nature. Flowers and gardening, in fact, are major themes in *Our Village*, but not in the lives of those who own and work the land. Furthermore, those who own and those who work the land hardly appear in *Our Village*, or appear as figures of satire, or as decidedly minor persons.

The dominant concern and the social models of *Our Village* are the rural middle classes, especially the independent yeoman farmers and their families and the commercial people, what the narrator calls 'the whole farmerage and shopkeepery of the place' ('A Christmas Party'). The gentry hardly appear at all; rural labourers appear often, but usually as minor characters except when useful to point a moral or adorn a tale. Even work is mostly a source of aesthetic pleasure and contemplation to the narrator of *Our Village*, so that what is on the margin of rural life is in the centre of the material of *Our Village*, and what is central to rural life is relentlessly marginalized *and* aestheticized. The 'reality' of rural life and the 'realism' that depicts it are decidedly partial.

This representation and the narrative 'voice' of *Our Village* are one; as the narrator remarks at the end of the last series of sketches, she bids farewell to the 'locality' with regret, for it 'has become almost identified with myself' ('Farewell to Our Village'). Moreover, she refers to her writing-desk as 'that important part of me' ('The Lost Keys'). The locality, the perceiving self, and the writing are almost one. The perceiving and writing 'self', the consciousness represented by the narrative voice, is obviously literary and aesthetic. The text is full of quotations and allusions from a wide range of serious literature and *belles lettres*, and the narrator informs us in passing of her other writing activity in the eminently literary genre of tragedy. Perhaps, too, these references serve to emphasize that the familiar and quotidian 'reality' of a rural world is far removed in several senses from the world of literary tragedy. The text is also decorated with or punctuated by samples of the narrator's own verse – one sonnet in particular, though pastiche Wordsworth, reinforces a connection with the attitude that nature transcends merely social relativities, seen in Wordsworth's shorter lyrics in *Lyrical Ballads*.

More obvious is the repeated framing of natural scenes or scenes with characters by references to painting, usually Dutch. Whenever a description is to be marked as particularly pleasing, it is described as though it were a painting, and the terms 'picture' and 'picturesque' are used frequently. This is a device often used by Walter Scott, and *Our Village*, too, is a description novel, but its descriptions serve an aesthetic, moral, and personal rather than a historical and public understanding of the matter. Furthermore, the style of *Our Village* is literary in its effects of expressiveness and immediacy (slipping into the present tense, addresses to the reader, use of deictic pronouns such as 'this' and 'that', and use of exclamations and dashes). Finally, the narrator invokes – or rather creates – a particular literary (and fictional) tradition of writing about the country, its people, and aspects.

This line of writing includes the novelists Charlotte Smith, Elizabeth Le Noir, and Jane Austen, the poet Cowper, and the naturalist Gilbert White. Admiring references are made to all of these writers, but the strongest affinity is claimed with Austen, in the early 1820s not yet a classic or even particularly well-known novelist. What Mitford does, however, is to make Austen over into a novelist who deals in Mitford's own kind of snug ruralism and insistent modesty of scale and subject. In the process, Mitford rejects the contemporary literature of grand romance, of operatic scale, of cosmopolitan culture; she rejects the rampant Byronism in poetry and fiction, the novels of passion and high society, and the explicit handling of national issues. As she remarks in her first sketch:

> Even in books I like a confined locality. . . . Nothing is so tiresome as to be whirled half over Europe at the chariot-wheels of a hero . . . it produces a real fatigue, a weariness of spirit. On the other hand, nothing is so delightful as to sit down in a country village in one of Miss Austen's delicious novels, quite sure before we leave it to become intimate with every spot and every person it contains; or to ramble with Mr. White over his own parish of Selborne. . . .

In a sense, *Our Village* does combine the social world of Austen's novels with the natural world of White's *Natural History of Selborne*, which Mitford describes as 'one of the most fascinating books ever written' ('Our Village'); but it should be clear by now how different Mitford's *embourgeoisement* of the country is from Austen's. Ironically, therefore, *Our Village* made Mary Mitford a literary lion in, of all places, the highest circles of fashion in smokey, crowded, dirty London; and in 1830 she was rewarded with a government literary pension (only the second ever awarded to a woman – the first went to Lady Morgan). Nevertheless, these rewards were just, for in *Our Village* Mitford had created a powerful national myth, one that is as vigorous now as it was in the 1820s.

Just before Mitford invented the archetypal English village, however, an Irishman and general writer scored an equally brilliant success and helped to establish another national myth by celebrating the life of the metropolis, London, with a different kind of domestic and social realism. Yet even he could not, ultimately, resist the myth of country life. In one way, Pierce Egan's *Life in London* (1820–21) was simply the culmination of a commercially successful popular literary product, developing for over a decade or so, in which were combined fiction, highly topical and 'realistic' subject matter, lively narrative style, great play with language, literariness, and sociolinguistic relativities, a widely disseminated culture of fashion and emulation, a renewed interest in urban life at all levels, and energetically executed illustrations. The tendency to associate the 'real' with the 'low' had already been exploited in Romantic folklore and 'national tales'; Egan simply focused on the 'low' in the rapidly changing yet apparently 'traditional' folk life of the city. His success gave rise to a renewed interest in urban popular literature and culture. By the end of the 1820s this popular literature was developed further by middle-class fiction in scenes of 'underworld' life in 'silver-fork novels' such as Bulwer's

*Pelham* (1828) and in 'Newgate novels' such as Bulwer's *Paul Clifford* (1830). The *topos* was then developed by Dickens in *Oliver Twist* (1837–39) and exploited by a host of 'shilling shockers' and 'Salisbury Square fiction'. In the second half of the nineteenth century, with the work of Emile Zola and Continental 'realists', the association of the 'real' with the 'low', and the moral and social function of such 'realism', became major critical issues.

The plot of Egan's *Life in London* is as desultory and disconnected as that of any earlier picaresque social survey, but it does pertain to the novel of education in which a young man or woman is introduced to the intricacies and intrigues, the risks and relativities of fashionable life. For young Jerry Hawthorn's aim in 'seeing life' in London is to return home to Hawthorn Hall, Somerset, a 'wiser' man, ready to take on the responsibilities of a landed gentleman – this he eventually does in Egan's sequel, *Finish to Life in London* (1828). Emulation of a kind, then, is the subject of Egan's novel, too; but it is emulation of an attitude to life found in elements of the very lowest classes in society but shared by the truly genteel of all classes, an attitude to life as a series of 'scenes' of 'fun'.

These themes are developed by several techniques. There is the bird's-eye view of London in Book I, chapter 1, a brief social and topographical survey of the rich human variety of this best school for the true and complete gentleman. There are the contrasting scenes, such as 'All-Max', the low gin-shop ('max' is slang for 'gin') in the lower-class East End of London, contrasted to Almack's, the famous upper-class dances held in the fashionable West End (Book II, ch. 5), and suggesting the richer, more authentic human life to be found in the former rather than the latter. There is also the general resemblance between the amorous activities of Corinthian Tom and those of his King (when younger), as well as the indulgent attitude to other sorts of genteel but not vicious dissipations. In short, Tom, Jerry, and Bob emulate their sovereign in a properly genteel way, and, more important, form a link between him and the common people through their visits to sites of royal and of common life, circumventing both the merely fashionable nobility and the puritanical yet materialistic middle classes. These contrasts, parallels, and connections are strongly reinforced by the justly celebrated plates supplied by the brothers Cruikshank.

But the form and style of *Life in London* have a richness and complexity that the plates, for all their vigour and vitality, do not. Egan brings to the novel the racy literariness, the linguistic extravagance and self-consciousness, the effects of immediacy and spontaneity found in much contemporary journalism and magazine writing. Egan aims for a personal and immediate, desultory and 'nervous', yet complex and highly wrought narrative 'voice' of his own, with numerous puns, parallelisms, complex sentences, and heavy use of typography (italics, several sizes of capitals, dashes, exclamations) to give a 'speaking' emphasis to the writing. The novel is also full of quotations and allusions to all manner of literature from the classics to street ballads. At the same time, true to the genre of the description novel, Egan loads his pages with mock-pedantic, mock-scholarly, mock-antiquarian footnotes, to such an extent that the footnotes usurp most of the space on the page. These techniques, the generally anecdotal narrative method, and the 'nervous' narrative style make *Life in London* a great example of disjunctive form in the Romantic novel and advertise its literariness as something distinct from usual kinds of moral-didactic fiction and fiction-with-a-purpose.

The variety of prose and verse discourses incorporated into *Life in London* is paralleled by its wide range of ephemeral and particular language, dialects of one kind or another, including upper-class slang, sportsmen's slang, thieves' and beggar's cant, Cockney, the peculiar accent of blacks, and professional jargon. These marginal or 'substandard' forms of English are played with to a degree by use of italics to draw the reader's attention to them and by Egan's often facetiously studious footnote translations and explanations. Embracing all these diverse discourses and registers of language is the narrator's self-consciously literary, punning, playful 'voice', the voice of one who uses language for 'fun'. The 'voice' narrating *Life in London* is the correlative of the vision of life for which the novel argues. Furthermore, Egan incorporates sub-literary discourse in his text, notably a Gothic chapbook romance written by one of the characters and quoted verbatim in Book II, chapter 8 (just the sort of chapbook Egan himself used to write in the 1810s), and a variety of poems patterned after the street ballads being sold by John Pitts, James Catnach, and others in Grub Street – indeed, the novel opens with a reference to Grub Street, one of whose most successful denizens was, of course, Pierce Egan. In short, *Life in London* deliberately incorporates elements of the non-literary and the sub-literary, lifting them up, as it were, and giving them a literary function, just as the novel suggests the reader should refresh and educate himself (Life in London *is* mainly for men) in the authentic life of the common people.

Egan's success made him a literary and social lion, and made him conscious of his own importance – so much so that he decided finally to moralize *Life in London*, to retrench its rather too aristocratically libertine morality, its too enthusiastically urban point of view on England and Englishness, its too playful literariness. In *The Finish to the Adventures of Tom, Jerry, and Logic in their Pursuits through Life in and out of London* (1828) Jerry falls in love with a good English country girl,

Mary Rosebud (an 'English Rose'); Bob Logic dies of a wasted constitution, Corinthian Tom is killed in a fall from his horse while fox
hunting, and Jerry marries Miss Rosebud and becomes a '*"settled
being"*', devoting his life henceforth to domesticity, responsible
management of the Hawthorn and Rosebud estates (now united), and
promotion of 'LIFE IN THE COUNTRY'. Furthermore, *The Finish* makes
even sharper and clearer the distinction between the artificiality of fashionable society (somehow 'not English') and the fun of low life. *The
Finish* has far more seriousness, and far less of the allusiveness,
linguistic variety, satiric and parodic elements, footnotes, disjunction
of form, and stylistic verve found in *Life in London*. The moral is clear.
New model gentility, domesticity, moral and disciplined paternalism,
moral seriousness, and LIFE IN THE COUNTRY are to succeed and to
supercede the necessary, desirable, useful experience of LIFE IN LONDON.

While Mary Mitford was publishing the first series of sketches of
*Our Village* and Egan was riding the success of *Life in London*, John
Galt, a Scottish miscellaneous writer, traveller, failed businessman,
former law student, administrator, and friend of Lord Byron, was
publishing a number of 'Scottish novels' which appeared on the surface
to do for a small Ayrshire village what Mitford was doing for her little
corner of Berkshire and Egan for the slums of London. Unlike
Mitford, however, Galt had little interest in village life and natural
history as sources for literary figures of authentic living and values.
Unlike the writers of 'national tales', but like Scott, Galt was interested
less¹ in great historical events and personages than in history as change
lived out on the local level. More important, in what he called his
'theoretical histories', Galt was concerned to show economic change
as the basis for, or conspirator with social, cultural, and intellectual
change. This concern derived from his reading in Scottish Enlightenment historiography and its attempt to account for all aspects of human
and social activity as the work of the human will, free from transcendental or divine intervention.[11]

*Annals of the Parish* (1821) is one of the 'Scottish novels' and is as
good as anything Galt wrote; it also remained his most influential and
enduring work of fiction. Its major achievement is in its combination
of the two formal elements of the narrative 'voice' of the Scottish
village clergyman, Micah Balwhidder, and the apparently artless but
in fact complex and suggestive narrative structure of annals of half a
century in the life of the fictitious Ayrshire village of Dalmailing. Each
chapter treats of a year from 1760, the year of the accession of George
III to the throne of the United Kingdom and of Balwhidder to the cure
of souls of Dalmailing. Here is registered the historical irony of
disparity Galt was so fond of. Moreover, especially in his fiction of
the early 1820s, Galt liked to create situations of narrative irony, in

which a limited and unreliable narrator such as Balwhidder requires the reader to bring his or her broader historical perspective, more cosmopolitan culture, and sense of larger issues to bear on the text. This ironic distance between character and reader is lacking in Le Noir's *Village Anecdotes* and Mitford's *Our Village*, but as with Austen's novels, the reader of Galt's *Annals* is both drawn into a kind of participation in the central consciousness and required to judge it. At the same time, given the evident limitations of this narrating consciousness, the reader is forced by Galt to take up the modern, progressive, yet ironical attitude to human action for which the novel as a whole argues. This technique of narrative irony, parallel to dramatic irony, is the main rhetorical principle of *Annals of the Parish*.

Balwhidder's lack of a modern historical consciousness is shown in his choice of the simple annals form and in his attempts, often ludicrous, to interpret current events according to an older, partly Calvinistic, partly oral and popular tradition of divination and prophecy, of interpreting 'signs', omens, and portents. Balwhidder's consciousness is also 'pre-modern' in that he lacks much of a private inward self. When, at one point, he does go through a patch of melancholy subjectivity, he thinks it is a sign that he should write a book (ch. 5). Here Galt registers the association of subjectivity and print in modern culture, as distinct from the orality, sociability, and community-mindedness of 'pre-modern' culture to which Balwhidder – usually – belongs. But though he cannot write Enlightenment history, Balwhidder cannot escape the historical process, and he, too, is transformed, in part, by the changes he half blindly narrates. By the end of his annals he has come to accept 'progress' – a more secular and pluralist society, the dominance of print culture, greater religious tolerance, social egalitarianism, more liberal moral attitudes, economic change, and prosperity. Since the story Balwhidder has to tell is the story of that modernization, there is a tension between the style and intention of his discourse and what he discourses about.

This tension suggests that it is precisely the literary and the figural rather than the theoretical and objective that provide the appropriate code for reading history and society. Everyday objects and incidents such as tea-drinking signify whole complexes of human and social values; strange new objects, such as coconuts or pear-trees, and persons, such as Mr Cayenne, the American Loyalist, represent the wider national or even international economic and social community. Symbolism and metonymy are major figures of representation in *Annals of the Parish*. Readers would have recognized the invitation to a figural reading of *Annals* even in the names – Loremore the schoolmaster, Macskipnish the teacher of dancing – and Dalmailing itself (named on the very title page) could signify 'productive of little' or

'slovenly place', significances the parish of Dalmailing loses in its progress through economic and cultural modernization. This kind of
naming would associate *Annals* with a particular tradition of Enlightenment fiction of social satire and criticism rather than with the formal
realism of Le Noir's *Village Anecdotes*, Hamilton's *Cottagers of Glenburnie* – indeed, *Annals* is almost an anti-*Glenburnie* – or Mitford's *Our
Village*.

Finally, the sense of lived history and representativeness of the rich
and copious descriptive material is enhanced by the way Balwhidder
shapes his description – his tendency to look before and after, to retrospect and foreshadow, to reflect on the fragility of his own memory
and powers of observation, and to reflect on the nature of his own
sympathies and antipathies, relationships and failures of relating to
persons and things within the world he describes. Yet this authenticity
is simultaneously undercut by Balwhidder's inadequacies in just what
he prides himself on, his ability to read the 'signs of the times'. Thus
*Annals of the Parish*, as a novel of description, presents its reader with
a complex lesson in changing 'reality' and changing or diverse ways
of perceiving it; and once the reader has recognized the irony in
Balwhidder's pride, and grasped the full significance of what
Balwhidder sees and describes but cannot fully comprehend, he or she
might wonder about the fragility of any reading of the 'signs of the
times', including his or her own, precisely because such reading is
always figural. Who is to say that Balwhidder's Biblical and Presbyterian figuralism is not as 'true' as that of the writer and the reader of
*Annals of the Parish*?

This scepticism about reading history is reinforced by the novel's
depiction of the relationship between history and the individual living
it. For one thing, the historical plot here seems to show the 'progress'
of Dalmailing from a materially impoverished, culturally backward,
semi-feudal and paternalist society, still divided along religious-
political lines laid down in the seventeenth-century Civil War and its
aftermath, to a prosperous, almost cosmopolitan, egalitarian, capitalist
society, divided perhaps in more complex ways but fundamentally
pluralist and firmly in the hands of the commercial middle classes. But
we are hardly invited to read this plot with unqualified enthusiasm and
simple-minded approval. Our attitude to the plot of progress is modified by our tendency to sympathize and identify with Balwhidder's
resistance to the plot even while we see the blindness and folly of his
resistance. Furthermore, while the novel seems to hint that the moral
and cultural leaders of this modernized society should be the gentrified
professional men such as young Rev. Malcolm rather than the
'pushing' commercial men such as Mr Cayenne or the old-fashioned
and rather vulgar Rev. Balwhidder, for the reader both Malcolm and

Cayenne remain decidedly minor figures compared to the rich if limited character of Balwhidder.

The impression of ambivalence toward the plot of progress is reinforced by several other factors. First, optimism about progress in history is qualified by the nature of the relation between the individual and history. For history is depicted as originating elsewhere. History reaches Dalmailing and its individuals; and some of its individuals leave Dalmailing to join history (especially large events such as the American and French Revolutionary wars). Economic change, the main element of the historical process, may occasionally deposit in Dalmailing a coconut or exotic bird, new agricultural and manufactured products, an American Loyalist, or, eventually, a whole new village-full of factory workers, with their own religion, culture, and politics. People from Dalmailing may go far away to get rich, to fight, to die, or to return home sadder, wiser, or richer. But Dalmailing itself does not generate history, and the individual has only three alternatives – to participate in history's process, to resist it, or perhaps to stand aside from it. Firmly situated in the centre of his world, Balwhidder cannot see beyond its limits; the reader, however, is expected to do so, and moreover to see Dalmailing as marginal, not central.

Thus Galt's novels are profoundly provincial. Only the reader, able to appreciate the charming and amusing and occasionally tragic inadequacies of Balwhidder and the other victims of history in 'the parish', is presumably at the centre of history, and possessed of the fully informed historical and social consciousness that can discern the text's ironic themes and structure. At the same time, this is not supposed to be a merely literary consciousness, even though it is a consciousness constructed in the act of reading a novel. Galt claimed to set a distance between his fiction and 'mere novels', and one might suppose he wished his readers to be men like himself – well-read, well-informed, interested in making the most of the changing social and economic world they found themselves in, interested in fiction not as escape from that world but as a way of understanding it and thus contributing to history's transformation of it. This intention gives special force to his use of figural realism as anti-romance.

Novels of country, town, and region, along with 'national tales', were one way of defining British 'national' culture, using techniques of domestic and social realism with themes of authentic rural life, the vitality of folk culture, and modernization of society, economic activity, political institutions, and the very culture of the common people which was yet supposed to be the basis of transhistorical 'national' culture. This 'national' culture in turn was supposed to reconcile or override social and cultural differences within a society. But one of the inner contradictions of this 'modernized', profession-

alized national culture is that it is not truly national, as yet; the better
sort of professional middle-class people are shown to be more in tune
with it than others, principally participants in court society, the aristocracy, professional and middle-class people who emulate them, and
the 'pre-modern' common people. These contradictions are exposed
to some extent in Gothic novels, and even more clearly in 'national
tales' and regional novels. But the contradictions are perhaps clearest
in those novels that sought to define Britain by recourse to the exotic,
some culture very different from what Britain's was supposed to be.
Whereas Gothic novels are usually set in Spain, Italy, or Germany, and
use a vague background of court culture and Catholicism, the novels
of the exotic in the late 1810s and 1820s move to the contemporary
or ancient Levant or the Middle East to study what is 'not British',
in such novels as Thomas Hope's *Anastasius; or, Memoirs of a Greek*
(1819), Lady Caroline Lamb's *Ada Reis: A Tale* (1823), and James
Morier's *The Adventures of Hajjî Baba, of Ispahan* (1824), as well, of
course, as Scott's *The Talisman* (1825) and *Count Robert of Paris* (1831),
and in parts of Maturin's *Melmoth the Wanderer* (1820).

The sources of this interest in the Levant were partly political, partly
cultural, and the interest was shaped by certain themes of Enlightenment historiography of court cultures. Britain's war with France had
reached as far as Egypt, where Napoleon was defeated, and Persia was
being sought as an ally or a victim by France, Britain, and Russia.
Romantic interest in exotic cultures and religions, 'primitive' or pre-
modern societies, mythology, and literature was well established by
the 1820s, and developed from an Enlightenment interest in Eastern
societies and governments as critically useful comparisons with European despotisms or as contrasts to European liberalism and 'progress'.
Southey established interest in the matter of the Orient in his poems
*Thalaba the Destroyer* (1801) and *The Curse of Kehama* (1810). The
conquest of Spain by the Moors was used as an analogy for the invasion of Spain by Napoleon, in Landor's poem *Count Julian* (1812) and
Southey's *Roderick* (1814). Byron shed a further Romantic glow on the
Levant in his enormously successful poems of the 1810s, *Childe
Harold's Pilgrimage* and *Don Juan*; Thomas Moore's *Lalla Rookh* (1817)
was about Persia and its tales, and was enormously popular, too; and
it owed a good deal to the evergreen popular classic, *The Thousand and
One Nights*, in the 1820s more popular than ever thanks to popular
reprints. But the Enlightenment interest in the Middle East continued
to be the strongest intellectual line of development. Writers such as
Voltaire and Montesquieu in France and Goldsmith in England used
the device of the oriental placed in Europe in order to defamiliarize and
criticize European culture and politics; and the societies of the Middle
and Far East served many writers as examples of the harmful effects

of court government and culture on society as a whole. Finally, interest in the Levant and Far East had a powerful motive in colonialism, imperialism, and growing interest in and competition for overseas markets.[12]

The Enlightenment inheritance, mingled with Byronism, is very obvious in Thomas Hope's successful and influential novel, *Anastasius; or, Memoirs of a Greek* (1819). It is set in the 1770s, after the first, abortive Greek uprising against Turkish rule, and it was published in 1819 when Greek national consciousness was being formed as the necessary prelude for the successful rebellion of 1821. Hope also laid claim to factual realism, declaring that 'the historical and statistical parts' of his novel were 'strictly correct', and that 'the fictitious super-structure' was 'founded on personal observation', and that first-person narrative or 'the form of biographical memoirs was adopted solely with the view of affording greater facility for the introduction of minute and characteristic details'. Thus does Hope invite the reader to take *Anastasius* as a quasi-novel. More important, *Anastasius* joins criticism of court politics with anti-romance in the mode of the great eighteenth-century satiric novels such as Le Sage's *Gil Blas*. Yet Anastasius does have one romantic ideal: as he traverses the eastern Mediterranean world, Anastasius finds his self-interest often in conflict with his 'national' pride, just as he finds his attempts to get ahead in life repeatedly frustrated by the system of 'things as they are' under foreign rule and court government, spreading its corruption downward through society.

In a way, then, *Anastasius* is not so much a picture of Greece under its *ancien régime* as a picture of the common people of Britain or Europe before they have been instilled with middle-class moral values and ethical standards and with a proper sense of national pride and national interest. *Anastasius* offers a picture of the unregenerate common people that is quite similar to that found in Cheap Repository of the 1790s, Elizabeth Hamilton's *The Cottagers of Glenburnie*, Gothic novels such as *The Monk* and *Melmoth the Wanderer*, and some of the 'historical romances' of the 1810s. *Anastasius* uses the exotic setting of the near-contemporary Levant (with notes and much descriptive material) as it had been used in Enlightenment sociological history (both fictional and non-fictional) – to criticize court culture and government, social emulation, and the individual self-interest and unenlightened popular culture that resulted from both.

Hope's success must have spurred another man who knew the Levant even better, the retired diplomat James Morier, to write his two highly successful novels of the confrontation of East and West – *The Adventures of Hajji Baba, of Ispahan* (1824) and *The Adventures of Hajji Baba, of Ispahan, in England* (1828). Both novels are informed by late

Enlightenment socio-cultural assumptions and by the related emerging values of Romantic nationalism. No less a student of the Enlightenment and creator of British 'national' culture than Sir Walter Scott recognized the sociological dimensions and political implications of Morier's novel. He interpreted the Persians, as depicted by Morier, in terms of the 'pre-modern' or potentially revolutionary common people of Britain or Europe:

> They are powerfully affected by that which is presented
> before them at the moment – forgetful of the past, careless
> of the future – quick in observation, and correct as well as
> quick, when they give themselves leisure to examine the
> principles of their decision – but often contented to draw
> their conclusions too rashly and hastily.[13]

Secondly, Hajjî Baba's vicissitudes in his journey of life were seen by Scott as an illustration of the social effects of a despotic court government:

> The rapid and various changes of individual fortune,
> which in any other scene and country, might be thought
> improbable, are proper to, or rather inseparable from, the
> vicissitudes of a government at once barbaric and
> despotic, where an individual, especially if possessing
> talents, may rise and sink as often as a tennis-ball, and be
> subjected to the extraordinary variety of hazards in one
> life, which the other undergoes in the course of one game.

Both these remarks show that Scott was reading Morier's two novels in terms of the immediate political problems of Britain in the late 1820s, when people like Scott felt themselves confronted by a ruling class no longer fit to govern and a common people not yet fit to do so.

The purpose of *The Adventures of Hajjî Baba*, then, is to show how superficial and denaturing an autocratic court culture can be. Absolutism is shown to be the cause of all alienations and differentiations in the society it dominates by centring all power and thus all meaning and value in itself. The ruler of Persia, the Shah, is by no coincidence known to his subjects as 'the Centre of the Universe'. This kind of centring is to be contrasted, presumably, with the supposed pluralism yet social integration of the West and Britain. In particular, absolutism and the court system are shown to pervert human nature and 'natural' social relations in several main areas: social emulation, commercial activity, professional life, religious and ethnic conflict, everyday social relations, or 'manners', love and marriage, the lottery mentality, the culture of the self, and language. The Persian system of government leads to financial extravagance and pursuit of mere display, as individuals compete in offering gifts and hospitality to the Shah, to the Shah's officers and favourites, to their officers and favourites, and so on, as they seek to impress others with their own status and wealth. For in a society based on status and favouritism, without legally constituted and limited state authority and public officers, one's power and success depend on appearing to be powerful and successful. Here readers could find an obvious parallel to the European courtier's, aristocrat's, or gentleman's culture and code of conspicuous consumption, which ultimately leads to mere pursuit of luxury and which runs against 'rational' principles of conservation and accumulation of capital.

Commercial and professional life are also denatured by court culture. In business life the important thing is the appearance of goods and services, and cheating is routine in the selfish scramble to get ahead as quickly as possible, as Hajjî discovers when he meets merchants or becomes one himself. Professional conduct is similarly affected by the dissemination of a court culture of favouritism, emulation, and display. Professional men such as priests, doctors, lawyers, and soldiers – even poets – are more concerned with appearing to be competent than with giving real service, and with pursuing self-interest rather than the interests of clients or the people or the state; and they are more concerned with boasting of their achievements and securing flattery themselves, for, again, appearance is all. As Hajjî discovers when he takes up various professions, merely wearing the recognized costume of a particular profession and boasting of one's ability are enough.

The evils of court culture are seen most clearly, however, in the place of women and romantic love in Persian society, major themes in Hajjî's adventures in both Persia and Britain. The seraglio, of course, is the grand example in Enlightenment sociology of the evils of court government, and the spread of the 'mistress system' from the court to the rest of society. Women are forced to compete with one another in the arts of coquetry to gain and then hold the affections of their 'master' – a domestic version of court politics. Thus women's moral and affective equality with men is denied – indeed, women are denied souls altogether. Like everyone and everything in Persian society, women are reduced to mere external appearance. But as to women, Hajjî once again displays his difference. Although he endeavors, as he says, 'to show myself a true Mussulman by my contempt for womankind' (ch. 43), he falls in love with the fair Kurd, Zeenab, thereby exhibiting a further difference from his countrymen in loving beyond his own racial, ethnic, and religious community. Romantic love, with its emphasis on personal choice, authenticity of feeling, and candour in human relationship, is, according to Morier, hardly known in Persia and then is regarded as folly. Nevertheless, in Persia such love is not possible: Zeenab is seen and desired by the Shah; the episode ends in her death and Hajjî's bereavement.

Corresponding to dependence on external circumstances in a court-dominated society is lack of inner self-dependence or even lack of coherent inner selfhood. Indeed, as the Zeenab episode shows, to follow one's inner imperative may be dangerous or even fatal in a court society. Thus court society in effect suppresses rich inner selfhood – it is a luxury or an aberration. Furthermore, Hajjî is supposed to be unusual (for an Oriental) in his decision to write an autobiography. But Hajjî's inner self is balanced by a characteristically Persian sociability. Like the protagonists of the earlier European picaresque novels, Hajjî is continually in motion, continually engaged in society in some way or another. He has little time for reflection, for like everyone in his society he is immersed in sociability, always on the road, as he must be if he wants to get ahead (or even survive) in a society in which no man, and certainly no woman, controls his or her own destiny. This sociability is strongly associated with two other cultural aspects of 'pre-modern' society – orality and narrativity.

The external correlative of Hajjî's lack of self is his lack of a fixed social character and the frequency and variety of his assumed characters, roles, and offices. He seems always to be in a character not his own, often or usually against his will, as a means of escaping death, poverty, or the consequences of his actions, good or bad. And as far as he is concerned, there is no inner correspondence to outward character. It is all outward show, again. This theme would receive longer treatment in Bulwer's *Pelham* and then in Carlyle's quasi-novel, *Sartor Resartus* (1833–34). Hajjî's saving graces are, however, inward impulses – if not romantic love, then passions that nevertheless take him beyond the limits of his society's courtly and 'pre-modern' mentality, and even beyond the limits of Persia and Islam. Hajjî's great wish is to be 'somebody', a person of importance, of power and wealth, and, like Defoe's heroes and heroines, this desire is at least partly responsible for taking him on the road and forcing him into one disguise or false character after another, though curiosity, that affliction of Enlightenment truth-seekers, also plays a large part.

Significantly enough, these desires of ambition and curiosity were considered by several Enlightenment writers to be the agents of change and progress in human society and civilization. For while Hajji Baba is, in most respects, a representative of his 'pre-modern', unenlightened society, in certain important respects, as we have seen, he is also different, and thus open to the ways of the West. Appropriately, then, his last identity, and the one through which he fulfils the other desires, is as a member of the embassy from 'the Centre of the Universe' to Britain, implicitly the centre of meaning and value to the novel and its readers. His curiosity takes him beyond the limits of his world, and seems to promise him freedom from its limits on the self. It is in this role, and on the threshold of his longest journey of all, that Hajjî ends his adventures.

In a sense this is an appropriate closure, for the point of the adventures of Hajjî Baba has been to establish the 'boundless difference' between Persia and Britain; yet Hajjî's adventures have also established his own difference as a Persian, and thus his suitability to mediate the difference between Persia and Britain, as well as to record it, since he is to be the secretary of the embassy. Of course there is a paradox in Hajjî's availability to the ways of the West, for just as Hajjî is both Persian and not Persian, a 'pre-modern' and yet partly 'modernized' man, product of a court society and partly alienated from it, so the West is shown to be both 'modernized' and residually 'pre-modern', free from court society and still residually subject to it. Hence the logic of a sequel to *The Adventures of Hajjî Baba*, which appeared in 1828 as *The Adventures of Hajjî Baba, of Ispahan, in England*.

In these further adventures Morier draws on another well-established technique of eighteenth-century and Enlightenment satiric fiction, the innocent abroad, including Swift's *Gulliver's Travels*, Voltaire's *Candide*, Johnson's *Rasselas*, and Goldsmith's *Citizen of the World*. The essence of this kind of fiction is to defamiliarize the reader's own, familiar world, and so to expose it as a constructed world rather than a natural one – the implication being that what is constructed is artificial and unnatural, and what is constructed may be reconstructed. Thus the further adventures of Hajjî Baba show that the 'modern' and 'pre-modern' elements in Britain are not equally distributed: some classes and some people, mainly professionalized middle-class people, are enlightened, while others, principally the fashionable classes and the narrowly middle-class people, are made objects of satire. In the late 1820s, Morier has taken up the matter of the emerging 'silver-fork novel' and adapted it to his own purpose. As one of Hajjî's acquaintances in England tells him,

> 'we have a certain tyrant among us called "Fashion," much more despotic than even your king of kings, whose decrees are more powerful than either reason or sense of propriety, and who, as you see, overthrows decorum, and makes of us, a nation naturally inclined to admire every thing that improves the dignity of our nature, a nation of frivolous and ridiculous imitators.' (Vol. II, ch. 3)

Britain and Persia may not be so different after all.

The point of Hajji's adventures, then, is not to bridge the 'boundless difference' between Persia and Britain but to leave it in place, demonstrating the superiority of those elements of British society which are enlightened and professionalized to those parts which are not and which resemble Persian society. Even Hajji cannot be completely modernized. He returns home to 'the Centre of the Universe', where he finds that his acceptance of certain British ways is likely to land him in trouble with envious Persian mullahs and ministers and where the reluctance of 'the Centre of the Universe' to believe Hajji's accounts of the achievements of the West could have dire consequences. In any case, Hajji finds that the longer he is away from the West, the fainter grows his conviction that in certain respects the ways of the West are superior to those of his own country. And when he finally appears before 'the Centre of the Universe' he finds that once again he must play the court game of flattery, evasion, and lies. At the end of his further adventures Hajji remains dangling at court, fearful of his enemies, hoping for the reward that can only come from 'the Centre of the Universe', and filling in the time telling stories:

> I pass my days in exciting the wonder of my countrymen
> by the relation of my adventures. I am privileged to stand
> before the king. And who knows? time, opportunity, and
> my tongue, will not be wanting to help me in the
> accomplishment of my wishes, and in filling up the
> measure of my ambition. And now, gentle reader, Hajji
> Baba kisses your feet, seeks protection at the skirt of your
> coat, and hopes that your shadow may never be less.

Hajji is left immersed again in his own court-dominated, oral, narrative, fatalistic, opportunist, linguistically extravagant culture.

Ultimately, the fiction of the exotic, which was quite popular and influential in the 1810s and 1820s, and converged with the interests of Romantic and Victorian non-fiction literature of travel in exotic lands, is less about the exotic itself than it is interested in using the exotic as a grand figure for the 'not British', similar to earlier use of Catholic Mediterranean cultures in Gothic fiction. As Edward Said reminds us, in *Orientalism*,

> The Orient [which includes the Middle East] is not only
> adjacent to Europe; it is also the place of Europe's greatest
> and richest and oldest colonies, the source of its
> civilizations and languages, its cultural contestant, and one
> of its deepest and most recurring images of the Other.[14]

Not only does the matter of the exotic, especially the Levant and the Orient, reflect the growing sense of national imperial destiny in Romantic fiction from Sherwood's *Little Henry and His Bearer* to Morier's Hajjî Baba novels, it also became an important thematic focus for defining what was supposed to be English, British, European, or Western – again as Edward Said puts it, 'the Orient has helped to define Europe (or the West) as its contrasting image, idea, personality, experience'. For beyond Europe's geographical or cultural limits in the early nineteenth century lay what, for Europeans, was a mirror of Europe's 'premodern' past and, in Europe's imperialist success, an affirmation of Europe's 'modernized' present. That this 'modernity' was defined pre-eminently in professional middle-class terms and values has already been illustrated in the previous chapters of this book.

## Later Romantic Novels of Self versus Society: *'Silver-fork'* and *'Newgate Novels'*

Representing the self, in novels of passion and later Gothic romances, and representing locale (town or country), region, and nation, in 'rural sketches', novels of provincial life, and national or oriental tales, were major areas in the development of prose fiction (and even verse narrative) after the end of the French and Napoleonic wars. But the particular relationship of self and society was treated in other ways, too, especially as a series of economic, political, and institutional crises, as well as the accelerating pace of population growth, urbanization, industrialization, and commercialization of culture, forced attention increasingly on questions of institutional reform and social leadership. Certainly these issues were addressed in the novels of Scott and in the novels discussed earlier in this chapter; but in the late 1820s and early 1830s they were addressed particularly in so-called 'silver-fork' and 'Newgate novels'.[15]

Silver-fork and Newgate novels were very popular in the late 1820s and 1830s, but, like earlier forms of Romantic fiction they were regarded by many critics with fear and contempt. In the late 1820s they were usually referred to, derisively, as merely 'fashionable novels'. In the first recorded use of 'silver fork' to refer to fiction, *The Times* of 15 December 1831 welcomed a reprint of the novels of Fielding and Smollett ('classic' novels in 'elegant' reprints now being essential furniture for the homes of the professional middle-class people who read *The Times*) with the declaration, 'A single chapter of any one of them is worth more than the whole bundle of those contemptible productions of the silver fork school, which are called "fashionable novels"'. Newgate novels were simply any novels that contained characters and scenes that could conceivably have been drawn from the great late eighteenth-century compilation of criminal biography, the *Newgate Calendar*.[16]

Thus Newgate novels were closely related to a major category of 'street literature', the popular criminal life and 'last dying words and confession' in chapbook or broadside form, popular for over two centuries but never more so than in the 1810s and 1820s. Reaction against silver-fork and Newgate novels by conservative middle-class critics was at times violent. In 1830, the formidable former member of the 'Noctes Ambrosianæ' set, William Maginn, in his new periodical, *Fraser's Magazine*, roundly condemned silver-fork and Newgate novels for spreading false values of social emulation of aristocracy, false glamorization of the lower classes, and contempt for the 'merely' middle class. Worse still, these false values were being spread among the largely middle-class readers of such fiction.[17] Then in *Sartor Resartus*, written in 1831 and published in *Fraser's* in 1833 and 1834, Thomas Carlyle took the silver-fork novel and its protagonist, the dandy, especially as found in the clothes-conscious hero of Bulwer's *Pelham*, as the basis for his comprehensive critique of a society based, as he saw it, on external and merely social values.

The silver-fork novel marked an important transition from Romantic to Victorian culture and values. Yet there were also many at the time and later, especially in France, who took the values and attitudes of some silver-fork novels and their dandiacal heroes as a model for protest against bourgeois utilitarianism, puritanism, domesticity, and chauvinism, and against Romantic culture insofar as it embodied these bourgeois values.[18] But the silver-fork and Newgate novels also participated in, mediated, and disseminated commercialized Romantic culture insofar as Romantic culture was a form of upper-class culture mass produced and marketed for the growing and increasingly fashion-conscious professional and middle classes. An outstanding example is the firm of Wedgwood, which carefully obtained information on changing tastes among aristocratic leaders of fashion, quickly adapted this information in new designs and lines, and skilfully promoted the new wares through association with aristocratic and royal 'patrons'.[19] Henry Colburn was the Wedgwood of the circulating-library novel. Colburn marketed his novels with the same methods and skill that Wedgwood used, recruiting authors with aristocratic blood or connections and printing puffing reviews and advertisements strongly suggesting that his novels were *romans à clef*.

Silver-fork and Newgate novels, then, were regarded in their own time and later as glamorizing the trivial or criminal, and thus as themselves morally, socially, and intellectually corrupting. Yet there is no denying the ostensible aim of these novels to be searching critiques of British society and its institutions in the last years of the decadent George IV. For example, both silver-fork and Newgate novels are, as their names suggest, novels of social description; moreover, both are concerned less with plot than with the familiar late Enlightenment view of the relationship of social and material circumstance to social and individual character. Silver-fork novels such as Robert Plumer Ward's *Tremaine; or, The Man of Refinement* (1825), T. H. Lister's *Granby* (1826), Benjamin Disraeli's *Vivian Grey* (1826–27), Edward Bulwer Lytton's *Pelham; or, The Adventures of a Gentleman* (1828), Theodore Hook's *Maxwell* (1830), and numerous novels by Lady Charlotte Bury, Countess Blessington, Lord Normanby, and others, are in effect later novels of manners, sentiment, and emulation, built on earlier fiction by such writers as Fanny Burney, Maria Edgeworth, T. S. Surr, 'Horace' Smith, and many others.

Newgate novels, such as Thomas Gaspey's *Richmond; or, Scenes in the Life of a Bow Street Officer* (1827) and *History of George Godfrey* (1828), Bulwer's *Paul Clifford* (1830) and *Eugene Aram* (1832), and later novels by Harrison Ainsworth, Dickens, and others, go back, quite consciously and overtly, to themes, characters, and techniques of the classic criminal picaresque novels of the eighteenth century, such as Le Sage's *Gil Blas*, and, more important, to English Jacobin protest novels such as Godwin's *Caleb Williams* and Holcroft's *Bryan Perdue*. Yet Newgate novels, too, are novels of manners, sentiment, and emulation, with more emphasis on scenes of low life, the criminal underworld, crime and detection, and the urban slums that were virtually unknown country to middle-class novel readers (as unknown as silver-fork society). Moreover, both silver-fork and Newgate novels often include scenes of both high and low life and use these scenes for the purpose of comprehensive social satire.

Thus both silver-fork and Newgate novels adapt established forms of the novel as social criticism in order to express, in the late 1820s, a deepening sense of social, cultural, and political crisis, a fresh sense of the inadequacy of 'Old Corruption', of court and aristocracy, the patronage system, and the hierarchical and paternalistic social order of gentry hegemony, both for the maintenance of social order and progress at home and the defence and expansion of empire abroad. Silver-fork and Newgate novels, like earlier Sentimental and Romantic novels of criticism of contemporary life, deal with the related systems of social convention and emulation on one hand and institutionalized power on the other. It is important to remember that many of these novels, such as Ward's *Tremaine*, Disraeli's *Vivian Grey*, and Bulwer's *Pelham* and

*Paul Clifford*, describe not just fashionable society but specifically those elements of fashionable society directly involved in the leading circles of Parliament of the pre-Reform Bill constitution. Yet these people are shown to be, after all, merely 'silver-fork society', treating with equal attention amorous and political intrigue, fashions in clothes and fashions in ideas, social crises of the day and novels of the day.

Silver-fork and Newgate novels then show, in characteristic late Enlightenment fashion, the effect of this society on individuals within and, through emulation, outside it. More broadly, these novels aim to show, as Enlightenment and English Jacobin novels did, the effect of government, as the whole range of social and political institutions, from manners to main force (law, police), on the character of the individual and relations between individuals. The villain of Bulwer's *Paul Clifford*, for example, the lawyer, judge, and courtier William Brandon, is described as 'a man whom the social circumstances of the world were calculated, as if by system, to render eminently and basely wicked' (ch. 33), whereas, on true Godwinian principles, the highwayman hero of the same novel is represented as a man who, but for the corrupt institutions of society, might have been a model citizen and benefit to his country. Bulwer's novel is, indeed, acknowledged by its narrator to be 'a story in some measure designed to show, in the depravities of character, the depravities of that social state wherein characters are formed' (ch. 29).

Silver-fork and Newgate novels take over the familiar Romantic examination of the social construction of the individual as well as the familiar Romantic opposition of self and society; but they adapt these familiar themes to a particular phase of professional middle-class criticism of Britain's power-holding classes – the end of the reign of the now much-despised dandy-monarch George IV, the short reign of the shabby and almost as despised William IV, and the political infighting and uncertainty (1826–37) that followed the long and undistinguished leadership of Lord Liverpool (1813–26). Silver-fork and Newgate novels respond to these political and social crises by attempting to forge a new image of the social leader as gentleman – at least, as the professionalized gentleman already called for in several decades of Romantic fiction. This new image would turn out to be the Victorian ideal of the gentleman;[20] but in the late 1820s and 1830s there was still much uncertainty as to how to form this new image, and the uncertainty shows up clearly in the 'fashionable novels'.

Like Romantic novels of passion and Gothic romance, and more so than in the earlier novels of manners and 'political romances' of the Jacobins, silver-fork and Newgate novels show a fascination for what they condemn. Their ambivalence is seen clearly in their treatment of the familiar conflict of subjective versus social categories of meaning and value. In several of these novels – for example, *Granby* and *Paul Clifford* – the hero is a 'natural' (i.e., inward, moral) gentleman who turns out at the end to be a gentleman by rank or birth as well. This is the tired plot device of concealed or misrepresented parentage and social class. Furthermore, some of these novels, especially *Vivian Grey* and *Pelham*, make the hero into something like an amoral fop or intriguer who yet turns out to have a good heart or to be a virtuous man after all.

Thus the plots, characters, and settings of silver-fork and Newgate novels afforded their readers the same contradictory pleasures afforded by the earlier novels of manners, tales of fashionable life, and novels such as Egan's *Life in London*: the fascinating spectacle of upper- and lower-class vice and extravagance, and the ultimate condemnation of these, in the novels' moral drift or conclusion, in favour of central professional middle-class values of self-discipline, moral egalitarianism, sense of personal and public duty, and the domestic affections, even though these values are cast in the final figure of the professionalized gentry family inhabiting an independent country estate and operating the old system of paternalism with a new, gentrified middle-class set of values. This structure and this pattern recur so frequently, with such seemingly endless variation, that they must represent a central interest for those of the novel-reading classes at this time.

This central interest is in distinction, for, as the hero of Disraeli's *Vivian Grey* observes, 'In England, personal distinction is the only passport to the society of the great' (first edn., Book I, ch. 8), and that society is the centre of power and emulation. Distinction, here, means both the ability to distinguish and (thus) the power to distinguish oneself from the rest of society. Distinction is, then, a complex discourse of power, and both silver-fork and Newgate novels, but especially the former, present a rich and complex, relentlessly deployed language and social practice of distinction and discrimination, supposed to prevail among a certain social class, to readers most of whom must have come from quite different social classes. As that defiant defender of the middle classes, William Maginn, put it, 'The higher classes of society are made the staple of Messrs. Colburn and Bentley's novels of manners, and their private acts and modes of life are the subjects of description in those elegant truth denouncing volumes'; Maginn believed, further, that the curiosity of middle-class readers about those 'private acts and modes of life' was the only motive for reading them.[21]

The 'private acts and modes of life' include courtship, private emotion (*ennui*, melancholy, *weltschmerz*), cookery (or *cuisine*), conversation (especially repartee), dress (*Pelham* is supposed to have made black *de rigueur* as the colour for men's formal evening dress), duelling, interior decor, decorum, drinks, epistolary style, handling of servants and tradesmen, gambling (and gambling debts), choice of restaurant, choice of tailor, painting, music, architecture, gardening, travel, literature (including silver-fork novels), pronunciation, grammar, horsemanship, scholarship, pets, morals – the list could go on, with as much miscellaneousness. For the fundamental principle – and the scandal – of the silver-fork novel, as a specific type of the novel of manners, sentiment, and emulation, is that the intrinsic importance of the topic of discrimination matters less than the act of discrimination, the exercise of personal taste within a social discourse of discrimination and distinction. This discourse operates as a discourse of power in two ways.

First, taste distinguishes those within the discourse from one another; in the Romantic period especially, taste distinguishes the original, the individual, the 'artist', one might say, from the merely eccentric on one hand and the slavishly fashionable on the other. Second, taste distinguishes those within the discourse of distinction from those outside it, the 'vulgar'. Silver-fork novels display the operation of the discourse of distinction in both these ways; and Maginn was probably right – this display must have been a large part of the appeal of these novels to readers most of whom were outside the world of silver-fork society. Furthermore, authors of silver-fork novels were often accused of being in fact outsiders, not denizens of silver-fork society, though Colburn tried to suggest that all his silver-fork authors were insiders. Paradoxically, as we have seen, silver-fork novels seem to argue that silver-fork society and its distinctions are false, artificial, or trivial. Moreover, silver-fork novels were, as we have also seen, themselves part of the commercialized discourse of distinction in the real social world of the late 1820s.

In short, readers of silver-fork novels could have it three ways: they could participate vicariously in the world of distinction depicted in the novels, they could share the novels' ultimate (if often hypocritical and ambivalent) condemnation of that world, and they could consume (by reading) a prominent article of fashionable distinction. Fashion being what it is, however, the vogue of the silver-fork novel – at least in the specific form it took in the late 1820s and 1830s – had to be short.

These contradictions in the silver-fork novel and its vogue have a simple enough explanation. Practices of taste, discrimination, and distinction, applied across the whole range of personal, social, and cultural life, had for centuries constituted a discourse of power within court society and for the defence of court society.[22] This discourse spread through the whole of society by complex processes of social emulation. But the commercialization of culture in the later eighteenth century opened new and powerful avenues for the operation and exploitation of this discourse beyond court society. By the 1810s and

1820s this discourse was no longer of much use in defending court or aristocratic privilege; rather, it became a field of struggle for ideological leadership within the classes that constituted the largest market for commodities of commercialized taste and distinction, the professional and middle classes.[23] But the old tension within these classes, between submission to and criticism of the court, aristocracy, and gentry, remained strong, especially in the classes closest to the gentry, the professional classes. In the 1810s and 1820s this tension resulted in the development of various attempts to fuse the old aristocratic codes of distinction with Romantic culture, particularly in the form of commercialized Byronism, the Regency dandy, and other anti-bourgeois cultural expressions. That is why silver-fork novels often contain what are in effect advertisements for particular merchants of particular articles of fashionable consumption. Yet silver-fork novels also mock fashionable consumption.

The Newgate novel shares in this ambiguous social critique. In spite of its emphasis on the criminal underworld and low life rather than high society, the Newgate novel shares with the silver-fork novel an interest in particular kinds of knowledge as power, or power-knowledge, to use a concept of Michel Foucault's.[24] For criminal society, like silver-fork society, is a society of insiders clearly distinguished from and even barricaded against outsiders. Paradoxically, these insiders are outsiders *par excellence* – outside the law that marks off 'legitimate' society, in fact, as the Newgate novels aim to show, as a society governed by injustice of which the criminal society is the product. And so, perforce, Newgate novels depict the criminal society as more authentic than, though at the same time a parody of the insider society of the power-holding classes. Furthermore, the outsiders often have an understanding of society's power structures that the powerful themselves lack. This alignment is represented in a long tradition of underworld literature, including Renaissance rogue novels, Fielding's *Jonathan Wild*, Gay's *Beggar's Opera*, the Raymond gang in Godwin's *Caleb Williams*, Holcroft's Jacobin novel *Bryan Perdue*, numerous banditti in Gothic melodrama and Gothic novels such as Dacre's *Zofloya*, scenes in such novels as Scott's *Heart of Midlothian*, parts of Egan's *Life in London*, the world of Job Johnson in Bulwer's *Pelham*, and chapter 16 of Bulwer's *Paul Clifford*. The criminal underworld is an emanation of silver-fork society; both represent for the middle-class readers of silver-fork and Newgate novels their linked social enemies – the courtly and gentry classes on one hand and the lower classes on the other.

Both worlds are described in terms of complex and mysterious codes of conduct, discrimination, and language, almost as secret societies, a preoccupation of this age of revolutions – revolutions often blamed on the machinations of secret societies. Yet both high society and the criminal underworld have to be penetrated or even mastered by the hero in order for him to carry out the ethical action that proves his 'real', virtuous (bourgeois) character and earns him the reward of true love, authentic domestic life, and public usefulness. Significantly, the hero usually has to adopt a social mask or actual disguise, to conceal his true identity, in order to achieve the necessary penetration or mastery, as happens in *Granby, Pelham,* and *Paul Clifford.* The vicissitudes and crisis of identity so central to the topos of self-recognition and self-transformation in the literature of Sensibility and Romanticism here take a somewhat glamorous form. At the same time, the corruption and unredeemed sociability of the lower classes are shown to issue from corruption and mere sociability in silver-fork society, and both are seen to be ripe for the kind of moral and social reform, through mastery of silver-fork and Newgate society, figured in the self-reform or self-criticism of the dandy or criminal hero such as Pelham or Paul Clifford.

As the system of courtly and aristocratic power faced ever sharper challenges from the professional and commercial middle classes in the late 1820s and early 1830s – the threshold of a prolonged but comprehensive process of political, administrative, and cultural reform – the tension within the novel-reading classes (still largely the professional and other middle ranks) between challenge to and emulation of the power-holding classes reached a parallel crisis, expressed forcibly if simplistically in the silver-fork and Newgate novel. This tension might seem to be resolved in the earlier silver-fork novels, such as *Vivian Grey* and *Pelham,* in the dandiacal protagonist closely associated with the author – in both cases there is a suggestion that the dandy transcends both the decadent aristocracy and the emulative or resolutely vulgar bourgeoisie. Significantly, both Disraeli and Bulwer became much more serious and earnest in their later novels, and even revised *Vivian Grey* and *Pelham* to make them much less dandiacal and bring them closer to the new model professionalized gentleman – moral, self-disciplined, socially responsible – being turned out of new model public schools such as Thomas Arnold's Rugby. The course of revision of *Vivian Grey* and *Pelham* and the careers of Disraeli and Bulwer as novelists (and as public figures and politicians) trace the transition from middle-class emulation of aristocracy to the formulation of a new synthesis of professional middle classes and gentry, a synthesis figured, as we have seen, in many other kinds of Romantic fiction, and, as stated several times in this book already, one that provided the basis for a social coalition that would dominate Britain and its empire for the rest of the century.

## Artists and Utilitarians: The Limits of Romantic Culture

Silver-fork and Newgate novels were designed to show the limitations of a society and institutions still dominated by court and aristocracy; but they also showed the limits of certain aspects of Romantic culture. They did so ambivalently, however, as writers and ideologues struggled to depict a fusion or coalition of gentry and professional middle classes, their values, social practices, and institutions, that could form a new governing class and remake British (and colonial) society in its own image. To a great extent, then, silver-fork and Newgate novels are satiric novels, though finally they remain romances of self-transformation and (thus) social regeneration.

Nevertheless, the period abounded with expressly satirical fiction – or rather, fiction in which satire outweighs romance. Early examples are the Jacobin and Anti-Jacobin novels of the 1790s. But as Romantic culture, commercialized, became the dominant new culture after 1800, satirists turned their attention to it, as earlier they had turned to Sensibility, recognizing the ideological and thus the political edge to the new artistic and cultural movements. Not surprisingly, Romantic fiction of certain kinds became leading topics of satire by the 1810s, as seen, for example, in Austen's *Northanger Abbey* and *Sense and Sensibility*. A comprehensive and well-known satire on Romantic and Sentimental fiction was Eaton Stannard Barrett's *The Heroine; or, Adventures of a Fair Romance Reader* (1813). Typically, Barrett focuses on the association of gender and genre, as well as class and genre. In this novel, the heroine, Cherubina, becomes discontented with herself, her comfortable middle-class life, the condition of women, and 'things as they are' in society at large. In a pattern made familiar by *Don Quixote*, such eighteenth-century satirical novels as Richard Graves's *The Spiritual Quixote* and Charlotte Lennox's *The Female Quixote*, and Anti-Jacobin novels of the 1790s, but given a new accent by Romantic novels of passion and domestic and social rebellion such as Mme de Staël's *Corinne*, Barrett's 'heroine' sets out to find romance and change the world, taking up residence in a ruined castle and leading a mob of discontented labourers, until she comes up against reality and is schooled into more rational and self-disciplined reading practices by her husband-to-be.

In Barrett's novel, gender, genre, and a whole range of intellectual, cultural, and social values and practices are aligned in opposing camps, and one camp (led by the rational, professional middle-class hero) is shown to be superior to the other. In the process, Romantic culture comes in for considerable satire and criticism; but the important point is that literary, artistic, and narrowly cultural values and attitudes are shown to participate in a language of symbols and symbolic structures, values and practices, that embraces all of subjective and social life, and reading novels (of the wrong or the right kind) can have profound local and national consequences. This was no mere exaggeration for the sake of satiric argument, but a recognition of the growing importance of the novel, literature, art, and culture as social institutions of ideological dissemination and mediation.

In the mid to late 1810s and 1820s such fictional exploration of Romantic culture and fiction became increasingly prominent as new social and economic crises challenged old as well as emergent social identities, institutions, and coalitions. Thus, when the feminine but well-read heroine of Jane Austen's *Persuasion* recommends to a young, recently bereaved naval officer that he read less of the Romantic poetry of Byron and Scott and more reflective prose in order to regain his self-control, Austen is evoking a public controversy well-known to novel readers of the mid-1810s and suggesting at the same time that one's choice of reading matter can have personal and perhaps national and even military consequences. More obvious and comprehensive treatments of Romantic culture, however, are found in the satirical 'novels of opinion' of Thomas Love Peacock.

Peacock's special concern was with Romantic intellectual and artistic culture, including such movements as utilitarianism – in the 1810s he was associated with the circle of the radical poet Percy Shelley, and in the 1820s his fellow workers at East India House included leading utilitarians such as James and John Stuart Mill. Peacock himself took up a position midway between these two manifestations of Romantic culture – a position prefigurative of a dominant strain of Victorian gentrified intellectual life. It could indeed be argued that Peacock's novels were for the gentrified professional intellectual – 'for' in the sense of 'addressed to' as well as 'toward the construction of'. Thus, like many other Romantic novelists, Peacock satirized 'Old Corruption'; but he also satirized both what he saw as partial or bogus cultural and intellectual movements within the professional middle classes and what he saw as crassly materialistic and self-interested practices of the commercial bourgeoisie. Peacock's novels represent the contradictions and ambivalences of the Romantic intellectual and professional torn between admiration for an idealized, gentry-dominated society and desire for thorough social and cultural reform.

This ambivalence is represented as a positive frame of value by Peacock's combination of classical and Enlightenment literary form with highly topical contemporary themes. Peacock wrote 'satirical romances' or 'novels of opinion' – 'opinion' as used on the title page of Laurence Sterne's encyclopaedic satire on theory and theorizing, *The*

*Life and Opinions of Tristram Shandy*, that is, sentiment or unproven conviction as distinct from action – in Greek, *dogmata* as distinct from *pragmata*. As Marilyn Butler puts it, 'opinion' for Peacock is 'in the most literal sense . . . a familiar contemporary controversy'.[25] Romance itself Peacock takes to be the theorizing, systematizing, projecting impulse, satirized in Greek Old Comedy by Aristophanes, in Lucian, Rabelais, Cervantes, Samuel Butler's *Hudibras*, Swift, Sterne, French Enlightenment writers such as Voltaire and Diderot, French comic writers such as Pigault-Lebrun, Anti-Jacobin writers such as Isaac D'Israeli, parodists such as Eaton Stannard Barrett, and a number of reviewers in the leading professional middle-class British periodicals of the 1810s and 1820s.

The purpose of such satire was socially reformative, for in a review of 1859, Peacock declared that Lucian's (and Voltaire's) objective was, 'by sweeping away false dogmas, to teach toleration'. Another branch of this kind of satiric fiction, Rabelais's carnivalesque novels and the French comic novels down to his own day, also provided Peacock with models for the way fiction of the right sort could intervene directly in social-historical change, 'directing the stream of opinion against the mass of delusions and abuses' of the *ancien régime* – what we would now call demystification.[26] As 'novels of opinion' in this sense, Peacock's 'philosophical romances' resemble some of the quasi-novels of the time, such as 'Noctes Ambrosianæ', which participated in the same ideological struggle for self-definition within the professional middle classes.

The particular ideological combatants satirized in Peacock's 'novels of opinion' could be divided into two main groups, both known to him personally and directly. First there are the Romantic writers, especially the poets, whom Peacock knew or knew of through Shelley and his circle. Peacock recognized the importance of Romantic literature, and much of it he deplored, especially the excesses of subjectivity, the consequent facile anti-social attitudes, and the theorizing, idealizing, transcendental tendencies. These he satirized particularly in *Nightmare Abbey* (1818). The second group of combatants may be seen as anti-Romantics, with their emphasis on reason, progress, science, technology, capitalist finance, productivity, and social engineering. These were the 'political economists' or 'utilitarians', led in Peacock's day by Jeremy Bentham, whom Peacock knew, James Mill, Bentham's disciple and Peacock's administrative superior at East India House, and Mill's son, John Stuart Mill, who also worked for the East India Company and whom Peacock found more congenial. These thinkers are satirized particularly in Peacock's *Crotchet Castle* (1831).

Peacock's first novel, *Headlong Hall* (1815; dated 1816), raises many issues, such as landscape gardening and the picturesque, the 'march of mind', the new 'science' of psychology, along with the pseudo-sciences of physiognomy and craniology, industrialization and the factory system, 'Scottish philosophy', musical theory and practice (Peacock was a lifelong follower of opera and his novels are studded with songs, glees, and choruses), geological history and topography, individualism, and utilitarianism. *Melincourt* (1817) is Peacock's longest novel and the one closest to conventional novel form and to the conventional plots and characters of the 'modern novel'. It, too, however, is full of talk, and continues many of the themes broached in its predecessor, as well as developing new ones, such as the primitive nature of man, the evils of paper money, Parliamentary representation, population theory and the poor laws, the spread of print and popular journalism, the slavery question, the condition of women, the medieval revival, paleontology, mythography, the ballad revival, statistical political economy, the institution of marriage, the dependence of professional men on their social superiors, urbanization, waltzing, the routinization of work, the relationship of nature to individual moral character, Anti-Jacobinism, religious toleration, and the relationship of politics and literature.

*Nightmare Abbey* (1818) narrows the range of intellectual issues to concentrate on certain aspects of Romantic literature, and these are related to political and social controversy. Though not the best, it is the best known of Peacock's novels because its characters are 'based on' well-known Romantic poets – Scythrop as Shelley, Flosky as Coleridge, and Cypress as Byron; other members of the Shelley circle may also have supplied Peacock with ideas for characters. But Peacock is less interested in these individuals than in the elements of Romantic culture which they represent. As he put it in a letter to Shelley,

> I think it necessary to 'make a stand' against the 'encroachments' of black bile. The fourth canto of 'Childe Harold' [published in 1818] is really too bad. I cannot consent to be *auditor tantum* of systematical 'poisoning' of the 'mind' of the 'reading public.'[27]

The novel is particularly concerned with the development of the Sentimental and Romantic culture of the self into what Peacock saw as excessive celebration of melancholy and subjectivity.

The literature Peacock has in mind here comprises 'philosophical novels', such as Godwin's *Caleb Williams* (ch. 8); 'Gothic romances' and novels of passion, such as Godwin's *Mandeville* (1817) and Lady Caroline Lamb's *Glenarvon* (ch. 6); autobiographical narrative poems, such as Byron's *Childe Harold's Pilgrimage* (ch. 11); 'dismal ballads', such as Coleridge's 'Rime of the Ancient Mariner' and 'Christabel'; and German dramas and novels, such as Schiller's plays (ch. 13) and

Goethe's *Sorrows of Werther* (ch. 14). Just as self-centred, though, is what the bored fine gentleman, the Honourable Mr Listless, calls '"drawing-room-table literature"' and what Mr Asterias, the ichthyologist calls '"the literature of society"', which, like the manners of society, has been infected with '"the inexhaustible varieties of *ennui*: spleen, chagrin, vapours, blue devils, time-killing, discontent, misanthropy, and all their interminable train of fretfulness, querulousness, suspicions, jealousies, and fears"'. Worse still, according to Mr Asterias, this cult of subjectivity and the literature that celebrates it infect moral and ethical ideas as well as social and political attitudes. Nevertheless, Asterias's view is not necessarily the novel's, for it immediately becomes clear that he has his own form of egotism and transcendental ideal – a passion for scientific enquiry that amounts to the absurd: he is trying to find a real mermaid.

The effect on women of such fashionable literature of self is to make them into social rebels and nonconformists, political radicals and feminists, as seen in the character Celinda Toobad, daughter of the Bible-quoting 'Manichæan Millenarian', Mr Toobad. He believes the world is in the grip of '"the Evil One"' and the modern period, '"commonly called the enlightened age"', is the height of his evil power. Celinda, having read German novels, the works of the Illuminati, and Mary Wollstonecraft, is in favour of absolute love and against arranged marriages and marriages for money. Perhaps somewhat like the heroine of Wollstonecraft's *The Wrongs of Woman*, she flees the 'persecution' of a marriage her father has arranged with Scythrop. Disguised as 'Stella' (a name taken from a sexually liberated character in a German play), she seeks refuge with a young man, who turns out to be Scythrop (though she does not realize it), and she tells him,

> 'I submit not to be an accomplice in my sex's slavery. I
> am, like yourself, a lover of freedom, and I carry my
> theory into practice. *They alone are subject to blind authority*
> *who have no reliance on their own strength.*' (ch. 10; Peacock
> uses italics to indicate a direct quotation from
> Wollstonecraft's *Vindication of the Rights of Woman*.)

Considering their common reading and interests, it is not surprising that 'Stella' and Scythrop fall in love; but Scythrop also loves (so much for fictional conventions of romantic love) the superficial, coquettish, but happy Marionetta O'Carroll (she is always singing, as her last name suggests, and the Irishness of her name also suggests a parody of 'the Wild Irish Girl', Lady Morgan; her first name indicates that she is too easily influenced by others, quite unlike 'Stella'). When Scythrop cannot choose between the two women, Celinda marries the Kantian, Mr Flosky, and Marionetta marries the Honourable Mr Listless, probably out of a desire to have a good 'settlement' – such, Peacock argues, is the nature of women and love in the age of moral and political egotism inspired by Romantic literature.

The relationship of Romantic literature, subjectivity, transcendental philosophy, obscurantism, social nonconformity, and even Jacobinism is set forth in the reading and intellectual development of the novel's central character, Scythrop, after his first disappointment in love early in the novel:

> He began to devour romances and German tragedies, and,
> by the recommendation of Mr Flosky, to pore over
> ponderous tomes of transcendental philosophy, which
> reconciled him to the labour of studying them by their
> mystical jargon and necromantic imagery. (ch. 2)

Peacock then seems to suggest that a natural outcome of this training in subjectivity is dissatisfaction with 'things as they are' in society, and a confused mixture of Jacobinism, secret intrigue, and paranoia. Scythrop 'now became troubled with the *passion for reforming the world*'.

> He built many castles in the air, and peopled them
> with secret tribunals, and bands of illuminati, who were
> always the imaginary instruments of his projected
> regeneration of the human species. As he intended to
> institute a perfect republic, he invested himself with
> absolute sovereignty over these mystical dispensers of
> liberty. He slept with Horrid Mysteries [a German Gothic
> novel] under his pillow, and dreamed of venerable
> eleutherarchs and ghastly confederates holding midnight
> conventions in subterranean caves. (ch. 2)

Scythrop's politics clearly owe more to novel reading than to any social realities; moreover, his interest in secret societies reflects both a political paranoia bred of excessive subjectivity and the contents of Shelley's early Gothic novels, *Zastrozzi* and *St. Irvyne*.

Against these characters of egotism, gloom, theory, obscurity, and rebellion are the spokesmen of 'sunshine and music' – or happiness, sociability, and common sense – principally the aptly named Mr Hilary and the epicurean Rev. Mr Larynx (named for the throat, channel for food and drink and source of song). Significantly Mr Hilary does not express himself in the jargon and in the obscurity that characterize the utterances of the egotists and misanthropes, for he is a classicist. Hilary also argues against transcendentalism and rejection of 'things as they are' for mere theory; rather, one should take the world as it is, and accept 'physical and moral nature', as the ancients did. The themes and characters of *Nightmare Abbey*, then, refer generally and specifically to Romantic literature and particularly Romantic fiction (often helped by Peacock's footnotes) as purveyors of a cult of subjectivity leading to dangerous social nonconformity and revolutionary politics.

In his next two novels, *Maid Marian* (1822) and *The Misfortunes of Elphin* (1829), Peacock turned his attention to the assumptions of the Romantic historical romance and national tale, as well as Romantic antiquarianism and folklore, though on the whole with less penetration than in his treatment of Romantic subjectivity. *Maid Marian* deals with the world of Robin Hood, as re-imagined in the Romantic period with the help of the antiquarian Joseph Ritson's collection of Robin Hood ballads, tales, and lore. The re-imagining involved seeing in the Robin Hood material a picture of an authentic, harmonious, contentedly hierarchical society, to be contrasted with the artificial, conflicted, competitive, and emulative society of Peacock's present. Scott used the same material in *Ivanhoe*, but Peacock uses it to mount a blatant criticism of aristocratic culture and court politics. As Peacock told Shelley, 'I am writing a comic Romance of the Twelfth Century which I shall make the vehicle of much oblique satire on the oppressions that are done under the sun.'[28] He would return to this theme of Romantic medievalism again in *Crotchet Castle*. In *The Misfortunes of Elphin* Peacock turned to medieval Wales to satirize court government and social oppression, at a time in the late 1820s when there was increasing and widespread dissatisfaction with the court and aristocratic leadership of Britain.

Thus in these two novels Peacock was responding to the political dimensions or uses of Romantic medievalism, in a post-Napoleonic Europe rapidly inventing traditions of all kinds in order to justify restoration of monarchic and court government as somehow suited to the 'national' character and culture. The novels take the cynical view that might usually makes both right and write – in the sense of what historians 'record' as history. Romantic historiography, in its renewed and more sympathetic interest in the distant 'national' past, was, as Peacock knew, writing to attack or justify the present. Moreover, the popularization of history in the 'national tale' and 'historical romance', along with the use of 'popular antiquities' or folklore to invent a 'national' culture for the present, could be seen by Peacock as further attempts to cover harsh political and social realities with pseudo-historical justification and the glamour of *belles lettres* or 'polite literature'. Like James Hogg in *The Three Perils of Man* (1822), Peacock tries to resist these literary developments partly by showing the brutality and insecurity of medieval life, but also by depicting his characters as very much like modern people caught in a less-than-modern world.

With *Crotchet Castle* (written 1830; published 1831) Peacock returned to the mode and many of the matters of *Headlong Hall*, but he continued the thematic line taken in *The Misfortunes of Elphin*, though now at a time when things looked much better for reform and enlightenment and 'the march of mind'. *Crotchet Castle* has the thematic breadth of *Melincourt* and the formal vitality of *Nightmare Abbey*, but there is a stronger sense of the interrelatedness of Romantic culture and literature, issues of social conflict, and theories and policies of social progress and management. The treatment of political economy, in the character of Mr Mac Quedy (i.e., son of Q.E.D., a philosophical demonstration), is particularly sharp, as public debate moved toward the Reform Bill of 1832 and the Poor Law Reform Act of 1834, and other systemic and institutional reforms. Peacock's handling of this theme anticipates that of Dickens in *Hard Times*.

There are other topics, of course, many of them already dealt with in earlier novels, and now very clearly related to what Peacock saw as the evils of bourgeois utilitarianism, topics such as the condition of women, the relationship of the gentry and the middle classes, social emulation, the suppression of the rural poor; other topics are related to the limits of Romantic culture, topics such as the ancients versus the moderns, fashionable literature (including the silver-fork novel), transcendental philosophy, the cult of the Middle Ages, antiquarianism; still other topics are related to contemporary scandals, problems, and issues, such as paper money and the banking system, the rash of bankruptcies in the late 1820s, education of the common people, Owenite socialism, experimental science, exploration and navigation, the charity commission, university education, and the outbreak of rural unrest under the name of 'Captain Swing'. The persistent arguments in all of Peacock's novels, for a fusion of the values of gentry and professionals and for social leadership in the national interest, are illustrated more clearly than ever before when the various genteel, middle-class, and professional people assembled for Christmas at Chainmail Hall have to forget their individual 'crotchets' and unite to repel an attack by 'Captain Swing' rioters.

In its integration of these various issues with literary form *Crotchet Castle* is as successful as anything Peacock wrote. Once again Peacock uses certain types of character and characterization, especially sociolect or jargon, intellectual talk set against singing and eating and drinking as sociable, convivial activities, and a story in two main sections or movements. The organizing principle of the themes, characters, and plot is the opposition of romantic love and commercialism or self-interest. Commercialism manifests itself most obviously in the life and character of Ebenezer Crotchet, half Scot and half Jew, formerly Mac Crotchet, who has made a fortune in the City and naturally removes himself to a country estate in pursuit of gentility. This pursuit requires him to invent a family tradition, first with a purchased coat of arms:

> Crest, a crotchet rampant, in A sharp: Arms, three empty bladders, turgescent, to show how opinions are formed; three bags of gold, pendent, to show why they are maintained; three naked swords, trenchant, to show how they are administered; and three barbers' blocks, gaspant, to show how they are swallowed. (ch. 1)

But he also needs a country mansion: this is in fact a villa (Peacock's satirical glance at pseudo-genteel suburbanization of architecture, led by such figures as J. C. Loudon), named inappropriately, after a nearby supposed Roman ruin, Crotchet Castle. Then he tries to sell his son and daughter on the marriage market to acquire some 'high blood'. His daughter is married off to Lord Bossnowl, son of the Earl of Foolincourt, and M.P. for the rotten borough (i.e., a borough which had so decayed that it no longer had a constituency to be represented) of Rogueingrain. These names speak for themselves, indicating clearly the novel's point of view on court politics and parliamentary reform. Crotchet's son, well educated and set up in the City, is to marry Lord Bossnowl's sister, the Lady Clarinda.

She is the novel's witty and cultivated heroine, and loves the impecunious water-colour artist, Captain Fitzchrome (i.e., son of colour); but she is so awed by the commercialism all around her that she seems convinced that she needs a rich husband and therefore may rightly be sold off to one by her father. Her tone, however, strongly suggests that she is not mercenary. When Fitzchrome protests that he does not want to see her 'sacrificed on the shrine of Mammon', she replies, "'I dare say, love in a cottage is very pleasant; but then it positively must be a cottage ornée: but would not the same love be a great deal safer in a castle, even if Mammon furnished the fortification?'" (ch. 3). Significantly, however, her intended, Crochet, Jr, has already jilted one woman, Susannah Touchandgo, when her father went bankrupt and absconded with remaining funds to the new territories of the United States, where he has set up a bank, based on paper money, in Dotandcarryonetown (dot and carry one: a schoolboys' term for simple arithmetic, suggesting that the town is based on paper wealth only).

Commercialism, most open and evident in the New World, has in fact penetrated every aspect of modern culture, though transmuted into various forms. Here Peacock remounts his satire on Romantic literature and culture, already inscribed in *Nightmare Abbey* and in *Maid Marian* and *The Misfortunes of Elphin*. Once again Peacock depicts certain aspects of Romantic culture as self-centred, narrowly professional, and merely the riding of hobby-horses. He also suggests that certain aspects of modern culture, particularly 'the march of intellect', led and celebrated by 'the learned friend' (i.e., Lord Brougham) and the Steam Intellect Society (i.e., Brougham's Society for the Diffusion of Useful Knowledge, founded in 1827), are too closely allied to the new industrial and commercial spirit that is behind other dangerous institutions of specious value, such as paper money and stocks. Even Romantic fiction and poetry are seen to be commercialized and self-interested, in more ways than one, and tied in to the corrupting pattern of social emulation.

*Crotchet Castle*, as its title suggests (crotchet: a whimsical or idiosyncratic fancy), satirizes hobby-horses, as *Headlong Hall* and *Nightmare Abbey* had. Peacock shows his admiration for the political journalist William Cobbett when he has his narrator point out that Mr Crotchet does not like the usual country gentleman's diversions of

> game-bagging, poacher-shooting, trespasser-pounding,
> footpath-stopping, common-enclosing, rack-renting, and
> all the other liberal pursuits and pastimes which make a
> country gentleman an ornament to the world, and a
> blessing to the poor. . . . (ch. 1)

Instead, being Scottish, Crotchet has an 'inborn love of disputation'; and so, being also 'very hospitable in his establishment, and liberal in his invitations, a numerous detachment from the advanced guard of the "march of intellect," often marched down to Crotchet Castle', where, of course, they display their crotchets. There is Mac Quedy the Scottish political economist, Toogood the Owenite socialist, Firedamp the meteorologist (who blames all human ills on '*malaria*'), Philpot the 'geographer' (who sees water as a cure-all and wants to discover the source of the Nile and the mouth of the Niger), Trillo the opera-writer (formerly O'Trill, who moved the 'O' in his name because Italian composers are fashionable while Irish ones are not, and who sees opera as a social cure-all), Henbane the toxicologist (who spends all his time seeking poisons and antidotes, which merely cancel each other out), Chainmail the antiquarian (who advocates a return to the twelfth century), Skionar the transcendental poet and Kantian, and Folliott the clergyman, hellenophile, and epicure. Minor appearances are made by Wilful Wontsee and Rumblesack Shantsee, friends of Skionar, modelled on William Wordsworth and Robert Southey (the poet laureate, hence 'Rumblesack'), who were formerly social visionaries and are now loyal and well-rewarded Tories.

'Progress' is a continuing theme in Peacock's novels, and strongly associated with new forms of social control (summarized in the portrait of Sir Simon Steeltrap's activities); with the new and modern in culture, including the pointless experimental sciences of Philpot, Henbane, and Dr Morbific; with the impractical theories of Mac Quedy, Toogood, and Skionar; and the frivolous or sycophantic writings of Wontsee, Shantsee, and the fashionable novelist Eavesdrop. Even the more positive characters, Fitzchrome, Chainmail, Toogood, Trillo, and especially the Rev. Folliott, ride hobby-horses that represent the impractically visionary: Fitzchrome is too obviously merely a lover and an artistic amateur; Trillo wants to build opera-houses to assuage society's discontents; Chainmail rejects progress and wants to return to an imaginary harmonious, paternalist society of the twelfth century; Toogood wants to found a new communalism on steam technology; and Folliott also rejects progress and wants a return to the virtues and culture of the ancient Greeks, as well as more emphasis on the pleasures of the table, other than the pleasures of table talk. The spirit of reform and progress through legislation and the 'march of intellect' collides with the spirit of rural paternalism and 'merry England' in chapter 8, when Rev. Dr Folliott is attacked, first by thieves, whom he accuses of being members of the Steam Intellect Society, and then by the Charity Commissioners appointed by Parliament to investigate administration of parish charities, but powerless or unwilling actually to reform them. According to Folliott, both the robbers and the Commissioners are examples of the way the 'march of mind' and 'progress' merely cause discontent.

*Crotchet Castle* does include discussion of Romantic literature and fiction as part of its survey of culture and ideas of the Romantic period, though this element is not in the foreground as it is in *Nightmare Abbey*. The Romantic poets, Skionar, Wontsee, and Shantsee, are treated as mere government pensioners; discussion of fiction is more in the foreground here, and takes two directions. In the first place, there is the fashionable novelist Mr Eavesdrop, described by Lady Clarinda as '"a man who, by dint of a certain something like smartness, has got into good society. He is a sort of bookseller's tool, and coins all his acquaintance in reminiscences and sketches of character"' (ch. 5). This is probably a reference to Benjamin Disraeli and his silver-fork novel, *Vivian Grey*.[29] Later in the same chapter, when Fitzchrome compliments Lady Clarinda on her observation and especially her 'attention to opinions', she admits it is because she is writing a novel:

> 'Yes, a novel. . . . You must know I have been reading
> several fashionable novels . . . and I thought to myself,
> why I can do better than any of these myself. So I wrote

a chapter or two, and sent them as a specimen to Mr
Puffall, the bookseller, telling him they were to be a part
of the fashionable something or other, and he offered me,
I will not say how much, to finish it in three volumes,
and let him pay all the newspapers for recommending it as
the work of a lady of quality, who had made very free
with the characters of her acquaintance.'

This is a reference to Henry Colburn, one of the leading publishers of
silver-fork novels.

*Crotchet Castle* also looks at the other great phenomenon of novel
writing in the 1820s, the achievement of Sir Walter Scott, although
Peacock had already tried his hand at satirizing 'historical romance' in
*Maid Marian* and *The Misfortunes of Elphin*. In chapter 9, while the
Crotchet Castle party are on their voyage up the Thames, they fall into
discussion of what the narrator calls 'legendary histories'. Lady Clarinda takes a very hackneyed line when she says,

'History is but a tiresome thing in itself; it becomes more
agreeable the more romance is mixed up with it. The
great enchanter [Scott] has made me learn many things
which I should never have dreamed of studying, if they
had not come to me in the form of amusement.'

The Rev. Dr Folliott is not sure which enchanter she means, Scott or
'"the enchanter of Covent Garden"' (the pantomime producer Charles
Farley). Lady Clarinda is shocked: '"Surely you do not class literature
with pantomime?"' Folliott replies, '"They are both one, with a slight
difference. The one is the literature of pantomime, the other is the
pantomime of literature."' The discussion then turns to the merits of
the twelfth century and is led by Mac Quedy and Chainmail, who both
feel that 'the great enchanter' of the North has misrepresented that
time, but they feel so for different reasons. Folliott closes, though he
doesn't conclude the argument, by declaring,

'If the enchanter has represented the twelfth century too
brightly for one, and too darkly for the other of you, I
should say, as an impartial man, he has represented it
fairly. My quarrel with him is, that his works contain
nothing worth quoting; and a book that furnishes no
quotations, is, *me judice*, no book – it is a plaything.'

For Folliott, literature can be reduced to the most mundane kind of
intertextuality.

These, of course, are comments by characters, and thus relative to the dramatic situations and relationships of the characters within the novel, rather than direct expressions of the author's point of view. And once again views at variance are not so much resolved as turned away from by the chapter's end. More direct is the narrator's comment on 'modern literature' in chapter 15, the Welsh idyll during which Chainmail falls in love with Susannah Touchandgo, whose bankrupt father had abandoned her and who retired to live with the simple Welsh farming family, the Ap-Llymrys. When Chainmail follows Susannah to the farmhouse, the situation seems ripe for a touch of domestic detail and realism, which the narrator declines:

> We shall leave this tempting field of interesting expatiation
> to those whose brains are high-pressure steam engines for
> spinning prose by the furlong, to be trumpeted in paid-for
> paragraphs in the quack's corner of newspapers: modern
> literature having attained the honourable distinction of
> sharing with blacking and macassar oil, the space which
> used to be monopolized by razor-strops and the lottery,
> whereby that very enlightened community, the reading
> public, is tricked into the perusal of much exemplary
> nonsense; though the few who see through the trickery
> have no reason to complain, since as 'good wine needs no
> bush' . . . these bushes of venal panegyric point out very
> clearly that the things they celebrate are not worth
> reading.

Quite clearly, commercialized literature and fiction are set against what 'the few who see through the trickery' are likely to read. Such comments, even those clearly related to particular characters in the novel, would make a reader reflect on their relevance to the novel in his or her hands – a 'novel of opinion', or 'novel of talk'.

For, more obviously than Peacock's other novels, *Crotchet Castle* sets itself apart from 'modern literature' and 'fashionable fiction' as they are depicted here, first in its satirical treatment of the themes and forms of modern literature, second by considering 'modern literature' as only one aspect of larger cultural, social, and ideological issues and conflicts, and third by refusing the usual novelistic methods of social and cultural criticism, found for example in the English Jacobin novelists, in novelists such as Maria Edgeworth, or the later and more pertinent silver-fork novels such as Bulwer's *Pelham*. *Crotchet Castle*, like all of Peacock's novels, makes its most penetrating criticism of the 'modern novel' by insisting on its own artificiality and its 'philosophical' character – 'philosophical' in the sense of resembling the 'philosophical' novels and tales of eighteenth-century Enlightenment writers such as Voltaire and Diderot, or the earlier masterpieces of satirical fiction by Rabelais or Lucian. *Crotchet Castle*, in particular, in its comprehensive treatment of Romantic culture and ideology, seems to challenge attempts to present similar critical surveys in more 're-alistic' fictional mode in novels such as *Vivian Grey* and *Pelham*, as though Peacock were insisting on the superior validity of his own form of fiction, and its superior value to 'the few who see through the trickery' of 'modern literature' in all its aspects. Significantly, *Crotchet Castle* was Peacock's last novel for many years, until, with *Gryll Grange*, published just before his death, he produced a final novel in the vein of *Crotchet Castle*, but taking up the intellectual and social issues of the 1850s – the age of Dickens, Kingsley, Trollope, Carlyle, Browning, Ruskin, and Tennyson.

In Peacock's novels, then, the argument is not to be found in a paraphrase of this or that dialogue, or in the relationship of a fictional character to a real-life person in Peacock's circle or the intellectual and literary world of his time. Peacock's novels are neither *romans à clef* nor quasi-novels. For if Peacock's are novels of talk, the talk is shaped and given its significance by Peacock's use of the novel form and the elements of prose fiction, composed in such a way as to constitute an argument beyond the arguments aired in the novel and transcended by form. They are not novels that represent talk realistically or even alle-gorically; they are, as Romantic novels of national or regional culture are, specifically literary expropriations of talk, only this time the talk is that of the professional classes and especially professional intellectuals – mere professionals, one should say – rather than the talk of national or regional representative types. More important, the talk is always situated in a particular plot and setting, and it unfolds relationships between characters (even though the characters are Peacockian versions of the Theophrastan Character). All of the talkers are shown to be more or less limited because the form of Peacock's novels implies the necessity of a broader, more cultivated, transcendental consciousness. The nearest approximation to that implied consciousness is the pro-fessionalized gentleman for which major Romantic novelists such as Edgeworth, Austen, and Scott also argued. Peacock represents this consciousness in five main ways: his handling of burlesque form; his handling of dialogue; his use of narrative voice; his deployment of character and characterization through language; and his use of the love plot.

Peacock's satiric handling of Romantic fictional form is seen most obviously in his early novel, *Nightmare Abbey*. Peacock uses here, as frequently in all his novels, the appropriate narrative figure of bathos, or descending from the sublime to the ridiculous, with the sudden end of highfalutin talk by comic or even slapstick action, or by more practical and physical aspects of human 'nature' and everyday life. Thus Nightmare Abbey is, suitably enough, 'in a highly picturesque state of semi-dilapidation', probably from poor management; but its setting is very unpicturesque, on the flat land of Lincolnshire between the fens and the sea, rather than on some darkly-forested mountain in the south of Europe or north of Scotland. The novel also has no hero, no heroine, and neither a romantic happy ending nor a grotesquely Gothic one. The narrative tone is resolutely dry and ironic. As for the narrative figures – talk is often broken off for eating, drinking, or singing, and there are several rather hackneyed slapstick incidents. Notable, too, is the figural use of songs, as in chapter 11, when the argument between the gloomy characters and the cheerful becomes a singing contest with the former led by Mr Cypress and his 'tragical ballad' (a pastiche of *Childe Harold's Pilgrimage*), and the latter led by Mr Hilary and the Rev. Mr Larynx with their 'catch' (a round song for three or more equal voices, often with punning or humorous lyrics and sung while drinking). Significantly, the 'tragical ballad' is sung by a solo voice, and the catch by a duet and then a chorus, a more sociable music altogether. For the upshot of the singing contest gives a clear indication of the novel's meaning:

> This catch was so well executed by the spirit and science
> of Mr Hilary, and the deep tri-une [three-in-one, a play
> on the trinitarian theology of the Anglicans] voice of the
> reverend gentleman, that the whole party, in spite of
> themselves, caught the contagion, and joined in chorus at
> the conclusion, each raising a bumper to his lips. . . .

In sum, *Nightmare Abbey* is a satire on Romantic culture and literature, in its form as well as in its thematic content. In particular, in its naming of characters, abandonment of the 'realistic' yet 'romantic' representation of people, places, or psychology, its rough handling of love conventions, and its detached narrative voice, *Nightmare Abbey* cocks a snook at Romantic fiction of several kinds examined earlier in this chapter.

Of course, as novels of talk, Peacock's novels obviously use a great deal of dialogue; but as suggested earlier in considering Peacock's themes, the significance of the dialogue cannot be reduced to positions expressed by individual speakers. Talk is relative; indeed, language is relative. Peacock does not present a relativist view of language and speech, and there is a master dialect of English in his novels, as in Scott's, Austen's, and Radcliffe's. But Peacock is also aware of the social nature of language, and especially speech, and seems to be suspicious of Romantic attitudes to language as authentic self-expression. Romantic love and poetry might be two areas in which authentic language could be seen in use; but, as we have noticed, Romantic poetry, especially that of the poets of presence, Wordsworth and Coleridge, is satirized in Peacock's novels, and other Romantic poets and poetic modes are dismissed as mere egotists or as sycophants to power. As for romantic love, the narrator in *Nightmare Abbey* acknowledges the Sentimental opposition of self as romantic love and society as 'mere' material and social interest, and notes the popular Romantic idea, derived from writers such as Rousseau and Mackenzie and shared to some extent by Peacock's friend Shelley, of the inadequacy of language to express inward subjectivity. But the ironic tone of the narrator clearly indicates disapproval of such ideas of sublime experience beyond language (see ch. 9).

On the whole, however, such direct intervention by the narrator in the action-through-dialogue is uncommon. Peacock prefers to absent the narrator by setting up most of the novels' talk as dialogue in the text of a play, eliminating narration for long stretches. Thus the reader can immerse himself or herself in the play of character-ideas. These dialogues proceed openly, and various views are expressed, and the reader is left to follow the arguments and do the adjudicating almost as a silent participant. Some help is given. The limited forms of language – jargon, idiolect, dialect, or sociolect – mark the limitations of the views expressed. Stage 'business', such as slapstick incident, can cut off the talk, as when the philosophical discussion of ghosts in chapter 12 of *Nightmare Abbey* is interrupted by the appearance of one, producing a variety of unphilosophical panic-stricken reactions. Often, too, there is the turning aside from talk to eat, or drink, or pursue some other, more down-to-earth interest, undermining the lofty ideas and theoretical nature of much of the talk. Finally, Peacock also manages dialogue by having 'reality' intrude on the theorizing, in a narrative figure of bathos. This figure is one that Byron used a great deal in *Don Juan* (which Peacock liked very much), and it was a favourite device in Anti-Jacobin novels of the 1790s and Barrett's anti-romance, *The Heroine*. Indeed, it had been a commonplace of conservative criticism of theory and theorizing since Burke's writings on the French Revolution.

On the whole, then, the dialogues proceed openly and are not resolved within themselves but rather by the formal situation of the talk. The talk is certainly not indeterminate, merely putting ideas into play, refusing to lead to a conclusion. Rather, the implicitly 'correct' view is precisely that, implied, or an overview or synthesis properly 'above it all' but not detached from the particular points of view set in play in the dialogue. Moreover, it is not just that certain views are implicitly recommended, but that a transcendental critical judgment is called into play – in itself a kind of resolution of the clash of opinions dramatized in the novel's dialogues. Just as the novels, in their fictionality and (therefore) literariness expropriate conflicting opinions from the real social world of the 1810s and 1820s and stay outside the struggle for ideological dominance of the professional middle classes, so the implied model consciousness in (and reading) Peacock's novels expropriates aspects of particular views expressed in the novels' dialogues, implicitly resolves the conflicts therein by means of literary form, and thus rises above those particularities and partialities. It is precisely a literary, formal solution to the ideological warfare of the time.

The narrative voice is the principal formal guide to this model consciousness. It is true, as noticed earlier, that the narrator does not intervene much in the novels' talk; and this detachment – an ironic detachment – is in itself significant, indicating perhaps Peacock's own position as a writer of reports on others' correspondence for the East India Company, indicating certainly his solution to the ideological conflicts within and about Romantic culture. This is not to say, then, that Peacock, or the narrator, is against or has no intellectual commitment, but that his commitment is to an ironic and detached, transcendentally intellectual attitude to the commitments of others; this attitude became embodied in a range of professional intellectual and cultural institutions, including literature and criticism, in the nineteenth century. So although the narrator in Peacock's novels does not adjudicate the novels' talk, the narrative voice plays a major role in the novels' argument by implying a certain kind of consciousness, by adding another, different kind of voice to the polyphony within the text. Whereas the polyphony of characters within the novel establishes the relativity of the characters' views, one might describe the discourse of the narrator as self-relative, though it is not self-undermining. It does not take away the ground on which it stands, but rather models in language (including classical languages, Latin and Greek) and style a consciousness that might be described as at once learned and witty, professional and genteel.

The narrator's style, fuller, more comprehensive, and more urbane than that of any one character in the novel, also reminds the reader that the meaning and value of statements are relative to the utterer of them, and the situation in which they are made. This dialogical structure within Peacock's novels continues a controversy about truth and discourse going back to Socrates and the Sophists. Irony is clearly the chief attribute of the narrative 'voice', combined with a 'nervous' energy of style (associated with 'genius' as uniqueness in late eighteenth-century rhetoric books), an allusive method, and a punning, linguistically playful attitude, with recondite words, neologisms, and circumlocutions – a highbrow counterpart, one might say, to Pierce Egan's narrator in *Life in London*. Literary quotation, deft play with philosophical terminology, passages of self-conscious circumlocution and grandiloquence, and juxtaposition of the mythic and the mundane all advertise a mind at once broad, deep, and well-stocked.

It is through such 'voicing' of a model consciousness that Peacock directs response to the other, lesser voices in his novels. For the well-informed reader implied by Peacock's novels will also see that Peacock's characters are characterized by their talk, by the rhetorical figures they use and the language with which they express themselves and the ideas they embody. For in Peacock, as in so many Romantic novelists, language is structured in a hierarchy of value, which is implicit and which the reader must grasp in order to make sense of the novel. Like his great predecessor in the satirico-intellectual novel, Sterne in *Tristram Shandy*, Peacock gives each character his or her hobby-horse and the jargon to go with it. But rather more like a conventional Sentimental novelist he also includes a few 'rounded' characters ('rounded' being a relative rather than an absolute scale of value), who have their own hobby-horses but who tend to have a larger, closer to standard, fuller range of language in their talk. This fact is meant to suggest to the reader that they are more in the right than the other, narrowly professional and intellectual characters or the merely fashionable ones. These characters who are more richly endowed linguistically seem 'rounder' because of their language; they are, however, just as allegorical and ideologically representative as the other characters. The hero and heroine are usually included in this group, too, and their central place in the novel's moral and social vision, already suggested in their language, is confirmed by the novel's love plot.

The romantic love plot runs alongside the chain of dialogues, resolving conflict of another kind by means of a plot of romantic comedy. This conflict is one of marriage for love versus marriage for money or for some other motive of material self-interest or social advancement. These bad motives are thematized in other ways in the novel, as well. True love is the expression and index of character, distinguishing those characters that are not intriguers and hypocrites from those that are. Thus true love also distinguishes the characters that have fullness and authenticity of being from those that are all talk. Marriage for money is a recurring theme, reflecting Peacock's larger theme that merely monetary values are replacing human values and relations in a world increasingly dominated by capitalist values and practices. No doubt this theme is very old, but Peacock places it in relation to dialogues on such contemporary topics as political economy and thereby gives it topical relevance to the public issues of the 1810s and 1820s. In fact, Peacock virtually ignores the old romantic comedy plot of marriage and disparity of social rank, the concern of a society more preoccupied with gentry values, and thus a plot more prominent in fictional and dramatic romantic comedies of the eighteenth century. At the same time, Peacock treats the conventions of romantic comedy with obvious nonchalance and playfulness, setting up blatant conflicts of love and self-interest, as in *Nightmare Abbey* and *Crotchet Castle*, and resolving such conflicts (or not resolving them) romantically in a perfunctory way.

The main love-plot in Peacock's novels usually features a vivacious, intelligent, well-educated, cultivated, and independent-minded heroine, somewhat after the model of the new woman (of the middle and upper classes) designed by Mary Wollstonecraft in the 1790s – a woman, that is, beyond the decadent courtly culture of coquetry and sexual intrigue, but no less feminine than the usual heroines of 'modern novels'. Such a character is also beyond the narrow peculiarities of the merely professional characters in the novels, the ones who spend much of their time engaged in talk. The heroes singled out to match such heroines *are* numbered among the talkers; but as suitors they are also men of action of some kind (especially in *Maid Marian* and *The Misfortunes of Elphin*), and thus somewhat set apart from the mere talkers. Furthermore, their betrothal to the scintillating heroines indicates that they have potential beyond the hobby-horses on which they discourse with the other talkers. Thus, while the heroes may not dominate the dialogues in Peacock's novels, the love plot tacitly validates their views as somehow, if only potentially, above and broader than the particularities and partialities of the mere jargon-users. The heroines rarely use jargon; often they are witty; frequently they seem above or beyond all the male talk, though they are marked out for the heroes by sympathy of views. They are figures for the full humanity which the heroes are striving and fighting toward in their dialogues with the other men in the novels. In fact, one could argue that the real match for heroines such as Lady Clarinda is not the hero such as Captain Fitzchrome, but the novels' implicit, gentrified, intellectual (male) reader.

Finally, Peacock uses the controlling hand of art, revealed through evident symmetries of structure, to convey to the reader the sense of a god-like, transcendental intelligence – that of the conscious artist – controlling meaning and value within the text. This almost musical sense of form is perhaps not surprising in a writer deeply interested in music and one who, moreover, uses songs frequently in his novels. Marilyn Butler makes a convincing case for Peacock's tendency to organize his material into three-part balanced structures, with an opening, theme-setting phase, largely static and repetitive in form; a central, 'active', mobile phase, in which the fixities of the first phase are unsettled, shocked, or displaced; and a closing, explanatory, resolving, settling, though by no means utterly conclusive phase – for closure would work against the authority of the implicit structure discussed earlier. It may be that this triadic structure was taken by Peacock from the song-form, or ternary form, in music; or perhaps he was influenced by the sonata-form, reaching its major phase of dominance in musical composition during the Romantic period. In any case, the triadic form is seen clearly, as an example, in *Crotchet Castle*.

The first eight chapters are centred on one setting and are dominated by talk among a more or less fixed set of idea-characters. The central two chapters, 'The Voyage' and 'The Voyage, Continued', shift the scene, and contain discussions of the historical novel and perception of the twelfth century as better or worse than the present. Here relativity of 'opinions' is clearly set forth. Of the remaining eight chapters, six are set in Wales, are highly descriptive, and deal with happy rusticity and true love, and the last two round up the characters again for a finale that ends in a twelfth-century banquet, more modern talk, a very timely and topical fight, and a pair of medieval songs. The 'Conclusion' speaks for itself. In this structure, it is important to emphasize, character, setting, plot, themes, and dominant type of discourse (dialogue, description) all interact. Furthermore, this is a structure that is shapely, but not predictable; complete, but not closed; open to chance and co-incidence, yet with a 'logic' of art and 'poetic' justness of its own. It is a literary, not a utilitarian shaping; yet it avoids, or plays with, conventional kinds of fictional shaping (as with the tying-up-loose-ends 'Conclusion').

The meaning that one of Peacock's novels has to communicate, then, resides not in particular statements or even the sum of statements made in its dialogues, but in the novel's formal and thematic elements considered in their interrelationship and as a whole. This kind of consideration calls for a reader different from the reader called for by most Romantic fiction or by the Waverley Novels, say; perhaps it is the kind of reader called for by Austen's novels, but more likely to be a man than a woman. It is a reader with a particular literary and critical frame of mind. This reader also needs to understand contemporary public issues, and will be able to see Peacock's 'novels of talk' as an alternative to or a transcendence of the discourses of utilitarianism, modern science, transcendental philosophy, Evangelicalism, or even 'modern literature' and culture. Peacock shows the limits of Romantic culture and Romantic fiction not only thematically but also formally, in his refusal to write a 'realistic' novel with 'realistic' characters, in his practice of having a narrator who is learned and highly allusive yet witty and detached, in his play with conventions of romantic plotting and resolution. Peacock wrote intellectual novels, if we might use the term 'intellectual' in a descriptive rather than evaluative sense; he wrote neither for mass amusement, as he thought Scott did, nor for a specialist few, as he thought most utilitarians, scientists, Kantians, and others did, though he did write for the few, or rather, he wrote in such a way as to suggest to readers that they were a select few. This few could be defined in sociological terms as the gentrified professional intellectuals with a broadly 'humanist' culture who came to dominate intellectual and then academic life – perhaps they still do. As Peacock's friend Shelley put it in a verse-letter of 1820, though Peacock's 'fine wit' was 'a strain too learned for a shallow age', he 'charms the chosen spirits of the time'.[30]

More recently Bryan Burns acknowledges that Peacock's novels 'have always been highly regarded by a small, discriminating section of the reading public'.[31] Yet the discriminating few called for in Peacock's novels are neither the denizens of fashionable silver-fork society nor mere professional littérateurs, but the few in command of an emerging culture in which literature itself, as distinct from mere commercialized amusement on one hand and mere journalism and utilitarian 'fact' on the other, would have a central role. Peacock is a literary novelist in this ambiguous sense of self-defining exclusiveness, rather than a reflexively literary novelist such as Sterne or a comprehensively literary novelist such as Scott. To this extent, Peacock's novels are designed, in their peculiar limitedness and exclusivity, to show the limits and limitations of other kinds of Romantic discourse and discourse of the Romantic period, including Romantic fiction.

# Notes

1. See Eric J. Evans, *The Forging of the Modern State: Early Industrial Britain 1783–1870* (London and New York, 1983), chs 19 and 22.

2. The definition of Romanticism is a long-standing controversy. See, among numerous others, L. R. Furst, *Romanticism in Perspective* (London and New York, 1969); *Romanticism Reconsidered*, edited by Northrop Frye (New York and London, 1963); and the works listed in the Bibliography at the end of this book.

3. See Irene Tayler and Gina Luria, 'Gender and Genre: Women in British Romantic Literature', in *What Manner of Woman: Essays on English and American Life and Literature*, edited by Marlene Springer (New York, 1977).

4. See Ellen Moers, 'Female Gothic', in *Literary Women* (New York, 1974).

5. See Lee Sterrenburg, 'Mary Shelley's Monster: Politics and Psyche in *Frankenstein*', in *The Endurance of Frankenstein*, edited by George Levine and U. C. Knoepflmacher (Berkeley, 1979), pp. 143–71.

6. See Peter Dale Scott, 'Vital Artifice: Mary, Percy, and the Psychopolitical Integrity of *Frankenstein*', in *The Endurance of Frankenstein*, pp. 172–202 (p. 173).

7. See David Punter, *The Literature of Terror: A History of Gothic Fiction from 1765 to the Present Day* (London and New York, 1980), pp. 121–28.

8. See Peter Brooks, '"Godlike Science/Unhallowed Arts": Language, Nature, and Monstrosity', in *The Endurance of Frankenstein*, pp. 205–20.

9. Lee Sterrenburg, 'Mary Shelley's Monster', in *The Endurance of Frankenstein*, p. 171.

10. *Scots Magazine*, new series, 11 (Sept. 1822), 315–22 (p. 317).

11. See Keith M. Costain, 'Theoretical History and the Novel: The Scottish Fiction of John Galt', *ELH: A Journal of English Literary History*, 43 (1976), 342–65.

12. See Andrew Martin, *The Knowledge of Ignorance: From Genesis to Jules Verne* (Cambridge, 1985), p. 63.

13. *Quarterly Review*, 39 (Jan. 1829), 73–99. This is principally a review of *Hajji Baba in England*; the portion of the review relating to *Hajjî Baba* is reprinted in the Everyman's Library edition of the work (London and New York, n.d.), pp. vii–xi.

14. Edward W. Said, *Orientalism* (London and Henley, 1978), pp. 1–2.

15. See M. W. Rosa, *The Silver Fork School: Novels of Fashion Preceding 'Vanity Fair'* (New York, 1936); Alison Adburgham, *Silver Fork Society: Fashionable Life and Literature from 1814 to 1840* (1983); and Keith Hollingsworth, *The Newgate Novel 1830–1847* (Detroit, 1963).

16. Hollingsworth, *The Newgate Novel*, p. 14.

17. *Fraser's Magazine*, 1 (June 1830), 514–15.

18. Ellen Moers, *The Dandy: Brummell to Beerbohm* (1960), p. 69.

19. See Neil McKendrick, 'Josiah Wedgwood and the Commercialization of the Potteries', in Neil McKendrick, John Brewer, and J. H. Plumb, *The Birth of a Consumer Society: The Commercialization of Eighteenth-Century England* (1982).

20. See Mark Girouard, *The Return to Camelot: Chivalry and the English Gentleman* (New Haven and London, 1981).

21. *Fraser's Magazine*, 1 (April 1830), 320.

22. Norbert Elias, *The Civilizing Process*; vol. 2, *Power and Civility*, translated by Edmund Jephcott (New York, 1982), pp. 313–16.

23. Pierre Bourdieu, *Distinction: A Social Critique of the Judgement of Taste*, translated by Richard Nice (Cambridge Mass., 1984), pp. 1–7.

24. Michel Foucault, *Power/Knowledge: Selected Interviews and Other Writings 1972–1977*, translated by Colin Gordon, Leo Marshall, John Mepham, and Kate Soper (New York, 1980).

25. Marilyn Butler, *Peacock Displayed: A Satirist in His Context* (1979). p. 19.

26. Quoted in Butler, *Peacock Displayed*, p. 267 and p. 18 (from a review of 1836).

27. Letter to Shelley, 30 May 1818, in *Thomas Love Peacock: Letters to Edward Hookham and Percy B. Shelley*, edited by Richard Garnett (Boston, 1910), p. 64.

28. Letter to Shelley, 29 Nov. 1818, in *Peacock: Letters*, edited by Garnett, p. 81.

29. Marilyn Butler says that Eavesdrop is a reference to Leigh Hunt and Thomas Moore, and their published reminiscences of Byron; *Peacock Displayed*, p. 184.

30. Quoted in Butler, *Peacock Displayed*, p. 20.

31. Bryan Burns, *The Novels of Thomas Love Peacock* (London and Sydney, 1985), p. 1.

# Chapter 7
# Conclusion: The Limits of Romantic Fiction

The preceding chapters have described the variety of form and motive in British prose fiction from the outbreak of the French Revolution to the death of Britain's modern merry monarch, George IV, and the threshold of major political and institutional transformations in Britain itself. We have seen that fiction was made to serve many functions in the social conflicts and re-alignments of this period, and was made to 'represent' different versions of reality, actual or potential, within the range of interests of those who wrote and read, produced and consumed prose fiction. We have also seen signs of anxiety about the limitations of prose fiction, or the validity of particular novels' representations of subjective and social reality, and about the limits of prose fiction, or fiction's ability to represent actual or potential subjective and social reality at all. As we saw in Chapter 1, anxieties about the limitations of the 'modern novel' were rife in the Romantic period, though gradually diminished by the achievement of novelists such as the English Jacobins, Edgeworth, Austen, and Scott. Such anxiety was directed not so much at the aesthetic as at the moral effect, especially in women readers, of fiction in general and certain 'bad' kinds of fiction in particular – generally, forms of 'romance' and novels of emulation. This anxiety led to various attempts, from Jacobin novels to historical fiction, to reclaim 'the trash of circulating libraries' or merely commercialized fiction for serious moral discourse and social criticism of contemporary life. Evangelicals and writers for children, in particular, agonized over the awful necessity of sugaring the pill of moral and ethical instruction with the delight of fiction, though they seem to have resigned themselves to it by the early 1800s.

Another moral, aesthetic, and intellectual concern, in spite of Scott's achievement, was with the mingling of 'romance' and 'reality' or history in the historical novel. Finally, we have seen the anxiety of many novelists to establish the literariness of their genre, to demonstrate the importance of prose fiction and especially the novel not only as useful moral, intellectual, and critical discourse but also as verbal art, part of the emergent institution of 'national' literature seen as a classless and timeless (or 'classic') master-discourse. For how could the novel or fiction be both propaganda – a means of intervening, for good or for ill, in actual moral and social change and conflict – and yet, as art, also above such change and conflict? Or, to put the question another way, when fiction aspired to art was it not simply trying to mask its own partiality, tendentiousness, and bias in order to achieve greater rhetorical effectiveness in pursuit of its particular political or class- and gender-based goals? Is art or literature apolitical or simply another way of being political?

The limitations of prose fiction of the Romantic period were widely canvassed in criticism, in prefaces to novels, and in fiction itself, as we have seen. But some texts put in question the limits of Romantic fiction, just as prose fiction, and especially the novel, were becoming the most widely disseminated forms of verbal art within a 'national' culture that was based on writing and print and that was largely represented in and through the novel. Most of these questioning texts were quasi-novels, addressed to literary intellectuals or to readers liable to harbour deep suspicions of fiction and fictionality; at least one of these texts, James Hogg's *Confessions of a Justified Sinner* (1824), attempted to deconstruct the great institution of the Romantic social-historical novel. Not surprisingly, however, these texts failed to halt the steady progress of the novel to central place in nineteenth-century literary culture, if not to highest status in the institution of Literature (that place was and is reserved by most critics and canonizers for poetry). Nevertheless, these texts explore and exhibit, not just the limitations, but the limits of Romantic fiction, the necessary failure of Romantic fiction to be a comprehensive and closed system of meaning, value, and representation, either by its generic nature or by its particular representation of subjective and social reality.

## The Limits of Genre: The Romantic Quasi-Novel

Romantic writers in general exhibited a disregard for generic limits. They did this partly as a way of contesting artistic categories and hier-archies associated with or serving questionable social institutions and hierarchies, partly as a quest for an authentic or natural language of form, partly as a transgression of artistic limits in a bid for creative freedom, and partly, too, as an accommodation with commercializ-ation of culture or the market for fashion and novelty, even in art. As

we have seen, moreover, novelists of the Romantic period incorporated elements of other, accepted literary discourses, particularly
history and the *belles lettres*, into their novels in various ways in order
to dignify the sub-literary form of the novel and give it more rhetorical
effectiveness with a 'reading public' very aware of differences of
cultural status between different discourses. In some cases, though, the
elements from other discourses could be seen to dominate the text as
a whole, lending it new authority, or requiring the reader to attend
more carefully to the text or to question received generic limits. Such
texts could be called quasi-novels. Of course there had been such quasi-
novels in the past: Sidney's *Arcadia* (1590), Bunyan's *Pilgrim's Progress*
(1678), Defoe's *A Journal of the Plague Year* (1722), Swift's *Tale of a Tub*
(1704), *Gulliver's Travels* (1726), and his other allegories – indeed, allegories in general – along with numerous philosophical, literary, and
political dialogues with fictitious characters, such as Clara Reeve's
*Progress of Romance* (1785), and oriental tales such as Samuel Johnson's
*Rasselas* (1759). But the Romantic period and especially the high
Romantic period of the 1810s and 1820s in Britain seem to have seen
a resurgence and flowering of the quasi-novel.

Certainly many novels or texts of these years seem to contain or
to be dominated by material not considered to be usual in novels.
When any of these elements are perceived to dominate in a text that
otherwise is a prose fiction, then readers and critics will tend to regard
the text as not really a novel, but something else. This kind of perception may, of course, vary according to changing literary conventions
and expectations. Good examples are lyrical writing, including narrative poetry, as in Moore's *Lalla Rookh*, or lyrical, expressive prose, as
in Hazlitt's *Liber Amoris*; drama, especially dialogue, often set up on
the page as it would be for a play, as in Dibdin's *Bibliomania* or
Wilson's 'Noctes Ambrosianæ'; and essayistic or expository prose, as
in Scott's *Paul's Letters*, Lockhart's *Peter's Letters*, Southey's *The Doctor*,
and a large number of books on history, geography, nature, and other
subjects cast in fictitious narrative form for children and young people,
by writers such as Sarah Trimmer, Anna Barbauld, Barbara Hofland,
Jane and Ann Taylor, and others.

Thus quasi-novels are often frame narratives, in which a prose
fiction frame contains inset material, such as verse, dialogues, or factual
essays, normally appropriate to other genres. Often the form is disconnected and desultory, to accommodate these diverse materials or to
allow for serial form of publication, and is only loosely held together
by a narrative frame of recurring characters, as in 'Noctes
Ambrosianæ'. The form is also open-ended, and the series just stops,
although other quasi-novels have definite opening and closure and an
obvious line of plot or development of material. Some quasi-novels

also tend to be carnivalesque, with rich allusiveness, referentiality, inter-textuality, and continuing play on and with recondite learning, ancient and modern languages, varieties of one language (English), and the nature of language itself. But this element of the encyclopaedic text tends to draw on the philosophical and critical attitudes, materials, and discourses of Enlightenment and Romantic learned culture rather than on popular culture, as in the Rabelaisian tradition. In short, the quasi-novel and especially the Romantic quasi-novel often reflect the rise of the professional writer as well as a continuing reservation about professionalism and continuing desire to see writing and literature as genteel avocations.

One Romantic quasi-novel which eschews the carnivalesque for the piously factual, however, is the Rev. Legh Richmond's *Annals of the Poor* (1809–14). It purports to describe the Rev. Richmond's experiences among the poor in a country parish on the Isle of Wight; it was reprinted many times, into the twentieth century, had a powerful effect on images of 'reformed' rural life, and stimulated a small tourist industry in the part of the Isle of Wight it claims for a setting. It was probably the best-known, most widely distributed religious text of the first half of the nineteenth century, apart from the Bible, the Book of Common Prayer, and the Hymnal. Here the elements of authentic description and the factual register the Evangelicals' persistent anxiety that fiction is a kind of lying and therefore not godly and therefore not rhetorically effective, even though the Lord Himself taught in parables. A secular version of this quasi-fictional depiction of the *embourgeoisement* of rural society, Mary Mitford's *Our Village*, was examined in the last chapter.

Another, very different yet strangely similar example is the Rev. Thomas Frognall Dibdin's *Bibliomania; or, Book Madness: A Bibliographical Romance* (1809; greatly expanded 1811; expanded again 1842). *Bibliomania* is a frame narrative and most of the text is made up of dialogues dealing with the history, symptoms, and cure of bibliomania. But there are also extensive bibliographical footnotes, often usurping most of each page and spilling over for many pages at a time, and containing, for example, entire book-sale catalogues with prices, as well as all kinds of bibliographical information. Appropriately, *Bibliomania* explicitly invokes the tradition of the farrago text going back at least to Burton's *Anatomy of Melancholy*. Yet *Bibliomania* is also aware of itself as, paradoxically, a kind of text which is a monument to its proposed topic: as one of the characters asks another, '"do BIBLIOMANIACS ever *read* books?"' (part I, p. 4). The very bookish excess of *Bibliomania* – its visibly divided page, with 'main' text above and copious, complex notes below; its evident love of the recondite; its supplements; its detailed indexes; its exploitation of the full repertory of printer's resources of typography, layout, and illustration – all these pull against the book's earnest argument 'on the right uses of literature'. Like so many romances of the 1810s and 1820s, *Bibliomania* is both moral and extravagant, a self-contradictory text.

Different again are the quasi-novels of Walter Scott and John Gibson Lockhart – respectively, *Paul's Letters to His Kinsfolk* (1816) and *Peter's Letters to His Kinsfolk* (1819). These are descriptive quasi-novels, the first giving an account by a fictitious Scot (Scott himself) of the state of Belgium and France after Waterloo, the second giving a fictitious Englishman's account of Scotland, especially its literary, intellectual, and cultural life. *Peter's Letters* contains numerous written portraits of Scotland's luminaries, accompanied by engraved portraits bound in, thus making obvious the non-fictional elements of the text.

Tom Moore's very popular *Lalla Rookh: An Oriental Romance* (1817), on the other hand, is usually considered to be a poem. Like several narrative poems of this period, it contains a number of different verse tales, in different verse forms; but in *Lalla Rookh* the frame narrative is in prose. Moreover, the text is larded with footnotes, in the manner of Byron and other narrative poets of the 1810s. Like the *Thousand and One Nights*, which was one of the most popular frame narratives of the time, reprinted in various cheap formats, *Lalla Rookh* employs the inset tales as a kind of delaying tactic for the main plot conducted in the prose frame. The frame is not just a convenience to bring together a handful of verse narratives, however; it is the basic story of the text and, moreover, affects the way the verse tales are to be read. Moore also wrote a novel, *The Epicurean: A Tale* (1827), and a quasi-novel in prose, *Memoirs of Captain Rock, the Celebrated Irish Chieftain, with Some Account of His Ancestors* (1824). The latter purports to be the autobiography of an Irish equivalent to Captain Swing, a combination of Robin Hood figure and social rebel; Rock's 'ancestors' are Irish rebels against the Anglo-Irish, going back several centuries. Later, Moore wrote another quasi-novel on a similar theme, *Travels of an Irish Gentleman in Search of Religion* (1833). On the other hand, some of Moore's verse narratives, such as *The Fudge Family in Paris* (1818), are, like Byron's enormously popular *Don Juan*, really satiric and comic novels in verse.

Perhaps the most richly literary and topical of the Romantic quasi-novels is 'Noctes Ambrosianæ' by John Wilson, William Maginn, J. G. Lockhart, James Hogg, and others, published serially in *Blackwood's Magazine* from 1822 to 1835 (a few preliminary sketches were published in 1819). Led by 'Christopher North' (John Wilson), the various characters gathered to drink and talk at Ambrose's in Edinburgh, to discourse on literature, politics, and characters of the day in free-wheeling, lively, joking, rambunctious dialogues. These are filled with puns, quips, dialect, poems, quotations, and allusions and are accompanied and often interrupted by a certain amount of buffoonery and action – in short, many tokens of professional literary and intellectual culture in an attitude of genteel, off-duty play, with the various characters exercising their well-stocked and creative minds in their 'authentic' voices (Hogg's dialect, for example), merely for the sake of it, rather than for pay.

This is a pretense, of course; Wilson was paid for contributing most of the 'Noctes' to *Blackwood's*, and the series made his reputation and his career. It even made him over in the public's mind to 'Christopher North', just as James Hogg's persona as 'the Ettrick Shepherd' became a real-life identity he could not shake off. It is also ironic that the dramatization, individualization, and vocalization of professional intellectual and critical written discourse in the 'Noctes' would have set up a tension with the normal tenor of such discourse in the rest of a particular number of *Blackwood's Magazine*, where the same issues and topics are discussed but in a more objective style, where the articles are usually anonymous and, in spite of variations of tone and style, where the aim is to create the impression of a transcendental master-discourse of critical writing (this, too, was a fiction, since everyone who read magazines such as *Blackwood's* knew the magazine's particular political and social bias). The 'Noctes' fictionalizes the norms of the rest of the magazine – indeed, professional, intellectual, non-fiction writing in general – and takes them out of the domain of professional activity altogether, into the domain of play that is at once leisured and cultivated. By putting the themes of professional criticism in a fictionalized social situation, especially by interrupting and breaking up a long-winded elevated discourse by a bit of slapstick, or a lively song, or a diverting play on words, the 'Noctes' deflates the rhetoric of professional critical discourse and seems to restore it to a particular individual and social situation. The 'Noctes' de-professionalizes professional writing.

Yet the 'Noctes' is no democracy of individualized voices, no polyvocal republic of ideas. Within the 'Noctes', as within an apparently polyvocal fictional text such as Smollett's *Humphry Clinker*, there is one voice closer to the implied centre than the others, one voice that centres and dominates – that of 'Christopher North'. In contrast to the rude contentiousness (especially of 'North's' chief foil, the 'Ettrick Shepherd') or frivolity or apathy of the other fictional characters, or the less dramatic articulateness of the 'real' characters who show up, such as Francis Jeffrey or William Cobbett, 'North's' urbanity, wit, learnedness, and suavity prevail. Gentility is once more at issue here, for as 'North' himself says in the last of the 'Noctes' (February, 1835), 'Without literature or manners, I hardly see how a man can be a gentleman.' Oddly enough, 'North' here commits an unprofessional grammatical solecism, making himself the one 'without literature or manners'. Nevertheless, 'Noctes Ambrosianæ' is perhaps the great Romantic professional carnivalesque novel, a carnival of the professional non-fiction writer's world of language. Appropriately, too, each of the principal contributors to the 'Noctes' was a Romantic novelist in his own right, though none was known primarily as a novelist.

The other great Romantic encyclopaedic and carnivalesque novel, *The Doctor, &c.* (1834–47), was written from 1813 to just before his death by the poet laureate, Robert Southey. It purports to tell the life and opinions of the narrator's mentor, Doctor Daniel Dove, of Doncaster; in effect it is a celebration of the character of the gentrified rural professional man, domestic in his habits, scholarly in his interests (though no author), and conservative in his views – the kind of rural professional to be found just before the 'modern' age of urbanization, industrialization, professionalization, commercialization, and revolution. In fact it is a compendium of topics, issues, and discourses, facts, opinions, and fantasies, essays, stories, and poems (and scraps of music), references, quotations, and allusions of many different kinds, in at least six languages, and many different styles, ranging from the fussily pedantic to thick dialect, to the classic children's story 'The Three Bears'. Thus the story and character of The Doctor disappear for many chapters ('interchapters', 'arch-chapters', and 'extraordinary chapters') at a time. Southey also claimed to participate in a tradition of learned folly (the title page is printed in 'motley', i.e., red and black) that includes Rabelais, Montaigne, Burton's *Anatomy of Melancholy*, and Sterne's *Tristram Shandy*, and suggests analogies between *The Doctor, &c.* and such miscellany texts as D'Israeli's *Curiosities of Literature* and *The Gentleman's Magazine*, 'that great lumber-room wherein smallware of all kinds has been laid up higgledy-piggledy' (ch. I.A.I.).

This is not to say that *The Doctor, &c.* is not an expressive Romantic text: the narrator tells us he wrote it with a Peacock quill and we are repeatedly reminded of the act of text-making going on before us, often with reference to a weaving metaphor. But it is an open weave, too: the reader is often addressed directly, and there are episodes of immediacy, as when the narrator takes the reader into his garden (ch. 139) and proceeds to list all that may be seen there. The reader is challenged and provoked, urged to reflect on the nature of the text, of text-making and the interpretation of texts, for good (wisdom, originality) or for ill (censorship, criticism, bibliomania). For text-making is acknowledged here to be as much a question of the reader's interpretation as of the author's construction, a question made visible by textual play (in several senses). Thus the reader is allowed at one point to ask the Author, '"If your book is intended to be either useful or delightful, why have you filled it with such a parcel of nonsense?"' The Author replies, '"What you are pleased to call by that name, Mr. Reader, may be either sense or nonsense according to the understanding which it meets with"', and refers the Reader to another book (*the* Book, the Bible – though the reference is to an Apocryphal book of the Bible) for an answer (interchapter 23). In fact, like 'Noctes Ambrosianæ' and other major Romantic texts, *The Doctor, &c.* represents textually as well as thematically or formally a specifically professional middle-class kind of gentility within or expressed through intellectual and literary culture.

Related to 'Noctes Ambrosianæ' and *The Doctor, &c.*, though apparently so different from them, is the great Romantic lyrical quasi-novel, William Hazlitt's *Liber Amoris; or, The New Pygmalion* (1823). *Liber Amoris* is in fact constructed from actual documents of Hazlitt's life, and although, like Lady Caroline Lamb's *Glenarvon*, it is based on known facts, it, too, could easily and more properly be treated as a novel of passion. The text is made up almost entirely of three kinds of material. The first part seems to be a transcript of dialogues between H., the writer, and S., the daughter of the landlord of the boarding-house in which H., separated from his wife, lives. The second part is made up of letters from H. to C.P. The last part is made up of letters from H. to J.S.K. This complex text obliquely unfolds H.'s unhappy and unrequited passion for S., and is rendered almost entirely from his point of view. Much of the writing is highly lyrical and impassioned, and H.'s passion is foregrounded everywhere.

Thus *Liber Amoris* is pre-eminently a text of Romantic expressivity. But H.'s writing is also filled with references and allusions to literature and the arts, and there are numerous quotations or unmarked phrases from classic literature. The title and situation, in fact, suggest a parallel to the Roman poet Catullus's unhappy love affair, celebrated in the best-known of Latin love poetry. The subtitle, 'The New Pygmalion', suggests the classical myth of the sculptor who fell in love with his own creation, whereupon Venus brought the statue to life to become Pygmalion's mate. This classical myth, however, had also undergone refashioning in several texts by one of Hazlitt's literary heroes, Jean-Jacques Rousseau. For Rousseau, the Pygmalion myth signified the power (and the danger) of the creative (male) imagination. *Liber Amoris* is, from the title page on, evidently and richly literary and artistic, apparently in the great tradition, going back to classical antiquity, of literature celebrating love, even (or especially) unrequited love, and the love object, usually a woman, as emanations of the male creative/erotic imagination.

The point of the amorousness here is not, as some reviewers

thought, to display a vulgar and unconventional realism about sexual desire, though that is one element in Hazlitt's use of the erotic. Rather, the point is to write the self, to express and fix what is internal, fleeting, and subjective. In this respect, the 'truth' about S. is irrelevant; in the fullest sense, S. is merely a pretext for H.'s textualizing of his creative imagination, and remains forever beyond H.'s passion, the passion's text, and the text's ability to represent anything beyond or outside H. H.'s passion is also played off against the sordidness of the boarding-house, H.'s divorce, and the petty civility of his surroundings, as well as his reverence for a fallen political idol, Napoleon (a statuette – diminished image – of the great man is a love token from H. to S.). Like so many novels of passion of the 1810s and 1820s, Hazlitt's quasi-novel is based on romantic irony – the impasse of infinite desire in the face of material, social, and historical relativities and limitations, including those of language and literary form.

Indeed, in January 1821, in the early phase of his infatuation with Sarah Walker, Hazlitt wrote a major critical essay, 'On Great and Little Things', dealing with general principles of intensity of feeling and relativity of perception, with evident allusions to his own fantasy of Sarah Walker, to Napoleon, to art and literature as worthy of belief and passion even if not 'true' in themselves, or only temporarily true. That is why Hazlitt gives no clear indication as to whether *Liber Amoris* is to be taken for fact or fiction, and why attempts to establish it as one or the other miss the point.[1] Like all key Romantic texts, *Liber Amoris* is designed, among other things, to bring into question conventional distinctions of discourse and genre and thus to seize a reality beyond the literary and even beyond language. The Romantic text must undermine itself in the cause of an ultimate realism of representation. Most liable to interpretation by the generic canons of fiction or autobiography, or both, it refuses, finally, to be even a quasi-novel, except insofar as, like some of the other quasi-novels considered in this section, it reflects the interests and problems of the professional intellectual and literary artist in the Romantic age.

The Romantic quasi-novel seems designed particularly to raise and deal with issues of defining art, and especially literature and criticism, as a central kind of social practice, at once genteel in the breadth of its culture, in its urbanity, cosmopolitan outlook, and contempt for merely commercial considerations, and yet professional in all other respects. One might say that if the superior value of the culture of the written text is a central assumption of professional ideology, then Romantic writers wished to establish the artistic written text as the preeminent form of that culture of print and writing. But already the literary critic, journalist, or scholar was in an ambiguous position, as at once a mediator and a dependent on the literary text; and it is striking that the most original Romantic quasi-novels were written by men who were primarily literary critics, journalists, or scholars, or who were known for achievement in one or more of the conventional literary genres. For, positively, the quasi-novel displays the Romantic writers' willingness to break down received conventional and generic distinctions and limits in order to found a written discourse at once artistic and true to 'reality', where generic distinctions are not to be found – at least, not in the Romantic vision of Nature. Negatively, the quasi-novel reveals some Romantic writers' persistent anxiety and doubt about the 'authenticity' of any writing, including literature, and especially fiction.

## 'What Kind of Book Is This?': The Limits of Romantic Fiction

Both Romantic quasi-novels and Romantic satirical novels, however, share many common assumptions with what they question and satirize. During the high Romantic period of the 1820s one novelist did attempt to expose the artificiality of the common ground and the limits of the Romantic novel, especially as constructed by Scott, the dominant novelist of those years. In part, James Hogg's *The Private Memoirs and Confesssions of a Justified Sinner, Written by Himself, with a Detail of Curious Traditionary Facts and Other Evidence by the Editor* (1824) is a satire on central themes of Romantic literature and fiction – Romantic subjectivity and late Scottish Enlightenment rationalism, middle-class expropriation of 'traditionary' popular culture (or folklore) and the invention of a 'national' culture from these materials, the liquidation of 'pre-modern' customary society in the interests of modern 'progress' and 'improvement', the subjection of orality and speech to writing, the suppression of popular amorous culture by middle-class puritanism and propriety, the marginalization of women within middle-class society and the exploitation of them outside of it, the glamorization of gentry culture, and the rewriting of history so as to justify the values and the power of the professional and middle classes against those of both the gentry and the common people. In a sense, therefore, Hogg's novel – indeed, his series of novels – is a reply to a host of texts, represented in earlier chapters of this book by More's Cheap Repository, Edgeworth's *Castle Rackrent*, Hamilton's *The Cottagers of Glenburnie*, Porter's *The Scottish Chiefs*, Scott's novels, Galt's *Annals of the Parish*, Mitford's *Our Village*, and even the theme of the 'pre-modern' Orient.

Hogg first came to literary prominence in the 1810s as a parodist and mimic, but in *The Private Memoirs and Confessions* he uses parody to deconstruct the myths and the professional middle-class literary culture he had served. He uses parody's technique of repetition and doubling to expose the artifice of what is parodied; for parody doubles with a difference in order to lay bare the claims of the parodied text to represent some reality when in fact it constructs that 'reality'. *The Private Memoirs and Confessions* is about a man who apparently has a double, and it is a novel which tells the same story twice, once in 'The Editor's Narrative' and once in the Sinner's 'Private Memoirs and Confessions', contained within 'The Editor's Narrative'. Hogg's novel accomplishes its unveiling of the premises of the Romantic novel by doubling discourses in ways that relativize them or that invert their 'normal' ordering. It uses doubling and doubles to insist on indeterminacy in the face of the attempt to unify and make coherent according to one, class-based code of unity and coherence.

*The Private Memoirs and Confessions* does this in three ways. First, by showing how attempts to re-present the 'reality' of the self in writing only defer the presence of the self and open it up to further interpretation, Hogg's novel puts in question late eighteenth- and early nineteenth-century assumptions about the coherence of the self, about the power of writing to make the inward self present to others, and about the self-validating authority of autobiographical and expressive writing. Second, by showing how historical writing fails to close off the past by definitive explanation and interpretation, Hogg's novel puts in question the ability of Enlightenment historiography, or Enlightenment-influenced Romantic historical fiction, to make the past present to the present. Finally, by making speech (or reported, 'transcribed' speech) bear truth in his novel when writing does not, Hogg insists, against the tide of thought in his time, on the wisdom and perspicacity of the speech community of the folk (of which he could be one) in the face of the pretensions to truth of Scottish Enlightenment, professional intellectual culture, even when that culture was professing to celebrate and appropriate the folk and their oral culture. But Hogg satirizes, exposes, and deconstructs with a purpose – to present his own version, the marginalized or outsider's version of 'modern' social history. In order to do so, Hogg presents in the career of his Sinner a case of the social construction of the individual as self-divided *and* a social rebel and reformer because of the divisions of class, religion, gender, culture, language, and national identity in the society into which he (in this instance) is born. It is interesting, but by no means decisive or even important to the effect of Hogg's argument, that his own domestic and professional experience qualified him to speak on these divisions as few other Romantic writers could. Thus the life of the Sinner takes in the entire spectrum of related issues, central to Romantic fiction and literature, outlined in Chapter 1 of this book.

To begin with, the division between country and town gentry, represented by Wringhim's actual father, the laird of Colwan, and his mother, daughter of a Glasgow merchant, is not resolved by a marriage that is arranged for money on one side and enhanced social status on the other. This division is comically dramatized by the disharmonies of the couple's wedding-night and is underlined by their religious differences. The suggestion, treated rather lightly by the 'Editor', is that the marriage is finally consummated by an act of rape. The couple soon part, though a son, George, is born. The division is then exacerbated by the intervention of a self-righteous professional man, the Rev. Wringhim. Mrs Colwan then bears another son, Robert, but the laird disclaims him, declaring that he is the Rev. Wringhim's bastard. The division in the family is represented by the divided house – Lady Dalcastle and Robert live in the upper floors, the Laird and George in the lower (the moral associations of upper and lower supersede the social ones here). The brothers are raised apart, in the classic situation of late eighteenth-century novels of education. George grows up to be what his position as first son prepares him to be, a flower of the gentry, while young Robert Wringhim (he takes his adoptive father's last name) grows up to be a caricature of the late eighteenth-century novel's version of the narrow professional – self-disciplined, self-righteous, puritanical, and jargon-spouting.

Now the class divisions of the parents, reinforced by the class differences between brothers in a property system based on primogeniture, are reinforced or defined further (as we know they were in reality) by religious differences, in a house (familiar emblem of the body of the state) divided within and against itself. As George and Robert become young men, these divisions are inserted into larger social divisions of the time. George, bred as a gentleman, becomes a sociable person in accordance with his Episcopalian religion of true faith *and* good works; but religion only reinforces his character as a Christian *gentleman*. Wringhim's religion is another matter. As second (and moreover disowned) son requiring a profession, he does find a 'calling', and one which conveniently justifies his hostility to his brother and his father and convinces him of his own superiority to both. In fact, his 'calling' is on a cosmic scale, through 'election' by predestination to salvation in eternity. He believes he has joined a community superior not only to that of his brother and father but superior to any on earth, a transcendental community, the 'community of the just upon earth'.[2] Here faith is absolutely prior to deeds – indeed, it 'justifies' deeds of any kind, even sinful deeds. Appropriately, too, membership in this community enables Robert to eschew society and sociability here below (except the company of his double, Gil-Martin), especially the company of women (p. 113). He becomes a solitary, self-justified individualist. This self-abstraction from community and society as well as from the social, amatory, procreative intercourse between the sexes accords perfectly with Gil-Martin's exhortation to Wringhim to '''raise himself above common humanity''' to the extent that he can murder his brother and father. Later he is accused of seduction by promise of marriage.

Furthermore, Wringhim's view of the moral and religious differences between himself and his brother, readily explicable as the rivalry of older and younger sons within the gentry, is also converted into the terms of social-political conflicts between Whig and Tory, town and country, middle class and gentry. These conflicts are exacerbated by the controversy over the proposed constitutional union of Scotland and England to form Great Britain. The period of the debate on Union is chosen by Hogg as the setting for the brothers' conflict and the Sinner's exploits because that was widely supposed to be the decisive step in the 'modernization' of Scotland (Scott had already set a novel during this period – *The Bride of Lammermoor*). Perforce the union was also the decisive step in the Anglicizing of Scotland – a process clearly represented in the novel by the relationship of dialect and standard English, speech and writing. Thus Hogg has described the social construction of 'reality' – personal, religious, social, 'national', and linguistic – in the person of his self-divided protagonist, Robert Wringhim, the 'justified sinner'. Not surprisingly, Robert goes' on to become a sociopath and, probably, a suicide.

Here another allegorical interpretation of the Sinner's career becomes possible, an allegory of the social construction and the fate of the revolutionary. When Gil-Martin tempts Wringhim to destroy his brother and father, he argues that '''you ought to consider what great advantages would be derived to the cause of righteousness and truth, were the estate and riches of that opulent house [of Dalcastle] in your possession . . .''', to which Wringhim admits, 'I cannot but say that the desire of being enabled to do so much good, by the possession of these bad men's riches, made some impression on my heart' (p. 146). Here is precisely the self-justification of the Revolutionary bent on expropriating the aristocracy and gentry in the cause of general 'philanthropy' (echoes of *Frankenstein* occur several times in Hogg's novel). For though Wringhim proclaims citizens' 'rights' and brotherly love (or fraternity), he has no sympathy with the common people, and does not even regard himself as speaking the same language as his fellow Scots. His motives throughout are liable to two explanations – his own, self-justifying one, and the reader's (and, curiously enough, Gil-Martin's) more cynical and worldly-wise view that Robert is acting merely out of ambition and self-interest, as conservatives in Britain (of whom Hogg was one) thought that French Revolutionaries and English and Scottish Jacobins had done. Wringhim, like his double, Gil-Martin (the Devil), is ambiguous. This doubleness further serves to emphasize Wringhim's isolation in the prison of self, for his ambiguous self-justification could stand for either extreme Calvinism or Revolutionary zeal, or both, as they do in Scott's novels. Moreover, such confident individualism and zeal were widely regarded as socially destructive – this, too, Scott had shown, as did many conservative Romantic novelists, including Austen and Mary Shelley.

It is not surprising, then, that like *Frankenstein*, which it resembles in several important respects, *The Private Memoirs and Confessions* has overtones in its language and its plot that could well suggest a contemporary political 'parable' to readers aware of recent British and European history and interested in the growing political and social crisis of the 1820s, which was seen in many ways as a continuation of the crises of the 1790s and the Napoleonic wars. A parallel between 'Jacobin' fanaticism and seventeenth-century religious fanaticism was, of course, a commonplace of the French Revolution debate in Britain, and had been turned to account several times in the 1810s and early 1820s by Scott. For example, in 'The Editor's Narrative', Wringhim is described as an 'incendiary' and later Gil-Martin is described with the same term, often used in the 1790s to describe a violent revolutionary. When Wringhim interferes with a game of cricket being played by his brother and his friends, Wringhim declares that '"he was determined to assert his right, and the rights of his fellow-citizens, by keeping possession of whatsoever part of that common field he chose"' (p. 34). In fact, Wringhim manages to rouse the citizenry of Edinburgh against his brother by casting the quarrel between them as an issue of class conflict between the gentry and the townsfolk.

In Wringhim's own narrative the political language and the political dimension of religious language are even more obvious, and build up an association between passion for religious and political reform and desire for power – another commonplace of the French Revolution debate in Britain and discussion of reform during the decades after 1800. Wringhim sees himself, for example, as 'a scourge in the hand of the Lord; another Jehu, a Cyrus, or a Nebuchadnezzar' (p. 108), Old Testament conquerors who defeated and enslaved the chosen people of Israel when they had sunk into corruption. Wringhim speaks of his 'duty to slay' in a just cause (p. 133); and Gil-Martin tells him they will be great benefactors to mankind: '"We have much before our hands to perform for the benefit of mankind, both civil as well as religious.

Let us do what we have to do here, and then we must wend our way to other cities, and perhaps to other countries"' (p. 136). This kind of talk strongly suggests an analogy between Wringhim and Gil-Martin and the revolutionary Jacobins, convinced of the justness of their cause, of their freedom from the bonds of laws and conventions of the past, of their duty to kill in a just cause, of the benefits '"both civil and religious"' of their work '"to other cities"' and '"to other countries"'.

If Wringhim is analogous to the Jacobin revolutionary fanatic, then Gil-Martin, who supplies him with his theoretical justifications, is analogous to 'fathers' of the Revolution and of British Jacobinism such as Godwin and other writers of the English provincial and Nonconformist Enlightenments, writers of the Scottish Enlightenment, and writers of the French Enlightenment such as Jean-Jacques Rousseau. Certainly many conservative writers of the Romantic period blamed the Revolution and other forms of political and social rebellion on the ideas of the Enlightenment social critics, disseminated through books and secret societies. Wringhim calls Gil-Martin 'my enlightened and voluntary patron', and his religious views constitute '"the doctrine that was made to overturn the principalities and powers, the might and dominion of the kingdom of darkness"' (p. 121). As Satan, Gil-Martin is also the archetypal rebel in the Christian tradition, portrayed in *Paradise Lost* as a consummate orator (also like Jean-Jacques Rousseau and other 'fathers' of the Revolution). Wringhim – or his double – goes on to commit numerous crimes analogous to the ravages of the Revolution, including fratricide, justified by Revolutionary ideologues and, in the eyes of some, even justified by English Jacobins such as William Godwin, in the name of transcendental principles of general philanthropy and liberty, equality, and fraternity. Wringhim's self-justification by his Antinomianism (by which the 'justified' cannot be sinners, no matter what crimes they commit) thus becomes a satire on the Revolution, since according to both there is no such thing as transgression for the just.

The Sinner's story is not, however, the whole of Hogg's text, nor all that the text has to tell. The significance of Wringhim's story is enriched, complicated, extended by the structure of the text in which it is enclosed, in two main ways – its narrative structure and its structuring of language. If the Sinner's story seems to carry a meaning similar to that of many Romantic social-historical novels, the text's narrative and linguistic structures undermine and undo the certainties, assumptions, and authority of such novels. In the first place the novel contains no authoritative narrator or narrative voice. If we see easily enough the limitations of Robert Wringhim's understanding of himself and his world, we see more slowly but just as clearly the limitations of the 'Editor'. Moreover, in most social novels of the period the characters who speak in a way closest to standard written English are the most important characters and the characters whose accuracy of perception, judgment, and consequent ethical action are most important to the novel's argument. But in Hogg's novel it is the characters who speak in the 'deformed' variant of standard English, Scots dialect, who speak the truth – the servants, the common folk, and 'auld wives'.

For example, Wringhim decides, as a pastime, to put down in writing the sayings of his servant Samuel Scrape regarding Wringhim's double character, according to what '"the auld wives o' the clachan"', whom Samuel believes to be witches, say:

> 'they say, – lord have a care o' us! – they say the deil's often seen gaun sidie for sidie w'ye, whiles in ae shape, an' whiles in another. An' they say that he whiles takes your ain shape, or else enters into you, and then you turn a deil yourself.'

Wringhim is so astounded that he can make no reply and almost gives in to this 'popular belief'; 'but I was preserved from such a fatal error by an inward and unseen supporter' (pp. 195–96). Paradoxically, neither Wringhim nor the 'Editor' can accept the explanations of '"the auld wives"'; yet to the reader they can seem plausible. Furthermore, the reader is likely to entertain a suspicion that Samuel is only pretending to be the unwilling purveyor of the 'popular belief'. Samuel goes on to report the exact words of one of the 'auld wives', Lucky Shaw, and Lucky's summary of a story of '"'an auld carl, Robin Ruthven'"', a '"'cunning man'"' (i.e., a soothsayer) who '"'had been in the hands o' the fairies when he was young, an' a' kinds o' spirits were visible to his een, an' their language as familiar to him as his ain mother tongue'"' (p. 198). Significantly, too, while Wringhim records himself as speaking standard English, he seems to 'transcribe' the dialect of his informant very scrupulously. It is also significant that Samuel reports his version of the accusations against Wringhim by means of a story – traditional repository and channel of popular culture. And Wringhim's decision to record this story as it was told produces a curious, distracting complexity in his own text. For Samuel's story of Lucky Shaw, with its quoted dialogue in dialect, has dialect speech (that of the inhabitants of Auchtermuchty) within dialect speech (Lucky's) within dialect speech (Samuel's) within Wringhim's narrative in standard written English.

Wringhim's own narrative, undertaken as a pastime here, is so burdened with dialect that the reader's attention is drawn to the intricacy and oddness of the text: the dialect speakers and their reports of the supernatural, linked finally to Wringhim, take over – indeed, hijack – Wringhim's own text, his 'private memoirs and confessions' – surely, if anything can be, a text that is self-validated, validated by its author's authoritativeness about the subject on which he writes, and itself undertaken not as a pastime but as a self-defence, an apology. This authoritativeness should be reinforced by Wringhim's persistent Biblical turn of phrase. The Bible is the Word, or rather *the* Word, which Wringhim has (like good Christians depicted in religous tracts) internalized. The Word, transcendental language *par excellence*, should constitute the self, validate the self's 'confession', and relegate all other language to the fallen and divided world of time. Yet Wringhim's would-be self-authenticating and self-validating discourse is defeated or undermined from within, in spite of its author, by what it purports to marginalize or exclude – the 'popular belief' expressed in the popular language. In Scott's novels there are also truth-sayers and soothsayers from the folk, and they usually say in dialect; but in Scott's novels there is also authoritative narration, or at least narration that has relatively greater authority than either of the principal narrators in *Private Memoirs and Confessions*, Wringhim and his 'Editor'. The irony and exposure are indicated clearly, if subtly and fleetingly, in the revelation (which we should have expected) that the Sinner himself probably spoke in Scots. For we learn from Hogg's letter to *Blackwood's*, quoted by the 'Editor' in the concluding part of his narrative, that, according to 'the little traditionary history' that remains among the common people regarding the Sinner's life, the Sinner on the last day of his life was supposed to have said to a young lad who would not keep him company, '"Then, if ye winna stay with me, James, ye may depend on't I'll cut my throat afore ye come back again"' (p. 241).

Of course, the 'transcription' of Scots in this text is not real speech and is not intended to be; it is intended to set up a relationship of contrast between speech and writing, Scots and English, truth and self-delusion. Within the novel, 'speech' represents a kind and use of language different from that of the conventionalized writing styles of the 'Editor' and the Sinner – and different from that of James Hogg, the character in the text other than the Sinner who expresses himself in both writing and 'speech'; for if Hogg's actual letter to *Blackwood's* is couched in the standard written English of the rural antiquarian conveying curiosities of folklore to learned and lettered gentlemen's magazines (much in the mode of Hogg's own essays in *Blackwood's* under the heading 'The Shepherd's Calendar'), then the Hogg whose spoken refusal to act as guide to the Sinner's grave site as surely expresses himself in dialect, as he tells the 'Editor':

'Od bless ye, lad! I hae ither matters to mind. I hae a' thae
paulies to sell, an' a' yon Highland stotts down on the
green every ane; an' then I hae ten scores o' yowes to buy
after, an' if I canna first sell my ain stock, I canna buy nae
ither body's. I hae mair ado than I can manage the day,
foreby ganging to houk up hunder-year-auld banes.'
(p. 247)

The Hogg in the text is fully occupied with the present and the
pressing realities of pastoral economy, and rather contemptuous of the
idle gentle-folk with nothing better to do than 'to houk up hunder-
year-auld banes'. As Hogg says to the 'Editor', who is pretending to
be a wool merchant in order to get the co-operation of the common
folk for his quest, '"It was a queer fancy for a woo-stapler to tak."'
Like the Sinner, the 'Editor' has to quote a criticism and rebuke of
himself by someone lower down the social scale, and the spoken truths
speak directly to the reader, neatly undoing the stability and centred-
ness of the 'Editor's' written discourse as a representation of a model
consciousness.[3]

There are two other important aspects of the play of language in
Hogg's novel: equivocation and ambiguity. Equivocation is, of course,
the speciality of Gil-Martin, Wringhim's double and dæmon (in the
sense of that word used in *Frankenstein*), and this fact is apparent to
the reader but eludes Wringhim, as in the passage where Wringhim
is persuaded by Gil-Martin to murder the virtuous minister Blanchard
(p. 134). Here Wringhim is not only persuaded in a way the reader
cannot be, and thus unable to 'read' Gil-Martin's equivocation, but he
is unable to see even the ambiguity in his own words, as he says things
the full significance of which are available to the reader, who is thus
placed in the knowing position of Gil-Martin, the Devil. Significantly,
Gil-Martin himself has a book from which he reads and which he keeps
in his bosom, but, unlike Wringhim's books, it is in a language
Wringhim cannot understand, just as the other interpreter or 'reader'
in Hogg's text, the 'Editor', does not seem to understand or even
perceive the equivocations and ambiguities reported in the Sinner's
text, or, indeed, of the Sinner's text itself. This fact undercuts the authoritativeness of *his* narrative, and puts him on the same level as the
Sinner, as far as the reader outside the novel is concerned. The result
is that both principal narratives in Hogg's novel come to be read as
kinds of dramatic irony, and so the rhetorical authority of both is
undermined. Equivocation and ambiguity work with the opposition
of writing and speech and the structural relationships of sociolect and
dialect to expose the pretension of self-assumed discursive authority
and to establish that meaning resides in the circumstances of an utter-

ance, its relationship to other actual or potential kinds of utterance, and in the situation of the hearer or reader of the utterance.

Finally, Hogg's shaping of the history of Wringhim's text – its writing, printing, and dissemination – not only undermines further the would-be authoritative textualizing of life, but also challenges the confident assumptions about the power of print and writing held by Hogg's contemporary professional intellectuals, writers, and social reformers both liberal and conservative, secular and religious. The history of the Sinner's text reminds us that, whatever else they may be, texts are physical objects, objects of material culture, and reminds us that writing and print, as much as speech, are dependent on circumstances for their very existence as well as for the meaning(s) they are able to divulge or that readers are able to construct from them. Writing seems to remove itself from history; but writers, readers, and texts are inescapably bound to history. The Sinner first has the idea of writing up his memoirs as a self-vindication and an instrument of social and ideological changes when, fleeing from Gil-Martin, he gets a job in a printing-house. His employer agrees to print the Sinner's memoir, and Wringhim exults because he imagines that his life-work (in more than one sense) will be disseminated by the wondrous power of print, so as to effect a direct intervention in social-historical reality.

Like the Enlightenment philosophers, English Jacobin novelists and polemicists, and Evangelical tract writers and distributors, Wringhim has an almost religious faith in the power of print to transform the world. But unreason seems to prevail even in the printing-house, for as Wringhim's chapbook was being printed, the Devil, dressed in a Circassian hunting coat and turban (thus bearing a curious resemblance to the father of the Revolution, Rousseau), appears in the printing shop to help in the work (giving a twist to the phrase 'printer's devil'); the workmen are frightened, Wringhim's employer reads the printed sheets of Wringhim's pamphlet, calls it 'a medley of lies and blasphemy', and orders it to be burnt. Is the employer's reading, his interpretation of Wringhim's text, correct? In any case, his action clearly represents the power of printers and publishers as 'gate-keepers' of print culture and the dissemination of ideas. Wringhim saves a proof copy of his text, however, and flees toward the border, to England (to freedom from what limits in Scotland?), recording his further adventures in a manuscript journal (a 'sample' of the handwriting was printed as a frontispiece to the novel).

He later commits suicide, and his printed memoirs and manuscript journal are buried with him, but his mysterious life is already turning into a text of a different kind and passing into folklore: as the 'Editor' puts it, 'the numerous distorted traditions, &c. which remain . . . may be attributable to the work having been printed and burnt, and of course the story known to all the printers, with their families and gossips'. Thus the Sinner's life, in the sense of autobiography, may have been buried with him as a printed (and written) text, but it came down to the present nevertheless, by word of mouth, from the printing house itself. Furthermore, if the Sinner's life spread by 'gossip', it spread by the kind of word-of-mouth dissemination traditionally ascribed to women. Just as the Sinner, who abhors women and avoids them, finds himself at several points in his adventures bound by women, physically or verbally, so in the end one version of his life may depend on them for its continued existence and propagation.

Over a century after his death, the Sinner's body is dug up by some young country men. James Hogg, another local man, then writes down the 'traditionary history' of the Sinner insofar as he can collect it and adds the detailed and strikingly realistic account of the partial exhumation of the Sinner's wonderfully preserved body; Hogg sends this report to a literary and philosophical magazine, *Blackwood's*. A gentleman reads the account and, while in Edinburgh on business, decides to travel down and see the Sinner's body for himself. Accompanied by his friend Mr. L——t (i.e., John Gibson Lockhart, Scott's son-in-law and editor of the Tory *Quarterly Review*), and another man, Mr. L——w (i.e., William Laidlaw, Scott's estate agent), he finds the body and exhumes all of it, for only the top half had been uncovered before. On the lower half of the Sinner's body (upper and lower again have moral significance) they find his printed and written texts, which are left in the 'Editor's' hands and he decides to print them, even though he admits that he doesn't understand their 'drift'. He writes his own 'Narrative' of the Sinner's life from what he can gather from 'history, justiciary records, and tradition' (p. 92), as well as his account of the expedition to find the body (again, recounted with strikingly realistic details), and prints the Sinner's memoir and journal set in his own frame narrative.

But this frame does not exhume the 'truth' about the Sinner, nor does it conclude, close, or terminate the Sinner's story, because the 'Editor' cannot formulate a secure interpretation that will resolve the contradictions between his own 'Narrative' and the Sinner's memoir and journal, or resolve the elements of the supernatural in the Sinner's life. Like Samuel Scrape's narrative in the Sinner's autobiography, the Sinner's narrative usurps its frame. The 'Editor' ends by declaring, 'With regard to the work itself, I dare not venture a judgment, for I do not understand it. I believe no person, man or woman, will ever peruse it with the same attention that I have done, and yet I confess that I do not comprehend the writer's drift' (pp. 253–54). Apart from the murder of George Colwan, all the rest is 'either dreaming or madness'. The 'Editor' admits that the Sinner's account of himself 'corresponds so minutely with traditionary facts, that it could scarcely have missed to have been received as authentic; but in this day, and with the present generation, it will not go down' – a view amply supported by the contemporary reviews of Hogg's novel – because it is not 'at all consistent with reason' (p. 254). It must, the 'Editor' concludes, be the work of a writing madman, a 'religious maniac, who wrote and wrote about a deluded creature, till he arrived at that height of madness, that he believed himself the very object whom he had been all along describing' (p. 254). It is appropriate, yet paradoxical, that the 'Editor', by definition a mediator of the text of another, should seek to explain the memoirs and confessions by inventing a double for the Sinner – an author whose madness was caused by writing, writing until he confused his 'subject', his personal identity, with his subject, the 'Sinner', who, as autobiographer, is both subject and object of the memoirs and confession. In one sense, of course, this is no explanation at all, but an abandonment of explanation, an admission that knowledge is not possible here.

The 'Editor's' attempt to enclose the Sinner's narrative, like the Sinner's attempt to enclose himself in self-validation, only produces a doubling, a dissemination beyond individual control, but rather subject to the modifications of dissemination through actual social and historical institutions, from class- or gender-based distributions of language, to 'superstition', printing practices, popular story-telling, and conventions of narrative and genre. It is no accident that this anti-hero seeks to justify himself and spread his beliefs (the fruit of his life-experience, as in an English Jacobin novel of the 1790s) through print, in standard English – through, that is, the dialect and the language medium of the professional middle classes who wrote, commanded, and consumed Romantic literature and especially Romantic fiction. But it is also largely a male-dominated language medium; not only are the truth speakers and critics of Wringhim within the novel dialect speakers, they are also usually women, and Wringhim is physically bound up by women twice in the novel. Like Frankenstein, Wringhim chooses a non-sexual mode of self-dissemination, or a mode of self-dissemination that is a replacement for the 'natural' and social one of physical procreation. This possibility is certainly suggested by the rolled-up phallic shape of the Sinner's texts when they are found with his body, and by the fact that they are found with the lower part of his body. The possibility is reinforced by the speculation by one of the 'Editor's' friends that the body of the Sinner has been preserved because of the mysterious texts, so that the Sinner's life might be passed down to posterity. This may seem like a coarse joke, but it is certainly not beyond Hogg, and even has its subtle and appropriate violence toward class-based literary decorums of the period, decorums Hogg was often accused, in his own person or as the quasi-fictional 'Ettrick Shepherd', of violating.

Appropriately, then, it is the 'Editor', who admits that he doesn't understand the Sinner or his texts, who yet becomes their disseminator. With his hand-me-down Enlightenment rationalism he is doomed to uncomprehending otherness from the self and the writing that his own writing contains. In his Enlightenment antiquarian zeal he exhumes what was buried, publishes what was 'private', and unwittingly centres what was marginal; but rather than illuminating and thus closing off or closing the book on the Sinner and his text, the 'Editor's' exhumation disseminates them. There is, obviously, a moral in this: the limits of Romantic culture, Romantic literature, and Romantic fiction in pretending to speak for all parts, regions, classes, and levels of society but in fact only speaking for the professional middle classes who practise this culture, literature, and fiction, and who think they have seized the living culture and language of the common people, such as 'the Ettrick Shepherd'. The novel rejects both the anti-social revolutionary egotism of the Sinner and the uncomprehending, Anglicized, gentrified, professional and literary culture of the 'Editor' and his associates for the truth of speech, represented by good Scots 'dialect', and representative of a traditional, popular, oral culture, which Enlightenment and Romantic literary culture dismissed as 'superstition' or expropriated in order to construct its own enabling fictions of imagined community.

Hogg's novel is an *exposé* of the assumptions of the professional culture which, whether revolutionary or conservative, was, Hogg could see, bent on destroying or expropriating the popular culture of the common people, including traditional oral and print narrative, and of which Hogg had been, throughout his career as a writer, a partly self-appointed and partly involuntary voice. That voice was versatile; like Gil-Martin, Hogg could assume many guises and imitate many styles, especially in the cultural margin where the traditional and oral came to be written, and commercialized, as a central element in the new Romantic 'national' culture and 'national' literature. But Hogg also found himself trapped in one of those voices, supposedly his 'real' voice, as 'the Ettrick Shepherd' of the 'Noctes Ambrosianæ'. *The Private Memoirs and Confessions of a Justified Sinner* let Hogg turn the tables, in more ways than one, on the culture he was, in order to get on in the world, willing to serve. In this sense his novel is, after all, an expressive act, more expressive than any Romantic personal lyric or self-validating autobiography. This does not mean, however, that Hogg's novel is merely self-expressive or self-vindicating, for Hogg was a serious writer participating fully in the practice of novel-writing as an important form of ideological communication among the professional and middle-class readers of early nineteenth-century Britain; but as an outsider he had a perspective from which to view the professional middle classes, their preoccupations and conflicts, and their literary and cultural institutions. Hogg's novel lays bare the assumptions on which those preoccupations, conflicts, and institutions were based, and in which we are still implicated today. Because it did so, Hogg's novel failed in its time, while the kind of Romantic culture and Romantic fiction he tried to expose and to put in question lived on through the nineteenth century, and even down to the present.

## Notes

1. See *Liber Amoris; or, The New Pygmalion, By William Hazlitt, with Additional Matter now Printed for the First Time from the Original Manuscripts*, edited by Richard Le Gallienne (1894), which purports to be 'a repository of the genuine material, so far as it survives, for arriving at a solution of a most extraordinary, most involved, and most painful episode in the career of one of the leading men of letters' of the Romantic period.

2. James Hogg, *The Private Memoirs and Confessions of a Justified Sinner*, edited by John Carey (1970), p. 115. All subsequent references are to this edition. Note that the edition does not contain the facsimile 'sample' of the Sinner's handwriting, published as frontispiece in the original edition.

3. See Emma Letley, 'Some Literary Uses of Scots in Hogg's *Confessions of a Justified Sinner* and *The Brownie of Bodsbeck*', in *Papers Given at the First James Hogg Society Conference*, edited by Gillian Hughes (Stirling, 1983), pp. 32–39.

# Chronology

*Note: Dates normally refer to first publication in any form; for further information on publication of novels and other fiction, see notes on Individual Authors (pp. 293–321).*

| DATE | WORKS OF FICTION | OTHER WORKS | HISTORICAL/CULTURAL EVENTS |
|---|---|---|---|
| 1789 | Cumberland<br>*Arundel*<br><br>J. Moore<br>*Zeluco*<br><br>Radcliffe<br>*Castles of Athlin and Dunbayne*<br><br>C. Smith<br>*Ethelinde* | Blake<br>*Songs of Innocence*<br><br>Darwin<br>*Botanic Garden*<br><br>White<br>*Natural History of Selborne* | End of 'Regency Crisis'<br>Storming of Bastille |
| **1790** | Radcliffe<br>*Sicilian Romance*<br><br>Williams<br>*Julia* | Alison<br>*Essays on Taste*<br><br>Bruce<br>*Travels to Source of Nile*<br><br>Burke<br>*Reflections on the Revolution in France* | Motions for repeal of Test and Corporation Acts withdrawn<br>Breach between Burke and Fox on French Revolution |
| 1791 | Inchbald<br>*A Simple Story*<br><br>Radcliffe<br>*Romance of the Forest*<br><br>C. Smith<br>*Celestina* | Boswell<br>*Life of Johnson*<br><br>Gilpin<br>*Forest Scenery*<br><br>Paine<br>*Rights of Man* | Birmingham Riots<br>Canada Act |

| DATE | WORKS OF FICTION | OTHER WORKS | HISTORICAL/CULTURAL EVENTS |
|---|---|---|---|
| 1792 | Bage<br>*Man As He Is*<br><br>Holcroft<br>*Anna St. Ives*<br><br>More<br>*Village Politics*<br><br>C. Smith<br>*Desmond* | Gilpin<br>*Essay on Picturesque Beauty*<br><br>Wollstonecraft<br>*Vindication of the Rights of Woman*<br><br>Young<br>*Travels in France* | London Corresponding Society formed<br>Association for the Preservation of Liberty and Property against Republicans and Levellers formed |
| 1793 | Parsons<br>*Castle of Wolfenbach*<br><br>C. Smith<br>*The Old Manor House*<br><br>West<br>*Advantages of Education* | Blake<br>*Visions of the Daughters of Albion*<br><br>Godwin<br>*Political Justice* | January<br>Execution of Louis XVI<br>May<br>Grey's motion for reform defeated in House of Commons<br>October<br>'British Convention' meets at Edinburgh |
| 1794 | Godwin<br>*Caleb Williams*<br><br>Holcroft<br>*Hugh Trevor* (−1797)<br><br>Radcliffe<br>*Mysteries of Udolpho*<br><br>C. Smith<br>*The Banished Man* | Blake<br>*Songs of Experience*<br><br>Darwin<br>*Zoonomia*<br><br>Paine<br>*Age of Reason*<br><br>Paley<br>*Evidences of Christianity* | Portland Whigs join Pitt<br>Treason Trials |
| 1795 | Cumberland<br>*Henry*<br><br>C. Smith<br>*Montalbert*<br><br>Kelly<br>*Abbey of St. Asaph* | Blake<br>*Book of Los*<br><br>Coleridge<br>*Conciones ad populum*<br><br>Roscoe<br>*Life of Lorenzo de' Medici* | May<br>Speenhamland System<br>Food Riots<br>Methodist secession from Church of England<br>November<br>Government introduces 'Two Acts' |

| DATE | WORKS OF FICTION | OTHER WORKS | HISTORICAL/CULTURAL EVENTS |
|---|---|---|---|
| 1796 | Bage<br>*Hermsprong*<br><br>Burney<br>*Camilla*<br><br>Hamilton<br>*Letters of a Hindoo Rajah*<br><br>Hays<br>*Memoirs of Emma Courtney*<br><br>Helme<br>*Farmer of Inglewood Forest*<br><br>Inchbald<br>*Nature and Art*<br><br>Lewis<br>*The Monk*<br><br>J. Moore<br>*Edward*<br><br>Roche<br>*Children of the Abbey*<br><br>C. Smith<br>*Marchmont*<br><br>Walker<br>*Theodore Cyphon* | Burke<br>*Letter to a Noble Lord*<br><br>Coleridge<br>*The Watchman; Poems*<br><br>Knight<br>*Progress of Civil Society*<br><br>Southey<br>*Joan of Arc*<br><br>Wollstonecraft<br>*Letters Written during a Short Residence in Sweden, Norway, and Denmark* | Failure of attempted French invasion of Ireland<br>Failure of peace negotiations with France |
| 1797 | D'Israeli<br>*Vaurien*<br><br>H. and S. Lee<br>*Canterbury Tales*<br>*(−1798)*<br><br>Radcliffe<br>*The Italian*<br><br>Robinson<br>*Walsingham* | Bewick<br>*History of British Birds*<br><br>Godwin<br>*The Enquirer*<br><br>Wilberforce<br>*Practical Christianity* | February<br>Bank Crisis<br>Failure of French landing in Wales<br>Naval mutinies<br>Defeat of Dutch fleet at Camperdown |

| DATE | WORKS OF FICTION | OTHER WORKS | HISTORICAL/CULTURAL EVENTS |
|---|---|---|---|
| 1798 | Charles Lamb *Rosamund Gray* <br><br> Lathom *Midnight Bell* <br><br> Lloyd *Edmund Oliver* <br><br> Roche *Clermont* <br><br> C. Smith *Young Philosopher* <br><br> Wollstonecraft *Wrongs of Woman* | Baillie *Plays on the Passions* (−1812) <br><br> M. and R.L.E. Edgeworth *Practical Education* <br><br> Lewis *Castle Spectre* <br><br> Malthus *Essay on Population* <br><br> Wordsworth and Coleridge *Lyrical Ballads* | May Rebellion in Ireland August French landing in Ireland Further Government attempts to control newspapers Nelson's victory at battle of the Nile |
| 1799 | Godwin *St. Leon* <br><br> Hays *Victim of Prejudice* <br><br> Walker *The Vagabond* <br><br> West *A Tale of the Times* | More *Strictures on Modern System of Female Education* <br><br> Sheridan *Pizarro* <br><br> Turner *History of the Anglo-Saxons* | Religious Tract Society formed April Pitt introduces ten per cent income tax July Combination Act; Act prohibiting certain political societies |
| **1800** | Edgeworth *Castle Rackrent* <br><br> Hamilton *Memoirs of Modern Philosophers* <br><br> J. Moore *Mordaunt* | Bloomfield *The Farmer's Boy* <br><br> Burns *Works* | Union of Ireland with Britain Widespread food riots Owen founds model factory at New Lanark |
| 1801 | Edgeworth *Belinda* <br><br> Opie *Father and Daughter* | Holcroft *Deaf and Dumb* <br><br> Southey *Thalaba* | Danish fleet destroyed at Copenhagen Economic distress and higher food prices |

| DATE | WORKS OF FICTION | OTHER WORKS | HISTORICAL/CULTURAL EVENTS |
|------|------------------|-------------|----------------------------|
| 1802 | Lathom<br>*Astonishment!!!*<br><br>Parsons<br>*The Mysterious Visit*<br><br>West<br>*The Infidel Father* | Holcroft<br>*A Tale of Mystery*<br><br>Scott (ed.)<br>*Minstrelsy of the Scottish Border* | Society for suppression of vice formed<br>Peace of Amiens with France<br>First Factory Act |
| 1803 | Owenson<br>*St. Clair*<br><br>J. Porter<br>*Thaddeus of Warsaw* | Godwin<br>*Life of Chaucer*<br><br>Lancaster<br>*Improvements in Education* | May<br>War with France resumed<br>Caledonian Canal begun |
| 1804 | Edgeworth<br>*Popular Tales*<br><br>Le Noir<br>*Village Anecdotes*<br><br>Opie<br>*Adeline Mowbray* | Blake<br>*Jerusalem; Milton* | British and Foreign Bible Society formed<br>July<br>Napolean prepares to invade England |
| 1805 | D'Israeli<br>*Flim-Flams!*<br><br>Edgeworth<br>*Modern Griselda*<br><br>Godwin<br>*Fleetwood*<br><br>Holcroft<br>*Memoirs of Bryan Perdue* | Knight<br>*Principles of Taste*<br><br>Lewis<br>*Bravo of Venice*<br><br>Scott<br>*Lay of the Last Minstrel*<br><br>Southey<br>*Madoc* | August<br>Britain, Austria, and Russia join in Third Coalition<br>October<br>Nelson's victory at Trafalgar |
| 1806 | Dacre<br>*Zofloya*<br><br>Opie<br>*Simple Tales*<br><br>Owenson<br>*Wild Irish Girl*<br><br>Surr<br>*A Winter in London* | Byron<br>*Fugitive Pieces*<br><br>Lancaster<br>*Plan for Educating Ten Thousand Poor Children*<br><br>Peacock<br>*Palmyra* | January<br>Death of Pitt<br>September<br>Death of Fox<br>November<br>Napoleon closes Continental ports to British ships |

| DATE | WORKS OF FICTION | OTHER WORKS | HISTORICAL/CULTURAL EVENTS |
|------|-----------------|-------------|----------------------------|
| 1807 | Charles and Mary Lamb *Tales from Shakespeare* <br> Maturin *Fatal Revenge* <br> A. Porter *Hungarian Brothers* <br> H. Smith *Horatio* | Bowdler (editor) *The Family Shakespeare* <br> Byron *Hours of Idleness* <br> Crabbe *The Parish Register* | May Abolition of slave trade |
| 1808 | Hamilton *Cottagers of Glenburnie* <br> Le Noir *Clara de Montfier* <br> Maturin *Wild Irish Boy* <br> More *Cælebs in Search of a Wife* | Hemans *Poems* <br> Jamieson *Dictionary of the Scottish Tongue* <br> T. Moore *Irish Melodies* <br> Scott *Marmion* | Beginning of repeal of laws requiring death penalty for minor crimes <br> August Convention of Cintra |
| 1809 | Edgeworth *Tales of Fashionable Life* (–1812) <br> Hofland *Officer's Widow* <br> Charles and Mary Lamb *Mrs Leicester's School* <br> Owenson *Woman; or, Ida of Athens* <br> A. Porter *Don Sebastian* | Byron *English Bards and Scotch Reviewers* <br> Coleridge *The Friend* (–1810) <br> R. L. E. and M. Edgeworth *Professional Education* <br> *Quarterly Review* | June Motion for Parliamentary reform defeated in the House of Commons |

| DATE | WORKS OF FICTION | OTHER WORKS | HISTORICAL/CULTURAL EVENTS |
|---|---|---|---|
| **1810** | Brunton<br>*Self-Control*<br><br>J. Porter<br>*Scottish Chiefs*<br><br>P. Shelley<br>*Zastrozzi*<br><br>West<br>*The Refusal* | Crabbe<br>*The Borough*<br><br>Hogg<br>*The Forest Minstrel*<br><br>Scott<br>*Lady of the Lake*<br><br>Southey<br>*Curse of Kehama* | London riots in<br>　support of Burdett<br>October<br>George III suffers from<br>　renewed bout of<br>　mental illness |
| 1811 | Austen<br>*Sense and Sensibility*<br><br>Dacre<br>*The Passions*<br><br>P. Shelley<br>*St. Irvyne* | More<br>*Practical Piety*<br><br>Scott<br>*Vision of Don Roderick* | February<br>Prince of Wales acts as<br>　Prince Regent<br>March<br>Luddite disturbances in<br>　Midlands |
| 1812 | Hofland<br>*Son of a Genius*<br><br>Maturin<br>*Milesian Chief*<br><br>Opie<br>*Temper*<br><br>West<br>*The Loyalists* | Byron<br>*Childe Harold's<br>　Pilgrimage*, cantos I<br>　and II<br><br>Crabbe<br>*Tales*<br><br>Egan<br>*Boxiana* (−1829)<br><br>H. and J. Smith<br>*Rejected Addresses* | January<br>Spread of Luddism<br>May<br>Assassination of<br>　Spencer Perceval<br>June<br>Liverpool<br>　administration formed |
| 1813 | Austen<br>*Pride and Prejudice*<br><br>Barrett<br>*The Heroine*<br><br>Opie<br>*Tales of Real Life* | Byron<br>*Giaour*<br><br>Owen<br>*New View of Society*<br><br>Scott<br>*Rokeby*<br><br>Shelley<br>*Queen Mab* | June<br>Wellington's victory at<br>　Vittoria<br>October<br>Defeat of Napoleon at<br>　Leipzig<br>East India Co.<br>　monopoly in India<br>　ended |

| DATE | WORKS OF FICTION | OTHER WORKS | HISTORICAL/CULTURAL EVENTS |
|------|------------------|-------------|----------------------------|
| 1814 | Austen<br>*Mansfield Park*<br><br>Brunton<br>*Discipline*<br><br>Burney<br>*The Wanderer*<br><br>Edgeworth<br>*Patronage*<br><br>Scott<br>*Waverley*<br><br>Sherwood<br>*Little Henry and His Bearer* | Byron<br>*The Corsair*<br><br>Scott (ed.)<br>*Works of Swift*<br><br>Turner<br>*England from the Norman Conquest to Edward I*<br><br>Wordsworth<br>*The Excursion* | April<br>Abdication of Napoleon<br>End of war with USA<br>Stephenson builds steam locomotive |
| 1815 | Johnstone<br>*Clan-Albin*<br><br>Peacock<br>*Headlong Hall*<br><br>Scott<br>*Guy Mannering* | Byron<br>*Hebrew Melodies*<br><br>Scott<br>*Lord of the Isles*<br><br>Wordsworth<br>*White Doe of Rylstone* | March<br>Napoleon returns from Elba<br>June<br>Napoleon defeated at Waterloo<br>Corn law passed |
| 1816 | Austen<br>*Emma*<br><br>Lady C. Lamb<br>*Glenarvon*<br><br>Opie<br>*Valentine's Eve*<br><br>Scott<br>*The Antiquary; The Black Dwarf; Old Mortality* | Byron<br>*Childe Harold*, canto III<br><br>Maturin<br>*Bertram*<br><br>Shelley<br>*Alastor*<br><br>Cobbett<br>*Political Register* | April<br>Income Tax abolished<br>Riots in East Anglia and manufacturing districts |

| DATE | WORKS OF FICTION | OTHER WORKS | HISTORICAL/CULTURAL EVENTS |
|---|---|---|---|
| 1817 | Edgeworth<br>*Harrington* and *Ormond*<br><br>Godwin<br>*Mandeville*<br><br>T. Moore<br>*Lalla Rookh*<br><br>Peacock<br>*Melincourt*<br><br>Scott<br>*Rob Roy* | Byron<br>*Manfred*<br><br>Coleridge<br>*Biographia Literaria*<br><br>Keats<br>*Poems* | January<br>Attack on Prince Regent's coach leads to 'Gag Acts'<br>March<br>March of 'blanketeers' broken up<br>June<br>Pentrick uprising in Derbyshire |
| 1818 | Austen<br>*Northanger Abbey;*<br>*Persuasion*<br><br>Ferrier<br>*Marriage*<br><br>Hogg<br>*Brownie of Bodsbeck*<br><br>Opie<br>*New Tales*<br><br>Peacock<br>*Nightmare Abbey*<br><br>Scott<br>*Heart of Midlothian*<br><br>M. Shelley<br>*Frankenstein*<br><br>Sherwood<br>*Fairchild Family* (−1847) | Byron<br>*Childe Harold*, canto IV<br><br>Coleridge<br>*The Friend*<br><br>Hallam<br>*Europe during the Middle Ages*<br><br>Hazlitt<br>*Lectures on the English Poets*<br><br>Keats<br>*Endymion*<br><br>Shelley<br>*Revolt of Islam* | Defeat of Burdett's and Heron's motions for reform<br>Vestries Act |
| 1819 | Hope<br>*Anastasius*<br><br>Scott<br>*Bride of Lammermoor*<br>and *Legend of Montrose;*<br>*Ivanhoe* | Byron<br>*Don Juan*, cantos I and II<br><br>Crabbe<br>*Tales of the Hall*<br><br>Hazlitt<br>*Lectures on English Comic Writers*<br><br>Hone<br>*Political House that Jack Built* | August<br>'Peterloo' massacre<br>'Six Acts'<br>Poor Relief Act |

| DATE | WORKS OF FICTION | OTHER WORKS | HISTORICAL/CULTURAL EVENTS |
|------|-----------------|-------------|----------------------------|
| **1820** | Egan<br>*Life in London* (–1821)<br><br>Galt<br>*Ayrshire Legatees*<br><br>Maturin<br>*Melmoth the Wanderer*<br><br>Opie<br>*Tales of the Heart*<br><br>Scott<br>*The Monastery; The Abbot* | Clare<br>*Poems Descriptive of Rural Life*<br><br>Keats<br>*Lamia, Isabella, The Eve of St. Agnes, and Other Poems*<br><br>Moncrieff<br>*Lear of Private Life*<br><br>Shelley<br>*Prometheus Unbound* | January<br>Death of George III;<br>accession of George IV<br>February<br>Cato Street conspiracy<br>Controversy over Queen Caroline's attempts to claim her rights<br>First iron steamship |
| 1821 | Lockhart<br>*Valerius*<br><br>Galt<br>*Annals of the Parish*<br><br>Scott<br>*Kenilworth; The Pirate* | Byron<br>*Don Juan*; cantos III–V<br><br>Mill<br>*Elements of Political Economy* | Defeat of Durham's reform bill |
| 1822 | Galt<br>*The Provost; The Entail*<br><br>Hogg<br>*Three Perils of Man*<br><br>Lockhart<br>*Adam Blair*<br><br>Opie<br>*Madeline*<br><br>Peacock<br>*Maid Marian*<br><br>Scott<br>*Fortunes of Nigel* | Byron<br>*Vision of Judgement*<br><br>De Quincey<br>*Confessions of an English Opium Eater*<br><br>Digby<br>*Broad Stone of Honour*<br><br>Rogers<br>*Italy* (–1828) | January<br>Sidmouth replaced by Peel<br>August<br>Suicide of Castlereagh;<br>Canning becomes foreign secretary |

| DATE | WORKS OF FICTION | OTHER WORKS | HISTORICAL/CULTURAL EVENTS |
|------|------------------|-------------|----------------------------|
| 1823 | Galt<br>*Ringan Gilhaize*<br><br>Hazlitt<br>*Liber Amoris*<br><br>Hogg<br>*Three Perils of Woman*<br><br>Scott<br>*Peveril of the Peak;<br>  Quentin Durward; St.<br>  Ronan's Well*<br><br>M. Shelley<br>*Valperga* | Byron<br>*Don Juan*, cantos<br>  VI–XIV<br><br>Hazlitt<br>*Characteristics*<br><br>Lamb<br>*Essays of Elia* | |
| 1824 | Hogg<br>*Confessions of a Justified<br>  Sinner*<br><br>Hook<br>*Sayings and Doings*<br>  *(–1828)*<br><br>Morier<br>*Adventures of Hajjî Baba*<br><br>Scott<br>*Redgauntlet* | Byron<br>*Don Juan*, cantos<br>  XV–XVI<br><br>Godwin<br>*History of the<br>  Commonwealth of<br>  England*<br><br>Landor<br>*Imaginary Conversations*<br>  *(–1828)* | Repeal of Combination<br>Acts |
| 1825 | Lauder<br>*Lochindhu*<br><br>Scott<br>*The Betrothed; The<br>  Talisman*<br><br>Ward<br>*Tremaine* | Brougham<br>*Observations on the<br>  Education of the People*<br><br>Coleridge<br>*Aids to Reflection*<br><br>Hazlitt<br>*Spirit of the Age*<br><br>Mill<br>*Essays on Government* | November<br>Financial crisis<br>Catholic relief bill fails<br>  House of Lords<br>Stockton and<br>  Darlington railway |

| DATE | WORKS OF FICTION | OTHER WORKS | HISTORICAL/CULTURAL EVENTS |
|---|---|---|---|
| 1826 | Disraeli<br>*Vivian Grey* (−1827)<br><br>Galt<br>*Last of the Lairds*<br><br>Lister<br>*Granby*<br><br>Scott<br>*Woodstock*<br><br>M. Shelley<br>*The Last Man*<br><br>H. Smith<br>*Brambletye House* | Barrett (Browning)<br>*Essay on Mind*<br><br>Hogg<br>*Queen Hynde*<br><br>Scott<br>*Letters of Malachi<br>  Malagrowther* | Russell's proposals on<br>  reform defeated<br>Destruction of<br>  powerlooms by<br>  unemployed weavers |
| 1827 | Scott<br>*Chronicles of the<br>  Canongate*<br><br>Ward<br>*De Vere* | Keble<br>*Christian Year*<br><br>Scott<br>*Life of Napoleon* | Brougham founds<br>Society for the<br>Diffusion of Useful<br>Knowledge |
| 1828 | Bulwer<br>*Pelham*<br><br>Bury<br>*Flirtation*<br><br>Croly<br>*Salathiel*<br><br>Moir<br>*Mansie Wauch*<br><br>Scott<br>*Fair Maid of Perth* | Elliott<br>*Corn Law Rhymes*<br><br>Mitford<br>*Rienzi*<br><br>Tytler<br>*History of Scotland*<br>  (−1843) | January<br>Wellington<br>  administration<br>February<br>Repeal of Test and<br>  Corporation Acts<br>Thomas Arnold<br>  becomes head of<br>  Rugby School |
| 1829 | Bulwer<br>*The Disowned;<br>  Devereux*<br><br>Marryat<br>*Frank Mildmay*<br><br>Peacock<br>*Misfortunes of Elphin*<br><br>Scott<br>*Anne of Geierstein* | Hogg<br>*Shepherd's Calendar*<br><br>Mill<br>*Analysis of the Human<br>  Mind* | April<br>Catholic emancipation<br>September<br>Metropolitan Police<br>  Act |

| DATE | WORKS OF FICTION | OTHER WORKS | HISTORICAL/CULTURAL EVENTS |
|------|------------------|-------------|----------------------------|
| **1830** | Bulwer<br>*Paul Clifford*<br><br>Carleton<br>*Traits and Stories of the Irish Peasantry*<br><br>Galt<br>*Lawrie Todd*<br><br>Godwin<br>*Cloudesley*<br><br>Hook<br>*Maxwell*<br><br>James<br>*De L'Orme*<br><br>Marryat<br>*The King's Own*<br><br>M. Shelley<br>*Perkin Warbeck* | Cobbett<br>*Rural Rides; Twopenny Trash* (–1833)<br><br>Coleridge<br>*On the Constitution of Church and State*<br><br>T. Moore<br>*Life of Byron*<br><br>Scott<br>*Letters on Demonology and Witchcraft*<br><br>Tennyson<br>*Poems, Chiefly Lyrical* | June<br>Death of George IV; accession of William IV<br>November<br>Wellington opposes reform; resigns: Grey administration comes in |

# General Bibliographies

*Note: Each section is arranged alphabetically by last name of author. Place of publication is London unless otherwise stated.*

## (i) English fiction: history and criticism

Baker, E. A.    *The History of the English Novel*, 10 vols (1924–36; reprinted New York, 1950–67); supplement (vol. XI) by Lionel Stevenson (1967). (Still a reliable and useful history.)

Bakhtin, M. M.    *The Dialogic Imagination*, translated by C. Emerson and M. Holquist (Austin, 1981). (Essays on nature of novel discourse; with Bakhtin's book on Dostoevsky, major contribution to understanding nature and function of novel in Western culture.)

Barthes, R.    'Introduction to the Structural Analysis of Narratives', translated by Stephen Heath, in *Image Music Text* (Glasgow, 1977) and *A Barthes Reader*, edited by Susan Sontag (1982). (Stimulating essay, from Barthes's structuralist phase, drawing on work of Russian formalists and structural linguists.) *S/Z*, translated by R. Miller (1975). (*Tour de force* of semiotic criticism, exhibiting the reader's freedom as interpreter, yet his or her dependence on interpretative codes.)

Booth, W. C.    *The Rhetoric of Fiction* (Chicago and London, 1961). (Deals with narrative method.)

Fowler, A.    *Linguistics and the Novel* (1977). (Summary of structuralist and linguistic approaches to prose fiction.)

Frye, H. N.    *The Secular Scripture: A Study of the Structure of Romance* (Cambridge, Mass., and London, 1976). (Stimulating and wide-ranging essay on romance as myth and genre, high art and popular entertainment.)

Kettle, A.    *An Introduction to the English Novel*, 2 vols (1951–53). (Using exemplary texts shows the relation of social history and fictional themes and forms.)

Leavis, F. R.    *The Great Tradition: George Eliot, Henry James, Joseph Conrad* (1948; Harmondsworth, 1962). (Major text in development of language of criticism for the novel; unhistorical and anti-historicist and highly influential with both academic and non-academic critics.)

Leavis, Q. D.    *Fiction and the Reading Public* (1932; reprinted 1965). (Important attempt to found an English school of sociology of fiction and literature, but lacks sense of the richness and moral dimension of popular culture and its varieties of fiction.)

Lodge, D.    *The Language of Fiction: Essays in Criticism and Verbal Analysis of the English Novel* (1966). (Considers various issues in modern formalist and rhetorical criticism of the novel.)

Spilka, M., ed.    *Towards a Poetics of Fiction* (Bloomington and London, 1977). (Valuable collection of essays from the periodical *Novel: A Forum on Fiction*; includes essays on some novelists of the Romantic period.)

Van Ghent, D.    *The English Novel: Form and Function* (1953; reprinted New York, 1961). (Excellent formalist criticism of selected novels.)

## (ii) Romantic background: social, historical, cultural

Anderson, B.    *Imagined Communities: Reflections on the Origin and Spread of Nationalism* (1983). (Stimulating book on Romantic nationalism and its relation to form of social-historical novel.)

Brown, F. K.    *Fathers of the Victorians: The Age of Wilberforce* (Cambridge, 1961). (Lively and detailed critical examination of Romantic Evangelicals.)

Butler, Marilyn    *Romantics, Rebels and Reactionaries: English Literature and its Background 1760–1830* (Oxford, 1981). (Good study of the complexities of the period.)

Evans, Eric J.    *The Forging of the Modern State: Early Industrial Britain 1783–1870* (London and New York, 1983). (Excellent historical survey, with valuable compendium of dates and other facts.)

Gilbert, A. D.    *Religion and Society in Industrial England: Church, Chapel, and Social Change 1740–1914* (London and New York, 1976). (The best general survey available.)

Goodwin, A.  *The Friends of Liberty: The English Democratic Movement in the Age of the French Revolution* (1979). (Study of the 'English Jacobins'.)

McKendrick, N., John Brewer and J. H. Plumb  *The Birth of a Consumer Society: The Commercialization of Eighteenth-Century England* (1982). (Important book on social change of which novel reading was a part.)

Marshall, D.  *Industrial England 1776–1851* (1973; 1982). (General survey of economic and social change.)

Mingay, G. E.  *The Gentry: The Rise and Fall of a Ruling Class* (London and New York, 1976). (Good study of the dominant social class during the Romantic period.)

Morris, R. J.  *Class and Class Consciousness in the Industrial Revolution 1780–1850* (London and Basingstoke, 1979). (Good brief survey of the major arguments on this issue.)

Perkin, H.  *The Origins of Modern English Society 1780–1880* (1969). (Argues interconnectedness of social and cultural institutions with social and economic change.)

Thompson, E. P.  *The Making of the English Working Class* (1963; reprinted Harmondsworth, 1968). (Still controversial, but by now classic study of economic and cultural change.)

Williams, R.  *Culture and Society 1780–1950* (1958; reprinted Harmondsworth, 1961). (Attempt to trace broad movements of English social and cultural change since the Romantic period.)

## (iii) Romantic Fiction

## A. Bibliographies and reference guides

Block, A.  *The English Novel 1740–1850: A Catalogue Including Prose Romances, Short Stories, and Translations of Foreign Fiction* (1939). (Still useful; needs to be corrected and supplemented by reference to other, more recent bibliographies.)

Leclaire, L.  *A General Analytical Bibliography of the Regional Novelists of the British Isles, 1800–1950* (Clermont-Ferrand, 1954).

Mayo, R. D  *The English Novel in the Magazines, 1740–1815* (Evanston, Illinois, 1962). (Important book on a neglected subject; includes extensive bibliography, but now needs to be supplemented from more recent work by other bibliographers; does not include mass of short stories, tales, fictional anecdotes, sketches, etc., published in the magazines.)

Orr, L. *A Catalogue Checklist of English Prose Fiction, 1750–1800* (Troy, New York, 1979). (Includes chronological checklist, author index, and essay on 'The Audience for the Novel, 1750–1800'.)

Spector, R. D. *The English Gothic: A Bibliographic Guide to Writers from Horace Walpole to Mary Shelley* (Westport, Conn., and London, 1984). (Review of recent criticism, with bibliography.)

Vinson, J. and D. L. Kirkpatrick *The Novel to 1900*, Great Writers Student Library (1980). (Includes brief biography, critical essay, and bibliography on major and some minor novelists of Romantic period.)

Watson, G. and I. Willison, eds *New Cambridge Bibliography of English Literature*, 5 vols (Cambridge, 1969–77), vols II and III. (The standard bibliography; lists individual works and works of criticism; occasionally unreliable on dates, authorship, and number of publications of Romantic novelists.)

## B. Readership, authorship, publication, and distribution

Altick, R. D. *The English Common Reader: A Social History of the Mass Reading Public 1800–1900* (Chicago, 1957).

Collins, A. S. *The Profession of Letters: A Study of the Relation of Author to Patron, Publisher and Public, 1780–1832* (1928).

Kaufman, P. *Libraries and Their Users* (1969). (Several essays on distribution of books in Romantic period.)

Klancher, Jon P. *The Making of English Reading Audiences, 1790–1832* (Madison Wisconsin, 1987). (Important conjunction of social, cultural, and literary history.)

Neuburg, V. E. *Popular Literature: A History and Guide* (Harmondsworth, 1977). (Rapid survey of popular chapbooks and broadsheets.)

Ong, W. J. *Orality and Literacy: The Technology of the Word* (London and New York, 1982). (Important essay on differences between culture of writing and oral culture.)

Varma, D. P. *The Evergreen Tree of Diabolical Knowledge* (Washington, 1972). (Much information on circulating libraries.)

Webb, R. K. *The British Working Class Reader 1790–1848: Literacy and Social Tension* (1955).

## C. History and criticism (general)

Brissenden, R. F.    *Virtue in Distress: Studies in the Novel of Sentiment from Richardson to Sade* (London and Basingstoke, 1974). (Good treatment of the varieties of fiction inherited by.novelists of the Romantic period.)

Foster, J. R.    *History of the Pre-Romantic Novel in England* (New York, 1949).

Karl, F. R.    *A Reader's Guide to the Development of the English Novel in the Eighteenth Century* (1975). (A useful survey; argues relation of novel to eighteenth-century 'common sense' philosophy and its service to bourgeois culture; deals with some novels of the 1790s.)

Kiely, R.    *The Romantic Novel in England* (Cambridge Mass., 1972). (Good critical essays on novels from *The Castle of Otranto* to *Wuthering Heights*.)

Tompkins, J. M. S.    *The Popular Novel in England 1770–1800* (1932; reprinted Lincoln Nebraska, 1961). (Excellent treatment of the 'trash of the circulating libraries' as well as other varieties of late eighteenth-century novel; includes discussion of conditions of authorship.)

## D. Themes, aspects of form, sub-genres

Adburgham, A.    *Silver Fork Society: Fashionable Life and Literature from 1814 to 1840* (1983).

Birkhead, E.    *The Tale of Terror: A Study of Gothic Romance* (1921).

Cox, S.D.    *'The Stranger within Thee': Concepts of the Self in Late-Eighteenth-Century Literature* (Pittsburgh, 1980). (Good book on a major topic.)

Eagleton, M., and D. Pierce    *Attitudes to Class in the English Novel from Walter Scott to David Storey* (1979).

Harris, W. V.    *British Short Fiction in the Nineteenth Century: A Literary and Bibliographic Guide* (Detroit, 1979).

Kelly, G.    *The English Jacobin Novel 1780–1805* (Oxford, 1976). (Formal and contextual study of Bage, Inchbald, Holcroft, and Godwin.)

Levine, G.    *The Realistic Imagination: English Fiction from Frankenstein to Lady Chatterley* (Chicago and London, 1981). (On the rhetoric and problematics of realism in fiction.)

Lukác, G.    *The Historical Novel*, translated by H. and S. Mitchell (1962; reprinted Harmondsworth, 1969). (Classic Marxist essay; includes long section on Scott.)

Lyons, J. O.    *The Invention of the Self: The Hinge of Consciousness in the Eighteenth Century* (Carbondale and Edwardsville, Illinois, 1978).

Poovey, M.    *The Proper Lady and the Woman Writer: Ideology as Style in the Works of Mary Wollstonecraft, Mary Shelley, and Jane Austen* (Chicago and London, 1984).

Punter, D.    *The Literature of Terror: A History of Gothic Fictions from 1765 to the Present Day* (London and New York, 1980).

Reed, W. L.    *An Exemplary History of the Novel: The Quixotic versus the Picaresque* (Chicago and London, 1981).

Spacks, P. M.    *Imagining a Self: Autobiography and Novel in Eighteenth-Century England* (Cambridge Mass. and London, 1976).

Summers, M.    *The Gothic Quest: A History of the Gothic Novel* (1938; reprinted New York, 1964).

Thorslev, P. L.    *The Byronic Hero: Types and Prototypes* (Minneapolis, 1962).

Todd, J.    *Women's Friendship in Literature* (New York and Guildford, 1980). (A major topic in Sentimental and Romantic fiction and culture; ranges from early eighteenth to early nineteenth century, through French and English fiction.)

Utter, R. P. and G. B. Needham    *Pamela's Daughters* (New York, 1937). (On women characters and writers after Richardson.)

Wilson, J. D.    *The Romantic Heroic Ideal* (Baton Rouge and London, 1982).

# Individual Authors

## Notes on biography, major works, and criticism

Each entry that follows is in three sections:
(1) *Outline of author's life and literary career.* Date of publication of novels and other literary works is that of first appearance in volume form, unless otherwise indicated.
(2) *Selected autobiographies, letters, and biographies.*
(3) *Selected critical works.* Listed in chronological order of publication.

In all cases, place of publication is London, unless otherwise indicated. Editions of novels are not cited, but modern critical editions of many of the novels discussed in this book are available in the Penguin English Library, the Oxford World's Classics, and editions published by Norton and Riverside. In addition, many novels by women authors of this period are becoming available in Pandora's Mothers of the Novel series and from Virago Press. Reprints of original editions of many novels of this period have been published for libraries by Garland.

Collections of reprinted critical essays are not included here, but are available for the major canonical writers in anthologies published by Macmillan (Casebook series), Routledge and Kegan Paul (Critical Heritage series), Prentice-Hall (Twentieth-Century Views series), and others.

AUSTEN, Jane (1775–1817), born at Steventon, Hampshire, second daughter, seventh child of well-to-do Church of England clergyman. Had six brothers and elder sister, Cassandra. Her brothers were all successful in various professions, including the clergy and the navy, except one brother who was adopted by a gentry family and another who suffered from an undisclosed mental illness. Attended boarding schools, but mostly educated at home. Always a great novel reader. She and sister did not marry, but lived together. Lived at Steventon until twenty-five. Wrote parodies and satires for family amusement and began writing novels in 1790s. Moved with family to Bath in 1801; after father's death moved to brother's home in Southampton, and then, in 1809, to house owned by another brother at Chawton in Hampshire, where she remained until just before her death. Revised novels begun in the 1790s and early 1800s, and published *Sense and Sensibility* (1811), *Pride and Prejudice* (1813), *Mansfield Park* (1814), *Emma* (1815; dated 1816), and *Persuasion* (1818), with *Northanger Abbey* (sold some years earlier but not published). Last piece of fiction, 'Sanditon', remained incomplete. Died at Winchester.

> *Jane Austen's Letters to her Sister Cassandra and Others*, edited by R. W. Chapman, second edition, corrected (1959). (Definitive edition.)

Laski, Marghanita, *Jane Austen and her World* (1969). (Illustrated profusely; mainly biographical.)

Hodge, J. A., *The Double Life of Jane Austen* (1972).

Cecil, Lord David, *A Portrait of Jane Austen* (1978). (Illustrated; mainly biographical.)

Halperin, John, *The Life of Jane Austen* (Baltimore, 1984).

See:   Lascelles, Mary, *Jane Austen and Her Art* (Oxford, 1939). (Major critical study.)

Leavis, Q. D., *Collected Essays* (Cambridge, 1983). ('A critical theory of Jane Austen's writings', pp. 61–146, originally published in *Scrutiny*, x and xii; good treatment of the formal elements and their composition.)

Mudrick, Marvin, *Jane Austen: Irony as Defense and Discovery* (Princeton, 1952). (Stimulating and controversial.)

Wright, A. H., *Jane Austen's Novels: A Study in Structure* (1953).

Trilling, Lionel, 'Mansfield Park', in *The Opposing Self* (1955; reprinted Oxford and Melbourne, 1980); 'Emma and the Legend of Jane Austen', in *Beyond Culture* (1965; reprinted Oxford and Melbourne, 1980).

Babb, Howard, S., *Jane Austen's Novels: The Fabric of Dialogue* (Columbus Ohio, 1962).

Southam, B. C., *Jane Austen's Literary Manuscripts: A Study of the Novelist's Development through the Surviving Papers* (1964). (Important textual study.)

Litz, A. W., *Jane Austen: A Study of her Artistic Development* (New York, 1965). (Excellent study of the formal techniques and Austen's transformation of the fictional conventions of her day.)

Bradbrook, F. W., *Jane Austen and Her Predecessors* (Cambridge, 1966).

Moler, Kenneth L., *Jane Austen's Art of Allusion* (Lincoln, Nebraska, 1968). (Valuable study of common themes and techniques of Austen and her contemporaries and predecessors.)

Duckworth, A. M., *The Improvement of the Estate: A Study of Jane Austen's Novels* (Baltimore, 1971). (Important study of Austen and her ideas on society as represented in the novels.)

Page, Norman, *The Language of Jane Austen* (Oxford, 1972).

Brown, Lloyd W., *Bits of Ivory: Narrative Techniques in Jane Austen's Fiction* (Baton Rouge, 1973).

Butler, M., *Jane Austen and the War of Ideas* (Oxford, 1975). (Austen in relation to controversies of the day.)

Hardy, Barbara, *A Reading of Jane Austen* (1975).

Devlin, D. D., *Jane Austen and Education* (1975). (On the intellectual background; focuses on *Mansfield Park*.)

Brown, Julia Prewitt, *Jane Austen's Novels: Social Change and Literary Form* (Cambridge, Mass. and London, 1979). (Focuses on marriage and the family in relation to individual subjectivity.)

Roberts, Warren, *Jane Austen and the French Revolution* (New York, 1979). (Shows contemporary relevance of Austen's major themes.)

Monaghan, David, *Jane Austen and Social Vision* (London and Basingstoke, 1980). (On Austen's use of the formal social occasion in her novels.)

Morgan, Susan, *In the Meantime: Character and Perception in Jane Austen's Fiction* (Chicago and London, 1980).

Kirkham, M., *Jane Austen, Feminism and Fiction* (Brighton and
Totowa, New Jersey, 1983).
Cottom, D., *The Civilized Imagination: A Study of Ann Radcliffe,
Jane Austen, and Sir Walter Scott* (Cambridge, 1985).

BAGE, Robert (1728–1801), born in Derbyshire, son of paper-maker; educated at
common schools and then trained for father's business. Married and
moved to Elford in Staffordshire; established paper-mill which he ran until
his death. Well connected with leaders in science, technology, and industry
in Midlands, as well as with leaders in English Nonconformist and
provincial Enlightenments. Studied mathematics; taught himself music and
languages. Began writing novels in late middle age: *Mount Henneth* (1782),
*Barham Downs* (1784), *The Fair Syrian* (1787), *James Wallace* (1788), *Man As
He Is* (1792), *Hermsprong; or, Man As He is Not* (1796). His work much
admired by urban intellectuals and reformers such as Holcroft and
Godwin.

> Memoir by his daughter, in Sir Walter Scott's preface to selection of
> Bage's novels reprinted in Ballantyne's Novelist's Library, vol. 9
> (1824).

> See:   Steeves, H. R., *Before Jane Austen* (1966). (Has an essay on Bage.)
> Butler, Marilyn, *Jane Austen and the War of Ideas* (Oxford, 1975).
> (Has a chapter on Bage.)
> Kelly, G., *The English Jacobin Novel* (Oxford, 1976). (Has a chapter
> on Bage; focuses on his novels of the 1790s.)
> Faulkner, P., *Robert Bage*, Twayne's English Authors, 249 (Boston,
> 1979). (A general survey of life and novels.)

BRUNTON, Mary (1778–1818), born in Orkney Islands, daughter of Scottish
officer. After mother's death, became father's housekeeper in the Orkneys.
Married a Presbyterian country clergyman around 1798. In 1803 Bruntons
moved to Edinburgh. Published two novels, *Self-Control* (1810) and
*Discipline* (1814). They adapt elements of late eighteenth-century novel of
manners and sentiment to themes of national culture, opposition of
country and city, study of motive and psychology of passion and desire,
and evangelical religion. Died of fever after delivering still-born child.

> 'Memoir' by her husband, Alexander Brunton, in *Emmeline: With
> Some Other Pieces* (Edinburgh and London, 1819); reprinted in the
> Standard Novels edition of *Discipline* (1832).

BRYDGES, Sir Samuel Egerton (1762–1837), one of a few novelists born into
landed gentry. Second son of gentleman of Kent; educated at Cambridge
and for law; purchased own estate in 1792 and gave himself up to life of
literature and bibliophily. Adopted Sentimental idea of genius as standard
of true, inward, personal aristocracy. Despised everything bourgeois, yet
as poet and novelist pursued themes and values of professional middle-class
culture and held neighbouring 'book-hating squires' in contempt. Published
several books of poems and number of novels and tales; latter include
*Mary de-Clifford: A Story* (1792), *Arthur Fitz-Albini* (1798), *Le Forester: A
Novel* (1802), *Coningsby: A Tragic Tale* (1819), *Lord Brokenhurst* (1819), *Sir
Ralph Willoughby: An Historical Tale of the Sixteenth Century* (1820), and
*The Hall of Hellingsley: A Tale* (1821). Believed that novel should differ
little from poetry in that it should focus on the 'real' self – the subjective
self – rather than on the merely social self revealed through plot and

character. Edited and printed large number of Medieval and Renaissance texts. Obsessively pursued his family's claims to aristocratic title; created baronet in 1814. In 1812 elected MP and sat in Parliament until 1818, speaking on bills to do with poor laws and copyright. After 1818 lived mainly at Geneva; died in Switzerland.

> Brydges, Sir Samuel Egerton, *The Autobiography, Times, Opinions, and Contemporaries of Sir Egerton Brydges*, 2 vols (1834). (Interesting self-portrait of mind riddled with social and cultural contradictions of his age.)

See:   Woodworth, Mary K., *The Literary Career of Sir Samuel Egerton Brydges* (Oxford, 1935). (Mainly critical.)

BURNEY (later d'Arblay), Frances (1752–1840), known as 'Fanny', born in King's Lynn, Norfolk, daughter of musician and teacher; moved to London with family in 1760; mother died 1762. Began writing diaries as child; influenced by intellectual interests and social views of father and family friends. Unknown to father, wrote epistolary novel, *Evelina; or, The History of a Young Lady's Entrance into the World* (1778); an enormous success and overshadowed all her later novels. In 1782 published *Cecilia; or, Memoirs of an Heiress*, in third-person narration, on same themes dealt with in *Evelina*. Partly because of her literary reputation, appointed Second Keeper of the Robes to Queen Charlotte in 1786; hated Court life; resigned position because of ill health in 1791. In 1793 married French officer and *émigré* nobleman, Alexandre d'Arblay, after earlier family objections. Another novel, *Camilla; or, A Picture of Youth*, published in 1796 by subscription in order to maximize profits. In 1802 d'Arblays moved to Paris during brief peace of Amiens; caught there when war resumed; Burney returned to England with her son in 1812. Published last novel, *The Wanderer; or, Female Difficulties*, in 1814. After death of father, returned briefly to France; husband died in 1818. Her numerous letters and diaries published after her death.

> *The Journals and Letters of Fanny Burney*, edited by Joyce Hemlow and others, 7 vols (Oxford, 1972–78).
> Hemlow, Joyce, *The History of Fanny Burney* (Oxford, 1958). (The definitive biography.)

See:   Adelstein, M. E., *Fanny Burney*, Twayne's English Authors, 67 (New York, 1968). (General survey.)
      Schrank, B. G. and D. J. Supino, editors, *The Famous Fanny Burney* (New York, 1976).
      Voss-Clesly, P., *Tendencies of Character Description in the Domestic Novels of Burney, Edgeworth, and Austen: A Consideration of Subjective and Objective World*, 3 vols (Salzburg, 1979).
      Kilpatrick, Sarah, *Fanny Burney* (1980).

CUMBERLAND, Richard (1732–1811), born at Trinity College, Cambridge, son of archdeacon of Northampton; sent to school at Bury St Edmunds and Westminster, where he lodged with poet Cowper; entered Trinity College, Cambridge, at fourteen; elected to fellowship. Began successful career as playwright in London. Married 1759; appointed Crown Agent to Nova Scotia. Play *The West Indian* bought in 1770 by Garrick and had long life on stage. Appointed Secretary to Board of Trade; travelled to Spain on government business. Published *Anecdotes of Eminent Painters in Spain* (1782). Returned to play writing; numerous plays in the 1780s, such as *The Jew* (1794), established him as one of leading dramatists of the day. A philosophical novel, *Arundel* (1789), followed by another, *Henry* (1795); last novel, *John de Lancaster* (1809); published interesting autobiography. Died at Tunbridge Wells and buried in Westminster Abbey.

> *Memoirs of Richard Cumberland, Written by Himself* (1806–07); edited by H. Flanders (1856; reprinted New York, 1969).

See: Dircks, R. J., *Richard Cumberland*, Twayne's English Authors, 196 (Boston, 1976). (General critical survey.)

DACRE, Charlotte (1782–1842?), like many contributors to 'the trash of the circulating libraries', remains a figure about whom little is known. Married to editor of *The Morning Post* newspaper and known as 'Rosa Matilda' in Della Cruscan circle of English Sentimental-Romantic poets. Wrote poetry such as *Hours of Solitude* (1805) and published four successful 'Gothic romances': *Confessions of the Nun of St. Omer* (1805), *Zofloya; or, The Moor* (1806), *The Libertine* (1807), and *The Passions* (1811).

> Summers, Montague, 'Byron's "Lovely Rosa"', in *Essays in Petto* (1928; reprinted Freeport, 1967).

D'ISRAELI, Isaac (1766–1848), born in London of Italian and Portuguese Jewish descent, son of merchant and stockbroker; decided to be a poet, but parents insisted on his entering business life. In 1791 began publishing *Curiosities of Literature, Consisting of Anecdotes, Characters, Sketches and Observations, Literary, Critical, and Historical*, an immediate success (2nd vol., 1793; 3rd 1817; 4th and 5th, 1823; 6th and last, 1834). In 1797 published Anti-Jacobin novel, *Vaurien; or, Sketches of the Times*. Another novel published in 1805, *Flim-Flams! or, The Life and Errors of My Uncle, and the Amours of My Aunt!* (enlarged 1806), which looks forward to Peacock's novels of opinion of 1810s and 1820s. Last novel, *Despotism; or, The Fall of the Jesuits*, published 1811. Published poems, miscellaneous works, and *The Genius of Judaism* (1833), history of sufferings of the Jews. By then had for some time been associated with Church of England. Blind from 1831, but with help of daughter completed *Amenities of Literature* (1841) and continued to revise *Curiosities of Literature*.

> Disraeli, Benjamin, *The Life and Writings of Mr Disraeli [sic; By His Son*, vol. 1 of *The Writings of Isaac D'Israeli*, 7 vols (1858–59).

See: Ogden, James, *Isaac D'Israeli* (Oxford, 1969). (Mainly biographical.)

EDGEWORTH, Maria (1767–1849), daughter of Anglo-Irish gentleman, Richard Lovell Edgeworth; he had several wives in succession and many children, some of whom Maria helped to educate. Family moved to their Irish estate of Edgeworthstown in 1773, but Maria Edgeworth educated in England; returned to Ireland to work closely with her father in his many projects for 'improvement', social and economic. Father forbade her to read most novels of the day, but she subscribed to Burney's *Camilla*. In 1795 published *Letters for Literary Ladies*. Wrote many books for children and young people; *The Parent's Assistant; or, Stories for Children* published 1796. *Practical Education* (1798), a treatise, written with her father. Edgeworths caught in turmoil of Irish rebellion of 1798 and political agitation over union with Britain. First novel, *Castle Rackrent* (1800), first of several 'Irish tales', attempts to transcend political and social conflicts revealed by troubles of 1798, calling for moral reform of Anglo-Irish gentry and Irish peasantry. Published ten volumes of *Early Lessons* for children between 1800 and 1802, and in 1801 *Moral Tales for Young People* as well as *Belinda*, novel of manners and sentiment in line of Fanny Burney. Visited France in 1802; met a Swedish count, who proposed to her; she declined, not wishing to be separated from her family and Ireland. Published *Popular Tales* (1804) and *The Modern Griselda: A Tale* (1805). Two sets of *Tales of Fashionable Life*, including the 'Irish tales' 'The Absentee' and 'Ennui', published in 1809 and 1812; established her reputation as leading writer of 'serious' fiction of early 1800s. Again with father wrote *Essays on Professional Education* (1809). In 1814 published novel she considered her major work to date, *Patronage*; in 1817 published *Harrington* and *Ormond*. Father died in same year; best fiction behind her. Completed *Memoirs of Richard Lovell Edgeworth* (1820) and three sequels to *Early Lessons* (1821–23); during these years spent much time running family estate; also met and visited many writers, including great admirer of her work, Sir Walter Scott. *Helen*, last novel, published 1834, by which time her reputation waning.

> *Letters from England 1813–1844*, edited by Christina Colvin (Oxford, 1971).
> Butler, Marilyn, *Maria Edgeworth: A Literary Biography* (Oxford, 1972). (The definitive biography; excellent criticism of the fiction.)

See:  Hurst, M. C., *Maria Edgeworth and the Public Scene: Fine Feeling and Landlordism in the Age of Reform* (Coral Gables, 1969).
Newcomer, J., *Maria Edgeworth*, Irish Writers Series (Lewisburg, 1973).
Butler, Marilyn, *Jane Austen and the War of Ideas* (Oxford, 1975). (Includes section on Edgeworth.)
Voss-Clesly, P., *Tendencies of Character Description in the Domestic Novels of Burney, Edgeworth, and Austen: A Consideration of Subjective and Objective World*, 3 vols (Salzburg, 1979). (Interesting comparative essay on techniques of depicting inward self and social world.)
Dunne, Tom, *Maria Edgeworth and the Colonial Mind* (Cork, 1984). (On Edgeworth's 'Irish tales' and her social situation, by a historian.)

EGAN, Pierce (1774 or 1775–1849), born in Ireland or London of Protestant Irish descent; father a labourer, though rest of family was quite successful. Apprenticed to London printer; followed sports of all kinds and gained considerable reputation in 1800s as sports journalist. Wrote and published chapbooks.

*Boxiana*, serial publication on boxing during great Romantic era of the sport, enormously popular (collected 1812, 1818, 1821, 1828, 1829). In 1820 and 1821, serial publication of novel *Life in London; or, The Day and Night Scenes of Jerry Hawthorn, Esq. and His Elegant Friend, Corinthian Tom, in Their Rambles and Sprees through the Metropolis*: another great success, inspired several imitations, and quickly adapted to stage. During 1820s wrote chapbooks and criminal trials; in 1824 began editing *Pierce Egan's*

*Life in London and Sporting Guide*, a weekly newspaper. Published another novel, *The Life of an Actor* (1825), dedicated to Edmund Kean. *Finish to the Adventures of Tom, Jerry, and Logic* published 1828. Spent last years in peaceful retirement.

See: Reid, J. C., *Bucks and Bruisers: Pierce Egan and Regency England* (1971). (Valuable biographical and critical study.)

FERRIER, Susan (1782–1854), born in Edinburgh, youngest of ten children of Scottish lawyer, estate manager, and colleague of Sir Walter Scott; privately educated; death of mother in 1797 and marriage of sister in 1804 left her in role of father's housekeeper until his death in 1829. Began writing in 1810 and published first novel, *Marriage* (1818), in Burney and Edgeworth line of novels of manners and sentiment, dealing with problems of social emulation. It was so successful Blackwood gave her £1000 for her next, *The Inheritance* (1824). In spite of literary success, avoided public life, like so many other women authors of this period. In 1820s began to go blind. Third and last novel, *Destiny; or The Chief's Daughter*, published 1831; thanks to Scott's help in bargaining with publisher, she received £1700 for it. Later years spent in blindness in Edinburgh.

> *Memoir and Correspondence of Susan Ferrier . . . Collected by . . . John Ferrier*, edited by John A. Doyle (1898).

See: Parker, W. M., *Susan Ferrier and John Galt* (1965).
Bushnell, N. S., 'Susan Ferrier's *Marriage* as a Novel of Manners', *Studies in Scottish Literature*, 5 (1968), 216–28.
Paxton, Nancy L., 'Subversive Feminism: A Reassessment of Susan Ferrier's *Marriage*', *Women and Literature*, 4 (1976), 18–29.
*Susan Ferrier*, National Library of Scotland exhibition catalogue (Edinburgh, 1982). (Contains essay by Ian Campbell on Ferrier's novels, and texts for beginning of an unfinished novel, *Maplehurst Manor*.)
Cullinan, Mary, *Susan Ferrier*, Twayne's English Authors, 392 (Boston, 1984). (Critical survey with biographical introduction.)

GALT, John (1779–1839), born in Irvine, Ayrshire, son of sea-captain; educated privately and at schools in Irvine and Greenock. Prepared for career in commercial shipping. Moved to London in 1804 to combine business and literary pursuits; studied law, but not called to bar. Travelled on Continent and in Mediterranean; met Byron and travelled with him, returning to England in 1811. Published travel book and *The Life and Administration of Cardinal Wolsey* (1812). Published plays: badly received. Turned to commerce again; unsuccessful; settled into life of authorship. Published *Letters from the Levant* (1813) and in 1814–15 edited *The New British Theatre*, including plays of his own. First work of fiction *The Majolo: A Tale* (1815–16). Published *The Life and Studies of Benjamin West*, the painter (1816–20). Acted as London agent for canal company. In 1820s began most active period as fiction writer, especially dealing with Scottish provincial life; fiction sometimes published in *Blackwood's Magazine* before it appeared in volume form. *The Ayrshire Legatees* (1820–21; in volume form, 1822), an epistolary novel; *Annals of the Parish* (1821), study of economic development and social change in Scotland from 1760 to the early nineteenth century; *The Provost* (1822) deals with town rather than village life. *Sir Andrew Wylie of that Ilk* (1822), *The Entail; or, The Lairds of Grippy* (1822), and *The Last of the Lairds* (1826) more concerned with old and new Scottish gentry caught in 'modernization' of Britain. Other fiction of these years includes *The Earthquake* (1820), *Glenfell; or, Macdonalds and Campbells* (1820), *The Steam-Boat* (1821; in volume form, 1822), and *The Gathering of the West* (1822; in volume form, 1823), a social satire. In 1823 turned to historical fiction with *Ringan Gilhaize*. Three more historical novels, *The Spaewife: A Tale of the Scottish Chronicles* (1823), *Rothelan: A Romance of the English Histories* (1824), and *Southennan* (1830), failed to equal *Ringan Gilhaize*. Another fiction, *The Omen* (1826), a study of mind under stress.

Went to Canada in 1820s for company involved in settlement; *Lawrie Todd: or, The Settlers in the Woods* (1830) and *Bogle Corbet; or, The Emigrants* (1831) make use of North American experiences. Published biography of Byron (1830) and *The Lives of the Players* (1831); more novels, *The Member: An Autobiography* (1832) and *The Radical: An Autobiography* (1832), deal with themes of public life and private man; *Stanley Buxton; or The Schoolfellows* (1832) another study of English and Scottish provincial life. In 1832, suffered first of several paralysing strokes, but continued to work to support family. More fiction: *Eben Erskine; or, The Traveller* (1833), *The Stolen Child: A Tale of the Town* (1833), *The Ouranoulogos; or, The Celestial Volume* (1833; illustrated by John Martin), and *Stories of the Study* (1833), all dictated. Published autobiography (1833). Retired to family house in Greenock in 1834, where he died. Two posthumous volumes of tales, *The Howdie and Other Tales* and *A Rich Man and Other Stories*.

Galt, John, *Autobiography*, 2 vols (1833).

See:    Aberdein, J. W., *John Galt* (1936). (Biographical and critical study.)
   Frykman, E., *Galt's Scottish Stories* (Uppsala, 1959). (Sensitive critical study of most lasting fiction.)
   Parker, W. M., *Susan Ferrier and John Galt* (1965).
   Gordon, I. A., *John Galt: The Life of a Writer* (1972). (Authoritative biography focusing on Galt's literary activities.)
   Costain, K. M., 'Theoretical History and the Novel: the Scottish Fiction of John Galt', *ELH: A Journal of English Literary History*, 43 (1976), 342–65. (Important essay on Galt and Scottish Enlightenment.)
   Aldrich, R. I., *John Galt*, Twayne's English Authors, 231 (Boston, 1978). (General survey, concentrating on fiction.)
   Scott, P. H., *John Galt*, Scottish Writers Series (Edinburgh, 1985). (Critical study; concentrates on the Scottish novels.)

GODWIN, William (1756–1836), 7th of 13 children born at Wisbech to modestly circumstanced Dissenting minister and wife, daughter of a King's Lynn shipowner. Very bookish as child; well educated at schools in the country, at Norwich, and at Hoxton Dissenting Academy. After several unsuccessful attempts at ministry, settled around 1783 to life as professional author and intellectual, perhaps angling for political patronage. Wrote three novels for money in early 1780s, though they show serious interest in novel form: *Damon and Delia* (1784), *Italian Letters* (1784), and *Imogen: A Pastoral Romance* (1784). In 1780s met Thomas Holcroft, with whom he formed powerful and rich intellectual and literary association.

Their ideas appeared first in Holcroft's novel, *Anna St. Ives* (1792), and then in Godwin's treatise, *Enquiry Concerning Political Justice* (1793). Godwin's first major 'English Jacobin' novel, *Things As they Are; or, The Adventures of Caleb Williams* (1794), intended as exposé of evils of gentry hegemony and deficiencies of aristocratic culture of chivalry praised by Edmund Burke in *Reflections on the Revolution in France*. In 1794 and 1795 became involved in public controversy; during these years also had close friendships with several intellectual and literary women, including Elizabeth Inchbald, Mary Hays, Eliza Fenwick, Amelia Alderson (later Opie), and others. In 1796 met and fell in love with Mary Wollstonecraft. Her pregnancy led them to marry, though they regarded marriage as only an institution of property. A daughter born, later to become Mary Shelley; Wollstonecraft died of the complications of childbirth. Godwin's *Memoir* of her (1798) made them both marks for conservative obloquy. In 1799 published a 'historical romance', *St. Leon: A Tale of the Sixteenth Century*; tried his hand at plays that were Romantic versions of seventeenth-century Heroic Drama. Close friend of Charles Lamb and greatly influenced by Coleridge, then in the depths of 'abasement' to Wordsworth and his ideas. These influences show up not so much in Godwin's Enlightenment historiographical project, *The Life of Chaucer* (1803), as in his next novel, *Fleetwood; or, The New Man of Feeling* (1805). Remarried in 1802; by second wife had one son. Godwin and his wife began business publishing children's books. Intrusion into the family of young Percy Shelley, ardent admirer of Godwin's ideas, led to elopement of Shelley and young Mary Godwin. In 1817 published another novel of psychological aberration, *Mandeville: A Tale of the Seventeenth Century in England*; also engaged in controversy with Thomas Malthus on the population question. Published massive *History of the Commonwealth of England* (1824–28). In 1820s in increasing financial difficulties, caused by poor management of publishing business. In 1830s published several more books, including two novels, *Cloudesley: A Tale* (1830) and *Deloraine* (1833); *Thoughts on Man* (1831), a philosophical essay; and *Lives of the Necromancers* (1834). Died in London.

> *Godwin and Mary: Letters of William Godwin and Mary Wollstonecraft*, edited by R. M. Wardle (Lawrence, Kansas, 1967).
>
> Paul, C. Kegan, *William Godwin: His Friends and Contemporaries*, 2 vols (1876). (Still a valuable source of information, with extracts from many of Godwin's letters and journals.)
>
> Marshall, Peter H., *William Godwin* (New Haven and London, 1984). (Now the definitive biography.)

See: Grylls, R. G., *William Godwin and His World* (1953). (Lively and detailed study of Godwin in his political and social context.)

Pollin, B. R., *Education and Enlightenment in the Works of William Godwin* (New York, 1962). (Interesting study of sources and ideas.)

Smith, E. E. and E. G., *William Godwin*, Twayne's English Authors, 27 (New York, 1965).

Butler, M., *Jane Austen and the War of Ideas* (Oxford, 1975). (Has section on *Caleb Williams*.)

Kelly, G., *The English Jacobin Novel 1780–1805* (Oxford, 1976). (Has chapter on Godwin's novels.)

Locke, D., *A Fantasy of Reason: The Life and Thought of William Godwin* (1980).

Tysdal, B. J., *William Godwin as Novelist* (1981).

GORE, Lady Catherine (Moody) (1799–1861), born in Nottinghamshire, daughter of wine merchant. In 1823 married Captain Charles Gore of Life Guards, and from this time poured out stream of about seventy different works, consisting of nearly 200 volumes, including translations of French novels. First novel published in 1824, *Theresa Marchmont; or, The Maid of Honour*. In 1827 published *The Lettre de Cachet*. In 1831, began to write plays; also wrote popular parlour songs from late 1820s on. By this time, considered one of queens of 'silver-fork' novel, especially in such works as *The Manners of the Day; or, Women as They Are* (1830). In 1832, moved to France for a few years, but continued producing novels.

See:   Rosa, M. W., *The Silver-Fork School: Novels of Fashion Preceding 'Vanity Fair'* (New York, 1936).
       Anderson, Bonnie, 'The Writings of Catherine Gore', *Journal of Popular Culture*, 10 (1976), 404–23.

HAMILTON, Elizabeth (1758–1816), born at Belfast, youngest child of Scottish merchant; raised by father's sister after early death of parents; a studious child. Very close to brother Charles and kept up correspondence with him while he was in India; touched deeply by his death in 1792. In 1796 published Anti-Jacobin novel, *Letters of a Hindoo Rajah*, followed by another, *Memoirs of Modern Philosophers* (1800), which includes satire on contemporary middle-class feminism and feminists, such as Mary Wollstonecraft. In 1801, published *Letters on the Elementary Principles of Education*; in 1804, *Memoirs of the Life of Agrippina, the Wife of Germanicus*, antiquarian, historical footnote novel. In 1806 published *Letters Addressed to the Daughter of a Nobleman, on the Formation of the Religious and Moral Principle*. In 1808 wrote moral-didactic tale on Scottish provincial life, *The Cottagers of Glenburnie*, widely read for several decades. In 1809 wrote *Exercises in Religious Knowledge* for inmates of Female House of Industry in Edinburgh, which she helped to found. Died at Harrogate.

       Benger, E. O., *Memoirs of the Late Mrs. Elizabeth Hamilton, with a Selection from Her Correspondence and Other Unpublished Writings* (1818).

HAYS, Mary (1759/60–1843), one of several sisters in Dissenting family; father died some time in later 1770s; largely self-educated. After fiancé died, associated and corresponded with leading liberal Dissenters; published pamphlet on public worship (1792). Enthusiastically embraced Wollstonecraft's *Vindication of the Rights of Woman*; knew Godwin circle and Romantic poets and writers such as Coleridge and Charles Lamb; also knew many women writers, including Wollstonecraft, Elizabeth Inchbald, Amelia Alderson (later Opie), Anna Laetitia Barbauld, and others. In 1793 published *Letters and Essays, Moral and Miscellaneous*, which includes some pieces of fiction and essay on novel reading. In 1796 published partly autobiographical novel on problems of autonomous selfhood for intelligent, cultivated women, *Memoirs of Emma Courtney*. In same year, responsible for bringing Wollstonecraft and Godwin together. Second novel, *The Victim of Prejudice* (1799), again sets self against society and again tries to find authentic rhetoric of female subjectivity, passion, and desire. In 1803 published *Female Biography*, attempt to argue against trivialization of women in society past and present. In 1821 published a similar project, *Memoirs of Queens, Illustrious and Celebrated*.

*The Love Letters of Mary Hays (1779–1780)*, edited by A. F. Wedd (1925).

See:   Tompkins, J. M. S., 'Mary Hays, Philosophess', in *The Polite Marriage* (Cambridge, 1938).
Adams, M. Ray, 'Mary Hays, Disciple of William Godwin', *Publications of the Modern Language Association*, 55 (1940), 472–83.

HOFLAND, Barbara (1770–1844), born in Sheffield, daughter of prosperous iron dealer; he died in 1773, leaving widow to bring up daughter and son. Mother re-married; taken into care of aunt; well educated. First published work in new liberal Sheffield newspaper, *The Iris*. By 1795 running her own milliner's shop in Sheffield. Married Thomas Hoole; Sheffield businessman. He died of consumption in 1799 and his business collapsed soon after. Determined to support herself; turned to writing; fell back on teaching, from 1807 to 1809. Writing career developed rapidly. *The History of an Officer's Widow, and Her Young Family* (1809) sold well. In 1810 married Thomas Hofland, son of an industrialist but educated to be a gentleman; his father's bankruptcy forced him, like his wife, to turn to the arts for a profession. In 1811 they moved to London to that end. In 1812 she had five books published, including *The Son of a Genius*, explicitly attacking Romantic culture and Romantic individualism. Books appeared in steady flow, with relentless pursuit of whatever was selling at the time: *Iwanowna; or, The Maid of Moscow* (1813), *A Father As He Should Be: A Novel* (1815), *Patience and Perseverance; or, The Modern Griselda: A Domestic Tale* (1813), and *The Blind Farmer and His Children* (1816), all of which were in Hofland's line of specialization, the 'domestic tale'. In 1820s continued to develop various forms of the tale, especially the tale for youth and the tale based on a moral abstraction: *Theodore; or, The Crusaders: A Tale for Youth* (1821) and *Adelaide; or, The Intrepid Daughter* (1823), both published by new leader in books for children and youths, John Harris; *Integrity: A Tale* (1823), and other similar works. By 1820s widely respected as a moral writer but by later 1820s struggling to keep up with fiction market; son died in 1833 and husband's health deteriorated; published some triple-decker novels.

Ramsay, Thomas, *The Life and Literary Remains of Barbara Hofland* (1849).

HOGG, James (1770–1835), son of Selkirkshire tenant farmer in poor circumstances; had little formal schooling; worked as shepherd. Mother was one of Scott's sources for popular ballads. In the 1790s began to write verse; in 1801 published first collection, *Scottish Pastorals, Poems, Songs*; main interest at this time still farming. Scott became friend and advisor. Published *The Mountain Bard* (1807). Failed as sheep farmer and moved to Edinburgh in 1810 to try luck at literature; published *The Queen's Wake: A Legendary Poem* (1813), his most successful poem; displayed remarkable ability to compose pastiches of whatever was doing well in poetry market. In 1817 involved in scandal of so-called 'Chaldee Manuscript' that enabled Tory *Blackwood's Magazine* to establish itself; from then on regular contributor to 'Maga', as it was familiarly known. First novel, *The Brownie of Bodsbeck* (1818), attempt to counter Scott's portrayal of Covenanters in *Old Mortality* (1816). In 1820 married and enjoyed happy and nourishing domestic life, though it cost him continual literary labour to support it; unlucky in dealings with book trade and over-confident as farmer. Published *Winter Evening Tales* in 1820, more poems, and two more unusual novels, *The Three Perils of Man* (1822) and *The Three Perils of Woman* (1823), both of which set popular culture of 'superstition' against rationalist Enlightenment discourses of narrative and historiography. Last novel, The Private Memoirs and Confessions of a Justified Sinner (1824). Visited London for first time in 1832; treated as literary lion. Published *The Shepherd's Calendar* (1829), *Songs, By the Ettrick Shepherd* (1831), *Altrive Tales* (1832), and memoir of Scott (1834), as well as other books and pieces.

> Hogg, James, *Memoir of the Author's Life* and *Familiar Anecdotes of Sir Walter Scott*, edited by D. S. Mack (Edinburgh and London, 1972). (The first of these is Hogg's autobiography, originally published 1807 and expanded several times thereafter.)
>
> Strout, A. L., *Life and Letters of James Hogg*, vol. I (only one published; Lubbock Texas, 1946). (Detailed, scholarly biography, covering years 1770 to 1825.)
>
> Parr, Norah, *James Hogg at Home* (Dollar, 1980). (Charming portrait of the domestic man.)

See: Batho, E. C., *The Ettrick Shepherd* (Cambridge, 1927; reprinted New York, 1969). (Biographical and critical, with extensive bibliography.)

> Simpson, L., *James Hogg: A Critical Study* (Edinburgh, 1962).
>
> Gifford, D., *James Hogg* (Edinburgh, 1976). (Stimulating critical essay on the major works.)
>
> Smith, Nelson C., *James Hogg*, Twayne's English Authors, 311 (Boston, 1980).

HOLCROFT, Thomas (1745–1809), like Hogg, a 'writer sprung from the people'; born in London, son of shoemaker and pedlar; no formal education. In 1757, became stable-boy at Newmarket; in 1761 returned to London to work in father's shoemaker's stall. Briefly taught reading in Liverpool; married for first time in 1765; contributed to *Whitehall Evening Post*; tried to set up school in the country. By 1771 a 'strolling' actor. After first wife's death married again in 1772; second wife also died, leaving him with daughter from first marriage and young son; married again in 1777. Wrote for various magazines; turned dramatist, and from then on a prolific author, producing plays, translations, periodical essays, novels, histories, and reviews, as well as editing various publications. In 1780s developed radical views on politics and religion. Met William Godwin and began life-long intellectual partnership. In 1790s associated with Godwin, Paine, Joel Barlow, David Williams, Mary Wollstonecraft, and other radicals. An avid amateur musician and collector of paintings and books. In 1792 published *Anna St. Ives*, novel in letters. In 1794, arrested for treason; the charge dropped. Son committed suicide. Published another novel, *The Adventures of Hugh Trevor*, satirical social-survey novel, in pseudo-autobiographical form. Continued to write plays, and helped introduce German melodrama, or 'music-drama', to England. In 1799 married Louise Mercier and, in financial difficulties, moved to Germany; returned to London in 1803; published final novel, *Memoirs of Bryan Perdue*. Like Godwin, now a marginal and obscure figure, as man and writer. Holcroft one of the great English auto-didacts, as his colleague Godwin was one of the outstanding products of formal intellectual education in late eighteenth-century England.

*Memoirs*, completed by William Hazlitt, 3 vols (1816); edited by Elbridge Colby as *The Life of Holcroft*, 2 vols (1925).

See: Baine, R. M., *Holcroft and the Revolutionary Novel* (Athens, Georgia, 1965).
Steeves, H. R., *Before Jane Austen* (1966).
Kelly, G., *The English Jacobin Novel 1700–1805* (Oxford, 1976). (Has a chapter on Holcroft.)

HOOK, Theodore (1788–1841), humourist, novelist, and socialite; probably the most amusing man in Britain in his lifetime; born in London, son of theatrical composer and song-writer. Composed songs and writing for the theatre. Quickly gained reputation as brilliant conversationalist, charming socializer, and man about town. Obtained government job in Mauritius, but mismanagement led to his disgrace, financial ruin, and imprisonment for debt on return to England. From 1820 to his death edited *John Bull*, type of scurrilous, satirical magazine with which these years abounded. Published nine very successful stories under general title *Sayings and Doings* (1824–28). Created problems for himself by not marrying the woman with whom he lived and who bore him five children. Published more novels, combining elements of romance plot, picaresque adventures, and scenes of 'silver-fork society', as in *Maxwell* (1830).

Lockhart, J. G., memoir of Hook in *Quarterly Review*, 72 (May 1843), 53–108.

See: Brightfield, M. F., *Theodore Hook and His Novels* (Cambridge, Mass., 1928).

HOPE, Thomas (1769–1831), son of rich Amsterdam merchant. Studied architecture, travelled throughout the Mediterranean, became a freethinker and liberal, and settled in England with his family when Holland was invaded by French in 1796. Tried by lavish hospitality to gain acceptance in fashionable society; soon became major art patron and collector; leader in the Greek Revival in the arts and in taste for Egyptian styles; published books on art, architecture, and costume. Married daughter of Archbishop of Tuam. His one novel, *Anastasius; or, The Memoirs of a Greek* (1819), was thought by many to have been written by Byron, and Byron said that he wished he had written it.

See: Watkin, D., *Thomas Hope 1769–1831 and the Neo-Classical Idea* (1968).

INCHBALD, Elizabeth (1753–1821), daughter of Suffolk farmer; raised as Roman Catholic; largely self-educated; ran away from home in her mid-teens and became an actress. Married the actor and painter Joseph Inchbald; they did not have children; toured together in various provincial companies; she specialized in comic and sentimental roles. Left a widow in 1779; refused several offers of marriage and maintained a reputation for chastity uncommon to both men and women in the theatre at that time. In 1784 first play was produced. Through the latter 1780s reworking a novel in letters, recast as a third-person narrative and published as *A Simple Story* in 1791; in completing it she was advised by her close friends William Godwin and Thomas Holcroft. It is a novel of domestic and psychological realism, and a study of moral, erotic, and psychological power struggle within a domestic relationship represented as at once paternal and filial and erotic. Second and last novel, *Nature and Art* (1796), more explicitly political. Godwin proposed to her in the early 1790s, but she refused him. Continued to write successful plays, usually sentimental comedies with edge of social criticism, but by early 1800s living in more or less quiet retirement. Wrote autobiography, but destroyed it as too worldly; in last years became religiose.

> Boaden, J., *Memoirs of Mrs. Inchbald*, 2 vols (1833). (Detailed but superficial biography.)
> Littlewood, S. R., *Mrs. Inchbald and Her Circle* (1921).

See: Mackee, W., *Elizabeth Inchbald, Novelist* (Washington, 1935).
> Kelly, G., *The English Jacobin Novel 1780–1805* (Oxford, 1976). (Has a chapter on Inchbald's novels.)
> Rogers, K. M., 'Inhibitions on Eighteenth-Century Women Novelists: Elizabeth Inchbald and Charlotte Smith', *Eighteenth-Century Studies*, 11 (1977).

LAMB, Lady Caroline (1785–1828), only daughter of Earl of Bessborough; raised in centre of fashionable Whig aristocracy during one of its most glittering and decadent periods; as a child spent six years in Italy; an omnivorous reader, especially of novels; showed early signs of eccentric character and psychological instability. In 1805 married Hon. William Lamb, but became involved with and obsessed by Lord Byron. The affair showed clearly the contradictions of upper-class code of amorous gallantry, especially in relation to treatment of women. Transformed her experience into *Glenarvon* (1816); second novel, *Graham Hamilton* (1822), different in form but similar in theme; last novel, *Ada Reis: A Tale* (1823), an extravaganza of Romantic orientalism. Problem of coherent personal identity, especially for women, major issue in her life as in her novels. Continued to cause stir in fashionable society, though husband remained fondly devoted to her. Died at Melbourne House, Whitehall, London.

> Cecil, Lord David, *The Young Melbourne, and the Story of His Marriage with Caroline Lamb* (1939).
> Jenkins, Elizabeth, *Lady Caroline Lamb* (1932; reprinted 1972).
> Blyth, H., *Caro – The Fatal Passion: The Life of Lady Caroline Lamb* (1972).

LAMB, Charles (1775–1834), born in London, son of domestic servant; early education modest; attended Christ's Hospital school; in 1792 apprenticed clerk of East India Company; stayed with Company for rest of working life. In 1790s became associated with young Romantic writers; published poems with Coleridge (1796) and with Charles Lloyd (1798). In 1796 sister Mary stabbed their mother to death in fit of temporary insanity. Between 1799 and 1825 lived quietly with sister, and wrote fictionalized versions of the classics, for children, such as *The Adventures of Ulysses* (1808) and, with sister, *Tales from Shakespeare* (1807); together they also wrote *Mrs. Leicester's School* (1809) for young people. In 1820 began contributing to *London Magazine* essays by which he is known as a major Romantic writer. In 1825 retired from East India Company to a comfortable independence.

> *The Letters of Charles Lamb, to which Are Added those of His Sister Mary Lamb*, edited by E. V. Lucas, 3 vols (1935).

*The Letters of Charles and Mary Anne Lamb*, edited by E. W. Marrs, 3 vols (1976–77).

Barnett, G. L., *Charles Lamb: The Evolution of Elia* (Bloomington, 1964).

Courtney, W. F., *Young Charles Lamb 1775–1802* (1982).

Cecil, Lord David, *A Portrait of Charles Lamb* (1983).

See: Randel, F. V., *The World of Elia: Charles Lamb's Essayistic Romanticism* (1975).

Monsman, G. C., *Confessions of a Prosaic Dreamer* (Durham, North Carolina, 1984).

LATHOM, Francis (1777–1832), born at Norwich, supposedly bastard son of nobleman, for he received annual stipend of £400 throughout his life. First wrote plays for Norwich theatre and a few novels, but then retired (was banished?) to rural Scotland; pursued life of local eccentric, drank whiskey, sang songs he wrote himself, dressed as an actor, and wrote string of novels through the next three decades, in main varieties of the novel of the day, but his 'Gothic romances' best known. At time of his death training some Scottish rural labourers as actors and had set up rural theatre. A few of his many novels are: *The Midnight Bell: A German Story* (1798); *Astonishment!!! A Romance of a Century Ago* (1802); *The Impenetrable Secret: Find It Out! A Novel* (1805); *The Romance of the Hebrides; or, Wonders Never Cease!* (1809); *Italian Mysteries; or, More Secrets than One: A Romance* (1820); *The Polish Bandit; or, Who Is My Bride? and Other Tales* (1824); *Young John Bull; or, Born Abroad and Bred at Home* (1828); and *Fashionable Mysteries; or, The Rival Duchesses and Other Tales* (1829).

LE NOIR, Elizabeth (1755?–1841), daughter of Christopher Smart, clergyman and early Romantic poet; mother was step-daughter of John Newbery, publisher of children's books. After Smart's death in debtor's prison in 1770, Newbery gave employment to Mrs Smart and her two daughters in office of *The Reading Mercury*; he then left this newspaper to Elizabeth and her sister when he died. In 1795 married French *émigré*. Gained interest and advice of Fanny Burney's father, who helped her publish one of her novels. In 1804 published *Village Anecdotes; or, The Journal of a Year, from Sophia to Edward*, and, in 1808, *Clara de Montfier: A Moral Tale*, novels of domestic realism and rural life.

LEWIS, Matthew Gregory (1775–1818), born in London, son of highly placed and wealthy civil servant and owner of West Indies estates; mother was cultivated daughter of baronet well connected at court. Lewis well educated at Westminster School, London, and Christ Church, Oxford; while at school, his parents separated; in 1794 began work as British Embassy attaché in The Hague and while there completed *The Monk* (1796). It caused sensation with reading public and conferred on him his nickname. After return to England held a seat in Parliament from 1796 to 1802. Turned to writing for theatre and achieved huge success with *The Castle Spectre* (1798). Had extensive literary social connections. On death of father in 1812, inherited sizeable fortune. In 1815 went to West Indies estates to institute reforms in treatment of slaves; published a book on his experiences. In 1816 spent time travelling on the continent; met Shelley and Byron. Undertook second journey to Jamaica in 1817 but died on return journey and buried at sea.

Peck, L. F., *A Life of Matthew G. Lewis* (Cambridge, Mass., 1961).

See:    Parreaux, A., *The Publication of* The Monk: *A Literary Event* (Paris, 1960).

Irwin, J. J., *M. G. 'Monk' Lewis*, Twayne's English Authors, 198 (Boston, 1976).

Conger, S. M., *Matthew G. Lewis, Charles Robert Maturin, and the Germans: An Interpretive Study of the Influence of German Literature on two Gothic Novels* (Salzburg, 1977).

LOCKHART, John Gibson (1794–1854), son of Presbyterian minister; well educated by father; entered Glasgow University in 1805; went on to Balliol College, Oxford. Returned to Glasgow in 1813; studied law in Edinburgh, but had little taste for it, preferring literary society. Contributed to *Blackwood's Magazine* when it was getting started, having a knack for burlesque and satire; published satirical novel about Edinburgh society, *Peter's Letters to his Kinsfolk* (1819). In 1818 met Scott and in 1820 married Scott's elder daughter, Sophia. In 1821 published historical novel, *Valerius: A Roman Story*; turned to more psychological kind of fiction with *Reginald Dalton: A Story of University Life* (1823). In 1822 published short novel of passion and transgression in life of Presbyterian minister, *Some Passages in the Life of Mr. Adam Blair*. Last novel, *The History of Matthew Wald*, published in 1824. In 1825 appointed editor of Tory *Quarterly Review* and moved to London. In 1828 published *Life of Burns*. After father-in-law's death, wrote biography of him. Deaths of his wife and several children darkened last years. Buried at feet of Sir Walter Scott in precincts of Dryburgh Abbey.

Lang, Andrew, *The Life and Letters of John Gibson Lockhart*, 2 vols (1897). (Detailed biography; includes many letters.)
Lochhead, M., *John Gibson Lockhart* (1954).

See:    Macbeth, G., *John Gibson Lockhart: A Critical Study*, University of Illinois Studies in Language and Literature, 17, nos 3–4 (Urbana Illinois, 1935). (Informative general survey of Lockhart's writings.)
Hart, R., *Lockhart as Romantic Biographer* (Edinburgh, 1971). (Indirectly illuminates Lockhart's own novels and Romantic psychological fiction in general.)

MATURIN, Charles Robert (1782–1824), born in Dublin, son of civil servant; educated at Trinity College, Dublin, and in 1803 ordained in Anglican Church of Ireland. Married in 1803; two years later became curate in Dublin, but like so many Romantic curates and vicars had literary tastes and ambitions. First novel, *Fatal Revenge; or, The Family of Montorio* (1807) published under pseudonym Dennis Jasper Murphy; *The Wild Irish Boy* (1808) attempted to cash in on success of Lady Morgan's *Wild Irish Girl* (1806). Always had to write for money. Published *The Milesian Chief* (1812), another 'national tale', then, through interposition of Scott and Byron, Maturin's play *Betram* produced by Kean in London in 1816; a great financial success. Another play, *Manuel* (1817); another novel, *Women; or, Pour et Contre* (1818); *Fredolfo*, a tragedy (1819); *Sermons* (1819), attacking Catholicism (one of the continuing themes of his fiction and plays); *Melmoth the Wanderer* (1820); and *The Albigenses* (1824), another novel. Died in Dublin in 1824, exhausted and despairing of escape from literary drudgery.

> The Correspondence of Sir Walter Scott and Charles Robert Maturin,
> edited by E. Ratchford and William H. McCarthy (Austin, Texas,
> 1937).

See:   Idman, N., *Charles Robert Maturin: His Life and Works* (Helsinki,
       1923).
       Kramer, Dale, *Charles Robert Maturin*, Twayne's English Authors,
       156 (New York, 1973).
       Fierobe, C., *Charles Robert Maturin (1780–1824): l'homme et l'œuvre*
       (Lille and Paris, 1974). (Detailed biographical and critical study.)
       Lougy, R. E., *Charles Maturin* (Lewisburg Pennsylvania, 1975).
       (Brief critical survey.)
       Conger, S. M., *Matthew G. Lewis, Charles Robert Maturin and the
       Germans: An Interpretive Study of the Influence of German Literature on
       two Gothic Novels* (Salzburg, 1977).
       Scott, Shirley C., *Myths of Consciousness in the Novels of Charles
       Maturin* (New York, 1980).

MOORE, John (1729–1802), born at Stirling, son of Presbyterian minister;
attended Glasgow University and apprenticed to surgeon. Made surgeon's
mate in Scottish regiment in 1747. Following active service went to Paris;
toured briefly with another Scottish medical man, Tobias Smollett. Set up
practice in Glasgow; married in 1757. Toured Europe for five years as
companion of Young Duke of Hamilton. In 1777 moved to London, and
in 1779 published *A View of Society and Manners in France, Switzerland, and
Germany*. In 1781 published a sequel, *A View of Society and Manners in
Italy*. In late 1780s became acquainted with Robert Burns. Also close friend
of Burney family and knew many other leading writers and intellectuals.
First novel, *Zeluco: Various Views of Human Nature, Taken from Life and
Manners, Foreign and Domestic* (1789). In 1792 went to France; wrote two
books about experiences there. In 1796 published second novel, *Edward:
Various Views of Human Nature, Taken from Life and Manners, Chiefly in
England*. In 1799 wrote biography of Smollett, with history of the novel,
printed with Moore's edition of Smollett's works. In 1800 published third
novel, this time in epistolary form, *Mordaunt: Sketches of Life, Character,
and Manners in Various Countries, Including the Memoirs of a French Lady of
Quality*. By now health failing; died at Richmond, Surrey.

> Memoir of Moore, by John Anderson, published with *The Works of
> John Moore, M. D.*, 7 vols (Edinburgh, 1820), vol. 1.
> Oman, Carola, *Sir John Moore* (1953). (Contains biographical
> information on Dr John Moore, General Sir John Moore's father.)

MORE, Hannah (1745–1833), born in Gloucestershire; father educated for clergy;
his expectations of inheriting an estate disappointed by a law-suit; then
became schoolmaster and married a farmer's daughter; Hannah fourth of
his five daughters. Well educated; with sisters ran boarding-school in
Bristol for daughters of professional classes and gentry; began writing
poems, plays, and translations. In early twenties jilted by an older
gentleman. In 1774 visited London and met Johnson's circle; a play, *Percy*
(1777), produced in London. In 1780s began associating with prominent
Anglican Evangelicals; in late 1780s and early 1790s published several
books attacking fashionable society and calling for commitment to
Christianity and social leadership. Took up Sunday school education of

poor as way to achieve greater social control of rural common people. In 1792 published chapbook, *Village Politics*, designed to show newly literate labouring people dangers of Jacobinism; in 1795 devised extensive project of chapbooks and broadsides, Cheap Repository, promoting Evangelical religion and social ideas and attacking every major aspect of traditional oral and print culture. Cheap Repository superseded by Religious Tract Society. After 1800 led a quieter life; in the late 1790s and early 1800s wrote books on education of women. In 1809, took on circulating-library novel and wrote her one novel, *Cœlebs in Search of a Wife*. Joined in other Evangelical crusades, such as anti-slavery campaign.

> Roberts, William, *Memoirs and Correspondence of Mrs. Hannah More*, 4 vols (1834). (The standard hagiography.)
> *Letters of Hannah More*, edited by R. B. Johnson (1925).
> Hopkins, M. A., *Hannah More and Her Circle* (New York and Toronto, 1947).
> Jones, Mary G., *Hannah More* (Cambridge, 1952). (Mainly biographical, but has a brief chapter on Cheap Repository, and considers More's other writings.)

See:    Pickering, Sam, 'The Cheap Repository Tracts and the Short Story', *Studies in Short Fiction*, 12 (1975), 15–21.
Pickering, Sam, 'Hannah More's *Cœlebs in Search of a Wife* and the Respectability of the Novel in the Nineteenth Century', *Neuphilologische Mitteilungen*, 78 (1977), 78–85.

MORGAN: see Owenson

MORIER, James (1780?–1849), born at what is now Izmir in Turkey into family of wealthy Levant merchants and diplomats; educated at Harrow, but joined father at Constantinople and entered diplomatic service in 1807. Published two lively and authoritative accounts of diplomatic missions to Persia (1812 and 1818). Retired with pension in 1817 and spent rest of life as society figure, amateur artist, collector, and novelist. Most successful novel was *The Adventures of Hajjî Baba, of Ispahan* (1824), followed by *The Adventures of Hajjî Baba in England* (1828). Other novels are mostly oriental tales and include *Zohrab the Hostage* (1832), *Ayesha, the Maid of Kars* (1834), *Abel Allnutt* (1837), *An Oriental Tale* (1839), *The Adventures of Tom Spicer* (1840), *The Mirza* (1841), *Misselmah: A Persian Tale* (1847), and *Martin Troutrond* (1849). Died at Brighton.

OPIE, Amelia (1769–1853), born at Norwich; father a Norwich doctor and Dissenter. Well educated; began publishing short poems. Mother died. Published a novel in 1790, *The Dangers of Coquetry*. In 1790s closely connected with English Jacobins in both Norwich and London, including William Godwin and Mary Wollstonecraft. Wrote some plays. In 1798 married painter John Opie; they did not have children; he died in 1807 and his widow returned to Norwich to keep house for her father. Published successful one volume tale, *The Father and Daughter* (1801). Published novel based on relation of Godwin and Wollstonecraft, *Adeline Mowbray* (1804), then a series of novels and collections of tales – *Simple Tales* (1806), *Temper; or, Domestic Scenes: A Tale* (1812), *Tales of Real Life* (1813), *Valentine's Eve* (1816), *New Tales* (1818), *Tales of the Heart* (1820), and *Madeline: A Tale* (1822). Friendship with the Quaker, Joseph John Gurney, led to her joining Society of Friends in 1825; henceforth published only didactic tales for youth and spent much time in philanthropic work, including anti-slavery movements. Died at Norwich and buried in her father's grave.

> Brightwell, Cecilia L., *Memorials of the Life of Amelia Opie* (Norwich and London, 1854). (Contains many letters; emphasizes Opie's conversion to Quakerism.)
> Macgregor, Margaret E., *Amelia Alderson Opie: Worldling and Friend*, Smith College Studies in Modern Languages, 14 (Northampton Mass., 1932–33). (Contains detailed bibliography.)
> Menzies-Wilson, Jacobine, and Helen Lloyd, *Amelia: The Tale of a Plain Friend* (1937).

OWENSON, Sydney, Lady Morgan (1783?–1859), eldest child of Irish actor and singer. Father had thorough knowledge of native Irish culture and music, passed on to his daughter. Raised in Dublin; often in company of father's theatrical friends. In 1801 first volume of poems published; turned to fiction: *St. Clair; or, the Heiress of Desmond* (1803), lyrical, epistolary novel of passion, influenced by Rousseau and Bernardin de St Pierre. Next novel, *The Novice of St. Dominick* (1805), a 'historical romance' set in France during reign of Henri IV. *The Wild Irish Girl: A National Tale* (1806) became rage of season and subject of considerable political controversy in Dublin because of its nationalist sentiments. Became literary lion as symbol of Ireland, carrying her harp from one fashionable assembly to another and known as 'the Wild Irish Girl' after her fictional heroine. Wrote an opera; published more 'Irish' verse; in 1809, inspired by éclat of Mme de Staël's *Corinne* (1807), wrote another 'national tale', *Woman; or, Ida of Athens*; went further afield, to India, for next fiction, *The Missionary: An Indian Tale* (1811). Became member of household of Marquis of Abercorn; mingled freely with fashionable society; in 1812 married Abercorn's surgeon, Thomas Morgan. In 1814 published *O'Donnel: A National Tale*, which earned £550, and in 1818 *Florence Macarthy: An Irish Tale*, which earned £1200. Published in the *New Monthly Magazine* a long essay on topical subject of Catholic emancipation and the Irish question. In 1827 published another novel, *The O'Briens and the O'Flahertys: A National Tale*; in 1829 published series of autobiographical sketches, *The Book of the Boudoir*. In 1833 professed to abandon plot and narration and published collection of novellas in dialogue form, *Dramatic Scenes from Real Life*. A historical novel, *The Princess; or, The Beguine*, published 1835. In 1837 received government pension for services to literature, first such pension given to a woman. In 1839 moved from Dublin to London; pursued social life to exclusion of writing, but in 1840 published another novel, *Woman and Her Master*. Husband died in 1843. At death left estate of over £15,000.

> *Lady Morgan's Memoirs: Autobiography, Diaries, and Correspondence*, edited by W. H. Dixon, 2 vols (1863; reprinted New York, 1975).
> Stevenson, Lionel, *The Wild Irish Girl: The Life of Sydney Owenson, Lady Morgan* (1936).

PEACOCK, Thomas Love (1785–1866), born in Weymouth, son of London glass merchant, who died when Peacock only three; mother was daughter of sailor, and vigorously encouraged Peacock's literary interests; moved to London when Peacock sixteen. Published verse in early 1800s; suffered disappointment in love in 1807; worked briefly as secretary for Navy; in

1810 and 1812 spent much time in North Wales. Published several more volumes of poetry in 1810s, some of it satirical. In 1812 met Shelley, most important friendship of his life. Thought of starting a school; arrested for debt after a love affair; received financial help from Shelley; considered emigrating to Canada. Began publishing satirical novels with *Headlong Hall* (1815; dated 1816); the others are *Melincourt* (1817), *Nightmare Abbey* (1818), *Maid Marian* (1822), *The Misfortunes of Elphin* (1829), *Crotchet Castle* (1831), and, many years later, *Gryll Grange* (1861). In 1819 joined East India Company and became their chief examiner of correspondence in 1836, succeeding James Mill. In 1820 married Jane Gryffydh, by whom he had four children; death of one child led to Jane having a nervous breakdown, and she was psychologically unstable for much of rest of her life. Also in 1820 Peacock published 'The Four Ages of Poetry', which inspired Shelley's 'Defense of Poetry'. In 1820s and 1830s devoted much attention to use of steamships for warfare and commerce. In mid-1820s channelled economic and social views into series of satirical poems, published in 1837 as *Paper Money Lyrics*. Also wrote essays on opera and food, two of his consuming interests. Later contributed articles to *Fraser's Magazine*, including important *Memoirs of Shelley*. Daughter married poet and novelist George Meredith, but marriage not a happy one. Peacock a life-long lover of Thames and its valley, and he lived there, at Halliford, most of his life.

See:   Stewart, J. I. M., *Thomas Love Peacock* (1963). (Brief, brisk critical study, concentrating on the novels.)
Dawson, C., *His Fine Wit: A Study of Thomas Love Peacock* (1970). (Detailed biographical and critical study.)
Butler, Marilyn, *Peacock Displayed: A Satirist in His Context* (1979). (Concentrates on the novels; rich detail of their intellectual context.)
Burns, Bryan, *The Novels of Thomas Love Peacock* (London and Sydney, 1985).

PORTER, Jane (1776–1850) and Anna (1780–1832), born at Durham, daughters of surgeon in regiment of dragoons; Anna born just after her father's death. Educated together in Edinburgh. Both sisters resolved to become writers and in 1790s Anna already writing tales. In 1797 she published *Walsh Colville* and in 1798 *Octavia*. By 1803 family settled in London, partly to further Robert Ker Porter's studies as painter. Jane's novel, *Thaddeus of Warsaw* (1803), very successful and made her a European reputation. It centres on Polish struggle for political independence, then a topical subject. Anna published some poetry, then two successful novels of her own, *The Hungarian Brothers* (1807), and *Don Sebastian; or, The House of Braganza* (1809), a 'historical romance'. In 1810 Jane scored her greatest literary success in Britain with Scottish 'historical romance', or 'biographical romance', as she preferred to call it, *The Scottish Chiefs*, based on life of Sir William Wallace, liberator of Scotland. In 1814 Anna published another novel, *The Recluse of Norway*, and in 1815 Jane published *The Pastor's Fireside*. Anna continued publishing romances – *The Knight of St. John* (1817), *The Fast of St. Magdalen* (1818), *The Village of Mariendorpt* (1821), *Roche-Blanche; or, The Hunter of the Pyrenees* (1822), *Honor O'Hara* (1826), and *The Barony* (1830). Meanwhile, Jane tried writing for theatre, without great success. Through his librarian, novel-loving George IV suggested subject for a romance to Jane; she dutifully produced *Duke Christian of Luneburg; or, Traditions of the Harz* (1824). Together the sisters

produced *Tales Round a Winter Hearth* in 1826 and *Coming Out* in 1828.
Both sisters contributed to the fashionable literary annuals of the 1820s.
Mother died in 1831; Anna died of typhus at Bristol in 1832. By 1840s,
Jane a venerable figure with international literary reputation.

> Hall, A. M., 'Memories of Miss Jane Porter', *Art Journal*, 12 (1850).
> (Interesting biographical sketch of both Porter sisters.)
> Wilson, Mona, *These Were Muses* (1924). (Contains sketch of life of
> Jane Porter.)

See: Hook, A. D., 'Jane Porter, Sir Walter Scott, and the Historical
Novel', *Clio*, 5 (1976), 181–92.

RADCLIFFE, Ann (1764–1823), born in London, daughter of haberdasher; his
wife had slightly higher social background. Most of childhood spent with
well-to-do relatives; may have attended school of Harriet and Sophia Lee
at Bath. Read widely, both in classics and more modern authors, and
knew something of art and music. In 1787 married William Radcliffe,
Oxford graduate and student of law; he did not practise law, but turned to
journalism and became proprietor and editor of *English Chronicle*. She
began writing as diversion; first novel, *The Castles of Athlin and Dunbayne:
A Highland Story*, appeared in 1789, followed by *A Sicilian Romance* (1790),
*The Romance of The Forest: Interspersed with some Pieces of Poetry* (1791), *The
Mysteries of Udolpho: A Romance, Interspersed with some Pieces of Poetry*
(1794), and *The Italian; or, The Confessional of the Black Penitents: A
Romance* (1797). This was, effectively, the end of her career as an author,
though after her death another novel was published, *Gaston de Blondeville;
or, The Court of Henry III keeping Festival in Ardenne: A Romance* [and] *St.
Alban's Abbey: A Metrical Tale; with some Poetical Pieces* (1826). Life almost
entirely private and domestic, and avoided literary circles and notoriety.
Spent good deal of time from 1790s on travelling around country with her
husband, and kept copious journals of these tours, one of which, *A Journey
Made in the Summer of 1794* (1795), was published. Died in London.

> Talfourd, Thomas Noon, 'Memoir' of Ann Radcliffe, in *Gaston de
> Blondeville* (1826). (Main source of information about Radcliffe's
> life and character; includes extracts from her travel journals.)

See: McIntyre, Clara, *Ann Radcliffe in Relation to her Time*, Yale Studies
in English, 62 (New Haven, Conn., 1920).
Ware, M., *Sublimity in the Novels of Ann Radcliffe: A Study of the
Influence upon Her Craft of Edmund Burke's Enquiry into the Origins of
Our Ideas of the Sublime and Beautiful*, Essays and Studies on
English Language and Literature, 25 (Uppsala and Copenhagen,
1963).
Murray, E. B., *Ann Radcliffe*, Twayne's English Authors, 149 (New
York, 1972).
Cottom, Daniel, *The Civilized Imagination: A Study of Ann Radcliffe,
Jane Austen, and Sir Walter Scott* (Cambridge, 1985).

ROBINSON, Mary (1758–1800), born Mary Darby in Bristol; educated in
Bristol at school run by Hannah More and her sisters, and at schools in
Chelsea. Married an articled clerk in 1774; husband neglected her and she
was pursued by various fashionable men about town. Published volume of
poems in 1775 and acted at Drury Lane. Often put in parts in which she
was disguised as a man, allowing her striking figure to be clearly seen by

the audience. As Perdita in *The Winter's Tale* seen by Prince of Wales, whose agents negotiated a settlement for her in exchange for her becoming his mistress. The Prince tired of her quickly and did not pay what he had agreed; then made the subject of numerous satires and cartoons. 'Perdita', as she was now known, turned to writing, and published a few poems before she hit public taste with series of novels of manners and sentiment in the 1790s. Novels written by or attributed to her are *Vancenza; or, The Dangers of Credulity* (1792); *The Shrine of Bertha* (1794); *The Widow; or, A Picture of Modern Times* (1794); *Angelina: A Novel* (1796); *Hubert de Sevrac: A Romance of the Eighteenth Century* (1797); *Walsingham; or, The Pupil of Nature* (1797); *The Natural Daughter* (1799); and *The False Friend: A Domestic Story* (1799). Knew many artists and literary people, but during 1790s one of her few friends was William Godwin. In last years was poor and crippled. Autobiography edited and published by her daughter after her death.

> *Memoirs of the Late Mrs. Robinson, Written by Herself: With Some Posthumous Pieces*, 4 vols (1801).
> Steen, Marguerite, *The Lost One: A Biography of Mary (Perdita) Robinson* (1937). (Racy biography; includes many portraits and caricatures of Robinson.)
> Bass, R. D., *The Green Dragoon: The Lives of Banastre Tarleton and Mary Robinson* (1957). (Contains many letters.)

ROCHE, Regina Maria (1764?–1845), born Regina Maria Dalton in southern Ireland and published two novels under this name, *The Vicar of Lansdowne* (1798) and *The Maid of the Hamlet: A Tale* (1793). Married a gentleman named Roche; became famous with *The Children of the Abbey: A Tale* (1796), one of most frequently reprinted 'Gothic romances'. Some of her other novels are: *Clermont: A Tale* (1798); *The Nocturnal Visit: A Tale* (1800); *The Discarded Son; or, Haunt of the Banditti: A Tale* (1807); *The Monastery of St. Colomb; or, The Atonement: A Tale* (1813); *The Munster Cottage Boy: A Tale* (1820); *The Tradition of the Castle; or, Scenes in the Emerald Isle* (1824); *The Castle Chapel: A Romantic Tale* (1825); and *The Nun's Picture: A Tale* (1834). Spent last years in obscurity and died at Waterford.

> See:    Schroeder, N., 'Regina Maria Roche, Popular Novelist, 1789–1834: The Rochean Canon', *Papers of the Bibliographical Society of America*, 73 (1979), 462–68.

SCOTT, Sir Walter (1771–1832), born in Edinburgh, son of Scottish lawyer and descendent of Border family. In 1773 afflicted with polio and spent much time at farm of grandfather in Border country; here acquired interest in sports and physical activity, love of Border country, and interest in popular stories and culture. In 1785 apprenticed to father as Writer to the Signet; followed courses of lectures at Edinburgh University and completed legal training; acquired familiarity with leading ideas of Scottish Enlightenment and interest in history. Called to bar in 1792; spent much time travelling about Scotland, particularly in Borders, in quest of folk-ballads. In early 1790s fell deeply in love; disappointment made life-long impression on Scott. In 1797 married French woman, Charlotte Carpenter, probably illegitimate daughter of Marquis of Downshire. In 1798 appointed Sheriff-Depute of Selkirkshire. In 1802 published first book of importance, edition of many ballads he had collected, *Minstrelsy of the*

*Scottish Border* (1802–03). Printer and publisher was young Kelso lawyer, James Ballantyne, and with him and his brother, John, Scott had close, life-long business and personal relationships.

In 1805 published long narrative poem, *The Lay of the Last Minstrel*, influenced by folk and art-ballad traditions; it made Scott into a rising literary figure. At same time working on edition of Dryden (1808). In 1806 obtained position as a Principal Clerk of Court of Session. For next poem, *Marmion* (1808), offered a thousand guineas by adventurous publisher Archibald Constable. Learned to pull strings of political patronage expertly and judiciously. In 1809 helped found Tory *Quarterly Review* as counterblast to more liberal *Edinburgh Review*. In 1809 and 1810 involved in reorganization of Royal Edinburgh Theatre; his novels were often adapted to stage and, later, made into operas. Published yet another best-selling poem, *The Lady of the Lake* (1810). Purchased estate on banks of Tweed and began building fake baronial castle named Abbotsford. Next poem, *Rokeby* (1813), another success. In 1814 published edition of *The Works of Jonathan Swift*.

In same year published first novel, *Waverley; or, 'Tis Sixty Years Since*, begun in 1805, advertised for publication in 1809–10, but only completed and published in 1814; published anonymously. In 1814 made journey to Orkney, Shetland, and Hebrides. Published another poem, *The Lord of the Isles* (1815), but course now set as novel writer. *Guy Mannering* (1815), *The Antiquary* (1816), *Old Mortality* and *The Black Dwarf* (1816; 1st series of Tales of My Landlord), *Rob Roy* (1817), *The Heart of Midlothian* (1818; Tales of My Landlord, 2nd series) and *The Bride of Lammermoor* and *A Legend of Montrose* (1819; Tales of My Landlord, 3rd series); all deal with Scottish history. In 1816 published semi-fictional travel book, *Paul's Letters to His Kinsfolk*. In 1819, with *Ivanhoe*, ventured further back in time and into English history, but just as successfully. Continued to write for magazines and to work on other books, keeping up killing pace of literary, social, business, and political activity. In 1818 baronetcy conferred on him (gazetted in 1820). *The Monastery* (1820) and sequel, *The Abbot* (1820), deal with social crisis of Protestant Reformation, *Kenilworth* (1821) with Elizabethan court intrigues, *The Pirate* (1821) with conflicting cultures in Orkney islands Scott had visited seven years earlier, and *The Fortunes of Nigel* (1822) with court and society during reign of James I.

In 1822 made stage-manager for visit of George IV to Scotland. Saw son Walter established in military career and daughter Sophia married to prominent critic, John Gibson Lockhart, in 1820. In 1823 published *Peveril of the Peak*, set in English Civil War period; *Quentin Durward*, set in contests between France and Burgandy; and *St. Ronan's Well*, Scott's homage to and revision of novel of manners and sentiment practised by Fanny Burney, Maria Edgeworth, Jane Austen, Scott's own friend Susan Ferrier, and other women novelists whose work he admired. Took on biography of Napoleon (published 1827). *Redgauntlet* (1824) returns to Scottish history, but contains brilliant inset short story, 'Wandering Willie's Tale', and an experiment in extended first person narrative. *The Betrothed* (1825) turns to Middle Ages and world of verse romances of chivalry that had absorbed him as a young man; but here Scott aims to show more sceptical, anti-romantic view of that society, as he does in treating 'antient chivalry's' great international adventure, the Crusades, in the companion novel, *The Talisman* (1825). Collapse of Constable's publishing house in 1826 meant financial ruin for Scott, though he managed to save Abbotsford for his heirs – this was his chief concern;

continued producing novels. *Woodstock* (1826) takes up period of English Commonwealth, and studies individual relations and loyalties in a period of uncertain political direction, similar perhaps to late 1820s; at same time, Scott plunged energetically into problems of national finance and Scottish independence with his *Letters of Malachi Malagrowther* (1826).

Wife died in 1826 and Scott's health began to deteriorate. Wrote collection of short tales, actually some of his very best writing, published as *Chronicles of the Canongate* (1827); wrote history of Scotland for children; prepared 'Magnum Opus' edition of Waverley Novels (1829–33). Produced two more good novels, *The Fair Maid of Perth* (1828), and *Anne of Geierstein* (1829). Early in 1830 suffered severe stroke, one of a series that would relentlessly erode his mind and health. Recovered sufficiently for a while to produce two more novels, *Count Robert of Paris* and *Castle Dangerous* (1831). Travelled to Mediterranean to regain his health; but on the way back suffered further strokes, rendering him helpless. Even to end, in lucid intervals he would call for pen and paper. Died at Abbotsford.

> *The Letters of Sir Walter Scott*, edited by H. J. C. Grierson, 12 vols (1932–37); J. C. Corson, *Notes and Index to Sir Herbert Grierson's Edition of the Letters of Sir Walter Scott* (Oxford, 1979).
>
> *The Journal of Sir Walter Scott*, edited by W. E. K. Anderson (Oxford, 1972).
>
> Lockhart, J. G., *Memoirs of the Life of Sir Walter Scott, Bart.*, 7 vols (Edinburgh and London, 1837); *Memoirs of Sir Walter Scott*, 10 vols (Edinburgh, 1882).
>
> Johnson, Edgar, *Sir Walter Scott: The Great Unknown*, 2 vols (New York, 1970). (Sensitive, detailed biography.)
>
> Daiches, David, *Sir Walter Scott and His World* (1971). (Profusely illustrated portrait of Scott in his time.)
>
> *Scott on Himself: A Selection of the Autobiographical Writings of Sir Walter Scott*, edited by David Hewitt (Edinburgh, 1981).

See:   Craig, David, *Scottish Literature and the Scottish People 1680–1830* (London, 1961). (Ch. 5 on 'The Age of Scott'; important essay in sociological literary history.)

Davie, Donald, *The Heyday of Sir Walter Scott* (1961).

Welsh, Alexander, *The Hero of the Waverley Novels* (New Haven and London, 1963).

Parsons, C. O., *Witchcraft and Demonology in Scott's Fiction* (Edinburgh and London, 1964). (Covers more ground than the title suggests; on Scott and popular culture.)

Hart, F. R., *Scott's Novels: The Plotting of Historic Survival* (Charlottesville, 1966).

Calder, Angus and Jenni, *Scott* (1969). (Brief critical survey.)

Cockshut, A. O. J., *The Achievement of Walter Scott* (1969).

Gordon, Robert C., *Under Which King? A Study of the Scottish Waverley Novels* (Edinburgh, 1969).

Devlin, D. D., *The Author of Waverley: A critical Study of Walter Scott* (1971).

Brown, David, *Walter Scott and the Historical Imagination* (1979). (Study of the Scottish works and the issue of historical authenticity.)

Lascelles, Mary, *The Story-Teller Retrieves the Past: Historical Fiction and Fictitious History in the Art of Scott, Stevenson, Kipling, and Some*

*Others* (Oxford, 1980). (Important book on relation of history and fiction.)

Reed, James, *Sir Walter Scott: Landscape and Locality* (1980).

Anderson, James, *Sir Walter Scott and History* (Edinburgh, 1981).

McMaster, Graham, *Scott and Society* (Cambridge, 1981). (Stimulating essay on Scott's social vision, as seen in his novels.)

Crawford, Thomas, *Walter Scott*, Scottish Writers Series (Edinburgh, 1982). (Best critical introduction available.)

Shaw, Harry E., *The Forms of Historical Fiction: Sir Walter Scott and His Successors* (Ithaca and London, 1983).

Millgate, Jane, *Walter Scott: The Making of the Novelist* (Toronto, 1984). (Good criticism of Scott's artistry and its development.)

Cottom, Daniel, *The Civilized Imagination: A Study of Ann Radcliffe, Jane Austen, and Sir Walter Scott* (Cambridge, 1985).

Wilt, Judith, *Secret Leaves: The Novels of Walter Scott* (Chicago, 1985).

SHELLEY, Mary (1797–1851), born in London, daughter of William Godwin and Mary Wollstonecraft; mother died from complications of childbirth; apparently did not get along well with step-mother, Godwin's second wife. In May 1814, after two-year period away from home, met Percy Shelley in her father's house; Shelley already married, but he and Mary eloped in the summer; travelled on Continent until September. Bore a daughter in February 1815, but she died within two weeks; early in 1816, bore a son, William; after suicide of Shelley's wife, Mary and Shelley married. In the summer, while staying near Geneva with Byron and some others, began work on *Frankenstein*. In 1817 at Marlow in Thames valley. Bore another daughter in September. *Frankenstein* published 1818. Left for Continent again, for an extended period. Daughter Clara died, followed by son William; bore another son, Percy Florence. In July 1822 Shelley and friend drowned in storm off Italian coast. Second novel, *Valperga; or The Life and Adventures of Castruccio, Prince of Lucca* (1823), her first historical novel, partly suggested and revised by Godwin, set in Italy in fourteenth century, during conflicts of Guelphs and Ghibellines, and argues for superiority of domestic affections over political faction or conflict. Later in same year, returned to England; edited Percy's poems; father-in-law, Sir Timothy Shelley, objected strongly to publication and the edition suppressed. Next novel, *The Last Man* (1826), takes seventeenth-century English Commonwealth and places it in twenty-first century in order to depict three-way struggle between court, gentry, and professional middle classes. Second historical novel, *The Fortunes of Perkin Warbeck: A Romance* (1830), deals with education, the formation of character, and sacrifice of domestic virtues and happiness to questionable ambitions for glory and power. Had several men admirers and two proposals of marriage, which she rejected out of loyalty to Shelley's memory. Another novel, *Lodore* (1835), takes theme of formation of character by early domestic education and social experience. After father's death in 1836 began no more new novels, but published *Falkner: A Novel* in 1837, another study of social rupture and reconciliation. Worked for a while on biography of late father, but unable to finish it. When publishing restrictions on Percy's work were lifted published *The Poetical Works of Percy Bysshe Shelley* with her own annotations (1839); edited his prose works (1840). Travelled with her son to Germany and Italy in early 1840s. Died in London.

*The Letters of Mary Wollstonecraft Shelley*, edited by Betty T. Bennett, 3 vols (Baltimore, 1980–).

*Mary Shelley's Journal*, edited by F. L. Jones (Norman, Oklahoma, 1947). (Valuable record of the Shelleys' reading.)

Grylls, R. G., *Mary Shelley: A Biography* (1938). (Well researched, using the extensive Shelley manuscripts.)

Dunn, Jane, *Moon in Eclipse: A Life of Mary Shelley* (1978). (Attempts to form a picture of Mary Shelley's mind and feelings.)

See:    Spark, Muriel, *Child of Light: A Reassessment of Mary Wollstonecraft Shelley* (Hadleigh Essex, 1951). (Interesting biographical and critical essay.)

Walling, W. A., *Mary Shelley*, Twayne's English Authors, 128 (Boston, 1972).

Tropp, Martin, *Mary Shelley's Monster: The Story of Frankenstein* (Boston, 1976).

Poovey, Mary, *The Proper Lady and the Woman Writer: Ideology as Style in the Works of Mary Wollstonecraft, Mary Shelley, and Jane Austen* (Chicago, 1984).

SHERWOOD, Mary Martha (1775–1851), born Mary Butt, daughter of country clergyman in Worcestershire; had happy childhood and well educated at Reading. Father died in 1796 and family settled at Bridgnorth; with sister Lucy did Sunday school work and published a few religious tales. In 1803 married cousin, an army officer, and went with him to India in 1805, where she did educational and charitable work. While in India, wrote *Little Henry and His Bearer* (1814). After return to England in 1816 ran boarding-school from 1818 to 1830 and wrote well over 200 fictional tracts, seconded by sister, Lucy Cameron, who was almost as prolific. Among most widely read works was *The History of the Fairchild Family* (1818–47). Published a few novels, but less successful in that line. Last years spent at Twickenham.

See:    Cutt, M. Nancy, *Mrs. Sherwood and Her Books for Children* (1974). (Biographical and critical introduction, with reprints of *The Little Woodman* and *Soffrona and Her Cat Muff* and a detailed bibliography.)

SMITH, Charlotte Turner (1749–1806), born in London, daughter of a witty and cultivated landed gentleman; mother died; placed under care of aunt; learned to read while very young and read everything that came her way. Attended school at Chichester and began writing verse; went to finishing school in London until twelve. In 1765 manoeuvred into marriage with Benjamin Smith, son of West Indies merchant, but of an unstable and improvident character; marriage not a happy one, though it produced twelve children; husband imprisoned for debt and family lived with him in confinement; finally separated from him in 1787. Began to write in order to support herself and children; published *Elegiac Sonnets* (1784); translated two French works, including Prévost's *Manon Lescaut*. In 1788 turned to Sentimental novel of manners with *Emmeline, The Orphan of the Castle*; published *Ethelinde; or, The Recluse of the Lake* (1789), *Celestina* (1791), *Desmond* (1792), *The Old Manor House* (1793), *The Wanderings of Warwick* (1794), *The Banished Man* (1794), *Montalbert* (1795), *Marchmont* (1796), *The Young Philosopher* (1798), and *Letters of a Solitary Wanderer* (1799, 1800–02). Also wrote a play, *What Is She?* (1799), several books of poetry, and a number of books for children. Died near Farnham.

Scott, Sir Walter, 'Charlotte Smith', in *Biographical Memoirs of Eminent Novelists*, vol. II (Edinburgh, 1834).

Hilbish, F. M. A., *Charlotte Smith, Poet and Novelist* (Philadelphia, 1941).

See: Foster, J. R., 'Charlotte Smith, Pre-Romantic Novelist', *PMLA*, 43 (1928), 463–75.

SMITH, Horatio (1779–1849), always known as 'Horace Smith'; second son of solicitor to Board of Ordnance; educated in school at Chigwell, then trained for stock exchange. Like so many others, preferred glamour and transferred gentility of theatrical and literary circles. Began writing novels, including *Horatio; or, Memoirs of the Davenport Family* (1807). With brother had enormous success with *Rejected Addresses* (1812), collection of their parodies of most popular poets of the day. Throve as stock broker and able to retire from business in 1820. By this time had met and helped many writers, including Shelley and Leigh Hunt; intended to join Shelley in Italy, but, when Shelley died, stopped at Versailles and lived there for three years; settled in Brighton. In his forties resumed interest in the novel, stimulated by success of Scott, and produced several pastiche Waverleys; *Brambletye House; or, Cavaliers and Roundheads* (1826), *The Tor Hill* (1826), and *Reuben Apsley* (1827) were successful, but he did not sustain his interest in historical romance or initial impact on reading public with later novels. Died at Tunbridge Wells.

WARD, Robert Plumer (1765–1846), lawyer, politician, and finally novelist; born in London's fashionable Mayfair, son of Gibraltar merchant; went to Westminster School and Christ Church, Oxford; in 1785 went to study law at Inner Temple, London. Called to bar in 1790; practised on western circuit. Married well; mixed in high society; published some books on international law; in 1802 brought into Parliament. From late 1800s to early 1820s held various minor Government posts; retired in 1823. Wrote two highly successful silver-fork novels, *Tremaine; or, The Man of Refinement* (1825) and *De Vere; or, The Man of Independence* (1827). Travelled; wrote more fiction. Died in London.

WEST, Jane (1758–1852), born in London and moved to Northamptonshire when eleven; self-educated and avid scribbler from early age. Married farmer, descendent of long line of country clergymen; looked after usual aspects of farm management left to women. One of her correspondents was Sarah Trimmer, author of books for children. Published some plays and books of verse, but known for novels of rural life and domestic realism, implicitly opposed to both novels of fashionable life and novels of English Jacobin tendency; her novels include *The Advantages of Education; or, The History of Maria Williams* (1793); *A Gossip's Story* (1796); *The History of Ned Evans: Interspersed with Moral and Critical Remarks* (1796); *The Church of Saint Siffrid* (1797); *A Tale of the Times* (1799); *The Infidel Father: A Novel* (1802); *The Refusal: A Novel* (1810); *The Loyalists: An Historical Novel* (1812); *Alicia de Lacy: An Historical Romance* (1814); and *Ringrove; or, Old-fashioned Notions* (1827). Also published book for children, *The Sorrows of Selfishness; or, The History of Miss Richmore* (1802); and two collections of moralizing letters, *Letters Addressed to a Young Man* (1801) and *Letters to a Young Lady* (1806), and contributed many pieces to *Gentleman's Magazine*. Survived husband and three sons; spent last years with failing sight and increasing sense of isolation. Died in Northamptonshire.

Lloyd, P. 'Some New Information on Jane West', *Notes and Queries*, 229 (Dec. 1984), 469–70.

WILLIAMS, Helen Maria (1762–1827), born in London, daughter of army officer; educated in Scotland by her mother. Went to London in early 1780s with mother; published several poems, helped by family friend and leading Dissenter, Andrew Kippis. From late 1780s spent most of life on Continent. In Paris during French Revolution, associating with leading Girondins, including Marie Roland; later lived with John Hurford Stone, unitarian, former member of Revolution Society in London, and active supporter of Girondin-led phase of Revolution. Imprisoned briefly by Robespierre, but stayed on in France and, with Stone, became French citizen in 1817. In 1790 published *Julia*, novel of liberal views; published popular translation of Bernardin de St Pierre's Sentimental tale, *Paul et Virginie*, in 1795; wrote several books on French Revolution and describing European society and politics. Died at Paris.

WILSON, John (1785–1854), born at Paisley, son of gauze manufacturer; educated at Paisley and Glasgow University. Deeply influenced by reading Wordsworth. Went to Oxford in 1803; travelled over much of Britain during university vacations. Planned to retire to cottage in Lake District; published some poems; married daughter of Liverpool merchant; lost fortune through incompetence of relative; decided to enter law; called to bar at Edinburgh. Soon became leading Edinburgh intellectual and writer, working for Tory *Blackwood's Magazine*, alongside Lockhart, Hogg, and others; from 1822 took over most widely-read section of *Blockwood's*, 'Noctes Ambrosianæ'. Elected to chair in Moral Philosophy at Edinburgh University amidst much controversy. In addition to poems, miscellaneous journalism and 'Noctes Ambrosianæ', wrote series of fictional sketches, *Lights and Shadows of Scottish Life* (1822), originally published serially in *Blackwood's*. Wrote two more novels, *The Trials of Margaret Lyndsay* (1823) and *The Foresters* (1825), both of which are interested in study of individual psychology. Died at Edinburgh.

Swann, Elsie, *Christopher North (John Wilson)* (Edinburgh and London, 1934). (Mainly biographical.)

WOLLSTONECRAFT, Mary (1759–1797), born in London, daughter of successful silk-weaver and property owner; father tried becoming gentleman farmer, but failed. Went to work to help support family, first as lady's companion, then as governess in Ireland. Belonged to Church of England but many of her intellectual contacts with leaders of English Dissent, such as Richard Price and the publisher Joseph Johnson; latter became her patron and publisher; published *Thoughts on the Education of Daughters* (1787) and novel *Mary: A Fiction* (1788). Did translations and wrote books on education; wrote for Johnson's *Analytical Review*, helped support and educate sisters and brothers. At Johnson's mingled with leading intellectuals, artists, and politicians of the day, including Paine, Blake, Godwin, Holcroft, and others; formed close intellectual relationship with Swiss painter Henry Fuseli. Published reply to Burke, *A Vindication of the Rights of Men* (1790). Publication of *A Vindication of the Rights of Woman* (1792) established her as leading feminist writer in Britain. Disappointed in relationship with Fuseli, went to Paris in December 1792, probably to associate with Girondin circle around Marie Roland. Relationship with

American Gilbert Imlay and registered as his wife; bore daughter, Fanny, in 1794; published *A Historical and Moral View of the Origin and Progress of the French Revolution* (1794); relationship with Imlay, now involved in breaking economic blockade against France, began to deteriorate. Travelled to Scandinavia for Imlay; sociological travel book, *Letters Written During a Short Residence in Sweden, Norway, and Denmark* (1796); on return to London found Imlay living with young actress and tried to drown herself. Returned to literary work for Johnson; renewed social and literary acquaintances; reintroduced to Godwin by Mary Hays in 1796. Began work on novel about condition of women; became pregnant and, in spite of philosophical and moral opposition to institution of marriage, she and Godwin married in March 1797 in order to relieve her from further public notoriety. Died in September 1797 from complications of childbirth, after birth of daughter, later Mary Shelley. Unfinished novel, *The Wrongs of Woman; or, Maria,* together with some other writings, published by Godwin in 1798 as *Posthumous Works of the Author of a Vindication of the Rights of Woman.* His *Memoir* of her, published at the same time, did much to wreck her reputation with conservative elements of reading public.

Godwin, William, *Memoirs of the Author of a Vindication of the Rights of Woman* (1798), reprinted as *Memoirs of Mary Wollstonecraft*, edited by W. Clark Durant (1927). (Durant edition includes much additional material, letters, etc.; Godwin's memoir indispensable.)
*Collected Letters of Mary Wollstonecraft*, edited by R. M. Wardle (Ithaca, New York, 1979).
*Godwin and Mary: Letters of William Godwin and Mary Wollstonecraft*, edited by R. M. Wardle (Lawrence Kansas, 1967).
Flexner, E., *Mary Wollstonecraft: A Biography* (New York, 1972). (Good on intellectual background of French Revolution phase.)
Sunstein, Emily, *A Different Face: The Life of Mary Wollstonecraft* (New York, 1974). (Good on family and social background.)
Tomalin, Claire, *The Life and Death of Mary Wollstonecraft* (1974). (Concerned with Wollstonecraft's moral and emotional life.)

See:    Poovey, Mary, *The Proper Lady and the Woman Writer: Ideology as Style in the Works of Mary Wollstonecraft, Mary Shelley, and Jane Austen* (Chicago and London, 1984).

# Index

attitudes to, 6, 14, 78–79, 88,
113, 115, 140, 182, 251, 253;
English Jacobin, 20, 28–42, 68,
96, 223, 228, 240, 251, 269, 271;
Enlightenment, 20, 26–28, 42;
epistolary, 31, 136; and fashion,
14; footnote, 17; formal elements,
20; Gothic, 18, 20, 25, 27, 36,
43, 45, 48–59, 71, 84, 94, 96, 98,
104–9, 128, 147, 153, 182,
195–201, 202, 213, 226, 231;
historical, 17, 33, 49, 92–98, 101,
142, 214, of manners, sentiment,
and emulation, 20, 25, 27, 42,
44–48, 49, 73, 79, 222, 224, 225;
Minerva Press, 72, 79; Newgate,
15, 207, 220–27, 228; Orientalist,
213–14; of passion, 57, 59, 84,
85, 142, 185–201, 231; pulp, 5;
quasi-novel, 21, 203, 252–60;
regional, 92, 209, 212, 241;
rogue, 226; versus romance, 7;
rural ('village anecdotes'), 71, 73,
74, 86–92, 201; Sentimental, 13,
20, 31, 45, 128, 184; 'silver-fork',
15, 72, 85, 218, 220–27, 228,
238, 240; and women readers, 7

Opie, Amelia, 37, 79, 83–86, 102,
105, 185, (310–11)
*Adeline Mowbray*, 60, 84, 85, 106;
*Dangers of Coquetry*, 29
Orientalism, 197, 213, 219–20, 260
Ossian, 97
Otway, Thomas, 49
Owenson, Sydney, Lady Morgan,
92–93, 206, (311)
*Wild Irish Girl*, 81, 82, 93–94, 95,
232

painting, 205
Parsons, Eliza, 105
passion, 43–44
Peacock, T. L., 21, 229–48 (311–12)
*Crotchet Castle*, 230, 235–41, 246,
247; *Gryll Grange*, 241; *Headlong
Hall*, 230–31, 235, 237; *Maid
Marian*, 234–35, 246; *Melincourt*,
231; *Misfortunes of Elphin*, 234–35,
246; *Nightmare Abbey*, 105, 230,
231–34, 235, 237, 241–43, 246
Petrarch, 31
Pigault-Lebrun, C., 230

Pitts, John, 208
Plutarch, 193, 194
Poor Law Reform, 235
popular culture, 5, 14, 90, 100, 140,
260, 261, 272; attitudes to, 6, 62,
71; Irish, 77
population increase, 15, 183
pornography, 58
Porter, Anna, 49, 94–95, (312–13)
*Don Sebastian*, 94–95; *Hungarian
Brothers*, 94
Porter, Jane, 15, 49, 94–95, 115, 186,
(312–13)
*Scottish Chiefs*, 82, 95–98, 260;
*Thaddeus of Warsaw*, 94
Presbyterianism, 90, 151, 154, 166,
211
Prévost, abbé, 161
prison reform, 43
professionalization, 13, 19, 91, 134,
213, 219, 223, 272–73
professions, 9, 10, 25, 30, 32, 45, 113,
182, 216, 241; ideology of, 10,
164; values of, 11, 13
'progress', 11, 141, 212, 213, 238, 260
Prometheus, 191, 192
proverbs, 171
Pygmalion, 189, 258

*Quarterly Review*, 12

Rabelais, 230, 241, 254, 257
race, 107
Radcliffe, Ann, 17, 18, 25, 26, 27, 46,
49, 50–55, 56, 57, 84, 94, 105,
107, 128, 147, 190, 199, 200, 242,
(313)
*The Italian*, 55; *Mysteries of Udolpho*,
36, 51–54, 58
radicalism, lower-class, 15
reading, 201; in Austen, 114–15, 127;
lower-class, 6
Reeve, Clara
*Progress of Romance*, 253
Reform Bill (1832), 163, 223, 235
Reformation, 34
regionalism, 17
religion, 12, 97, 197, 215, 262
Religious Tract Society, 5, 6, 103, 104
Renaissance humanism, 11
Restoration, 197
revenge, 26, 34
rhapsody, 65